JOURNEY
INTO
DARKNESS

JOURNEY
INTO
DARKNESS

Anthony Faramus

GRAFTON BOOKS

A Division of the Collins Publishing Group

LONDON GLASGOW
TORONTO SYDNEY AUCKLAND

Grafton Books
A Division of the Collins Publishing Group
8 Grafton Street, London W1X 3LA

Published by Grafton Books 1990

British Library Cataloguing in Publication Data

Faramus, Anthony
Journey into darkness
1. Jersey, 1936–1945 – Biographies
I. Title
942.341084

ISBN 0-246-13490-9

Printed in Great Britain by
William Collins Sons & Co. Ltd
Glasgow

To Mary for her patience, loyalty and love

And for the brave women of Romainville who
put inspiration into the men

Contents

*F*OREWORD BY GREVILLE JANNER, MP

Mauthausen is a hideous place, a relic of barbarity and a sink of death. Today, it is a memorial which every Austrian should be required to visit at least once, as a reminder of the past and a warning for the future.

As a young War Crimes Investigator in post-war Germany, I anguished at the frail resources with which we were expected to hunt down the SS killers, concentration camp guards, and murderers of escaped prisoners-of-war. All four of my grandparents had emigrated to Britain from the Baltic States. Every one of the family who had remained behind became a victim of Nazism. The chances of their killers being hunted down, prosecuted, convicted and sentenced to any penalty that could adequately reflect their crimes were nil.

At weekends, I worked in the Bergen-Belsen Displaced Persons' Camp. The old concentration camp site was a wilderness of death. The hope of new life in a Jewish State kept the DPs from total hopeless decay.

In later years, I paid homage at Auschwitz and trod the trails of Theresienstadt. I prayed at the gates of Stuttof and Natzweiler, and addressed a gathering at Hitler's first concentration camp, Dachau, to protest at President Reagan's visit to Nazi graves at Bitburg. And I mourned at Mauthausen.

Mauthausen is near Vienna. I refused to attend a conference in Austria's capital without visiting that awful place. It is right that we should remember the unique tragedy of the Jewish Holocaust, but wrong that we should forget the suffering and the deaths of others, caught up in the same flaming Hell. Mauthausen was for all those who opposed the Nazi regime.

I pay tribute to Tony Faramus, a survivor of Mauthausen. May the reopening of his wound prevent the creation of others.

PART 1

It had been a long, slow, hazardous and tiring drive from Budapest across the Austrian border into Vienna. The icy, unlit roads, combined with a sky without stars, had proved disastrous to many motorists; vehicles lay forsaken and crumpled in snow-filled ditches.

Clobbered up in a heavy overcoat, a woolly hat pulled down over my ears, gloves on my hands and two pairs of socks on my feet, I still felt the cold; the car's heater would have been efficient at the press of a button, but my travelling companion – my wife, bless her – is allergic to mechanical calories derived from petroleum, hence my discomfort. Why, I wondered again, had I chosen to tour Europe in the depths of winter?

Teeth chattering, I drove with extreme caution in the direction of the city centre, my heavy eyes squinting through the large snowflakes beating against the windscreen. 'Just think,' I said to Mary, 'it's mid-morning in Los Angeles, around seventy degrees and climbing.'

Mary popped her head out of the travelling rug. 'That's right,' she said, 'think warm.'

I was looking for a hotel or guest-house where we might take shelter for the night. When one loomed up out of the inky darkness, I slithered the wheels into the kerb with great relief. 'Looks somewhat majestic, expensive,' I said.

'It might be cheaper than driving on and falling asleep over the wheel,' Mary replied. 'We've arrived in one piece, let's count our blessings, not the schillings.'

The foyer of the hotel was warm, inviting and welcoming. The receptionist, a stout individual in a sombre suit and starched wing collar, greeted our entrance in a cordial and sympathetic manner, almost curtsying, and apologizing for the weather, 'schrecklich', the worst he could remember, okay for polar bears, not for human beings.

I had known worse, I might have told him. He pressed a bell. A uniformed porter braved the freezing cold to bring in our luggage, another was directed to the bar and hurried back with two generous glasses of brandy. 'Compliments of the management,' the beaming receptionist said in well-rehearsed English. 'Prosit!'

Mary smiled and said, 'How very kind!' To be truthful, I felt uncomfortable. I was not enraptured by Austrians or their country. I preferred to pay for the grace and favour, and dipped my hand into my pocket. I caught Mary's reproving look, raised my glass, said 'cheers' and swallowed the brandy and my pride.

The normal routine of passport inspection and form-filling was waived. There was time for a rest before dinner, we were informed. Would we be eating in the hotel? We had little choice; once showered and rested we had no desire to venture out in the streets. I answered 'Jawohl', but, I explained, we were vegetarian. A problem for the kitchen perhaps?

'Nein,' not at all. The chef was accustomed to cooking dishes to individual taste, and his 'Spezialität' was a Bavarian omelette. Patiently, he listed the ingredients. 'Schmecken gut,' I said. But, perhaps another little inconvenience? We ate eggs only from chickens free to run about.

The man's expression was pained. He half smiled. I waited for a post mortem. None came. All the 'Eier,' he said, were bought fresh daily, from a farm where 'die Hennen' were free as 'die Luft'. We had his absolute assurance.

'We're not the only freaks to stay here,' Mary said as we took the lift to the second floor. The room was cosy and tastefully furnished. 'Posh!' Mary said sinking into an armchair upholstered in rich velvet and gold braid. 'We can afford to splash out for a night or two,' she added with a yawn.

'People who stay here don't quibble about the cost,' I said. 'To garage the car alone is a rip-off.'

She laughed. 'Then why don't you sleep in it and cut out the expense of a double room.'

'This is an emergency, let's turn it to good account,' I retorted and spoke into the intercom to order myself a bourbon whisky. Our week in Greece, a few days in Yugoslavia and Hungary, had been in accommodation far less opulent, though clean and welcoming. One night in superior style would make a nasty hole in our budget but we were unlikely to have to beg for bread on our way back to England.

I took my turn in the shower and, in a good frame of mind, lay back on the bed to sip my Jack Daniels. The wind howled and buffeted the windows. But we were warm, safe and pleasantly relaxed.

Now dressed, we made our way down the broad, richly-carpeted staircase to the plush dining-room with all the spendour of glittering candelabra, pink table linen, ornately-uniformed attendants and a portly musical ensemble.

The 'Oberkellner' escorted us to our table. Seated, Mary scanned the menu; in a mischievous but humorous way and at full volume, she said: 'Blimey, mate! Fit for royalty! I don't want to put the wind up you, but this little lot is going to set you back more than you think. I hope you've got enough spondulicks, if you 'aven't I'll make do with a veggie faggot and chips.'

Heads turned, ears burning inquisitively.

Mary ordered a schooner of Harvey's Bristol Cream. Her brown eyes twinkled. 'Five quid's worth,' she said.

'Three gallons of four-star,' I answered. 'Enough to see us to the French border.'

Our fat waiter, all smiles, responded kindly to our allergies. He served us first with an onion soup with croutons, made wholly from vegetable stock, as he was anxious to explain. He opened the bottle of wine, a Pouilly chilled to a nicety. There followed the entrée, a fluffy omelette served on a silver tray and garnished with finely chopped shallots, peppers, whole baby mushrooms and spinach. For 'pudding' we chose from a selection of fresh pastries and, at the coffee and liqueur stage, the trio of violinists approached our table. They bowed.

Out of the corner of my mouth I said to Mary: 'Ask them to play "Deutschland über alles".'

She kicked me under the table and smiled up at the musicians. 'Please, Messieurs,' she said, 'will you play "La Cumparsita"?' A far cry from Strauss, Mary hummed a few bars and they caught on. On the final bow, she said, 'Tip them.' I was unstinting in my generosity.

Nicely grogged, but clear-minded, we made to leave our table. The Oberkellner barred our way. He clicked his heels. 'Monsieur ... Madame,' he said, 'our chef wishes to take champagne at your table. Will you do him the honour?'

I frowned and looked at Mary. 'Anxious to please, eh? I wonder why?'

Mary grinned and settled back in her chair. 'They've heard about you, no doubt.'

'One who got away.'

'Oh, come on! It's just a nice way of showing their hospitality. We've met good and bad everywhere, you know that.'

Champagne corks popping, it turned out to be an impromptu party; the chef was privileged to have been a prisoner-of-war in the hands of the British, he said; the manager, musicians and some untiring guests sang boisterously. Mary, with her know-how, put on a hilarious skit – a 'knees-up'. She belted out 'My Old Man's a Dustman' and 'Knocked 'em Down the Old Kent Road'. When, in the small hours, we returned to our room I readily admitted that it had been a most enjoyable evening.

Anxiously, I peered through the window down into the street below. The snow had stopped and the wind subsided. As I undressed, I thought about the road back. It had been my intention to avoid stopping in or driving through Germany, preferring to return the way we had travelled on the outward journey, via Italy, Switzerland and France. Now, that intention was out of the question, the radio news had warned us that the mountain passes were blocked.

'There's no alternative,' I said to Mary. 'We'll have to drive through parts of Germany.'

Without glancing up from a week-old copy of the *Sunday Times*, she answered: 'That's what I thought.'

'The autoroute will take us to Strasbourg and on to Nancy; if the roads are cleared we can reach the French border in one hop,' I said, tracing a finger over a map. 'Damn it! I had no idea we were so close to Linz.' I cursed softly. 'Mauthausen is clearly marked, just a few kilometres off the autoroute. Did you know?'

Mary rustled the newspaper before putting it aside. 'Yes, I knew,' she answered earnestly. 'You're not thinking of going there, are you? If you are, I don't want you to.'

My head sank back on the pillow. Knowing what was passing through my mind, Mary lectured me, briefly and with feeling. I yawned and closed my eyes. 'No more than a fleeting thought,' I said.

The next morning showered and dressed, we took a light breakfast of toast and marmalade in our room. I then left Mary to finish the packing and sauntered down into the hotel's lobby to settle the account. With time to spare, I looked into an ante-room and browsed along a shelf stocked with periodicals and books. My eyes fell on a copy of a guide book printed in English entitled *Visiting Austria*. I sat down in an easy chair. In the section, Upper Austria: City of Linz, a page was devoted to the village of Mauthausen with a colourful photograph depicting 'a pretty scene of happy innocence': old buildings, balconied guest-houses, a beautiful church spire, an old market square with its medieval stone whipping post, and an open-air swimming pool, 'all neatly spread along the banks of the river Danube'.

Happy innocence! I read on:

It is a village that has seen great violence. In times past Mauthausen was known as the Toll House on the river or Money House. Barbarossa, King Frederick I, refused to pay tax for passing through the village as he came up the Danube. He destroyed Mauthausen by fire. Between 1618 and 1648, Mauthausen was caught up in the Thirty Years War and in 1679 there was a serious outbreak of cholera.

Mauthausen will always suffer from the notoriety of its name. The village itself is a popular tourist attraction, but there is a marked difference in the attraction which brings many thousands of people from all over the world each year. The majority stay a few hours or a whole day, leaving before nightfall. Some refuse to sleep in the village; it is said that ghosts come down from the hills with the mist and the winds have voices. Local people are anxious not to talk about the historical monument on their doorsteps, the former concentration camp. In most cases they would prefer to see the evidence of the death camp obliterated into the ground. On the other hand, guest-house proprietors, bar-keepers and shop-keepers welcome the additional trade and make a good living because of the notorious camp.

And I spotted a well-thumbed booklet, a guide to Mauthausen Concentration Camp with an introduction in English:

Dear Visitor!
You are now on the grounds of the former German Concentration Camp of Mauthausen. It was one of the many camps set up over almost all Europe between the years 1933 and 1945 by the National Socialist regime of Adolf Hitler for the exploitation and extermination of its opponents. From 1938 to 1945 the name Mauthausen spread fear and terror; Mauthausen was a synonym for death by slave labour in the quarries. There were more than 206,000 people in this camp. The number of prisoners who were killed here or who perished as a result of the torments of camp life exceeded 110,000. The soil of this vast stronghold is soaked with the blood of thousands of innocent people. In order to remind future generations of what the Nationalist tyranny of Hitler's Germany meant to our people and to all mankind, the Austrian Federal Government has erected a museum and has transformed the remains of this camp into a worthy memorial, a place of warning and commemoration. Here, 110,000 people gave their greatest possession, their life, for the great ideals of love for humanity, of loyalty and comradeship in the struggle for their homeland against Nazi barbarity and war.

THINK ABOUT IT!

Flowery words! 'Love for humanity, loyalty and comradeship.' I paused to think about it for myself and I could see the flaws in the terminology. What, I wondered, would the good men and women, those with clean hands who gave 'their greatest possession, their life', think of a world still deeply entrenched in hate, in greed, in war and in murder? Every city in the 'civilized' world is plagued by evil factions, people still live in fear and terror of their neighbours, of villains who stalk the streets to prey on the weak, and of petty tyrants sanctioned by governments to persecute, condemn and demoralize those who oppose wicked laws and openly challenge them. The warnings and lessons of places like Auschwitz and Mauthausen have had little, if any, impact on the latter-day generation.

My late friend Lutchez often talked about the powers behind governments and about double-dealing politicians. And after the war the Austrian, Simon Wiesenthal, a fellow-prisoner at Buchenwald and Mauthausen, enlightened me further; unafraid, he spoke up about his country's role in the atrocities in his well-documented book *The Murderers Among Us*. 'If Germany wins the war, we are Germans; if Germany loses the war, we are Austrians.' So said the Austrian government of the time, deeply entangled as it was with crimes against humanity. And if the truth were known, postwar parliamentarians would have voted to see the evidence of the Fortress of Mauthausen, constructed by slave labour and with Austrian materials, bulldozed into the ground. It was the International Committee for Mauthausen, a body of influential ex-prisoners, who put pressure on the Austrian government to preserve the camp as a memorial.

Adolf Hitler was Austrian, born in Braunau on the River Inn, and went to school in Linz. Adolf Eichmann, the Chief of the Gestapo's Jewish section who promoted the use of gas chambers, grew up in Linz; and among the many hundreds of Austrians presiding over and staffing the numerous concentration camps and places of extermination on home ground was the obnoxious Anton Kaufmann who was born in the village of Mauthausen.

Simon Wiesenthal said there appeared to be no wide feeling of guilt in his native Austria because the crimes were carried out 'under German orders'. Years after the Germans began to make restitution payments to Jewish victims, the Austrian government maintained that they need not pay anything to victims of Nazi rule since *they* should get restitution from the Germans whose fault the 'whole thing' was anyway. And Chancellor Adenauer of Germany – he was twice arrested during the Nazi regime – who took part in founding the Christian Democratic Union, said: 'If the Austrians want something, we'll send them Hitler's bones.'

Later, Austria did receive 321 million marks for the victims of German atrocities. However, when it was decided to make some sort of payment, the Austrian government paid the *persecutors* first, not the persecuted. Money was given to Austrian Nazis to compensate them for loss of jobs and property after the end of the war and only later to the long-suffering victims.

The Austrian Minister of Justice, Broda, became exasperated with Simon Wiesenthal as he probed into the doubtful past of some eighteen hundred judges and public prosecutors occupying prominent legal positions in Germany and Austria, almost *all* of whom had signed death sentences 'in the name of the Führer, Adolf Hitler'. Trials of alleged war criminals in Austria were travesties of justice in many cases; it was almost impossible to form a jury, so many people asked to be excused on account of sickness and other reasons. Strange things happened in court cases, audiences applauded the defendants and laughed when Jewish witnesses were sworn on the Bible. Some of the worst criminal sadists were found not guilty, the court ruling that the defendants had acted under duress, 'executing orders from above'. Lenient sentences and acquittals, even for proven guilt of the most heinous crimes, created shockwaves among honourable Austrians seeking justice; students marched through Vienna carrying placards reading AUSTRIA – NATIONAL PARK FOR NAZI CRIMINALS.

On returning to the room, I said to Mary, 'D'you remember reading about the play *The Diary of Anne Frank*, when the performance was interrupted by an anti-Jewish demonstration of young people booing and hissing?'

She answered readily. 'At the Landestheater ... in Linz.'

'That's right,' I replied, picking up the luggage, ready to leave. 'A fake, they said! Anne Frank and the Amsterdam warehouse was an invention, a lie!* Concentration camps never existed, so say the new breed of Nazis and Fascists. Evil propaganda! The Germans were good at it. That little bastard, Goebbels, must be laughing in the grave. A hundred years from now, people will be firmly persuaded that it was all a damned hoax.'

Downstairs, and calmed, we were wished 'Auf wiedersehen' and 'Safe journey, come back soon'. In the car, Mary quipped: 'Like I said, there's good and there's bad everywhere.'

'That I don't deny,' I replied, taking the wheel and moving away gingerly. 'They were courteous, business-like, perhaps compensatory. Simon Wiesenthal, and he should know, says that the Austrians are divided into two groups, the guilty ones with blood on their hands who

---

* The Dutch author of *The Diary of a Young Girl* died in Belsen, aged 16, in 1944.

have got away scot-free, and the accomplices – those who didn't commit crimes but knew about them and did nothing to prevent them.'

'But,' Mary reasoned, 'you mustn't overlook those hundreds, perhaps thousands of decent Germans and Austrians who resisted Hitler and paid the price. Every country had its nasty bits of work, even the Channel Islands.'

Snowploughs were clearing the roads and gangs of men at work shovelled the snow into gigantic heaps. 'Efficient, these Austrians,' I muttered. I drove carefully over the slippery cobblestones, awake to the fact that the wheels of the car were rolling over a vast graveyard. Much of the granite paving had been cut and shaped by slave labour in the quarries of Mauthausen; the 'Wienergraben' there was the biggest source of granite supply in Austria and the property originally belonged to the city of Vienna, hence the name.

On the autoroute, I continued to drive with the utmost caution, not wishing to die in a mangled heap of metal. For all that, big fat luxurious Mercedes and suicidal Porsches roared by with horns blaring, spraying my windscreen with salty slush and hustling me off course. 'Arrogant bastards!' I yelled.

After more than two hours of sluggish motoring, often in a funereal procession of vehicles under the control of considerate drivers more alert to the conditions, we were attracted to a picturesque-looking tavern with smoke billowing from a chimney. Tempted to 'mittagessen', I turned the wheel, drove on to a slip road and stopped the car in a parking bay.

Inside the lively restaurant, we were guided to a table beside an open fire burning huge pine logs. Our waitress, a plump blonde 'Mädchen' with blush-coloured cheeks and in a short gingham dress with a white frilly apron, smiled and said a cheerful 'Willkommen.' Nothing was too much trouble, Mary and I agreed. The tomato soup we were served was vegetarian. There followed a 'Wintersalat', crisp lettuce, white beans, grated carrots, hard cheese and a side-plate of potatoes. A hot chocolate pudding and freshly ground coffee served in a tall glass with brandy left us nicely relaxed.

The room was a hubbub of conversation; burly men drank king-sized tankards of dark beer drawn from a wooden barrel; stout women, some with feathered hats, sipped a light-coloured wine, and properly-managed children relished something fizzy. Upper and middle class families relishing a Sunday lunch, chatting and enjoying a commanding view through a panoramic window of tall, white-flaked trees on the horizon. Skiers and tobogganers were making good sport of the snow-covered slopes and, within hearing, little children, frolicsome in woolly bonnets and ear-muffs, were engaged in a contest with frosty missiles whilst others were building a snowman. A scene of happy innocence! Children enjoying the conditions provided by nature, a gift denied to the children who perished in Auschwitz and Mauthausen.

'What place is this?' I asked turning to Mary.

She leaned her head towards me. 'You must have driven in with your eyes shut,' she whispered. 'We're at Amstetten.'

I choked on a lump in my throat. I stared through the window with more intensity; now my mind's eye saw a contrasting, unsightly tableau of slag heaps, of limp figures in tattered clothes, and of death and destruction; the shunting of engines, harsh voices, the crack of whips and screams reverberated in my head. I felt an urge to run out of the door, down to an embankment and call out 'Lucy ... Lucy ... '

'This is where she died,' Mary said tenderly, wanting to share my grief.

I nodded. 'Arbeitskommando Eisenbahn Konstruktion, Amstetten,' I said, hiding my emotion. 'Some five hundred women worked here. Killing work! There was no shortage of replacements. Somewhere here, perhaps where those children are playing, even under this very building, Lucy is buried.'

'You loved her, didn't you? Talk about her, I don't mind.'

'I think, now, it was no more than infatuation, foolish love, the extraordinary way we were brought together as so many men and women of Romainville were paired, and living on a tightrope, by the day, by the hour, capitalizing on opportunity, in blind happiness, setting too high a value on the future, disillusioned, and frequently in tears for friends leaving for deportation and execution. Brave, brave women of Romainville! God knows how we men looked to them in times of depression.'

I drove away from the car-park. Had I been journeying alone, I might have sheered off the motorway and stopped to cry myself blind. In the hazy windscreen images were miraged. My ears picked up voices, voices I easily recognized. 'Hé, copain! Viens nous voir, faire une petite visite.' Maria Baranbanov's radiant face was beamed in my vision. 'Don't pass us by without saying hello,' I heard her voice call.

'Tiens, Maria! You've never been far from my thoughts. I saw you, Maria. I was sick at heart, wanting to warn you, but there was nothing I could do ... '

'I saw you too ... I had no voice to cry out ... '

'Pauvre fille ... you looked so cold, so weak ... was it very bad, Maria?'

'I was frightened ... very frightened. But I wasn't fooled. Some of the women were heartened, thinking it was for the showers ... the door closed, the children cried, mothers screamed ... there were just a few

moments to think about all those I loved, Mamma, Papa ... you and
Marc ... Lucy and Paulette ... my pony, Domino ... then my eyes started
to burn ... I was suffocating ... choking ... '

Horns blared, brakes screeched. Mary nudged me. 'You're straying all
over the road!' she calmly warned me. A large black Mercedes shot across
my bow; another car kept pace, the driver looked my way and bunched
his fist. I drifted into the slow lane, out of harm's way. 'Bloody foreign
road-hogs!' Mary said, tongue in cheek.

The sky was darkening. We were approaching the first turn-off for
Mauthausen, the sign broke through the gloom, ten letters seemingly a
hundred feet high into the thickening clouds. 'I don't think we should
drive much further,' I said to Mary, 'another hour and we could meet up
with a snowstorm. It will be safer to stay in Linz for the night.'

Mary looked up from the illuminated road map. 'There's another
turn-off to Mauthausen coming in three kilometres,' she said patiently.
'Perhaps we can find a comfortable hotel in the village.'

I squeezed her hand. 'Thank you,' I said.

The short drive to the village was well marked; arrows were repeatedly
posted pointing to EHEM KZ MAUTHAUSEN, the aim being to protect the
peace and quiet of people living along the route and to persuade the
many thousands of visitors to the camp to proceed without stopping
even for a moment; straying foreign motorists, especially Americans
armed with Canons and Super 8s, were prone to put residents to
inconvenience, often in a wounding way, knocking on doors with pocket
dictionaries and inquiring in pidgin German, 'der Weg für der Lager' or,
thick-skinned, 'der ausrottung Lager' (extermination camp). And shop-
keepers had complained about Americans taking up their time, buying
nothing and subjecting them to no less than an interrogation, even a
trial, asking them where they were during the war, what they were doing
and if they knew what went on in the camps? They posed in groups
outside shops and premises, pointed their cameras and took pictures of
the bricks and mortar as if they had been cemented with guilt.

I drove slowly through a hamlet, picking out the droll name of
WINDPASSING, then over a level-crossing at St Pantaleon on a course
which took us parallel to the infamous railway line; thence, with headlamps at full beam, the massive outline of the iron bridge spanning the
river Danube came into view.

I stopped the car, turned off the ignition, wound down the window
and listened. The wind was whistling; a passing barge hooted; there was
a back-wash of water. Clean untrodden snow covered the railway track;
there was no tell-tale evidence, nothing to suggest the bloody theatre of

chaos, great violence and murder I had witnessed one night in late
October 1944.

Strong cross-winds buffeted the car as we crossed the river. The
village, misty, was niggardly lit by the glow of lighting in the windows of
small business premises and guest-houses soliciting eleventh-hour customers. The main thoroughfare was deserted when I drove into a
parking-bay reserved for patrons of the Gasthaus – Zum Schiff.

Heads down, we hurried across the quadrangle into a small lobby. I
rang the bell. The summons was immediately answered. A smiling Frau
Himmelbauer, rubbing her hands – from the cold or the promise of
business – invited us into a bar-cum-dining-room. She put the back of a
hand to Mary's flushed cheeks. 'Mein Liebling!' she sighed. 'Du bist kalt,
sehr kalt!'

Whilst we thawed out in front of an open fire, Herr Himmelbauer was
ordered out into the cold to bring in our luggage. Were we hungry? Frau
Himmelbauer still had a couple of servings of 'Gulasch mit Kartoffel
und Knödel' on the stove. Her jaw dropped when I explained we were
not meat-eaters. She shook her head, looked Mary up and down critically
and said Mary was too thin, she needed fat on her bones to ward off the
cold.

We enjoyed a light meal of sliced potatoes fried gently, brown sauce
and dark home-made bread. After a drink of hot lemon tea, we climbed a
short flight of stone stairs to the first floor. Our room was simple,
unadorned, scrupulously clean and nicely warmed. Sleep came easily; in
my brief moments of awareness, I heard nothing but the wind and the
gentle rattle of a window, no unearthly disturbances and no ghosts.

At breakfast time, we joined a few other people in the dining-room,
mainly visitors to the camp on the previous day now returning to their
homes by rail. Impoverished humble country-dwellers, living from hand
to mouth, they made great sacrifices to put a little money away to pay for
their annual pilgrimage. In sober tones, often tearful, they would tell
about the father, the mother, the son, the daughter and other close
members of the family who never returned from Mauthausen.

Beaming, Frau Himmelbauer served us boiled eggs fresh-laid by hens
allowed to exercise, not from 'gefangene Hühnchen', she said in a
booming voice. This was a cue for the village nosey parker and handyman around the place, who wanted to know 'Warum?' Why didn't we eat
eggs from the battery system? Not wanting to be drawn into an argument about the morality of imprisoning creatures in tiny cages so as to
increase profit, I patted my stomach and told the old man it was for
reasons of health.

He pulled up a chair and sat down. 'Das Geschwür?' he quizzed.

'Nein,' I replied. It wasn't an ulcer.

He had one. His doctor had advised surgery. But at this late stage in his life, he didn't want to be cut open. Not that he minded a little pain, God knew he had had his share of suffering. A bullet in the leg from the 1914 war, another in an arm and shrapnel in the back. 'Kognak' was all the medicine he took to ease the misery.

'Get him a glass,' Mary said.

Herr Himmelbauer put a large one in front of him. 'Prosit!' the old man said, knocking back half at one gulp. Cornered, we were obliged to listen to his experiences as a prisoner-of-war. The British, 'die Tommies', were 'okay'. They fed him well; 'der bully-beef mit Rosenkohl und rösten Kartoffeln', and 'Apfel puddings mit custard'. Big mugs of tea and he was never short of something to smoke. Mind you, there was always the 'Schweinkopf' who got up his 'Hintere' and called him 'Jerry' and 'figging Boche'. He scowled and jabbed a thumb into his chest. He wanted to make it known that he was not German but an Austrian, born in Linz.

As I don't smoke, I couldn't offer him a cigarette. He rolled his own, lit it and gave a jerk of his head. Were we intending to visit that place up on the hill? I said we were. He had never been nearer than a kilometre, nor did he wish to go any closer. 'Jawohl,' he said in answer to my question, he was living in the village throughout the last war, exempt from military service because of ill health.

I bought him another cognac. Then I asked, what did he know about the goings-on? 'Sicherlich,' he replied in a guarded voice; certainly, he knew something was taking place. Who didn't? But the villagers were frightened for themselves; they kept in the background, closed their shutters, and locked their doors when the trains arrived. It was a bad time, 'sehr schlecht', he said.

I ventured to ask him about Anton Kaufmann, the SS sergeant camp guard who was born in the village and charged with war crimes for which he was sentenced to death by an Allied Military Court sitting in the town of Dachau, Germany. The name Kaufmann was not an uncommon one in the village and I was curious to learn something about the vicious man's early history.

He was thoughtful whilst he rolled another cigarette. After putting a lighter to it, he said there were some matters best not talked about; one could not condemn the whole village because of one bad apple, with that one exception everybody, 'jedermann', conducted themselves properly.

Far from the truth. The village of Mauthausen, like many villages and hamlets in Austria, had a poor reputation. There had been trading with the camp guards in the effects 'requisitioned' from the many thousands of prisoners arriving at the station; good clothing, baggage, jewellery, anything of value or having some use, even children's toys, went onto the open market. Gold fillings extracted from prisoners before they were put to death and meant for Berlin were stolen and sold in the village. Civilian employers hired slave labour from the camp, a part of the fee charged went to the Kommandant and his cronies. A minority of those sent to work on private constructions, on farms and as domestic servants claimed they were treated well, sufficiently fed and allocated a warm corner to sleep in. The majority were less fortunate; their employers proved to be tyrants for labour was inexhaustible and dirt cheap; slaves, overworked and undernourished, were repeatedly eliminated by men and women in better shape, if only moderately so.

Not all transports arrived in the village screened by 'Nacht und Nebel' (night and fog). In clear daylight unscrupulous villagers hung about the station precinct like vultures looking for spoils; children of school age, indoctrinated with hate towards the 'Teufelmenschen' (devil folk), jeered and pelted stones at child-prisoners and the very old, cripples among them, who lagged behind the marching columns. Hitler was crazy, the old man whispered in my ear. Perhaps so, but it wasn't Hitler who killed people with great cruelty, who was trigger-happy, who slipped noose-wires over necks, who put a boot into pregnant women, and who led little children by the hand into gas-chambers; the real villains were the hirelings, from the high ranks down to the lowest, operating as a team or independently.

In heavy overcoats and strong walking shoes, we strolled out into the quadrangle; rosy-cheeked, well-fed and warmly-clad children were on their way to school, some with bicycles; they sounded their bells and put their riding skills to the test, back-pedalling and weaving in and out of the municipal earthenware pots for flowers and shrubs, children blessed with good health, happy, and with much to be thankful for.

In the market square, we paused to look at the site of the old whipping-post; over the balconies of apartments bed-linen hung out to air, stout women in dust-caps and with sleeves rolled up beat carpets and wielded yard-brooms. Passing a row of neat shops, a post office and a bank, our path through the narrow cobbled street brought us to the 'Bahnhof' lying hidden behind large hoardings with bill-stickers torn and flapping in the face of a wind coming across from the Danube.

The small station, well-kept and disciplined, makes a striking tableau, perhaps conscious that it is a sensitive point of focus for photographers and people who come just to stare and imagine. In the better seasons, the frontage is emblazoned with flowering tubs and hanging baskets; except for a new façade in the past decade, the small building remains as it was

when first constructed more than one hundred years ago, and there is
nothing to suggest that, since, many thousands of people from all four
corners of the world were mercilessly beaten through its portal.

Gottfried Weissengruber, the station-master, questioned my presence
on territory normally forbidden to members of the public. Whilst Mary
watched from the platform, I walked the length of the rails to the bridge
and back, peering down at the sleepers and shifting the cinders with the
toe of my shoe as if I were a detective searching for clues to a crime. If the
sleepers could communicate they would speak volumes.

An agreeable man, with one assistant who appeared to have many
roles, Herr Weissengruber invited us into his office-cum-parcel store. He
was born at St Georgen, yet another location where great cruelty and
murder prevailed in the construction of a railway line. He showed pride
in his job and his station, but I was bold enough to ask him if he had any
qualms as the appointed caretaker of the most infamous railway station
in the world. He frowned at the question. It was not one that had been
put to him before. At 'the time' he was a mere boy of eight; he had a clear
recollection of being warned by his schoolmaster not to speak to the
prisoners or go near them and, like other children of his age, he was led
to believe that all the prisoners were 'teuflisch Juden' (devil Jews) on
their way to Hell. On a happier note, he remembered the strange
aeroplanes flying low over the houses and the excitement among the
children when friendly soldiers gave them 'Kaugummi' and 'Zuckerwerk'
(chewing gum and candy).

Herr Weissengruber asked if I could name one railway station in the
whole of Austria, big or small, not touched by the 'Katastrophe' of war. I
doubted if anyone could, I had to admit. But, I told him, *his* station held
the distinction of being the point of no return; in the last weeks of the
war, convoys arriving came from hurriedly evacuated camps in Germany
and far-off Poland; they could go no further, Mauthausen was a
dead-end, the queues stretched from the station three and a half kilometres to the camp and led directly into the gas-chamber.

Gottfried Weissengruber had much to be thankful for in his job and
his mind was easy. He wasn't only in charge of a railway station, there
were supplementary unpaid activities which he valued. Very often
people arriving to visit the camp, ex-prisoners among them, refused to
go any further than his waiting-room; they broke down and cried, he
comforted them, even took hold of a hand.

After drinking a coffee and looking at an album of photographs of the
station staff and friends taken just prior to the war when the camp was
under construction by forced labour – Herr Weissengruber couldn't or
wouldn't point out the 'Bahnhofsvorsteher' of that treacherous era – we

took our leave of the site of sainted memories and walked along a pavement flanking 'la route de grande douleur', as the French had named it, the road of great grief. It was splayed out like an esplanade with a long row of neat pretty dwellings and business places on the lee-side of the river. Out from the centre of the village, the Danube diverged from view; we walked past a stonemason's store with a forecourt displaying chilling polished headstones and ornamental urns.

Houses were now on both sides of the rising ground. Some were mellow with age and others were contemporary. They were fronted by trim gardens with climbing plants and cultivated shrubs, the homes of diligent working-class and professional people with Volkswagen 'Beetles' and Mercedes-Benz standing in the open and in garages. A quiet wooded backwater in the dead of winter but devalued in the better seasons by an invasion of noisy motor-coaches, mini-buses and motor-cars belching fumes and kicking up the dust as they passed to and fro. Many disillusioned householders, saddled with loans and mortgages, would vote to see the monument on their doorsteps wiped off the map.

The short twisting hill which accounted for an untold number of lives is now widened and smoothly macadamized and furnished with benches for those wishing to halt for a moment. We were startled to hear shouting and guns firing, and I was amazed to come upon shooters in fancy clothing – hats decorated with colourful feathers, tweed hunting jackets, knickerbockers and ankle boots – taking up the exact stance of those sharp-eyed SS killers who once lined the verge with their weapons at the ready. In the densely-wooded 'grave-pit' area, hired lackeys yelled at the top of their voices and clouted the tree trunks with long-handled cudgels to frighten the wildlife into the sights of the shotguns. A deer, put in danger, leaped across the road, stumbled to its knees and scrambled up the bank out of harm's way, a fugitive for a short time.

I showed my anger and came within spitting distance of a puny-looking individual with a square of black moustache on his upper lip. 'Hey, du!' I shouted scornfully. 'This ground is sacred!' He shrugged his leather-faced shoulders and frowned. I drew closer. 'Compris? Dieser Grund heilig,' I said pointing at the one-time theatre of blood. 'Nix schiessen! Nix Gewehr! Compris?'

The man understood. He took a backward step for fear of my striking him. A colleague, taller and broader, ambled over, his shotgun cradled in his arms. 'Was ist los?' he asked in a peppery manner. 'Was gibt mit dir?'

I bunched my fists and reiterated my disapproval in stronger language, the words clipped but perfectly understandable to the bunch of countryside vandals looking on wide-eyed. 'Du und dein blutdurstig

Freunds hier kommen, schrein, schiessen und trampein über das Begräb-
nis. Blutig Raufbolde!'

The man glared in my face. He curled a lip and screwed his trigger-
finger into the side of his head. 'Du bist verrückt, ganz verrückt,' he
yelled. He pointed to the last bend in the hill. 'Weg! Partir! Schnell!'
Snarling, he gave me a warning.

'Come on!' Mary said. 'We're outnumbered.' She took my arm and we
walked away. 'What was he going on about?' she asked.

'He said I was a crackpot. He threatened to put a cartridge up my
backside. Charming people!'

Mary stopped and turned. 'Hey, you!' she shouted. She gave the man
a 'two-fingered' sign and had the last words: 'Figging Scheisskopf!'

The laughter coming from behind our backs was mocking, loud and
lasting.

'Qu'est-ce qu'il a fait?' What had I done? It was a question I was often going to be asked. Nothing had been told to me in detail. I did not have a clear conscience, yet, to my way of thinking, I had done nothing to be ashamed of; on the contrary, I had made a contribution, some might say a trivial one, to the appeal put out by the British government to go on the warpath.

According to the laws of the Occupation of the Channel Islands, I had been found guilty of misdemeanours by the German military authority and the British-Jersey judiciary for which I had been jailed. Time up, I was released; after a period of freedom, I was re-arrested by the civil police 'acting on the orders of the Feldgendarmerie', to be taken to the port of St Helier for deportation as an 'undesirable subject' to France. Apart from that, I was left in ignorance.

Now, as I waited in my police cage in Granville, Normandy, I realized how much of a fix I was in and how far from my home. My mother might have said, without meaning to be malevolent, 'You've made your bed, Son, now lie on it.' Perhaps I should have taken her advice. 'Get off the island before it's too late; you can still get on the last boat going to England,' she had said. Better than anyone she knew my character; she often said that I was impetuous, strong-minded and too ready to tempt providence, a 'Leo' whose horoscope was under the influence of the Devil himself.

My mother, née Ada Laura Floch and wed to a Faramus who was not in fact my father, a true Jerseyite whose English was garbled and laced with French and the local dialect, had gazed hard into her crystal ball and seen what was in store for me amongst the damp tea-leaves in the bottom of her cup. Too well did I remember her expletive: 'Christ-all-bloody-mighty, Son! I see nothing but trouble for you if you don't leave before the Jerries arrive. Ah, le malheur! Who knows what the buggers will do, eh?'

The wireless told us that the 'buggers' were well-established in France; Paris had been taken and they were fast approaching the Channel coast.

Only a few short miles separated the Channel Islands from the evil reported to be raping, murdering and butchering on their cross-country excursion. How frightening were the news bulletins! And the general talk! I made light of the warnings; even the neighbours and others among the village community of Beaumont advised me to cut and run. With the alarm bells ringing and the island bigwigs of local government making all sorts of dubious announcements, I was unwilling to join the long queues of evacuees waiting to board the boats at St Helier harbour, many of whom changed their minds before anchors were weighed. I was intrigued by the stirring events and curious to see these foreign bogeymen for myself when they arrived.

Like many young men of my age on the island, I saw war only as a madcap adventure, blind to all the destruction, pain and horror it produced. On the beach, in the coastal village of Beaumont, Parish of St Peter's, where I was born in a primitive whitewashed cottage, I had played at war games with my friends, machine-gunning imaginary enemies in their thousands as they approached the shore on the high tide. Never once did it occur to our callow minds that the Germans would one day break through the much-heralded strong-hold of France's Maginot Line and, almost a walk-over, proceed to occupy coastlines a mere pistol-shot from Jersey's eastern bays.

And when they came, in the summer of 1940, they were like tourists on a first visit, with broad grins, carrying baggage and cameras; they filled the deserted hotels and abandoned guest-houses, made themselves at home and were waited upon. And I listened to the old people in the village, some of whom had never ventured further than their front doors, my grandmother among them; stunned and confused by the formidable power of strangers in uniform and with great machines of war come to lord it over their domains, they were cast down by the sudden intrusion and upheaval in their lives. They were of accord: 'Jersai' was well-buggered.

Many of my school-day friends had enlisted in one of the services. I, too, had been ready and willing to volunteer, and it had been to the Royal Air Force that I presented myself. If my life was going to be forfeited, I told my father, then it was going to be the way I chose. My mother said: 'Get your hair cut before the interview, don't go looking like a girl.' The village barber, where I served an apprenticeship with clippers and comb after school hours and at week-ends, scoffed. 'Hey? The RAF? Not for the likes of you, my lad! A Spitfire pilot? Ha, ha! Not a chance in hell. They might take you in the Royal Army Service Corps.' My stylish 'Italian cut' lay ruined on the floor: he near-scalped my head.

Others agreed and I guessed why. The war in the air had not yet started in earnest. The RAF was choosy. College types and young men from impressive backgrounds were given preference; whereas my father and mother were very much working-class and, in financial terms, not worth a sou; and my education had been elementary, terminating with a black mark at the age of fourteen.

Undaunted, I dressed in my Burton's dark grey pin-striped suit. I might be twenty years old but my mother still gave my shoes and ears a last-minute inspection, as she always did when I was off somewhere special. 'Don't forget,' she said, 'stand up straight, keep your hands out of your pockets and, for Christ's sake, call the man "Sir".' And as I climbed into the bus going into St Helier, she called out for all the village to hear, 'Don't give out any lip if you're turned down.'

The eastern pier took me up a steep hill to Fort Regent. The recruiting officer was a gangling, middle-aged person with a sharp face and a thin, gingery moustache. I said a chirpy 'Good morning, Sir,' when I walked into his office. He nodded, pointed to a chair, stared me full in the face, opened a silver cigarette case, snapped the lid shut in a superior way and put a cork-tipped 'du Maurier' between his lips. I thought to myself: Here's a la-di-da bugger. He took several puffs at his cigarette before breaking the silence.

'So!' he said. 'First things first.' He studied my application form. I looked at a picture of a Spitfire in flight above his head and I counted the seconds to one hundred. 'Your name spells Greek to me!' he said frowning.

I didn't know whether he was being supercilious or nicely curious, nor did I make an attempt to correct the pronunciation. 'Rather an uncommon surname you might think, Sir,' I replied tongue in cheek.

'I'm confused,' he said crustily. 'Why is your father's name different from your mother's?'

It was a question I couldn't remember being asked before. My father was a 'Chevalier', my mother a 'Faramus'. A matter of fact. It was well-known. They were my true parents; if they were unmarried there was no bad odour; they were regarded with the highest respect in the Parish, if not the whole of the island. No one would dispute that. The recruiting officer wasn't a native, but imported into Jersey from England for the emergency. 'Oh,' I answered casually, 'it's not uncommon, something to do with old Jersey customs and religion, I believe, Sir.'

Tricky, I thought. Puzzled, he stroked his chin. I tried a smile to throw him off the scent. I was glad of the interruption when a cleaning lady in a white overall carried in a tray of tea and biscuits. There was only one cup and saucer. She set the refreshments at the man's elbow and retreated quietly. I watched the tea-spoon whisk around the cup like a propeller.

Bloody bad manners, I thought. Supping his tea and munching on a 'Marie', a popular square-shaped biscuit with fluted edges, he jerked a thumb at the picture of the Spitfire. 'You want to be a fighter-pilot, eh, my boy? Is that what you have in mind to fly?'

I answered politely and tactfully. 'I would very much like to be considered for training, Sir.'

'And what makes you think you have the ability to learn?'

'I catch on quick, Sir. I have a good head for things mechanical. I learned to drive my father's lorry in a matter of hours. Three tons fully loaded. Self-taught, Sir.'

'Remarkable! Quite an achievement!'

'Yes, Sir. That's what everybody said. I was only ten years old at the time.'

He finished his tea and lit up another du Maurier as if there was all the time in the world. I wanted to say: 'Get on with it man, the bloody Jerries will be up your backside before long.' I sat patiently, not too hopeful now; he was just killing time, bored at that.

Getting to his feet, he made a turn of the room. After a few moments of silent thought, he looked down at me. 'Let me tell you, my boy,' he drawled, 'there's a devil of a difference between forty miles an hour on the ground and four hundred above. Any fool can learn to drive a four-wheeled vehicle. A Spitfire, like any other warplane, has hundreds of gadgets. It's a sophisticated piece of equipment, technical this and technical that. You don't just climb into the bloody thing, start up, change gears and put your foot down: you have to know about revolutions, navigation, communications, atmospherics, gunnery and a thousand and one intricacies. And as if that's not enough, you must have the right disposition, a mind as sharp as a needle, cool and calculating; in short, you have to be intellectual, a bloody genius. Now, do you know what I mean?'

'Yes, Sir! Everyone has to start from scratch. Give me a couple of weeks and I could get the hang of things.'

'You could, eh! Smart fellow! Tell me, how much does a Spitfire cost, d'you think?'

'A great deal of money, Sir. Several thousands of pounds. Five or more I would guess.'

'At least you know that much.' He went to the door and opened it. Taking the hint, I stood up. 'Tell you what,' he said, beckoning me out, 'when Woolworth's sell Spitfires, come back and see me. Meanwhile, sound advice, my boy, since you have the ability to drive a heavy lorry and want to get into the war, pop in next door and see the army chappie; the Royal Army Service Corps will teach you to drive a tank in a day or so.'

The door closed on me. I turned on my heel. 'Toffee-nosed bloody twit!' I called out, loud enough for him to hear.

From the wide expanse of sandy beach, less than a running minute from my cottage home with its lilac tree and small front garden bursting with sweet-smelling summer flowers, I watched the last of the evacuation boats steaming across the graceful sweep of St Aubin's Bay. As its stern disappeared behind St Aubin's Fort and on to Noirmont Point, I felt somewhat isolated; my best friends were on board or had already gone to join the armed services. Now I was left wondering if I had made the wrong decision.

It was June, normally a month of gaiety with light-hearted visitors drowning their cares and making whoopee on duty-free drinks and cigarettes. 'Sunny Jersey' was living up to its holiday-brochure reputation, if only in climate. The sky was blue, the weather warm, the breeze invigorating, waves lazily lapped the breakwater and the golden sand was unsullied. Except for seagulls at rest on the mirror of water, small birds preening themselves and a solitary dog at loose ends, there was no sign of life. The air was filled with unmistakable despondency.

The States authority, under a powerful body of Connétables, Centeniers and Vingteniers – unpaid policemen made up of wealthy farmers, businessmen and retired brigadiers working in co-operation with the uniformed service – had, it was widely said, handled the evacuation clumsily. To leave, or not to leave? That was the question. In the last-minute scurry to join the queues at the harbour, homes, possessions and businesses had been sold cheaply or abandoned. Farm animals were left to fend for themselves; cattle and horses roamed the narrow country lanes tramping through property in search of water. Sadly, pets were cut loose; many dogs were locked into abandoned cars parked along the roads leading to the pier; they could be heard yelping and howling for their runaway masters. Truly, the island was in a turmoil of uncertainty.

The high tide having receded, and my mind ticking over, I trekked along the spongy shore, a three-mile stretch from the pretty little western port of St Aubin's to the heart of the capital, St Helier. Behind the high red granite seawall, the promenade covered an equal distance. Private dwellings on the north side of the broad road, the small bungalows and chalets – the 'Chez-Nous' and 'Mon Retreat' of the blessed – wash-painted in a spectrum of rainbow hues and with gardens crying for water, showed signs of forced entries; windows were broken and front doors splintered, all the hallmarks of vandals and looters, activity hitherto unknown on an island noted for its tranquillity and principles of honour among the natives. The excuses varied, from the thin to the frank.

'I'm looking after the stuff until "they" come back.' Or, 'Take what you can before the Jerries grab the lot.'

The superior guest-houses where, only yesterday it seemed, sun-worshippers basked lazily on the balconies and flat roofs sipping gin and chilled tonics and downing ice-cold lager-beers with lime, now hid behind drawn curtains, closed shutters, folded canopies and stacked deck-chairs; the 'Sea Views' and 'Marine Villas' were soon to be cast into a dismal shade by ugly concrete pillboxes and heavy gun emplacements.

At the 'stylish' end of the promenade, West Park, the causeway leading to Elizabeth Castle was deserted, as was the sea-water swim-ming pool. I walked up the broad granite slipway, stepping over para-phernalia that had been hurriedly and carelessly forsaken; rows of bathing cabins displayed discarded swim-costumes, rubber slip-ons, personalized towels and some with the crest of the nearby opulent Grand Hotel, others with markings from less superior houses, an inflated 'Mae West', children's buckets and spades, socks and stockings, the remains of picnic luncheons buzzing with large flies; a buckled 'Stop-me-and-buy-one' Eldorado ice-cream tricycle lay surrounded by broken cornets and wafers and, strewn about, a small fortune in empty lemonade and beer bottles on which the deposits would go unclaimed.

Across the wide esplanade stood the island's mecca of music, big bands, dancing and fond memories – the impressive, white-painted West Park Pavilion. Here, on many a balmy evening when I could afford the admittance through the front door – slipping in through the back when I couldn't – I had captured a few hearts, closely clinched to a partner in a slow foxtrot. I lingered a few moments, my ears pricked; alas, I felt a sensation of nostalgia and sadness, the saxophones, trom-bones and clarinets were as silent as death.

Looking westward along the elevated mile to First Tower, the avenue of the renowned Battle of Flowers was deserted, plans for the yearly spectacle buried. Where, as long as I could remember, a never-ending parade of exhibits bedecked with carnations, rhododendrons, lovely girls and those voted the most attractive – 'Miss Jersey' the plum – floated past cheering, happy crowds, multi-wheeled troop-carriers loaded with grey-green uniformed aliens, half-tracks and gun-carriages would soon be churning up the smooth tarmac.

By way of the esplanade, I made my way into the town, strolling past the Grand Hotel which I would soon have good reason to regard with nausea for the rest of my life. Catering staff, for the time being out of a job, and small groups of workers from warehouses, at a stalemate and speculating on the next source of wages, searched the blue sky for the swastika-emblazoned warplanes and parachutists the island had been promised.

Rumours were ten a penny, enlarged upon by scaremongers, and with a ring of truth. Some old people were nervous, thinking they might become superfluous, according to what one heard broadcast on foreign wireless wavebands, and young men expected to be put to hard labour on military projects. Titbits of information, of a shady kind, were being buzzed around; sticky fingers were being dipped into the States' coffers; heavy boxes and suitcases had been seen sneaking out of banks and depositories in the dead of night 'for preservation in a secure place' until, 'naturellement', Jerry had been chucked out and the rightful owners returned to the island to collect their valuables ... *if* they ever came back. Essential goods were fast disappearing from shops in preparation for a blackmarket. Suddenly, normal standards of conduct and morality mattered little as a rabble of States dignitaries at the Town Hall made ready to greet the expected enemy.

'Gaudins', the upper-crust tea-rooms where cream horns and French chocolate éclairs were the specialities amongst many other goodies served on delicate china plates and eaten with small silver-plated forks, were desperate for customers. In King Street and Queen Street, the prime shopping venues for precious stones, jewellery and packaged bottles of alcohol free from duty, businesses that thrived on holiday-makers were depressed or closed altogether. Notices saying 'Gone abroad' or 'Closed for the duration' were stuck on the inside of empty windows. Half a mile on, east of the town, the well trodden St Saviour's road was in mourning. Gone were the middle-class families who would have been pouring out of the bed-and-breakfast lodgings for the beach and the open sea-water pool at Havre des Pas – the one-time address of that celebrated deportee from France, the novelist, Victor Marie Hugo – or to the bus depot for a pleasure trip to explore the many nooks and crannies around the rugged north-west points; wondrous attractions with awesome-sounding names favoured by adventurous boys – 'Devil's Hole' and the 'Wolf's Caves'. Without delay, such breathtaking beauty spots would be fenced with barbed-wire, posted with forbidding sentinels, and watchwords stamped with the sinister death's-head would proclaim the area 'Verboten!'

Further along St Saviour's road, I turned into the half-circular driveway of the better-class Continental Hotel, my place of employment. Weeds had started to sprout up the lower face of the building and litter was strewn about; Fred, the car-park attendant and capable handyman, had been evacuated to England with his family.

I opened the front door with a key. Inside, the reception desk and

office were unstaffed. All the many bedroom keys rested on their
respective numbered hooks, and the niches for storing letters and
accounts were empty. Windows were bolted, curtains drawn, and heavy
furniture stacked against exterior doors. At vulnerable points around the
building, trip wires and alarms were installed, not in contemplation of a
warlike resistance when the enemy arrived, but to thwart the peepers and
snoopers among the local authority.

The bar was open and lively. I heard Joe, the Portuguese kitchen-
porter, singing. Elsie, his paramour, a plump woman in charge of
bedrooms and with no one to chamber for, was playing a ham-fisted
accompaniment on a piano. Lily, a pretty young waitress and my
current, was seated out of uniform on a tall stool, posing like a
member of high society with a scented 'Passing Cloud' cigarette in a
long holder between her fingers and sipping a port and lemon from an
ornamented glass. I made up the complement of the staff in occupation, a parlour-man, boot-boy and dish-washer no longer being in
service. Without legal title, we were squatters by permission of the
management in exile, having been granted open-sesame to lock, stock
and barrel.

Joe looked much happier than he had been for the past few days. He
had been suffering greatly from a raging toothache. Those dentists who
had not left the island were at a premium, asking for gold not currency.
Two bottles of Scotch whisky had settled Joe's bill for the treatment. We
had enough and more to spare. We were sitting on a reservoir of wines
and spirits, cigarettes and cigars. The larders were stocked with provisions and plans were in hand to protect these valuable assets from the
sequestrators at the Town Hall. And we were aware that our bastion was
under sentence. An informant in the constabulary was peddling us
news. Hotel accommodation for the impending guests was being earmarked by rumoured fifth columnists and local toadies in high office.
One, in particular, a Centenier of St Helier, Mr Arthur Tostevin was
prepared to assist.

The crunch came all too soon, just as Joe, Elsie, Lily and I were
enjoying a champagne and caviare existence. Lily and I were sharing one
of the better rooms on the top floor, complete with bathroom and
running hot water, a luxury I had not experienced before. Early one
morning, I was alerted to a great roar of engine power which almost split
my ears. I jumped out of my bed and threw open a window, Lily, in all
her nakedness, at my side. It was our very first glimpse of a swastika on
the tail of a twin-engined aeroplane, easily recognized from photographs
as a Dornier, better-known as the 'Flying Pencil' of the Luftwaffe. The
machine circled the town, terrifying pigeons and seagulls, and putting

the wind up people walking to work as it skimmed chimney-pots in a swaggering display of aerobatics.

On its second run, I pointed excitedly. 'Look, Lily, you can see the Jerry pilot!'

Brazen Lily, never short of spicy language, leaned dangerously out of the window, breasts quivering on the sill. 'Hey, you bloody *Schwein-hund*!' she shouted at the top of her voice. 'Show-off bastard! Fuck off!'

The Jerry pilot might have been huffed by Lily's furious gestures, for he returned with friends later in the day to drop small bombs indiscriminately on the town, and machine-gunning at random, shattering the nerves of the inhabitants and killing eleven people. Small damage was effected; the fourteenth-century Town Church was hit, boats and yachts moored in the harbour were set on fire, and a tobacconist and off-licence shuttered shop window was blown out; what remained of the stock was scattered into the road, quickly gathered up and conveyed away.

News of an air attack on Jersey's sister island, Guernsey, was even more grievous; many more people had been killed and injured. Such violence had not been contemplated by the inhabitants of Jersey. They had been led to believe that their property and lives would be respected; now, bitter words were levelled against the authorities at the Town Hall who had been instrumental in persuading individuals and whole families in a state of uncertainty to remain on the island and not run away 'like those vermin who had already deserted their holes'. Better to be a live rat than a murdered patriot, many islanders concluded.

The military occupation was imminent. Communications, in the form of 'orders', so one heard through the grapevine, were being received at the States offices from the enemy across the water. It was total surrender. White flags were flown from public buildings, and a large cross was painted on the tarmac in the harbour precinct so that it could be seen by reconnoitring aircraft. Heavy farm equipment, wooden stakes and concrete blocks which had been strewn about to block the airport runway at St Peter's and the golf course at La Moye by zealots opposed to an occupation were removed by a gang of workers sent by the States Labour Board.

At the Continental Hotel we were on the defensive resisting all callers bearing threats of eviction. Joe brandished kitchen carving knives from windows; Elsie and Lily rigged up a garden hose to a convenient tap and doused lurking figures with jets of water. In a rebellious mood, I claimed the hotel to be requisitioned on behalf of the German forces and, as their 'appointed agent', promised to report any infiltrator to the commander-in-chief on his arrival. Elsie typed out notices to this effect; Joe, who spoke and understood some German, underwrote the instruction in that language. Tacked to the front and back doors of the building, the 'Notizen' made a serious impression – 'Achtung!' and 'Eintritt Verboten' conveyed an intimation not to be ignored in a situation of mounting confusion and suspicion, and at a time when fifth columnists, a Swiss and an Austrian subject, both hotel managers, had come to the surface along with a few Jersey and English-born characters ready to collaborate with the enemy.

It was essential to make safe our stocks of drinks and tinned goods and anything that would keep, the likes of which would not appear in the shops for many long and tedious years. I went into the town and in broad daylight selected a car, one which had been abandoned and with enough petrol in its tank to make two trips into the country at St Peter's within a mile of my home at Beaumont. In a small piece of sloping woodland where I once collected chestnuts and picked wild cherries as a boy, Joe and I buried the cache.

It was the last day of June, a critical day. At dusk, by pre-arrangement, the town's hawker arrived at the back door, the rubber wheels of his handcart gliding silently over the narrow streets from his storehouse nearby. Encouraged by the British Broadcasting Corporation's wireless announcements urging people in occupied territory to sabotage the enemy's war efforts, by fair or foul means, one supposed, Elsie and Lily stripped the beds and the linen cupboards of the better quality blankets, sheets and towels. The better silverware, cutlery, drinking glasses, decanters and chinaware were packed into tea-chests. The hawker made several collections, carrying away goods and chattels which, in all probability would have been shipped to homes in Germany. Our act of 'patriotism' – that's how we saw it – would go unhonoured. Somewhat ashamedly, we made a handsome profit, not in the normal currency which one believed would be rendered valueless, but in golden sovereigns.

At midnight, the eve of the Occupation, we set about making the most of the last few hours of independence, throwing open the doors to friends in an orgy of eating, drinking and music and dancing. The shindig alerted the Town Hall; two uniformed constables raced to the hotel on their bicycles. But they were in no mood to lay down the law; seeing the drink and the company, they hung up their helmets and pocketed their cycling ankle-clips to join the dancers on the floor. And, when time was called, the more boozed up voted to burn down the hotel. After some argument, sense prevailed: wilfully setting fire to a building where the Germans intended to doss down could result in someone facing the firing-squad and there were several antagonists at the Town Hall who would point a finger at Joe and me.

Not since the year 1781, at 'The Battle of Jersey', when a French warring expedition under the command of one de Rullecour was defeated in the town's Royal Square, had the island been at the mercy of so great a turmoil. From my attic bedroom at Beaumont, I craned my neck out of the skylight window to see a procession of low-flying, troop-carrying Junkers aircraft – 'flying coffins' – approaching St Peter's airport.

I ran down the stairs and jumped onto the saddle of my bike. 'Where you off to, Son?' my mother shouted.

'Up the hill,' I shouted back as I went into low gear and increased the pressure on the pedals.

'Don't do anything, for Christ's sake … '

Head and toes down, I pedalled up the steep, winding St Peter's Hill. Aeroplanes were swarming over the perches and hectares of potato crops like angry hornets; in the meadows cattle stampeded, horses snorted and bucked, and chickens squawked and flapped their wings in terror. Breathless, I arrived outside the perimeter of the airport buildings and runway enclosed by a high wire fence, to join the growing group of spectators eager to see the 'fireworks' for themselves. There were grubby little lads playing truant from school with their hands clamped over their ears to shut out the shattering noise from the strange-looking aeroplanes with their swastika markings; farm labourers from around and about in muck-stained dungarees chewing on thick sandwiches of cheese and beetroot; round-shouldered old women in sackcloth aprons, with tired, yellowish-brown faces and potato-stained hands; and spotty-faced servant girls from the moneyed houses in fresh frocks flirting with horny youths; clerical types in grey suits, white starched collars and college ties, taking time off from their offices in the town and having arrived on a bus. It was an event that would go down in the history books. It had some people laughing, some clowning, some sneering, some weeping, no one having any idea or notion how their lives would change henceforth.

Above the roar of taxiing engines, amid the blasts of hot dust and grit stirred up by huge propellers, my ears picked up the opinions, the speculations and the sarcasm mouthed in the odd local dialect, French and patchy English. That 'Jersai' was in the shit, 'dans la merde', buggered, 'foutu' and up the fucking creek went without saying. 'Vraiment cochon!' (Truly pig!) And who would have thought the day would come when we would see our big-wigs shaking Jerry's hand, eh? 'Tu vas voir,' (you'll see) they'll be kissing their backsides before long. Who d'you think is going to feed all these fucking tourists? 'Les pauvres fermiers,' the poor farmers, that's who! 'Merde!' Shit! That bugger Goering has sent us the bloody works!

We stood in small groups, sweating in the heat of a Mediterranean-like July sun, hardly believing what our eyes were witnessing. We watched our bespoke-tailored leaders, the hawk-eyed Bailiff and Superior Judge of the Royal Court, Alexandre Montcrieff Coutanche, and the tall, weighty Attorney-General, Charles Walter Duret-Aubin, sweep by, back to the States parliamentary chamber in the rear seat of a gleaming black Humber limousine, the States' pennant hanging limp from its mounting on the roof. In their wake came a cavalcade of lesser civil dignitaries: senators, 'elder statesmen', Centeniers and Jurats, sitting prettily in a fleet of cars with senior German officers. Moved by awe and tradition, the more obedient among the gogglers raised their caps and stood to attention; the more loutish, vulgar young roustabouts whom I supported made vigorous gestures with fingers to nose, shouting rude words, cleared their throats and gobbed onto the hot tarmac.

The transformation of the island was speedy. I cycled into St Helier to see the town swarming with German uniforms: army, navy and air force. From the porticoes of the General Post Office in Broad Street and the Town Hall, the black, white and red swastika banner fluttered in the breeze. Commandeered cars, sedate Austins and Humbers, their petrol tanks replenished, had been turned into military taxi-cabs, ferrying troops and baggage to the Grand, the Mayfair, the Continental, and to hotels in the country districts. It was the first day of July 1940; by local States' government order, the people of Jersey bowed to the will of the occupying forces and German orders were registered in the Royal Court.

The enemy was firmly established and, as one would have guessed, the bootlickers came out into the open, in the firm belief that Britain would lose the war and the island would see a lasting occupation. Those wretches, in the main holding civil office, went out of their way to implement the rules and regulations instituted by the military Kommandant. They searched homes, confiscated wireless sets and property useful to the Germans, and reported irregularities, no matter how small. Loyal subjects suddenly found themselves in jail, convicted by a military tribunal and the States' civil courts; offences included the possession of propaganda leaflets dropped on the island by the Royal Air Force, chalking anti-German graffiti on walls, incivility to the Germans and scrapping with them, and violating the law of curfew. Unknown numbers were secretly to be deported as 'undesirables' to prisons in France and to concentration camps in Germany, to be swallowed up with the great masses of humanity who would disappear without trace. Along with the Jersey-born subjects who became victims were Irish subjects, conscientious objectors from England who had been sent to the island for harvesting and who were a cause of irritation to the local authority, friendly aliens and the few Jews remaining.

It was back to business with a marked difference at the Continental Hotel. The Italian contingent, mainly employed in catering, were freed from their short spell of internment in a camp on the east of the island. They showed great resentment at their treatment by the British army. Pietro Lucari, the former head waiter at the Continental and a friendly alien, looked gaunt and haggard and had lost all his hair, shorn to the skull on grounds of 'hygiene'. Under his new bosses, Lucari had been promoted to manager. The swarthy chef Sergio Bonetti, a fascist, lamented his shorn pate too. His dark curly hair was no more. 'Fucking bastard Tommies,' he went about his kitchen growling; it was nothing more than spite before they ran away, he complained. The conceited Italians, now self-conscious, hid their mutilations under hats whenever they went in to the town.

I was working for 'them', a byword which one would hear a hundred times a day. Joe, Elsie and Lily had also been recruited back to their former jobs at the Continental. 'Look,' the clerk at the States Labour Board said to me, 'it's not what I call forced labour, washing their dishes is not what I call going over to them. They'll feed you on duty and you'll get paid. You'll get something to eat on top of your normal rations. Is that so bad, eh? The only other work, and for the same firm I might add, is with a pick and bloody shovel. So take your choice, my lad.'

I did. It was little use arguing. No work, no pay, no rations. Directly, or indirectly, the working population was in the service of *them*. My duties in the pantry required far less skill than in the gala days gone by; there were no trays to prepare for room service, no eggs to boil for the breakfasts, no bread to cut and toast and arrange into silver racks, no newspapers to deliver, and no fresh Jersey butter to spread on thin Hovis which, like the dainty salmon and cucumber sandwiches and newly-baked scones, enriched the afternoon teas. And no tips! No longer did I hear a gentle knock at the pantry door – a glass of milk to take upstairs; hot water for my lady's senna-pods; shoes for a shine and a penny or two for my trouble.

A stark difference, too, when I peeped through the glass aperture in the swing door leading into what was once a dining-room of white linen-covered tables set with pyramid-like serviettes and posies of fresh flowers where stately guests conversed in low tones with neat uniformed wait-resses in white starched aprons and black stockings. Now I saw a scrummage, a noisy menagerie of rank and file with square jaws, close-cropped heads, coarse table manners, spooning Sergio Bonetti's thick 'kartoffel Gulasch' into their mouths and chomping on hunks of black

bread. A keen tennis player, Bonetti groused about those 'fuckin zher-
mans' who had taken over his favourite court. He was discontented with
the gallons of stew and the floury dumplings which he had to prepare
almost every day of the week, simple food which any idiot could cook.
His culinary skill was not for the likes of pigs, he was heard to say under
his breath.

Not all was well among the staff. Lily was far from happy with her new
guests. Gone was the will and the shine. Being groped as she passed the
long trestle tables in the dining-room was not a condition of service, she
complained to Pietro Lucari, the 'Geschäftsführer' (a title which he
disliked). Elsie was having a spot of bother upstairs. She back-handed a
loutish corporal and, by doing so, forfeited a week's pay whilst receiving
a severe reprimand.

There was trouble when a framed picture of Hitler hanging on a wall
in the dining-room was desecrated with juice from an overripe tomato.
The entire staff was lined up and severely lectured to by an Unteroffizier
who promised a reward to anyone who turned in the culprit. I stood
erect, eyes unblinking, wanting to look above suspicion.

Quietly, I was building up a dossier of 'crimes'. Chalking 'V' for
victory signs and 'Deutschland Kaputt' was a popular pastime. I was
pissing over 'Notizen' and 'Plakate', deflating military bicycle tyres,
uncoupling saddles and loosening handlebars. In another category, I was
'requisitioning' whole loaves of bread from the Continental military
store, whisking the booty away through the back door after hours. On
the occasion when I was stopped by the local constabulary for violating
the hour of curfew, a loaf and a handful of cigarettes got me out of
trouble. Indirectly, I was having some liaison with the Royal Air Force,
picking up news-sheets dropped at a point on the west of the island and
distributing them into earnest hands.

It was the well-groomed Pietro Lucari who brought me the fateful
message. The colour had returned to his cheeks and he was sprouting a
thick carpet of new hair. 'A telephone call from the Grand,' he said
glumly. 'Mistaire Tostevin wants to see you at his office.'

I was bitterly familiar with the name. 'Mistaire' Arthur Tostevin was
an honorary police officer with the eminent title of 'Centenier'. Within a
short time, he had acquired a disreputable nickname for himself, the
more forthright islanders calling him 'Goebbels' to his face.

Pietro Lucari looked at me with concern. 'What have you done?' he
asked.

I shrugged. 'I'm on my way to find out,' I said. I shook hands with
Lucari. He was a friendly man, always courteous and polite to the lower
orders, and he had pardoned the 'Breetish' for scalping his head. Before
leaving the hotel by the front door, I had a few words with Joe, Elsie and

Lily. The odds on my immediate return, they knew as well as I did, were stacked high against. They promised to provide my mother with goods from my share of the hidden mine. Given this assurance, I sauntered along St Saviour's road and turned west into La Motte street. What did Tostevin, the most dangerous among the enemy bootlickers, want of me? No questions had been asked about the sale of the hotel's better effects to the hawker, which could be construed as robbery; only Lucari had been mildly inquisitive after his return from detention. I knew that Tostevin and his plodding 'shadow', Detective Constable Benjamin Shenton, were making discreet enquiries about a grand theft at 'Clos de Tours', a house overlooking the tiny harbour at St Aubin's, the grandiose residence of the Bailiff, Alexandre Montcrieff Coutanche. Some time after Coutanche had published a civil order prohibiting the hoarding of foodstuffs under penalty of imprisonment, the 'Clos de Tours' larder was relieved of several hundreds of cans adorned with English, French and German labels. Tostevin and Shenton were out to catch the plunderers.

The narrow streets in the town were thronging with military personnel and noisy with huge vehicles which shook the foundations. Unhurried, I took a round-about route, west along the Esplanade from the once pompous Royal Yacht Hotel, a former hive for dark-blue blazers, white flannels, nautical caps and bloated faces, past the long row of warehouses – quaint storage depots of the seed and timber merchants which, by rights, should have been bustling with horses and wagons, handcarts and fussy little open-cab lorries. I stopped to look at a dusty window of a defunct travel bureau, smiling to myself. A fading poster advertised an excursion to St Malo for seven shillings and sixpence return; another offered a week-end in London for thirty shillings to take in a show.

I crossed the broad road and looked over the sea-wall. The ancient, fairy-like Elizabeth Castle – out of bounds to the locals – was bathed in a late morning hazy sun, a shimmering tide lapping its causeway access. Turning my head westwards, I could see the long narrow breakwater at Beaumont, more than two miles away. A lump came to my throat; here was my playground where I learned to swim as a five-year-old. Now? No-man's-land, inhabited only by seabirds. For a moment I was tempted to run the distance to my mother; there were many holes and corners on the island where I could hide and hold out until the day of deliverance.

When? A year, little more, said the optimists. I had no choice but to brave it out. Each short, unwilling step took me nearer to the building; it looked more imposing, more repellent than I had ever noticed before. Propped up against an outside wall, sticking out like a sore thumb, was a bicycle, a folded mackintosh strapped to the crossbar, the saddle and handlebars raised to fit the tall figure of Tostevin's crony, Detective Constable Shenton.

I walked up the steps: a German sentry barred my entrance into the great lobby. After my identity had been checked, I was directed up a wide staircase to a room on the first floor. I thumped on the door, determined to be bold. I was all too familiar with Tostevin's manner – unsympathetic, cold, a bully. Ben Shenton was little better: my mother called him a lèche cul, an arselicker. Still fresh in my memory was the occasion when Tostevin and Shenton arrived at my mother's home to arrest me, not yet eighteen, for the offence of taking away a motor-car without the consent of the owner.

'Borrowed,' said my tearful mother. 'Just a joyride. Don't make it hard for him,' she pleaded. 'He's not a thief.'

'He bloody well is in my book!' Tostevin retorted. 'Your boy has taken more than one! He's led me a right bloody song-and-dance! He needs a sharp lesson! A dose of the clink!'

Before the fearsome little magistrate, Pinel, in the lower court, I pleaded guilty. The court was empowered to fix a maximum custodial sentence of only one month. Tostevin recommended that the matter be dealt with at the Royal Court. Subsequently, the Bailiff and Superior Judge, Alexandre Coutanche, passed a term of three months 'avec les travaux forcés', an old Jersey punitive idiom meant to demoralize and degrade those condemned to hard labour in the fearsome prison stone-yard: even convicted debtors and intemperants were not exempt from this medieval form of punishment.

Tostevin looked at his pocket watch when I walked into the room, formerly a prime double guest room with a view over the harbour and St Aubin's bay. The Centenier was hunched over a knee-hole desk, his feet barely touching the carpeted floor. Detective Constable Shenton, with the face and physique of a clapped-out pugilist, stood over his stunted colleague, a bicycle trouser-clip gripping the cuffs of each ankle.

'You took your bloody time getting here,' Tostevin snapped.

Straightfaced, I answered: 'I took a swim on the high tide.'

'That could be your last swim for a long time, you cheeky bugger,' Tostevin retorted with a smirk. 'Mind your p's and q's, you're in enough trouble.'

'What sort?'

'I'm coming to that! I'll knock you off your high horse. I haven't had eyes in the back of my head, you know. I bet you had a right shindig in the Continental with that Portuguese wop and those two tarts. I could pin a few sins on your head but I haven't got time. One is enough to put you away for a long spell.'

My blood started to boil. Sneering about the company I kept and the terms he used were both objectionable. I had nothing to lose; I could afford to be provocative. 'Look here, Goebbels ...'

Ben Shenton was quick to interrupt. For a moment I thought he was going to thump me. He stuck a finger in my face. 'Watch your rotten little lip!' he said, red of face. 'Know your place! Have respect for the Centenier! What's this Goebbels lark, eh?'

A breeze came into the room through the open window. A hungry sea-gull perched on the sill, squawked and sheered off. I stood my ground, counting the flies on the ceiling. 'Not a lark,' I said after a moment. I pointed a finger at Tostevin; his face was half-hidden behind a large white handkerchief. 'He knows! He's heard the nickname! He's got a lot more to worry about than me! Jerry arsehole-crawler, poking your noses in every corner of the island on the look out for hidden cars and wirelesses. Betting on Jerry winning the war, eh? Well, I've got a good memory and when the time comes I'll have a big mouth.'

Tostevin seethed. I knew my explosion of feeling and anger would be to my cost but I was not regretful.

'Tell him why he's here,' Tostevin said impatiently.

Shenton didn't seem to relish the order. He fished into a pocket, pulled out a notebook and hesitated before opening it and reading: 'That you did, whilst in the employ of the States Labour Board for certain units of the German army in occupation at the Continental Hotel, over a period of nine weeks, fraudulently obtain the sum of nine pounds ... '

I hadn't bargained for that. It had been nothing to weigh on my mind. True, I had signed for wages each week claiming a small amount for a bogus dependant. At first it was a misunderstanding, but then I decided a deceit, petty at that, was all part of the stratagem to outwit the enemy. 'Is that the best you can do?' I taunted. 'Ninety Occupation Marks! Money specially printed! Cheating the Jerries is not an offence but worth a medal.'

'That's not for the Centenier to decide,' Ben Shenton said, unimpressed. He proceeded to search my clothing, the usual procedure before removal into custody. He pounced on a folded sheet of paper which I had lodged in the top pocket of my jacket, intending to take it home for my mother and neighbours to read. 'What have we got here?' he asked, spreading the damning evidence out on the desk before Tostevin's eyes.

'Where did you get it?' Tostevin challenged.

I could have kicked myself. I smiled, a little sickly. 'From Buckingham Palace,' I said insolently. I put a finger on the illicit newsletter. 'There's the King and Queen's picture. They sent it to me by special delivery.'

Tostevin shook his head and tutted. 'It's a pity you didn't keep a civil tongue in your head, my lad,' he said.

It was late September, and the Occupation was nearing the end of its third month. Up to this time, one could not criticize German behaviour on the island; apart from minor incidents, the military personnel had conducted themselves reasonably well, though some were ill-bred big-mouths. Trifling with married women and young girls caused dissension with husbands and boyfriends, and there were drunken brawls with an Irish involvement which resulted in black eyes and bloody noses, earning the participants a short spell in jail. As a result many islanders refused to believe the horror stories of murder and rape perpetrated throughout the invaded countries.

One had to be on guard not so much against the Germans, who often overlooked minor infringements of the Occupation's laws, but against an increasing number of informers, some motivated by a deep-rooted ill-will towards their neighbours and wanting to settle an old score. There were the fifth-columnists, Italian and Austrian hotel head-waiters and managers from pre-Occupation days among them. After the war two Englishmen were convicted by an English court for collaboration. Both served long prison sentences.

One was also chary of the 'Jerry-bags', married women and daughters who became intimately attached to German soldiers, airmen and sailors whilst husbands and fathers were serving with the British forces overseas; but none was more dangerous than certain prominent members of the States government who were seen to be hobnobbing socially with top-ranking German officers in hotels and returning the compliment in the privacy of their own homes.

On remand in a cell in St Helier's medieval jail, better known as 'the building on the wrong side of Gloucester Road', I thought it too much to expect Centenier Arthur Tostevin to find a spark of decency and destroy the telltale newsletter. I received a caller, a tall, gangling member of the Feldgendarmerie in his shining badge of office – a breast plate with an eagle emblem. A middle-aged man, he looked far less awesome when he removed his steel helmet and sat down on a stool in my cell. He was courteous, gentle and even fatherly, in sharp contrast to the antipathy shown to the prisoners by the warders and governor of the twenty-cell jail. The German policeman offered me a cigarette which I readily accepted, not because I was crying out for one, but it was an opportunity to flout the prison rule on tobacco prohibition.

He read from a thin document, interpreting the German wording slowly so that I might understand his halting English: 'On information received, you were found to be in possession of a British propaganda leaflet contrary to the laws of Occupation ... ' The informant's name, A. Tostevin, Centenier of St Helier, was typed at the bottom of the page.

A plea of guilty, he said, would not necessitate my appearance before a Military Tribunal. I had prepared myself for a stiff sentence, even stretching my imagination in my long nights of confinement to a firing-squad. Almost apologetically, I was asked to accept 'one month' of simple imprisonment. I had a right of appeal but I was advised against. He put a hand on my shoulder. 'When one is young,' he said, 'it is just a short time.'

I was committed for trial, on the charge of fraud, to the awe-inspiring Royal Court. I instructed my defence counsel, a faint-hearted advocate provided by the establishment, to argue the case beforehand with the prosecuting Attorney-General, the corpulent Charles Walter Duret-Aubin. The civil court, I said, had no jurisdiction in the matter, the offence was against the Occupiers, I had been working for 'them' and the money I had wrongfully appropriated was in German marks. Judging by the leniency with which the Feldgendarmerie had punished me in what was considered a more serious misdoing, I stood a better chance of fair play before a Military Tribunal. Pietro Lucari had promised to support me at a Tribunal; he would attest that I was a good worker and that my job at the Continental was open.

My request pooh-poohed, I stood in the dock facing a panel of familiar funereal faces — two Jurats and the presiding Judge, the formidable hawk-nosed Alexandre Montcrieff Coutanche. The court was filled: some of the audience had a genuine interest and some were oglers passing the time away. My first rebuke came from Duret-Aubin; he admonished me for turning my back on the judges and greeting my mother with a wave of a hand; she sat in the gallery, dressed in her Sunday best, a light-grey dress with a white lace collar and cuffs. Pinned below her throat was a good-luck charm — a silver horse-shoe which my grandmother had given her. A black cloche hat, adorned with a cluster of bright red artificial cherries, was set on her head and her greying hair was bunned at the nape of the neck. In her younger days, my mother's beauty was often compared to that of the brazen 'Jersey Lily', Emilie Langtry, the love of the Prince of Wales and other eminent men.

My mother had been allowed a brief visit whilst I was on remand. Her news was far from encouraging. My father was ailing and not at work. She had been reading the tea leaves. 'Don't expect to get off lightly, Son,' she warned me, 'nine pounds or nine hundred, that Coutanche is a hard man.' Lowering her voice and speaking in French so that the hovering warder might not hear or understand, she said: 'Ton père soupire après une boîte de poisson.'

My father craved a tin of fish. In a whisper, I said: 'Parle avec Joe.' I knew my father liked sardines, a commodity of the past, except for what was hidden away in our cache, and I could rely on Joe to dig up enough to satisfy my father's needs.

My advocate was unambitious in pleading my case. The result was inevitable. The nature of the currency obtained by deception mattered not; 'Neither here nor there,' said the Attorney-General, 'Fraud was fraud,' irrespective of the amount. I had been employed by the State; the offence was for a civil court to decide upon and not a German Military Tribunal.

Pietro Lucari was not called on my behalf, but in any case his support would have fallen on deaf ears. Mitigation? I was already a convicted felon, the Attorney-General told the court; 'car-borrowing' and contravening the laws of the German occupation were on my record. A stiff sentence was asked for.

I braced myself. Three months, I said to myself watching the bushy-browed Coutanche consult with his Jurats. With time off for good behaviour, I could be home for Christmas.

Coutanche looked down on me from his carved oak perch like a large bird of prey sharpening its beak before the kill. I needed a sharp lesson, he said. It was a doctrine I had heard many times before, when, at school, I put both hands out, or bent over to my headmaster to receive six of the best for small misdemeanours like playing truant, smoking and teasing the girls.

'Six months' imprisonment,' Coutanche trumpeted, deriving some pleasure in piling on the agony with 'hard labour'.

I was a convict in a jail noted for its stark, almost brutal, rigours, worsened by the Occupation. In a cell of thick red granite walls, I shivered in my white institutional cotton tunic and trousers. For five and a half days a week I was condemned to the notorious stone-yard, a narrow quadrangle of walled cages each equipped with a saddle-stool, wire eye-protectors, a short-handled hammer and the material – granite boulders – which one had to reduce to chippings. Normally in demand for repairing roads and laying out driveways to hotels and large country houses, now they were claimed for German military uses.

Squatting all the long day without exercise on a growing mound of chippings, limbs ached and contracted, ears buzzed, heads drummed and the palms of one's hands burned with huge bursting blisters. Scabbed backsides, like every other lesion, went untreated. The rules were strictly enforced by the governor and his warders, men, English and local-born, who had seen military service; the more case-hardened had proved themselves policing the 'glass-houses' of the British army. No speaking, no togetherness, one eked out one's time in complete silence and solitude.

Physically and morally, conditions were bad, designed to be so, to the extent that those sentenced to more than two years were transported to a prison on the English mainland after the maximum time permitted in Gloucester Road had been reached and at the States' expense. With the advent of the Occupation, conditions worsened rapidly in the jail. The population increased to an average of thirty; cells which had not been used for many decades were leased to the Military Tribunal for petty civil offenders, guarded by His Majesty's warders. Food rations for the public at large were less than desirable, but people were free to rummage around and trade for extras; gardens were turned into vegetable plots; rabbits and chickens, whilst not plentiful, provided stews and traditional Sunday roasts for the fortunate and those able to pay blackmarket prices.

Before the Occupation, food for prisoners was weighed to a gram, insufficient and of poor quality, a regime contrived by some cheese-paring dietician from the dark ages merely to ward off malnutrition. Now prisoners were vulnerable to rascally and cunning warders who dissected the prisoners' bread and dipped their fingers into their bowls.

With the tightening of belts, the characters and conduct of some people changed for the worse. The governor and his deputy had their own shabby scheme afoot to supplement their own beggarly larders. Whereas in normal circumstances food parcels were prohibited, the wily pair winked at the rule, and friends and families of the prisoners were encouraged to bring in foodstuffs; legitimate rations which had been scraped together and provisions bought on the black market were left at the gate for examination and then systematically nobbled, only a small proportion reaching the cells.

To have a prisoner among us who had been sentenced to death was emotionally disturbing. François Scornet, a handsome young French-man, had escaped from France in a small boat in an attempt to reach England; for that offence his execution was imminent. Breaching the rules, the prisoners sought to save Scornet's life; it was thought that a petition to the two most influential men among the States hierarchy, Alexandre Montcrieff Coutanche and Charles Walter Duret-Aubin, might prove effectual in having the sentence commuted to imprisonment.

On learning of the concern, Scornet took heart. But, to get word to the two exalted principals, one had first to go through a complicated channel, giving notice to the senior warder who would then inform his chief who, in turn, would approach the governor. The governor listened with half an ear; that the prisoners should dare put their names to a paper, for whatever reason, was contemptuous and against discipline, deserving only of punishment. François Scornet was executed by firing-squad at St Ouen's Manor in the north-west of the island on 17 March 1941. His body was then transported to the mortuary chapel at Almorah, St Helier, and buried in a holding grave.

A board of Commissioners who toured the jail each month, retired 'gentlefolk' in plus-fours and country tweeds, were unsympathetic to the complaints made by a minority of prisoners with the courage to tell of the wretched conditions, the cold and the need for warm clothing and bedding, and the short rations. 'We are all suffering,' they would say.

I was released in the early spring, calculating that my right to remission had been violated by twenty-one days for, off his own bat, the governor had decided that the sentence imposed by the Military Tribunal and the one imposed by the Civil Court should run consecutively; moreover, I had not been an exemplary prisoner, he said, I had complained incessantly about the food, my work had been below standard, I had dared to put my name to a petition and I had been insolent to the Commissioners.

'Good God!' my mother cried when I arrived home. 'You're as thin as a rake! What happened to all the bread puddings and gooseberry pies I left at the jail?' She led me across the road to a small farm holding where there was a commercial scale. I sat in the dish: the pointer registered little more than nine stone, two less than seven months before.

My mother fed me thick soups and rich stews; the meat ration was small but potatoes and other root vegetables were still available. She still had enough flour to bake her own bread, and 'honest' Joe, in my absence, had taken great care of my share of the cache; the supply would last out another year.

At liberty, I was walking a tightrope. 'Be on your guard, Son,' my father warned from his sick-bed, 'they'll be watching you like hawks.' And he didn't mean the Germans.

'When I feel up to it,' I said, 'I'm going into the Town Hall and blow cigar-smoke in Tostevin's face.'

My father's eyes twinkled, even in pain. 'And carry a bottle of whisky under your arm, Son,' he said.

The States required every able-bodied man to work, there were no free handouts. At the Labour Department, I reluctantly accepted a pick and shovel and, with three other jail-birds, as all ex-prisoners were tagged, I was driven in a military truck to St Peter's Valley, a picturesque rural locality of woodland, hillocks, green meadows and gurgling streams.

It was a blissful season in the year despite the inconveniences and the sad spectacle of the invaders having made themselves at home. Plants thrived, shrubs thickened and birds sang in the blossoming trees. But I was not enraptured by the delights of nature; it was late in the evening and pitch dark when I reported for work and there was a suggestion of evil lying in wait.

Powerful arc-lamps were beamed at a rockface in a tract of land bordering the country road. 'Hier graben,' one of the German civilian overseers said as he demonstrated with a pick, a sledge-hammer and broad chisels two feet long. I worked the night shifts, chipping and cleaving at the mass of stone and shovelling the deposits into wheel-barrows. The work was hard, but the pay in Marks was above average with an extra allowance of bread and meat.

'Back-breaking, eh?' my mother questioned when I arrived home in the mornings dog-tired. 'Not your kind of job, Son. What's it all for?'

'We're not to ask, Mum,' I replied. 'Some sort of tunnel, that's for sure.'*

From acts against the enemy, calculated to annoy rather than cause injury, I was escalating to something more aggressive. The project was well under construction, a tunnel fifteen or more feet high supported by a system of props and joists many yards deep into the interior. To speed up the work, additional labour was recruited and explosives brought into use. Holes were drilled into the rock and small charges inserted under supervision. But the two German overseers became lax, spending much of the night shift in a hut, eating and drinking and trafficking in second-hand goods. Little by little, amounts of explosive were pocketed and set aside.

Tensed up, I walked the three miles from the site to my home in the very early hours of the morning: my special pass permitted me to disregard the curfew. My mother had good reason to look surprised when I woke her up. She came down the stairs, a shawl over her nightdress. 'Hello!' she said. 'Have you been given the push?'

'Laid off,' I answered truthfully, but not looking at her straight in the eyes. 'Until further notice, we were told. There was an accident, Mum. The whole piddling thing came down. Surprised you didn't hear the bang.'

She boiled a kettle of water for cocoa. The brown powder was like gold dust. 'I heard something,' she said. 'The windows rattled, I thought it might be a clap of thunder or the Jerries letting off.'

I heard my father calling for me. I crept up the stairs into his bedroom; his life was on the ebb and he knew it. 'What's up, Son?' he asked.

I smiled, nervously. 'Nothing's up Dad, not now, the bloody thing is all down, a fine mess.' I told him what had happened. 'No one hurt,

---

* This was the beginning of a vast underground military hospital, destined to become a concrete tomb for countless starving and ill-used East European slave-labourers brought to Jersey under the TODT labour organization.

   Today, this grotesque creation, described as 'a spectacular feat of engineering', has been the subject of an extensive programme of work 'using artifacts with chilling realism' to make it into a museum and tourist attraction.

Dad,' I said. 'I think it might have been deliberate ... sabotage!' I whispered.

In the poor light, I saw his wink. 'You didn't have a hand in it, did you, Son?'

I never returned to the site. The two German overseers were found negligent and were returned to Germany, we learned. I was redirected by the States Labour Board to another vast military project, the reconstruction of the sea wall along the 'Five Mile Road' to the west of the island. The work was even more laborious than the tunnel project, mixing cement and ballast by hand and wheeling the heavy concrete on barrows to the beach in hot weather.

As a welcome respite, I was among those conveyed to St Peter's airport to clear away debris from huts on the encampment bombed by the RAF. The runway was peppered with small craters. Abandoned, ruptured anti-aircraft guns, covered in blood, bits of uniforms and human flesh had to be cleared away. I picked up a scarred forage-cap; the tab on the inside identified the owner as 'Oberge ... Wagner.' A workmate thought there might be some relationship to the great German composer of romantic music, Richard.

In my leisure time, with the beaches and the bays, rock climbing and exploring caves around the northern coastline out of bounds, I sought some form of counterbalance to the restrictions and monotony imposed on my freedom. At weekends, the long balmy summer evenings tempted me to challenge authority. After dark, I had made incursions into territory which I knew down to the ground, bent on what my patient mother called 'des bêtises'. More than just pranks: I was sticking my neck out, doing things which, if caught at them would at best put me in jail for a long time. At worst I would find myself facing a firing-squad.

I was at the wheel of a small military truck which I had 'borrowed'. Never before had I been in command of a machine as powerful and manoeuvrable. I raced over rough ground like a bucking bronco, a midnight breeze wafting in my face through the open cab. I steered the wheels along familiar roads, pointing the stub nose in the direction of the sea with the intention of committing the truck to the rocks.

Disaster was imminent. Driving on the north-west side of the island, along the narrow, twisting, high-banked lanes at Plemont, the masked headlamps fell on an obscure mass steering an erratic course towards me. 'Loose cattle,' I thought and braked. With the engine idling, I put my head out at the side. I heard singing, drunken singing. My reaction was impulsive. My foot moved sharply, off the brake pedal and onto the accelerator. I revved the engine until it screamed and crashed the gears; the truck bucked and charged like a goaded bull, full tilt at a squad of soldiers. Through the windscreen, I saw uniforms frantically scrambling up the six-foot grass banks; I heard dull thuds, screams and curses, but I drove on at maximum speed, telling myself that my coup, dastardly as it seemed, was a legitimate act of sabotage.

I abandoned the truck in a tucked-away place called Vinchelez, Parish of St Ouen. In the darkness, I had little difficulty in finding my way home, side tracking the patrols in St Ouen and St Peter's, taking to the fields and meadows and stepping into cowpats. I stopped for breath, crouching behind hedgerows, listening behind walls; I climbed over gates, trampled over gardens until I reached the safety of the cottage in Beaumont.

I tapped gently at the back door, it had never been locked in normal times. I heard the creak of the old staircase; through the curtained glass panel above the door, I saw a flicker of light; my mother was descending the stairs with an oil-lamp in her hand.

'Bon dieu!' she gasped as I swept past panting like a pair of bellows. 'You've been running! It's three o'clock! What have you been up to? Where have you been?'

She followed me into the living-room. I dropped into the armchair. 'Mum,' I said, 'I've broken all records for the cross-country.' More earnest, I said: 'I've had a bit of an accident.'

'What accident? Are you hurt?' She raised the lamp's wick and looked me over. 'Bugger me!' she let out. 'What's that you're wearing, eh? A Jerry jacket! And a cap! How d'you come by them?'

I calmed her down. Cocoa and a cigarette had a good effect in a crisis. I told her what had happened and tried to assure her, and myself, that there was little to worry about. I had put on the tunic and cap which I had found on the seat of the truck. In the confusion no one could prove that the hit-and-run driver was a civilian. Suspicion, I told her, would fall on one of their own; there were a number of renegade soldiers among the units.

'I hope to Christ you're right, Son,' she replied despairingly. 'How d'you know you haven't killed a couple of the buggers, eh?'

'Too bad,' I said under my breath. 'I didn't stop to look, Mum. There was some shouting, a few jolts, like running over bumps in the road, you know ... '

We drank our cocoa and smoked our cigarettes, weighing up the ifs and buts and listening to the sporadic traffic that lumbered up the hill and rattled the windows. 'Look, Mum,' I said, 'I'll chuck it in, before it gets out of hand.'

'For your own good, Son. But we'll have to watch out for that little devil Tostevin; if he finds out, he'll see you swinging by the ears outside the Town Hall.'

The thought made me shudder. We had heard how the Germans treated saboteurs in occupied countries, stringing them up from lamp-posts in public squares as a lesson to would-be troublemakers. We finished our drinks, then we crept out of the back door, down a narrow pathway to a stone-built shed which served as a wash house, shared by two neighbours. I built a wood fire in the grate under a large cauldron. When the flames were burning furiously, I stuffed the tunic and the cap deep into the inferno. We watched until nothing was left but the metal buttons, little blackened discs which my mother raked from the ashes, counted and dropped into the outdoor lavatory, washing them away with a bucket of water. Eventually, along with the waste and deposits, they might pass under the cottages and drift along the village sewer to end up a few hundred yards out on the high tide.

Lying in bed wide awake, I felt defeated. My hands were tied. It would be unfair to pursue my private vendetta against the enemy and put my mother at risk. And I was sorry that I could not relate my last adventure to my father, the good man was near to a coma, within days he would be buried in a grave in the parish of St Peter at Philadelphia Methodist church.

I was a privileged 'invité' frequenting the newly-opened military night spot in the town, the 'Bel Ami,' courtesy of a recent friend, a red-headed member of a troupe of 'can-can' girls imported from Paris. Tongues were wagging: I was 'hobnobbing' with Jerries, drinking their liquor, and shagging their tarts. Admittedly, I was drowning my cares in rum company, singing and dancing when the majority of the inhabitants were finding the long evenings hanging heavily on their shoulders in the darkness of their homes.

But my critics were well off track. I was not flirting with the enemy, just with one or two girls in good odour. Nor was I doing anything illegal. I slept in a dressing-room after closing time so as not to violate the ten o'clock curfew. But, an informant told me, the Town Hall was taking an active interest in my bold complacency, assigning two police constables to the door of the club on the nights I was present in case I was tempted to wander on to the streets after the crucial hour.

It appeared that the Town Hall had run out of patience. Sitting at a table watching frilly petticoats lifted waist high and nicely-shaped knicker-covered 'derrières' displayed for my eyes to pore over, and responding wildly to the 'ooh-la-la's,' I felt a heavy hand on my shoulder.

'Come with us,' said a police constable.

Startled, I asked: 'What for?'

'We'd like a word,' a second constable said.

'What about?' I burst out.

'Tell you downstairs. It won't take a minute.'

Foolishly, I left the table and walked down a flight of stairs, one constable in front, one behind. At the exit door, I hesitated, sensing a trap. The constable behind shoved with all his weight, sending me hurtling through the door into the dead of night. The ruse had worked. Arrested and taken to the Town Hall, I was charged with 'being abroad after the hour of curfew' and bailed in the sum of £1 to appear before a magistrate.

'Hey!' I turned my head at the call. I was walking along the Parade, a broad stretch of road west of the town. I recognized the policeman, 'Ginger' by nickname and one which he was sick of. He was breathless, blue in the face and with rainwater dripping from his helmet. 'Hey!' he repeated and dismounted from his bicycle. 'I've pedalled the bloody island looking for you and I'm soaking wet.'

I turned up the collar of my Harris tweed overcoat. The December wind was sharp. 'Wet inside as well as outside, eh Ginger,' I said cheekily. 'I've just come away from the barber's, getting spruced up for a party tonight.'

'You no-good fucker! Someone's going to cut you down to size, it's on the cards, Son.'

He had little reason to like me. He hadn't forgotten the day when I got in his hair. With other boys, I stood watching him walk by, stiff-necked, a pretty prudish village girl on his arm. She wore a beret to the side of her head. I called out: 'Red hat, no drawers!'

'What's up, Ginger?'

He blew into his hand. 'I tell you what,' he stuttered, 'you can forget the party, I got news for you.'

'What d'you mean?'

'I'll tell you this much, it's none of my doing, I'm just the messenger boy, but I've been told to bring you in.'

'By who?'

He dropped his voice. 'Goebbels. Don't ask me why, all I know is it spells trouble.'

Trouble! He wheeled his machine along the gutter and I kept pace on the pavement, weaving my way in between soldiers and civilians alike. I asked myself: What could it be? It was some time since the hit-and-run incident. There was a strong probability that I had escaped blame. What then? True, I had nettled 'Goebbels', giving him notice that I intended to plead 'not guilty' to the charge of breaking curfew; moreover, I was going to blab my head off and put him in hot water. I had engaged a

noted advocate to defend me, his fee an agreed package of food from the
cache. And Tostevin was nonplussed, wondering how I had been able to
produce such an extravagant influence.

'Ben Shenton is with the Centenier,' Ginger said as we walked into the
Town Hall. I could see that for myself, the tell-tale bike with the high
saddle leaned against the wall.

'You young sod!' Tostevin stormed when I walked into his office. 'I've
had half the force out looking for you! Where were you, eh?'

I answered with all the impudence I could muster, first lighting up a
cigarette from a full packet of Gold Flake and ignoring Ben Shenton's
'Put that bloody fag out.' After a couple of puffs, I said: 'I don't have to
account to you for my movements, Goebbels, but, if it matters that
much,' I said running my fingers through my damp head of hair, 'I was at
the barber's having a trim, shampoo and face massage. Any law against
that?'

Tostevin looked up at his towering colleague. He chuckled. 'He's
picked on the right day to get tarted up, Ben.' Still chuckling, he turned
to me. 'I hope you've washed the dirt out of your ears, you rotten
bugger, because I want you to prick them up.'

Something was afoot, something treacherous by the atmosphere. Talk
of undercover deportations was being circulated from mouth to mouth,
the prime instigator in the conspiracy to remove 'undesirables' from the
island being Tostevin. Two English-born Jews from the mainland, jailed
for burglary before the Occupation, had not surfaced when due for
release. Irishmen labelled 'troublemakers', lodging in the seedy houses of
Sand Street and Seaton Place, had disappeared from their usual haunts,
and many 'conscientious objectors' of English origin who refused to
work on German military projects went missing. Some of these 'rebels' I
would meet later.

I tried not to bat an eyelid, thinking how that cinema desperado,
Humphrey Bogart, might have reacted to being put on the spot.
Without curling a lip, I lit another Gold Flake, then glared at Tostevin
with malevolence and suspicion as I emptied the packet on to the floor
and pulverized the tobacco with the sole of a damp shoe. Ben Shenton
made a gurgling sound in his throat. 'Three months of your pay on the
blackmarket, Ben,' I said, 'you might try to put that little lot in your pipe
and smoke it.' I looked at the ruffled Tostevin. 'Look here,' I growled, 'I
haven't got all day, what d'you want me for?'

'Me!' he answered smugly. 'I don't want you for anything. I'm just
what you might call the go-between.' His eyes narrowed. He gave a little
laugh. 'It's your lucky day! You're going on a trip, my lad, not on a
five-bob charabanc jaunt around the island with tea and buns thrown in.

Oh, no!' He glanced at the clock on the wall. He leaned across his desk. 'This will take the wind out of your sails all right, there's a car coming for you in ten minutes, chauffeur-driven at that, they're carting you off ... to France.'

A turn-up I hadn't bargained for. There came a long moment of silence, both men looking at me as if they anticipated a miserable show of tears. I put on a bold face and smiled. 'You make it sound like hard lines, Goebbels,' I said. 'France, eh? La charme! Les belles filles! C'est la vie!'

I was to travel first class. On previous journeys by rail, not that many and over no great distance, it had always been the hard seat of a third-class compartment or standing in a crowded corridor; only once had I dared to sample the soft cosy luxury of the privileged ranks until an irate inspector had tossed me out of the 'fauteuil' by the ears.

Now, on this unlooked-for occasion, not only was my ticket 'free-gratis' but the compartment was reserved and, somewhat bewildered and apprehensive by the turn of events in my young life, I was escorted to 'la voiture Pullman' standing at a platform shrouded by a cold winter fog that would carry me and my two 'travelling companions' the 340 kilometres to Paris, a city which I had often heard described as 'Gay Paree'. But I had little reason to express a feeling of joy or excitement; I was damp and tired, fraught with tension and inclined to believe that I would never make the return journey to the place of my birth.

The sea-crossing to the port of Granville, in Normandy, from the small harbour of St Helier, Jersey, was one I would never forget – for a number of reasons. The pint-size, decrepit cargo boat had fought gallantly for its survival against a freezing December gale, dipping, smacking and shuddering to near-breaking point in a mountainous Channel sea.

I stood like a drunkard on the open deck, my face streaming wet and blue with cold, both arms entwined around a stout rope that tethered exposed cargo to an iron mounting forged into the bulwark. A flapping canvas tarpaulin that threatened to tear away from its anchorage offered me small protection from the full force of an icy, salty spray. My stomach was decidedly uneasy, but I felt far less wretched than my grouchy 'companions', who were clutching at a safety rail, cursing and spewing their breakfasts into the raging sea; only the seagulls rejoiced. I could feel no sympathy for their plight, only disgust; I might have warned them, but they had both been greedy and selfish with their first meal of the day, devouring large slices of black bread and fatty pork with raw onions immediately before the sailing. Now, it was all belching away and I had an urge to call out, 'Serves you bloody well right, you pair of bastards!'

As the boat veered a few degrees in its erratic course, the freezing spray continued to lash at my face. I turned my head and looked about the deck. Hanging on to a rope, I waddled a few steps and found shelter in the rear seat of a large black motor-car, a Studebaker Terraplane, one of several four-wheeled vehicles which the German military authority on Jersey island had requisitioned and were deporting to the French mainland and from there, in all probability, to private German homes: the spoils of war.

From the protection and comfort of my leather-upholstered retreat, I looked through a tinted windscreen covered with an oily spray; there, with its tarnished brass radiator and bulbous headlamps facing the long pointed nose of the Studebaker, was another 'déporté', a dark green Delahaye lorry emblazoned with the name of a dairy company. Alongside, square and haughty and seemingly resentful at being shackled by all four wheels, was a dapper, mustard yellow and black, four-door Essex saloon that had once motored along the byways and highways of the United States, the country of its origin. Hoodless, and unprotected from the salt water that doused its red-leather seats and wooden dashboard, was a coveted, sporty, two-seater, muck-stained MG, a 1938 model TA which the original and enthusiastic owner had lovingly spoiled with eye-catching extras – stone-guarded fog and spot lamps, a chrome bar arrayed with fancy club badges, green-tinted sun-deflectors, and – I managed a smile – an electric hooter which sounded off a wolf whistle, a 'floozy-puller'. There was evidence that it had lain doggo; straw and hay hung from the framework and spoked wheels like soiled streamers.

Lastly, the baby, someone's abducted treasure, a pretty little black-hooded Austin buggy which shivered in its yellow, wasp-like body, its two owlish headlamps seeming to gush tears of sorrow; for the sake of hearing my own voice, I muttered, addle-headedly, 'Don't cry, little tot, we are together in this fine how-d'ye-do, you, me, and three Jersey heifers mooing in the hold, that Raleigh three-speed bike and all the rest of the paraphernalia shanghaied from homes; chances are, pal, your new home will be a good one.'

In a darkening light made worse by a thickening pea-soup fog, the battered old boat with its seedy crew and even seedier small number of passengers limped into the basin of the port, mercifully coming to rest with a bump against the stanchions of its berth. Miraculously, we had arrived on *terra firma*. I said 'goodbye' and 'good luck' to the Studebaker. I patted the seat sympathetically as I went to open the door. 'You have no need to worry,' I said, 'you'll find a grand place somewhere in Germany with a chauffeur to take care of you, no doubt.'

My escorts were having difficulty in standing firm, their legs were wobbling like jellies and they both looked as if they might have been dragged out of the sea, their greatcoats were so drenched. I waited for an instruction, my handcuffed wrist deep into the pocket of my overcoat. Having come round, the senior in rank, a tall mean-looking Feldwebel, beckoned me. 'Kommen Engländer, we go,' he said weakly.

I pulled my hand out of my pocket and offered my chafed wrist to the other half of my escort, a short, green-faced Korporal whom my mother would have sniffed at and described as a 'gueule-de-con'. The 'cunt face' looked clapped out, his eyes rolled and he mopped vomit away from his cracked chin with the back of his hand. He hesitated, grabbed at a safety rail and let out foul wind. His fingers were so numbed with cold, he left it to me to snap the loose end of the handcuffs over his wrist.

The mean sergeant retrieved his black briefcase and jerked his head in the direction of a narrow, sloping gangway. I turned and glanced back in a last farewell to the forlorn assembly of four-wheeled deportees with the familiar 'J' registration number-plates and, in that brief moment, I sensed a feeling of deep sadness; the island paradise that I had known in times of bliss was lost to shame. The humiliation I had felt and the treachery I had seen was something I could never forgive or forget. One day those islanders who hobnobbed with the Germans – the ones my mother called 'jerry manderers' – would be brought to book.

As we disembarked, we slithered on icy rungs, shouldering past dock labourers coming aboard to unload the contraband of war. Under fuzzy arc-lamps, we gingerly stepped ashore. What next? Where next? My morose guards had not volunteered any information. Before sailing, and in a civil tongue, I had tried to ask: 'Bitte, Herr Feldwebel, wo gehen … ?' The sergeant cut me short, rudely growling: 'Halt's Maul! Nix parler. No speak! Compris?' I nodded, muttering, 'Fuck you,' under my breath. The only clue I had been able to glean from their conversation was a reference to Paris but, to my mind, it was inconceivable that the military authority on Jersey island would go to all the trouble of transporting one individual of little or no importance to such a distant place over sea and land; if it was the intention to imprison me for any length of time, or shoot me – as was well within the bounds of possibility – all the means to carry out one or the other were on the island.

The sky was a black umbrella, the wind cold and fierce. The street lighting was sickly, conforming to the emergency regulations. The narrow streets were deserted; swirling fog enveloped the buildings and we stumbled along blindly, crossing and re-crossing cobbled passages.

A shadowy figure loomed out of the murk. The sergeant pulled him up short and bawled in an old man's face. 'Du, Französe! Polizei Haus? Direktion poste de police? Compris?'

The man shrugged his shoulders, bent his head and hastened away. At a safe distance, I heard his voice utter 'merde'. The sergeant cursed the whole population of Granville. The corporal groaned and belched and the sound carried. Rankled, the sergeant waylaid a youth, putting a vice-like grip on an arm. 'Du, garçon,' he said, 'Polizei Französisch, poste ... tout de suite, compris?'

The sergeant released his grip, but not before the squirming lad had complied with the order to guide the sergeant right up to the door of the police station, and as he slipped quickly away into the darkness I heard his cheeky retort clearly – 'con Boche!' I gloated, thankful to know there were Frenchies who resented the alien squatters in their midst.

The door opened directly into what looked like the charge room; it was sizeable at first glance, untidy, but thankfully warm to anyone coming in out of the miserable cold. The lighting was austere, a discoloured, fly-stained electric bulb dangling on the end of a frayed length of flex over a cluttered desk. A uniformed figure, above the common rank, sat tongue in cheek in a stickleback chair scratching on a writing pad with pen and ink, a deep frown around the arches of the policeman's eyes was a clear enough indication that his concentration had been disturbed by our untimely and clumsy entrance.

The sickly corporal unlocked the cuff from his wrist, leaving it to hang on mine. Following a recently acquired habit, I stepped before the desk where many feet had preceded mine. A patch of dark lino had worn to the floorboards and the brads were hard under the thin soles of my brown suede shoes.

Suddenly, and without so much as an upward glance, the gendarme barked: 'La porte, s'il vous plaît! Schliessen!'

The sergeant responded with a scowl, slamming the street door shut with the toe of his boot; the force of the impact rocked a bottle perched on the edge of a shelf and it crashed to the floor. I saw the gendarme's heavy black moustache bristle. He closed his eyes and clenched his fists. There was a blob of ink on the writing paper. 'Nom de dieu!' he sighed.

Behind the steel bars of a cage in a murky recess of the room, a figure stirred restlessly. A cracked voice called out angrily. Never before had I heard such a mouthful of bad language from a woman. 'Hey là! Espèces de cons! Merde alors! Quel fracas! Arseholes!'

The gendarme grimaced. He called out: 'Ta gueule, Babette!' He shrugged. Ignoring the Germans, he absorbed the ink-stain with a corner of a piece of blotting-paper. This done, he resumed his writing. The slight was jumped upon. The sergeant pushed forward angrily. He pounded the edge of the desk with a fist, causing the inkwell to buck. 'Monsieur,' he hissed, 'attention! Ich bin müde!' He turned his head and pointed a finger at the corporal who was slumped on a bench. 'Mein Kamerad ist auch müde, fatigué, compris? Malade auch! Nix toute la nuit ici! Compris, Monsieur?' He opened his briefcase and took out a document. 'Der Engländer,' he said, 'reste ici, à la poste, deux ... trois heures, compris?'

The gendarme looked up at me. He nodded his head in salute. He leaned across his desk and offered me a handshake. 'Good evening!' he said cheerfully. Then, more seriously, he looked at the scowling sergeant. In garbled German, interposed with his own native tongue, he went to some lengths to explain the strain he was under. The 'Brief', he said, pointing at the letter, was a matter 'tout important', 'ganz wichtig'. He'd had a trying day, 'beaucoup d'interférence', he didn't want to miss the last post; placing the palms of his hands together, pleading for time and patience, 'der zwei oder drei minuten, Monsieur le sergent,' and then he would devote the whole of his attention 'à l'armée allemand'.

The sergeant turned hostile. He stepped back and mouthed 'französische Schweinerei' and promised his inert friend, Karl, he'd knock the 'Scheiss' (shit) out of the 'dumm' Frenchman after two minutes. The gendarme gave me a wink. Seemingly unconcerned by the threat, he obstinately continued with his writing, blotting each line with meticulous care. I took stock of my surroundings, shifting my eyes but not my feet lest I, too, incurred the wrath of the sergeant – I feared that it would be some time yet before we finally parted company.

It was not the first police station I had been formally acquainted with, but I had never seen one so unorderly, so slovenly even. Despite the circumstances of my presence my spirits were revived, if only for a few hours, and I knew I was among friendly allies, which had not been the case with fellow British-Jerseymen of the St Helier police at the Town Hall from whence I had started out in the morning.

The charge-room smelled of strong tobacco; empty wine bottles formed part of the gaudy decor, they spilled over the sides of a cardboard box to the floor, they stood upright on shelves like book-ends, and one, half-full, performed the duty of a paper-weight on the gendarme's desk. I looked longingly, with a craving almost as if I had not eaten since supper the night before, at a 'demi-pain', the kind of crusty white 'baguette' which I hadn't seen for many a long day; it was sliced longways and over-filled with hard cheese. It stood on top of a filing cabinet alongside a glass jar filled with haricot beans, probably the gendarme's supper.

For want of a screw, a wooden coat peg sagged loosely from its mounting on a yellowing wall; and behind the desk, above the gendarme's head, a photograph in a black frame hung at a cant – a nostalgic reminder of a police football team of bygone days. To the left of the desk there was a half-glazed door, a shadow of light penetrated through the glass which had long ago been treated to a thin coat of cream-coloured water paint, voices from within the adjacent room produced a low continuous humming and hawing as if a card game was in progress.

To the extreme right of the charge-room, in a broad recess, were three narrow cages; open steel bars reached from the base to the ceiling. In each confine was a wide wooden board on short legs with a wafer-thin mattress; a solid table, not unlike a butcher's block, was bolted to the floor. The woman, Babette, lay face down on her mattress, long unkempt hair straggling to the stone floor. Her breathing was heavy, intercepted by animal-like noises.

Twice the street door opened. Both times a civilian ambled in rubbing cold hands and greeting 'Albert' with a cheery 'bonsoir', habitués, I guessed. But the cordiality was brief when Albert's friends clapped their eyes on the two Germans; they accelerated their leave-taking with a 'tout à l'heure, mon vieux', Albert didn't look up, neither did he reply.

Albert was stretching his luck, I thought. His audacity was making me uneasy. I breathed with relief when his voice finally piped triumphantly, 'Et voilà!' He looked up. 'Brief fini!' he exclaimed. 'Fertig machen, mein Herr,' he added for good measure and pushed his chair away. 'Merci bien pour votre patience, Monsieur le sergent.' Albert spread out his hands. 'Maintenant, je suis à votre service. Was wollen Sie, bitte?'

I cringed. The smile on Albert's face was noticeably twisted. Understandably, the sergeant exploded. He stabbed a forefinger into his chest. 'Was will ich!' he stormed. 'Du,' he shouted into the unflinching face of Albert, 'du figging Komödiant! Frechheit! Schweinigel! Mal à tête … !'

Albert put on a pained expression. That he was a 'comedian, brazen-faced, a dirty-pig, sick in the head,' and that there was a 'figging Krieg' going on, and the sergeant needed only a simple signature on a piece of paper for me, before taking temporary leave of the police-station so as to dry out his and the corporal's uniform, eat and rest, did not produce an immediate effect.

Albert nodded. 'Compris,' he said. 'Signature pour prisonnier anglais.' Nothing more simple than that, he agreed. But there was no need for abuse, he told the enraged sergeant. And, Albert asked, 'pour le registre', could he be told for how long the prisoner would be detained in his station and for what reason?

'Nein!' It was none of Albert's 'figging' business.

'Très bien,' Albert replied with a shrug. He sat back in his chair, dipped his pen in the inkwell and, ignoring the piece of paper which the sergeant pushed under his nose, calmly addressed an envelope. That done, he reached into the depths of a trouser pocket, pulled out his purse and unfastened the clip; searching amongst the banknotes, he selected one which he neatly folded before tucking it into the envelope. Looking across his desk, he passed his tongue, backwards and forwards, over the gummed flap. Having sealed it firmly, he embraced the envelope before putting it to one side. 'Voilà tout!' he said. 'Un cadeau pour ma mère, mein liebling Mutter, achtzig Jahre alt,' he told the red-faced sergeant.

Albert, play-acting, wiped away an imaginary tear. His dear old mother was all he had in the world, he said glumly. 'Krieg oder nix Krieg,' the old lady was foremost in his mind. Christmas, 'Weihnachten, Monsieur le sergent,' was near, she would be watching for the postman, the money in the envelope would be enough to buy a blackmarket chicken, 'ein Huhn', a few eggs and a small bottle of cognac. 'Voyez-vous, Monsieur le sergent,' a good mother is to be treasured … !

The sergeant stamped a heel, he snorted like a maddened bull and for the second time made contact with the desk; the ink-well hiccuped, papers fluttered, and dust drifted about the air. The sergeant bellowed in Albert's face: 'Figg deine Mutter! Figg dich auch Dummkopf!' He thrust the piece of paper at Albert. Threatening to bust Albert's 'figging Kopf', he shouted 'Unterschrift, gottverdammt! Signature! Vite!'

Albert stiffened. He curled a lip at the tall sergeant. Albert's old mum had been grievously affronted and I thought he was about to take a swing at the sergeant. I took a step back, tempted to run for the door; there was nothing to stop me but the cold, unexplored outside. The corporal was bunched up on the bench, head back and mouth open.

Two gendarmes looked in from the adjacent room, cards in hand. One tutted impatiently. 'La bagarre, Albert! Qu'est-ce qui se passe?'

The 'bagarre' awakened Babette. She raised her head and squinted through the bars of her cage, spitting like a wild-cat at Albert. 'Diable!' What the hell was going on, she wanted to know? She yawned. And then her heavy eyes fell on the two Germans. She broke into a hysterical laugh. 'Hey, Albert,' she sallied, 'dites-moi, mon vieux, qu'est-ce qui se passe avec les deux cons Boches, eh?'

Albert put a finger to his lips. 'Gardez le silence, Babette!'

But Babette ignored Alfred's advice. She launched out at the two Germans with a volley of verbal abuse, making good use of her limited knowledge of German which was easy to understand. Screwing a finger into the side of her head, she said Adolf Hitler was 'verrückt' and an 'arschloch' and all 'Deutschland' was 'pourri avec la syphilis'.

The sergeant bunched his fists and sidled up to the cage. 'Du stinkende Frau!' he yelled. 'Hure! Putain!'

Babette was stung. To be called a stinking whore was wounding. She thrust an arm through the bars of her cage and struck the sergeant across the chest with a well-worn shoe. She spat at him. No ugly 'Boche salaud' was going to get away with such an insult. 'Putain, eh!' She had been charged with many complaints, but never, 'jamais dans ma vie', with selling her body. 'L'inspecteur Albert' would vouch for that and so would every gendarme in Granville. She had friends around and about who were big shots in the 'Maquis', she warned the sergeant. She slashed a finger across her throat. 'Fritz' and that paralytic 'serpent' on the bench had better be on guard, swimming the sewers of the town in December was no fun.

Albert quickly and wisely intervened in the slanging match. He handed Babette a full glass of red wine which immediately dampened down her anger. Half-apologetic for her outburst, he returned to his desk, picked up his pen and signed the paper with a flourish. He handed it to the sergeant grinning complaisantly as he did so. 'Signature complet, Monsieur,' he said, 'alles in Ordnung.'

All in order. The farce played out, I was forcefully steered into the cage next to Babette; the heavy door clanged shut and the key turned in the lock, the responsibility for my safe-keeping temporarily put on the head of Inspector Albert. An escape, said the sergeant patting his pistol-holster, would mean that Albert's old mother would never clap eyes on her son again.

That ominous warning discharged, the sergeant jerked the corporal to his feet. Heads down, and buffeted by a cold wind that blustered in to chill the room, the pair of Germans departed, the tempestuous Babette braying like a donkey as their heavy footsteps receded along the cobbled street. Albert growled. 'Bloody Boches! A pain in the derrière,' he said, pushing his cap to the back of his head and soothing a crimp on his forehead with finger-tips. He offered me a Gauloise cigarette and sniggered. 'Did you see how I shit in that ugly face? I know how to handle those buggers. Tell you a secret, mon ami, if it wasn't for my old mother I'd be fighting them with the Maquis.'

'Christ, Albert! That sergeant was seeing red, you were chancing your arm!' I shook my head at the cigarette. I told Albert I had never smoked anything as strong as a Gauloise; more than anything, I needed a wash and food.

'The Boche won't feed you,' Albert sneered. He summoned a colleague who unlocked my door and followed me closely to a washroom. My damp Harris tweed overcoat was taken to dry out in front of a stove. Albert gave me a clean blanket which I put around my shoulders on my return to the cage. After I had settled myself down on the wooden bunk,

Albert passed me a glass of red wine. 'Not good, not bad,' he said apologetically, anything 'réclamé' was seized by the Boches or one had to pay through the nose on the blackmarket. I was grateful for the hospitality, something which I had not experienced before when in police custody. The first gulp of wine warmed my empty stomach and lent me the fillip I needed. A nice surprise followed; a young gendarme with a pink wet face carried in my 'souper', a meal that was generous and bourgeoise; a bowl of hot thick potage of white beans flavoured with pork, a long crisp stick of bread sliced lengthwise, buttered and well-spread with a soft cheese.

After I had finished the repast to the last crumb, Albert pulled up a stool and refilled my glass. Another good samaritan had scoured the dock area for a handful of Virginian cigarettes. One was lit for me. I was a celebrity, at least I felt like one given the attention and the service.

'You will travel better on a full stomach,' Albert said.

'Where to, d'you think, Albert?' I asked.

'Over some distance you can be sure,' he replied. Albert rubbed the dark stubble around his chin with a finger and thumb. He pondered. Then he fished into a narrow pocket of his waistcoat. Pulling out a handsome-looking silver watch he flicked open the lid and cradled the ancient timepiece in the palm of a hand. 'This belonged to my father,' he proudly said. He held the watch through the bars for me to take a close look. 'He, too, was a "flic", in Abbeville, the watch was a presentation on his retirement and it was passed to me when he died.' Albert pointed to the photograph on the wall behind his desk. 'Le gardien, the goalie, one of the best.' Albert sighed. 'Ah, mon vieux, if he was alive today, he would fight the Boches single-handed. Merde alors! I hope the British know what they are taking on in this war, all France is counting on Churchill to get us out of the shit.'

Exactly my sentiments! It was not yet seven o'clock by Albert's treasured heirloom. He sat back at his desk and picked up the telephone. After a few moments he bellowed into the mouthpiece. I lit my second Gold Flake.

Babette stirred. She struggled into a sitting position and swept back the mass of tangled hair over her head. 'Hey, Albert!' she called out hoarsely. 'Encore un petit verre et une cigarette, s'il vous plaît, chéri.'

Albert silenced her. He put up a hand and shouted into the mouthpiece. 'Cherchez, nom de dieu! Look for the bugger! Oui ... oui ... oui ... j'attendrai jusqu'à la mort.' Albert turned his head. 'My cousin! A stupid bugger! Assistant to the chef-de-gare. Someone is gone to look for the crétin. We might get some information from him.'

I offered Babette a Gold Flake and lit it for her from mine. She gave

me a fierce stare and looked me up and down, then, slowly, her haggard
face broke into a smile. 'Gentil, mon petit garçon, merci bien,' she said
softly. She excused herself and turned her back. Searching through a
shabby handbag, she found a comb and a small round mirror and
proceeded to repair her hair and face, unravelling a jungle of snarls and
knots and swabbing her eyes and mouth with spit daubed on a corner of
a soiled handkerchief. That done, she turned around, looking somewhat
more presentable; despite the wrinkles on her face and a haunted
expression she was not unattractive to my mind. 'Seulement un jeune
homme, eh?' she asked of me.

'Twenty-one, Madame. Vingt-et-un.'

'Ah, British!'

'From Jersey.'

'Vous avez bonne mine! Good-looking! Regardez bien. J'ai trente-
deux and I look fifty. C'est la bouteille, the bottle is my trouble. Putain,
eh? Never! That Boche canaille! I hate them! This poste is my second
home. Albert, c'est un type chic, he brings me here for my own good.'

Jersey island she knew like the back of her hand. In the high seasons
before the Occupation, she had waited on tables at the Royal Yacht
Hotel and the Pomme d'Or. After a disastrous marriage at eighteen, she
had taken many lovers but, 'ma parole, au coeur sincère', never had she
asked for or accepted any money. She reached through the bars and took
my hand whilst she wept. 'Albert says I am "une femme perdue". I get
drunk and open my big mouth, but I am not a slut like that ugly Fritz
said.'

Albert sat up, one ear glued to the receiver. 'Leon?' he questioned into
the mouthpiece. 'Where have you been? Écoutez bien. Listen! I have a
lodger, un Anglais, understand? ... Bon! Now, on the night train to
Paris, do you know of any special arrangements? ... You do not? Pas
possible! Alors, you go and find out. I will wait ... '

Albert drummed his fingers on his desk impatiently. 'That one!' he
muttered. There was a long delay before Leon came back on the line and
Albert was quick to tear him off a strip. Then Albert listened intently. He
nodded and said: 'Bien, ça va, Leon. Bonne nuit!' Albert pushed back his
chair, picked up a bottle and replenished the glasses. 'Bon santé,' he said.
'As I thought, to Paris for you, my friend. My cousin put his nose to the
ground. There is a compartment reserved, de première classe rien moins,
for two Boches military and one civilian from Jersey on the nine o'clock
train.'

Into my third glass of wine, I was nicely fortified and ready to defy
anything that might come. 'Well, Albert, Paris is a place I've always
wanted to visit but could never afford,' I said jauntily. 'I've seen naughty

postcards, and I've heard about the Moulin Rouge and the pretty girls with nice legs who stroll the Champs-Élysées on a Sunday afternoon. Do I have a reason to be in the dumps?'

Albert pouted. 'Moment!' he said. 'La patience! I do not think the Boches cart you all the way from Jersey so that you can flirt with French girls. Non, mon vieux!'

'I guess not, Albert! Whatever the reason, it won't be fun, just the usual miserable four walls to look at and the rattle of keys to listen to. Unless, Albert, there are other designs for me!'

Albert was liberal with the wine. The alcohol would help me to sleep on the long journey ahead, I would need the energy to grapple with the unexpected when I reached my destination, he said. But after ruminating and taking counsel on the telephone, Albert did have a flash of hope for me. There was a civilian internment camp at St Denis, an industrial town less than ten kilometres from the city centre; British and American subjects were housed there. St Denis was not a bastille in the category of the notorious Paris prisons like Fresnes, Cherche-Midi or La Santé, it was revealed, but, by all accounts, 'un veritable camp de vacance' protected by the International Red Cross in neutral Geneva.

'Alors,' Albert chirped, 'that, I believe, is where you are going. But, of course, that depends on what you have done!'

I said 'au revoir' to the kindly inspector, Albert, who had made my brief stay in his police station comfortable, even interesting. Albert grasped my unfettered hand and wished me 'bon voyage et tenez-vous bien' and pushed two long sticks of buttered bread into the depths of my overcoat pocket.

My two guards, the sergeant, Erich, and the corporal, Karl, looked crumpled but dry and somewhat refreshed; neither had lost their crabbedness, which suggested a miserable journey ahead. The woman, Babette, did nothing to improve my lot; before I stepped out into the night, she blew me a kiss and called out: 'Vive la Grande-Bretagne!' and screaming, she delivered a tirade of abuse at the two Germans: 'Scheissköpfe! Deutschland kaputt! Hitler verrückt!' The sergeant stopped in his tracks, turned his head and yelled back: 'Stinkend alt Kuh!'

The rain had stopped. I turned my collar up and bent my head against an icy wind. We made rapid strides along the narrow, pitted streets, leaving behind rows of silent, shuttered dwellings; shadowy figures darted in and out of alley-ways and a lean dog stopped to growl at us before turning tail. The fog was dense in places, a black curtain in one street, uplifted in the next. Finally, a crescent of feeble light loomed up ahead and I was relieved to hear the sergeant say: 'Bahnhof, nur drei hundert Meter.'

The station was a hive of activity, red-faced porters in blue coarse cotton clothing, well-padded and muffled, pushed loaded trolleys ahead of heavy-coated travellers, civilian and military. Sharp calls, whistle-blasts and escaping steam added to the confusion. The sergeant produced an official-looking piece of paper at the guarded barrier; it was scrutinized before we were allowed access to the platform.

Our attendant – 'I am the cousin from Albert' – conducted us to a compartment in a carriage labelled: 'Réservé au personnel militaire, Feldgendarmerie.' In a flash of wit, Leon, a thin man with a moustache waxed to needle-like points, said: 'Courage, mon vieux! You go first class, en tout confort surtout!'

In all comfort! There was more than enough space for three; the seating was soft and luxurious and the compartment nicely heated. Karl, the corporal, lowered the window blinds and unlocked the handcuff attached to his wrist. 'Du,' he said venomously, pointing a finger at the floor, 'schlaf dort. Boden, compris!'

I understood. My 'bed' for the journey was to be the hard floor. Obediently, I slumped down; Karl juggled with the handcuffs and hooked up my left wrist to a steel bracket underneath one of the seats, according enough slack in the chain for me to stretch out or sit up as I chose. The Germans removed their greatcoats, unbuttoned their jackets, loosened their belts and prised off their boots.

Doors slammed. A whistle blew. Steam hissed. Couplings were drawn taut; in fits and starts, the train pulled slowly away from Granville into the Normandy countryside, 340 kilometres to the city of Paris and to a place destined to alter my mental and physical development significantly; a place of confinement which I would come to remember as a mythological heaven in my young life.

Wide-eyed, I listened to the dull metallic ring of the wheels as they turned an irregular pattern; a strong wind buffeted the carriage, but my two guards snored in their sleep indifferently. Chewing at a bread stick, I communed with myself; so much, in so short a space of time, had happened to me since stepping out of the barber's shop that morning. My poor mother would be wondering where I was. Tostevin wouldn't thaw; he wouldn't find the grace to tell her. Lily, the pretty waitress from the Continental Hotel, had been left high and dry on her birthday. And the party? I had made a deal with a farmer – half a bottle of whisky for an illicit leg of pork; the accompanying roast potatoes, carrots, cabbage and rich brown gravy would have been a blow-out haunting my imagination. Joe and Elsie would be there watching the clock and speculating on my absence.

The conductor banged on the door and called out: 'Dix minutes à

Paris'. I rubbed my eyes and stretched my aching limbs. A familiar smell of rancid bread and sausage filled the carriage; my guards were fully dressed, seated and munching on their breakfasts.

I was allowed a few moments of privacy; with the handcuffs hanging loose from my wrist, the corporal followed me to the door of the lavatory. On my return to the carriage, I made use of the mirror which was screwed into a wood panel above the sergeant's head. I wet the tips of my fingers with my tongue and freshened up my tacky eyelids. I rubbed my scalp with my knuckles and combed my hair, first down over my eyes and then back over the crown of my head with a parting, the insidious little runt, Karl, with a grin on his face following my actions; he winked at the sergeant.

It was daylight when we stepped down onto a crowded platform, the weather was dry and milder in the city. We mingled with the morning's rush, a mass of people, military and civilian, going to their places of work. The streets were congested with strange looking vehicles, commercial vans and lorries with tall wood-burning cylinders bolted to the bodies, horse-drawn pantechnicons, push-carts, perambulators and, strangest of all, two-wheeled fiacres and half-taxis pulled by riders on bicycles.

We were walking haphazardly, it seemed, crossing and re-crossing the streets and retracing our steps. The corporal became irritable, and persuaded the sergeant to ask the way. The sergeant stopped at a municipal-looking building where an elderly uniformed concierge was sweeping litter. 'Du,' he said tugging at the man's sleeve. 'Das Lager St Denis, Metro, compris?'

The old man propped the broom handle under an armpit, he delved into a pocket and pulled out a metal case. Unhurried, he opened the lid and breathed on the lenses of a pair of steel-rimmed spectacles, wiping them clear across a knee of his trousers. The corporal scowled and muttered that he was an old shit. The man peered closely at a paper which the sergeant held in his hand; he scratched at a growth of white stubble on a face that was blue and thin and turned to throw me a glance; he sniffed loudly and wiped the point of his nose with the cuff of his jacket before shaking his head.

'Dumme alte Scheisse! Komme, Erich,' the corporal growled.

The sergeant hailed the driver of a passing Kubelwagen marked: Polizei. It pulled up at the kerb. There was an exchange of salutes and the man at the wheel looked at the paper which the sergeant thrust under his nose. 'St Denis!' the man said. 'Ja, ja!' He twisted in his seat and pointed, the 'metro' was 'nur zwei hundert' metres away.

I was cheered. My destination was confirmed. I was going to the

civilian internment camp for British, Commonwealth and American
subjects. We squeezed into a carriage of the Metro. It was eight kilometres or so to the industrial town of St Denis. But bogus directions had
us going in circles, changing from one line to another; both guards were
becoming increasingly exasperated by the antics of the young French-
men who pulled faces and made animal noises.

I had time to study these Parisians – boys and girls developing, those
getting on and those whose lives had almost run its course – although
they were 'free' people it wasn't difficult to recognize the humiliation and
the strain in their pinched faces. Yet, over the page of an open book or a
newspaper, eyes expressed sympathy when they saw my manacled wrist.
Recognizing my nationality, perhaps because of my mould and my garb
– my dog-tooth, straw-coloured, Harris tweed overcoat on which there
were outstanding hire-purchase payments, my slate-blue serge,
RAF-type trousers and brown suede shoes were distinctly English –
some put their feelings into words at their point of departure, throwing
me an 'au revoir', a 'good luck', and a 'happy Christmas', which reminded
me that it was going to be yet another one in confinement; no bean-
feasts, no girls to kiss under the mistletoe and no gala Boxing-day night
for 'flappers' at the Pavilion dancing to romantic tangos and an interval
with an agreeable partner behind the potted palms in the half-shadows of
the gazebo.

My heart missed a beat when I looked at some of the young girls, a
variety easily distinguishable from the homely breed I had known on the
island. These Parisiennes showed intelligence; despite the shortages and
lack of resources, they were chic. They wore cloche hats and gaily-
coloured woollen bonnets, short skirts, and broad belts which strangled
their waists; lean rations had paled their cheeks and willowed their legs.
The more flippant threw me an affectionate glance as they left the
carriage, one pouting her cherry lips to blow me a kiss: a sight for sore
eyes.

To be deprived of the company of girls was a biting punishment in
itself. I valued their comfort and overtures more than ever before. Living
on an island, in a quiet, sparsely populated village, I was a late starter in
the field of birds and bees, a young man with parents of narrow means,
treading a path of moral righteousness. I attended Sunday school and
was a reluctant Boy Scout prevented from accompanying older boys on a
Saturday evening's frolic in the town. The beach and the sea at Beaumont were my place of recreation. I looked on unambitiously when
other boys, more lustfully inclined, played rough and tumble with girls
who flaunted their bulges and curves in risqué headstands and cart-
wheels, and when my friends were invited to investigate that which was

hidden under blouses, bloomers and bathing-costumes I kept well in the background.

Sooner or later, it had to come, the 'real thing', as Jenny put it. A Welsh girl, imported to work as a housemaid for a well-to-do family in the village, she was a unique breed of skivvy on the island: petite, dark and almond-eyed. The more courteous women among the villagers were complimentary about Jenny's looks, comparing her prettiness to those of the far-famed actress, Anna May Wong. But Jenny's voluptuous appearance and her working uniform – a short, tight-fitting black dress with a white collar and white cuffs, black stockings and black patent-leather high-heeled shoes – were fuel for the tongues of puritans and those envious of her freshness, shapely figure and cute looks. Disgusting! 'Vraiment dégoûtant,' they said of Jenny's red bathing-costume, a two-piece which curved high on the thighs and exposed an expanse of stomach with a navel 'big enough to lose a five-bob piece'.

Jenny had a regular caller, a dapper, blue-suited motor-car salesman from the town who drove up to the house in a variety of smart cars. A 'show-off' who chucked half-smoked, expensive cork-tipped cigarettes into the gutters for boys to scramble after, he had manners and style, opening and shutting car doors for Jenny and escorting her to fancy places like the Pomme d'Or and the Royal Yacht Hotel. No menial working-class lad could afford to compete in lavish spending.

Yet, without a penny to my name, I was on the brink of laying my innocent hands on what horny young men lusted after. It came to me suddenly and totally unanticipated. It was a balmy summer evening, near to dusk when I came out of the sea invigorated by a swim on the high tide. The incoming tide had lapped the breakwater; now it was receding, I stood on a narrow strip of drying sand to rub the water off my limbs with the palms of my hands. Thinking I was alone on the beach at the latish hour, I was startled by a voice calling from the dark shadows of a projecting granite boulder which had long become dislodged from the breakwater and which served as a windbreak.

'Hello!' the voice called. 'Would you like to use my towel?'

I froze. I said to myself: 'Christ! It's her!' It was Jenny. No one could fail to recognize her titillating voice. She was no more than twenty yards away, a white towel waving in her hand. 'Hello!' I replied.

She repeated the offer. 'Come on, you don't have to be shy!'

Hoping my blushes would go unnoticed in the near-darkness, I scampered over. 'Er … thank you,' I spluttered, unmanly. 'I forgot to bring one,' I fibbed, not wanting to admit that my mother's good towels were few and her second-best hardly fit to be exposed to general view.

'This one is large enough for two,' Jenny said. She patted the sand.

'Here, sit down.' I obeyed, promptly. 'Aren't you the young man who delivers the evening paper?' she asked.

'That's right. At about six o'clock. Six evenings a week.'

'I'm Jenny.'

'I know.'

She took a corner of the towel and rubbed my chest. 'How did you come to know my name, eh?'

Cautiously, I answered: 'Only because I've heard it mentioned.'

'Really!' She gave a little laugh. 'Am I talked about?'

I could hardly recount the gossip and the smut, which seemed unfair and in the worst possible taste. That little Welsh tart. Tits like life-savers. Worth a bob or two of anybody's wages. More pricks than you've had hot dinners. 'Oh!' I said. 'In a nice way. Because you're new to the village. You're different to the local girls.'

'How different?' she asked, taking more of the towel and rubbing my legs. 'Am I prettier?'

'Yes,' I answered truthfully.

'What else?'

'Well ... you dress nicely.'

'How old are you?'

'Seventeen.'

'You're tall for your age.'

'Six feet.'

'Good-looking too. You've lots of girlfriends, I bet.'

'None really. I know one or two, no one special.'

'Kissed or cuddled any?'

I was glowing red all over. I looked away, at the twinkling lights of a ship crossing St Aubin's Bay. 'Parties,' I said. 'Christmas times.'

'Ah, ah! Postman's Knock!' She slapped me lightly on the bottom. 'Naughty,' she said. 'That's the game when you get a girl on her own. I hope you didn't do anything bad.'

'No, nothing ... '

Suddenly, she grasped my hand and pressed it to a breast. Then she took my forefinger and traced it around her navel. A cold sweat came over me. I was grateful for the protection of the darkness. I could hear voices, a courting couple passed dangerously close by, a late bather was splashing about the water's edge and a loose dog was sniffing around.

'Kiss me,' she said, offering up her lips.

I went adrift for a moment. I was going to be late home. My mother would be watching the clock, preparing the milk for the Ovaltine. 'What time is it?' I asked.

She fumbled into a straw beach-bag then squinted into the face of her silver wrist watch by the light of a pencil-thin torch. 'Not quite half past nine,' she replied. 'You don't have to go yet, do you?'

'In a few minutes, I must,' I said with urgency.

'Time enough to make a man out of you,' she said eagerly. She took my head between her hands and clamped her lips to my mouth, a snap action which led to something more urgent and positive. She nestled up close to me and I felt the plump flesh of her breasts against my ribs. I had no expectation of what followed next. Her fingers flipped open the fly-buttons of my shorts; she tugged at my prick, stroked it with a hand, and when I hardened, she took it in her mouth. Wallowing in her gobbling grip, my intuition was to get on top of her but she resisted, turning me aside. 'You're only at half-cock,' she said. 'There'll be another time. I promise.'

I lay awake most of that night, not even my mother's delicious Ovaltine or counting sheep helped me to sleep. My eyes stared into the darkness, my brain fagged with speculation and, stretching my imagination, I could see nothing but a bright red bathing costume and Jenny's lusty thighs splayed out on a dazzling white sand. I kept repeating her parting words: 'I'll let you know when the time is right.' And I was not to tell a soul. I was unlikely to blab my mouth off, not even to my closest friends. I'd be cold-shouldered and my family put to shame if anyone found out that I had tampered with a girl, especially one generally seen as a 'poule'.

When a week turned into two, I became restless waiting for Jenny's call, thinking that she might have regretted her entanglement with a boy seven years younger than herself and lacking in earthy knowledge. But no! I was about to pedal away from her place of work after pushing a copy of the *Evening Post* through the letter box when the door opened. It was Jenny who greeted me with a smile. She put a finger up to her lips. 'Come to the back door after the family leave, just after eight,' she whispered.

My face flushed and all my pulses thumped. I jumped on the saddle of my bicycle and pedalled my newspaper round in record time. With time to spare, I took a dip in the sea, taking a bar of soap with me as I regularly did in the summer months – the cottage was severely primitive and unplumbed – and put on a clean shirt and bleached-white shorts for what I rated a momentous adventure in the offing.

I waited outside the village pub, the British Hotel, my eyes glued to the house, St Michael, one hundred yards along the main road. I was joined by two friends of legal drinking age, they sipped shandy beer and chatted about the threat of war and what they might do in the event. I half-listened, unconcerned by the convulsions shaking the political world; my nerves were all keyed up to a promise and I wanted to give a good account of myself.

'Hey! You don't have much to say for yourself,' one friend said.

'Spick-and-span for the middle of the week,' the other said with mild surprise. 'Combed and Brylcreemed too! What's on then?'

'Er ... nothing,' I muttered. 'Just that we had an aunt come to tea,' I lied. I was tempted to brag that I was about to pay a call on Jenny and that I had already sampled her passion. I'd have liked to see their faces. They'd have spewed in their beer jugs.

But I resisted the urge to let the cat out of the bag. Together, we watched the family saloon reversing from its garage. It cruised majestically by us, big, black and shiny and with Jenny's starchy employer at the driving wheel. 'Nice looking car,' was all I could say, feeling funky.

'Flying Standard, de luxe model,' one friend said. 'With a wireless and all.'

'Two hundred and more quid's worth,' the other estimated. 'Two years' wages to me.'

'Bugger all to old what's it. He's well-loaded.'

'Must be. His kid goes to college, a posh house and that bit of crumpet for a skivvy.'

'If he hasn't had his prick in that then I'm a Chinaman.'

Coarse laughter ringing in my ears, I made myself scarce, taking a roundabout way to the house, along a narrow footpath verging the railway line and the seawall. Approaching the rear gate, I crouched low, protected from inquisitive eyes by a row of tall flowering shrubs. The garden gate was unbolted. I crept through, treading on ground out of bounds to irrelevants like me. Jenny's employer was a big noise on the island, if he was to return to the house suddenly I'd be clobbered from one end to the other.

She was waiting at the opened kitchen door. She took my hand and squeezed it to put me at ease. 'Don't be nervous,' she said, 'the family is away for two hours.'

The kitchen smelled of delicious cooking. We passed through, into a carpeted hallway and then into the sitting-room. Jenny had already made preparations. Although it was still daylight, the curtains were drawn closely across the bay window, wall lamps with pink shades were glowing and the three-piece suite had been pushed clear of the pile carpet. For all her assurance, I was not completely at ease: sitting on top of a piano, a portrait of the 'master' posed in the grand manner scowled at me.

Jenny, without the frilly apron, was still in uniform. She wasted no time with preliminaries. In a pair of high-heeled black patent shoes, she stood on her toes to kiss me; at the same time, she unbuttoned my flies and fondled my prick. After a few minutes of insistence and sweet talk, she said: 'You're about ready, d'you want to try?'

Throbbing, I nodded. I watched, almost hypnotized. She wriggled her bottom and struggled to pull her dress over her hips. Apart from black stockings hooked up to a suspender-belt she wore nothing else. I had peeked at the likeness before when one of the more vulgar men of the village returned from an excursion to Paris with smutty pictures.

She squatted on the floor, lay back and fanned out her legs. 'Come on,' she said, holding her arms out, 'step out of your shorts and come down on me.' I followed her instructions, got down on my knees and settled myself on her stomach. Off-target, she twisted, first one way then the other. 'Now,' she urged, 'push hard.'

I did, until I became lost in dense black hair. She gurgled, jerked, jogged and clawed at my backside with her finger-nails. But I was oblivious to any hurt; and in my frantic excitement, my ears were deaf to the traffic of horse-drawn potato wagons returning from the quay and passing the window a few feet away; nor did I give a thought to the risk of Jenny's employer returning unexpectedly.

Jenny, my unblushing and rapacious tutor in eroticism, the idyllic village of Beaumont and the golden beach which had been my playground from infancy were now but pleasant memories in my troubled mind. I was in the district of St Denis, not loose in an open compound among other British and American civilian detainees, but provisionally in solitary confinement, which meant my imminent removal to another place.

To a place of execution? That had crossed my mind. My dossier was classified 'Sicherheitsgefangener politisch', that much I had been told. I was a political security prisoner. I saw no one to whom I could appeal for clear-cut information; someone, somewhere, would be making a decision on my destiny and I could only expect uncharitable intentions.

Throughout the long days, I paced the stone-flagged floor of my spacious cell in a single-storey building at the entrance to the camp. I performed basic exercises to counteract the damp cold. I saw nothing but dark clouds through a barred window built high above my head. With a swelling heart, I listened to voices, English-speaking voices, loud chatter, even laughter and what I took to be invigorating ball games. Loneliness was dismal; for the uninitiated, isolation and silence could have a traumatic effect. My term of imprisonment in Jersey's medieval jail with its rules of iron stood me in good stead.

I could not be too critical. I had a soft mattress to sleep on and blankets enough. Twice a day a guard entered my cell to bring me food and drink. Surprisingly, the soup was flavourful – thick, varied in content and always hot. Black bread, margarine and hard cheese made up the rest of my rations. And I knew when the month of December was coming to a close. Carolling came to my ears; a nice consolation for which I was grateful to an unknown source; the guard brought me a meal of fat bacon and fried potatoes, apple pudding, chocolate biscuits and a handful of Player's cigarettes. It was the season of goodwill.

'Auf! Schnell! Partir!' The guttural command echoed along the corridor leading to the heavy door of my cell. There had been no advance warning. I was leaving. A key turned in the lock and the door was pushed open. 'Komm,' a guard beckoned, 'partir St Denis, Camion wartet.'

On the defensive, I dared to ask: 'Wo bitte?'

An answer, a civil one at that, was unexpected. 'Nach Romainville. Das Fort. Viel besser.'

Romainville? The place meant nothing to me. The guard's hint that it was a much better place came as a relief.

I walked out into the crisp air and blinked in the bright daylight. Unfettered, I was conducted to a canvas-topped truck where I was invited to sit in the cab between the uniformed driver and a guard, two young Wehrmacht soldiers of different dispositions from the sour-faced oafs from Jersey who had deposited me in St Denis three weeks before.

The truck bumped over several kilometres of cobbled roads. My two escorts were friendly and talkative. Showing off, they pointed out places of significant interest, twice circling the Sacré-Coeur as if they were conducting me on a sight seeing tour; the driver slowed down to whistle at pretty girls, and both men huffed and puffed over the delights to be found in a place called 'Pigalle'. After three weeks with my tongue tied, I joined in with the banter and laughter.

Too soon, the truck climbed a zigzag gradient of narrow cobbled streets in the district of Les Lilas. Romainville's ancient battlement loomed conspicuously into view, a few flat acres of grey barren land surrounding squat ramparts blackened and decaying with age. We passed over a drawbridge, above a dry moat strewn with fragments of rock and covered by tall weeds and bracken, and then stopped beyond an archway. The driver turned off the engine. 'Heim kommen,' he said. Both men shook my hand and said 'auf Wiedersehen', and I stepped down on to a stage which was inhabited by an extraordinary cast: unbelievable, weird, exotic and outlandish people with whom I would associate in plot, in risk, in drama, in play and in love.

My reception was not exactly cordial. I was propelled into a guard-room by a scowling, masticating middle-aged corporal. He cursed at my departing escort; twice within minutes, he said, his meal had been interrupted. Barely giving me a glance, he tapped his pockmarked nose with a finger. 'Die Nase', he said, 'au mur, et silence. Compris?'

In a multinational community, I would quickly come to learn languages constructed with gestures and verbal 'mumbo-jumbo'. Hands at my side, I stood with my nose an inch from a wall, a ritual which was the recognized procedure in every prison and camp. My blank wall was being shared by another individual; straining my eyes sidelong, I caught a glimpse of a tall figure with a whiskered face and a head of long unkempt hair. Clearly, he was unwell, he was snuffling and breathing with a hissing sound.

The room was comfortably warm. Heat from a woodburning stove fanned my backside. I caught a whiff of stew of sorts. The corporal was a noisy eater, his spoon came into collision with his teeth and his tongue clucked with every mouthful swallowed.

A chair grated on the bare floorboards. I felt the stub of a finger in the small of my back. I turned my head. The corporal stared at me inquisitively, picking at his yellowed teeth with a finger-nail. 'Du bist Engländer, ja?' he asked.

'Britisch geboren,' I answered. 'Von Jersey Insel.'

'Bist du Spion?' he asked gruffly.

I shook my head negatively. In boyhood, reading fourpenny Sexton Blakes and spy stories, I fancied myself in the role of a romantic secret service agent flitting across foreign countries on missions of danger. Those pretend days were long behind me. Captured spies, as I had read and seen on the cinema screen, were blindfolded and shot. 'Nix Spion,' I assured the corporal; 'nichts,' nothing worth making a fuss about, I added.

I wondered if he would object to a question or two. With a polite 'Entschuldigung mir bitte, Herr Korporal,' I asked him if he knew what was intended for me.

He pointed to a clock on a wall and I had no trouble in decoding the answer. 'Der Kommandant, Hauptmann Bruchenbach, isst, compris?' He put a grubby finger in his mouth. 'Manger, compris? Manger fini, ausfragen.' The commandant was eating.

I dared to ask if there were other Britishers in the Fort.

He opened a small tin box and crammed snuff up his nose. Snorting, his eyes watered. 'Nein,' he answered. 'Beaucoup französisch, etwas ungarisch und polnisch,' a few 'italienisch und beaucoup Juden.' He jerked a thumb in the direction of my fellow-prisoner who stood deadlocked and uncomplaining. 'Jetzt,' he said, 'ein Amerikaner.'

For me that was a breath of good news. At least, circumstances permitting, I might have someone to speak English with. Could I speak to the 'Amerikaner?' I asked the corporal.

He went to a window, looked through it with caution before turning to tell me to be quick about it.

I shook hands with the emaciated American. His hand was limp and as cold as marble. We made our introductions. His speech was laboured; pain showed in his eyes and a growth of beard covered a gaunt face. I was the first human being he had spoken with in four long months, he said. His age couldn't be assessed with accuracy, but I guessed he was in his late twenties, nearing thirty. Clapped in the notorious La Santé prison of Paris, most of his time had been spent in solitary confinement. About Romainville, all he could offer was a chilling piece of news which conflicted with what I had been told on leaving St Denis. The Fort was 'some kinda depository' for Gestapo hostages.

There was no time to dwell on the unpleasant possibility of execution. The ringing of the telephone interrupted any further questions, answers or speculations. I jumped. The corporal grabbed the receiver. 'Wachposten,' he answered at full volume. He listened briefly. 'Jawohl, Herr Oberleutnant,' he said briskly. 'Sofort, Herr Oberleutnant.' Picking up a rifle, he slung it over his shoulder. 'Komm,' he beckoned, 'nach Kommandantur. Nix parler, compris?'

Out in the cold, we trudged along a wide gravel path lined with leafless trees towards an elegant-looking, three-storeyed house with a white-painted, stone-structured portico and slatted shutters to the windows. The front door opened. A white-jacketed, silver haired attendant presented himself. After dismissing the corporal he pointed down to a fibre mat and told us to wipe our feet. We wiped the soles of our shoes clean before stepping onto a tiled hallway. Very quietly, the elderly servant knocked at a door marked 'Privat'. Someone within called out, 'Eintretet.'

The room was reasonably large, square and lavish in furnishings; two hide, brass-studded armchairs rested either side of an old desk; the fitted carpet was spongy underfoot, a rich blue in colour, like the full-length curtains to the two windows. The four walls were partly obscured by tall wooden filing cabinets and shelving, the cream-coloured paintwork was heavily smoke-stained. Suspended from the high ornamental ceiling, a chandelier of crystal reeds reflected brilliantly in a gilded mirror which hung over a white marble mantelpiece. The opulence of the room was more befitting to an officer of a higher rank, I thought, and not to the little piddling figure who appeared to be nodding off where he sat perched like a bird in a high-backed chair with his elbows on the desk and the toes of his boots barely touching the carpet. Hauptmann Bruchenbach was owlish-looking behind spectacles with thick lenses. He was gnomish, with a head too large for narrow, sloping shoulders. His lips were fleshy and wet. The fingers of his right hand were heavily nicotine-stained and the curl of smoke which rose ceilingwards came from a Player's cigarette.

'Stand correctly, to attention.' The command was spoken in clear English and not offhanded. 'You are required to stand precisely at all times in the presence of a German officer, and you are not to speak unless you have first the permission or when it is necessary to answer questions. Is that understood?'

I nodded. My American companion let his chin fall on to his chest. The spokesman, Oberleutnant Frederic Kaiser, a tall, slim, pansified-looking individual with gold-rimmed spectacles, chose his words guardedly as if trying to avoid grammatical errors. Fair-haired, pale-faced, in his middle thirties, he was immaculately uniformed. His black leather riding boots seemed to be moulded to his legs. He stood to the side of the mantelpiece, his rear warming to a wood and coal fire crackling in a wrought-iron grate.

The Oberleutnant's runaway tongue was brought to a sudden halt. Bruchenbach put up a hand. 'Ein moment, Herr Kaiser,' he squawked. Speaking in his own language and with a slur which, by all facial traits, must have been induced by alcohol over many years, he said: 'Before you quack on, I would like to know who is who?'

The Oberleutnant was quick with an apology. Unbidden, and to save the American's fast-failing energy, I promptly disclosed my identity. The Oberleutnant said 'thank you' stiffly. He turned to the Hauptmann. 'Der Engländer, Herr Hauptmann. Von Jersey Insel.'

'Ach so!' the Hauptmann exclaimed with a snigger. 'Un petit peu d'Angleterre, ja? Pris par nous. Deutsch Soldaten.'

With a feeling of patriotism, I returned an explanation in the same two languages. All the Channel Islands, I said, were no more than 'un peu de chose', part of the United Kingdom, not militarily important. 'Nix bedeutend, Herr Hauptmann. Point de tout.' In my opinion, I told him, the German occupation of the islands was a waste of 'Zeit und Mann-kraft'.

I hadn't meant to antagonize the Hauptmann. He reacted by thumping the desk with his fist. 'Egal!' he snapped. 'Dummer Esel!' Silly fool! Who was I to judge? Was I a 'figging' military strategist?

The Oberleutnant interposed. Reading from my dossier, he said: 'Nur ein Hotelarbeiter, Herr Hauptmann.' A dishwasher!

Bruchenbach leaned forward. The Channel Islands, he pontificated, was a stepping-stone to England; within the year, the unbeatable German army would be in London, and Churchill, 'gross Jude', would be hung up by the 'Hoden'. Did I understand 'Hoden'?

'Balls, Herr Hauptmann!' Here, I could see, was a man inclined to be temperamental and easily needled. A few moments of silence whilst he sat back and sulked. The Oberleutnant took the opportunity to put a log on the fire. Then, after lighting up another Player's cigarette, Bruchen-bach said: 'Savez-vous London?'

I wasn't familiar with the city, having been there only briefly as a boy. I had read about the more important landmarks: 'Piccadilly, Herr Haupt-mann; Trafalgar Square, the Strand … '

Bruchenbach cut me short. 'Ach so! Der Strand!' He cursed. 'Gott-verdammt!' He turned to the Oberleutnant, punched the air and growled. 'Scheisse! Das ist der Name!' he said.

Bruchenbach recounted what appeared to be a wounding experience in his past life. Head bowed, the Oberleutnant listened grim-faced. I was able to follow the gist of the Hauptmann's complaint without the Oberleutnant's interpretation. 'The Hauptmann,' he said, 'was visiting England for the first time. Unfortunately, it is an unpleasant event which has come to his mind. The Hauptmann was a guest at a first-class hotel in the Strand. After only one day, the Hauptmann was approached by a female who spoke German in moderation. She said she was a guide. At first she was pleasant, escorting the Hauptmann to many places of interest. In the evening, when they returned to the hotel, the Haupt-mann paid her a fee. The Hauptmann then discovered that he had been cruelly imposed upon ... '

Bruchenbach, soured by the memory, interrupted. He rubbed two fingers together, 'Die Frau, la femme,' he said, 'nix figging gut. Demande la monnaie pour bett. Zwanzig schilling! Hure! Schlecht vooman! Compris?' But that wasn't all. To add injury to insult, the following day when Bruchenbach was out and about making his own rounds of the city, he returned to his room to change for dinner and, in the interval, someone had rifled his room. 'Parti' was his 'Brieftasche' with money, passport and 'Fahrkarte', his 'Kamera', a gold fountain-pen and a new shirt which was still in its wrapping.

Hoping this past misfortune wasn't going to rebound on me, I expressed my sorrow as best I could. 'Traurig, scandaleux, Herr Haupt-mann,' I said. In mitigation, I tried to defend the British, usually reliable for their probity and honesty. The 'Frau' who spoke German, I suggested, was one of many crooks who came from the continent to prey on tourists.

'Bah!' Bruchenbach retorted. I was stupid, he said. The 'figging Frau' was a member of a gang of robbers right enough. The hotel manager was 'Britisch' and in on the 'Schwindel'. The 'Britische Polizei' were 'Sch-weinerei'. Bruchenbach angrily stubbed a thumb in his weedy chest. 'Polizei say me, figging Nazi!' He shook his head slowly, defensively. 'Me nicht Nazi! Me gut deutsch Soldat! Compris?'

In different circumstances the story would have been worth a laugh. Prudence was essential. I nodded in understanding and kept my mouth firmly shut. The Oberleutnant then referred to the second document. Pointing to my feverish companion – 'him with the beard' – who seemed inattentive and indifferent to the procedure and who was allowed to sit down, 'name, Marcello Troska, acht und zwanzig Jahre alt, Herr Hauptmann,' the Oberleutnant read that Troska had been in France since 1938, living in Paris at an address on the Boulevard de Courcelles.

The address, fashionable from what I had been led to understand, excited Bruchenbach's attention. 'Feine Anschrift,' he said. The globes of his eyes contracted to pin-points. Staring at the American, he wanted to know if he was a Jew?

Sweating profusely, the American lifted his head. 'Half, halb Jude,' he volunteered the reply with an effort. 'Mein Vater arisch Polnisch und mein Mutter Jüdin von New York.'

Bruchenbach looked up at his aide. 'Haarspalterei,' he said icily. Hair-splitting. He could see no difference between a half Jew or a whole one. They were all the same. And to the Oberleutnant's discomfort, Bruchenbach seized on the opportunity to harangue the 'Judenschaft', blaming American Jews for starting the war; 'alle Juden' were selfish, greedy, cunning swindlers, according to him.

Asked by Bruchenbach what profession he followed, the American replied: 'Die Photographie.' And the 'Kategorie?' 'Kunst und Mode, Herr Hauptmann.'

Bruchenbach sneered. Photographic art and fashion, he said, was nothing but a disguise for smutty pictures. He lectured on French depravity and filth, but the Americans had an even worse standard of moral behaviour, the German people had been told. Unquestionably, Bruchenbach was an odd fish. I turned a deaf ear to this verbal assault on the American and slewed my eyes to a floorplan hanging on a wall. It was of a long, narrow building with three floors, fronted by a courtyard and dotted with black and red markers, some one hundred in total – evidently the prisoner building. A broad green line, off-centre, showed a division, the left-hand area stamped with an 'M'. On the opposite side, of smaller area, was the letter 'F'. Obviously, 'Frauen' were at the men's finger-tips, in about equal numbers, as far as I could judge.

This was refreshing evidence but it was overturned by bad tidings. We, the Oberleutnant revealed, were political prisoners of the German Military Tribunal in Paris, to be detained 'until further orders'. In a soft-spoken manner, arousing the suspicion that all was not well-intentioned, he laid stress on his and the Hauptmann's responsibility – solely to the administration of the prisoners during the time of their detention; other than that, neither he nor the Hauptmann had control over judgments or penalties to be conferred. It was information which bore an ominous note.

Bruchenbach brooded with his aide over a serious problem. My ears pricked up. The American and I presented an unforeseen handful. We were of an age when we would attract the attentions of the more promiscuous women and our nationalities would put us in good stead. In the event, Bruchenbach concluded it would be wise to take extra precautions.

Discipline, said the Oberleutnant, was important to the administration and prisoners alike. An attempt to undermine authority, engage in false intelligence, communicate with outside sources without permission or try to escape, would be an act of sabotage accountable to the special police. And the rule on fraternizing had strictly to be observed; it was an offence to communicate with the women by clandestine means; punishment was severe – several days or more in a darkened cell on bread and water.

Dusk was upon us as we left the Kommandantur. I took the American by the arm; we shivered in the cold, damp air as we moved slowly along a broad gravel path. Our escort, an amiable-enough corporal with a squint, muttered words of sympathy for the distressed American and explained that there was an infirmary within the building where he would receive attention. The middle-aged man hinted at 'heisse Suppe und warm Bett' awaiting us and that promise was heaven-sent.

We came upon the crown of a small hill. Lights twinkled from the building which was shrouded in a thin fog. It was a structure of stone, true to the plan I had seen in Bruchenbach's office; through small trees and shrubbery, I could see heavily-clad strollers within the barbed-wire perimeter of the courtyards. Our approach was being closely monitored. A voice carried to my ears. 'Voilà, deux nouveaux venus.' The news of our arrival was quickly passed on. More voices, searching for information, cried out: 'D'où venez-vous? Quelle nationalité?'

The building lay deep in the basin of the Fort. We took a narrow, unmade road, downhill between deep-rutted wheel grooves and mud-filled pot-holes. We rounded a bend at the rear of the building to be met by men at the open windows who saluted our approach with warm-hearted feelings, eager to know from what prison we had come and, 'par hasard', had we heard of a father, a son, a brother? Further along, a reception of women jostled for position over the sills of the first-floor windows. They were bubbly, boisterous, like unruly girls in a boarding-school. It was a heavenly vision. They waved their hands; they blew kisses and they were cheerfully vulgar. So much for the rule on fraternizing, I thought.

'Allo, Herman chéri! What have you brought us, eh?'

'Hey là, Herman! One for me?'

'Pour moi, Herman, the one with the biggest tail.'

The laughter was loud and long. The corporal, Herman, looked up at the windows and wagged a finger. 'Méchant,' he called out. 'Nix parler. Verboten, gottverdammt.' Heckled, he turned his head before we reached the far corner of the building and, grinning, made known our nationalities. A loud cheer went up.

We entered through a guarded gate and passed a lean-to which appeared to be the cookhouse. Warm air and steam gushed out of the open door and I caught a glimpse of women in sackcloth aprons with peelers and knives sitting at a trestle table. Once inside the women's courtyard, we were greeted with whistles, cries of 'allo darlings' and 'kiss me goodnight'. Inside the building, on the ground floor, women were in the stairwell and lining the bannisters from the first floor. More animated laughter and ribbing. For the briefest of moments, all my cares became buried under an avalanche of hugs, squeezes and embraces.

Still in the women's division, the patient Herman led us along a narrow corridor to a door marked: DOUCHES. In a stone-flagged ante-room fitted with slatted boards and wooden benches we undressed, the unstable American being helped by a gnarled old peasant woman with a club foot. Her short, bare brawny arms picked up the American with ease. She sat him down under a nozzle and pulled a chain. I followed the old woman's instructions and washed myself in luxuriously warm water which sprayed out of antiquated plumbing. I soaked my hairy parts with a dark liquid carbolic which brought tears to my eyes, guaranteed, the old woman said, to kill every last flea.

Rid of all dirt and impurities, we were dressed in temporary clothing, long flannel nightshirts with an institutional insignia which, said Herman with a laugh and a finger to the side of his head, came from an 'Irrenhaus'. The dressing-gowns, unlike the nightshirts, had not originated from a lunatic asylum; they were well-padded against the cold, braided with velvet, richly embroided and had lost little of their brilliance. Wiping away the steam from a mirror, I looked at myself and chuckled.

The number on the door was 26. Our accommodation on the first floor overlooking the courtyard came as a refreshing surprise. It was just like home, said a beaming Herman. The room was worthy of commendation. I had expected a cell with bars, scarcely equipped and cold. In length and breadth, the dimensions were adequate for two persons. It was nicely heated, a wood fire burned in a cast-iron pot-bellied stove. Behind the door, a two-tier wooden bunk was stacked against the wall; clean grey-white sheets and army type blankets were neatly spread over the mattresses. 'Gut schlafen,' said Herman, thumping the beds with a fist. And a touch of humour from the women; on the pillow of the upper tier lay a note scribbled in English and French: 'Hôtel de Romainville. Ring for service. Pour la fille de chambre et la masseuse.'

The room had been freshly scrubbed, it smelt of carbolic soap and the scuffed floorboards showed patches of damp. The furnishings were modest but practical; a heavily scorched table, two kitchen chairs, a small chest of drawers, a narrow steel locker for clothing, a food cabinet, and a vintage brown leather-upholstered armchair which had seen good usage. The decor was colourful; the smoke-stained walls were plastered with nostalgic reminiscences of Paris in peaceful times – a large poster of the river Seine on a sunny day with boater-hatted and parasol-shaded people strolling the banks; another of the sophisticated Champs-Élysées with canopy-fronted cafés and pavement tables bustling with fashionable 'habitués', and a saucy calendar featuring a pretty long-legged 'modèle' posing seductively in lingerie. Nailed to one wall and supported by sisal string, a shelf held a small library of books and magazines; well-thumbed crime novels and stories of adventure and romance; an encyclopaedia on wild animals; a holiday guide to the ski resorts of Switzerland; and, conspicuous by its tantalizing cover, a weighty book on haute cuisine and wines. On another shelf, convenient for the stove, were kitchen utensils and cutlery, a blackened stewpot, a frying pan, enamel plates, a kettle and drinking mugs – all the tackle for self-catering.

It seemed agreeable. I had expected a régime more like that of a conventional prison. I could not see, nor could I hear any evidence of high security: no bolt on the door, no Judas-spyhole, no heavy footsteps or the constant jangle of keys. On the contrary, there was a noticeable air of laxity about the building; beyond the door, voices rang out with surprising energy, even gaiety. I heard bursts of loud laughter and song; from some quarter, France's crooning idol, Tino Rossi, was performing on a gramophone record. Not immediately obvious, however, was the black spot to one's surroundings.

With the American, Marc Troska, tucked safely into his bed on the lower tier of the bunk – helped by the old, club-footed woman, Grand-mère Tauzin, who then left the room to go in search of 'le docteur' – I ventured to ask the affable Herman what prisoners were faced with. Was there a danger of execution?

Herman blinked and turned his head away. He rummaged in a pocket, found a half-smoked cigarette and lit it before replying: 'Nur wenige. Nix schiessen Romainville. Anderswo, compris?'

Shootings! A few. Not at Romainville, some other place. Pressed, Herman explained that executions were usually carried out at a place called Mont Valérien, near Longchamp racecourse, 'nur Menschen'.

Only men. Intending to calm me, Herman added that the Germans wouldn't shoot a 'Brite' or an 'Amerikaner', we would be sent to a labour camp until the end of the war.

'Krieg nix gut,' Herman said sadly. He opened his wallet and pulled out a photograph. His two sons, Wilhelm and Alex, both in their early twenties, were serving in an infantry regiment somewhere on the Eastern front. His wife, Herta, wrote regularly from their home in a suburb of Cologne but not with news of his boys. The next letter might tell him they were 'kaputt'. Herman lowered his voice to a whisper and said: 'Hitler verrückt.'

Herman departed, closing the door and turning the key in its lock. Minutes later, and true to Herman's promise, a meal was brought in. The bearer of the well-stacked tray introduced himself in English, in an accent thick as the sliced black bread arranged in a small shallow wickerwork basket. Ignoring the two middle-aged corporals who followed him into the room and stood quietly in the background, he said: 'Gentlemen, good evening. My name is Franz de Bruyne and I am from Antwerp. It is my pleasure to meet you.' And with a broad wink, he added, 'I am a merchant in diamonds in the world outside, here I am the chef de cuisine.'

The Belgian was a jovial man, given to showing off. He was in his early forties, loosely built, with a pale face and thinning dark hair parted in the middle of his head and flattened with an overload of brilliantine. He was unlike any chef I had known; he wore a pair of beige cavalry twill breeches with puttees wound around his legs, a turtle-neck jumper, and a cream-coloured double-breasted jacket with silver buttons, which might have once belonged to a swinging bandleader.

It was bizarre. I wanted to laugh. Marc Troska was on his back, blind and deaf to the proceedings. The corporals looked on, straight faced. Franz de Bruyne pointed to the food prepared to honour the first British and American to the Fort. He made a play of imitating a maître d'hôtel, first making it known that the components which made up the dishes were a contribution from some of the better off prisoners, men and women. 'À commencer,' he announced, 'le potage Romainville … lentilles et pommes de terre avec l'oignon et fines herbes; en suite, le pouding confiture d'orange; enfin, fromage de chèvre et du pain bien beurré.' And with a grand flourish, he took what he called 'la pièce de résistance', a half-bottle of red wine, from the hands of one of the corporals and set it down on the table. 'Avec les compliments de la chambre 40', Franz said; and pointing to the elder of the two Germans he added, with a bow, 'with the permission, die Erlaubnis, of Monsieur le chef caporal, Herr Laufer.'

I said 'danke schön' to Herr Laufer, a scraggy-looking man with a stub of grey-yellow hair to his upper lip and a painful expression on his face. It was all uncanny, unreal; the informality, the calmness, the food, the wine, and the whole packet of Player's cigarettes which Franz unveiled from his pocket. I began to think that the meal was a privilege granted to a prisoner about to go to the wall.

I was hungry, and sincere in my regret that the American was unable to partake in the feast. Whilst I ate, I was aware of being watched as if I were some kind of rare animal in a zoo at feeding time. Herr Laufer, thoughtful, stuffed tobacco into the bowl of a well-charred pipe. After a few puffs, he grimaced and muttered something about 'der Ritz, Franz, besser essen nix, gottverdammen!'

The other corporal, Weismann, a tall man with close-cropped fair hair and a large face, pink and round like a Dutch cheese ball, had a light-hearted grumble in support of his colleague. There were times, he told Franz in a peppery voice, when he would gladly change places; Romainville, he said, was more like a hotel than a prison.

The more fiery of the pair, Weismann, had news for us. The Kommandant, 'Herr Hauptmann Bruchenbach', had given instructions to impose special restrictions, nothing to do with the corporals, Weismann was quick to point out; it was a directive from the Hauptmann by telephone. First, said Weismann, moving to the window, the blackout blind was to be kept lowered 'Tag und Nacht'. A measure that would prevent us from ogling the women when they paraded in the courtyard. Perhaps more important, he said, grinning, the 'Hündinnen' (bitches) would be frustrated with disappointment looking up and seeing damn all. Our arrival had sent the women into a tizzy. 'Christus, Franz!' Weismann squawked. What, he asked, was it with these two? Did we have big 'Schwanzen'?

I could answer that lewd question for myself, not for the American who was comatose and breathing painfully. Disappointingly, our door would be kept under lock and key; we would be denied freedom of movement and association with other male prisoners until such time as 'Herr Hauptmann' decided otherwise. In mitigation, Laufer explained, we could be a lot worse off in any one of the prisons in Paris. With a full stomach and my cheeks glowing, I couldn't argue with Laufer's evaluation. Come what may, Romainville, at first glance, was acceptable as a place of incarceration, even with the restrictions.

It had been a tiring day. After the custodians and Franz had departed, I started to prepare myself for bed. I heard small footsteps in the corridor outside the door, then a gentle knock before a key turned in the lock. The door opened. My visitor was a woman in a three-quarter length white cotton coat, graceful at that. She was slender, sylph-like. Her height was accentuated by a towering turban wrapped around a head of fiery red hair. Small ringlets of curls showed underneath on her forehead and at the nape of her neck. She was attractive; even in the poor light I could see brownish spots on her pale cheeks. I put her age at thirty-five; indeed, she was surprisingly more, almost ten years, I was to learn.

She greeted me with a polite enough 'Monsieur, good evening' before colliding with the slop-bucket. Picking it up by its wire handle and placing it aside, she said, in good English and scoldingly: 'You will learn to keep this in a corner out of the way and with its cover on.'

'Yes, Madame,' I replied meekly. I could see a stethoscope tucked loosely into a pocket of her coat. At this early stage, I had no way of knowing if she was affiliated to the administration – she had come into the room with her own key and unescorted – until she introduced herself as 'Dr Beriot, a prisoner also, authorized to see to the health of all prisoners, and I have to make out a report on all new arrivals to the Fort.' However, she dispensed with the normal procedure 'for the time being', she was primarily concerned for 'your sick friend Monsieur Troska'.

For many long minutes she pored over the American. Her fingers drummed against his chest. She talked to him but, groaning apart, he made no response. She straightened up, deliberated silently, then muttered to herself: 'Il est bien malade.'

Madame Beriot left the room and returned promptly with Grandmère Tauzin. The old woman carried blankets and a hot water bottle. Madame Beriot gave me instructions. It was essential to keep Monsieur Troska warm. His lungs were inflamed, she said, and he was severely debilitated. There was little she could prescribe but for me to keep vigil, to heat up water for the bottle and to replenish the stove every two hours. I had to be prepared, she said solemnly, to find Monsieur Troska dead in the morning.

I was left alone with that thought. I strained to keep awake, pacing the room, dousing my face in cold water, drinking innumerable cups of hot sweetened acorn coffee and smoking cigarettes. I was faced with a trying situation, the stark reality of a man, a complete stranger, close to death and with little to offer him but a prayer. It could be me lying there in the same situation, convulsed in fits and starts and mumbling. Apart from aching in every muscle from fatigue, I was as sound as a bell. I was unfamiliar with sickness and death; coffins, funerals and graveyards made me shudder. But in times to come, I would be indifferent to humans in decay and with the rattle of death in their throats; and there would be critical intervals when I would yearn to fall into a deep unconscious sleep never to waken to the ferocity of my everyday existence.

My train of thought was suddenly interrupted by a cacophony of air-raid sirens. Beams of searchlights penetrated the black-out blind and illuminated the room with a whitish glow. Anti-aircraft guns boomed, the window rattled, and shrapnel fragments slithered off the roof tiles into the gravel of the courtyard beneath my window.

Disturbed by the clatter, Marc Troska twisted in his bunk. He sobbed and his mind rambled into the distant past. He was in a sad state of delirium, calling for 'mother' and 'dad'. I heard the name 'Sylvia' clearly in his utterings; and he spoke in fragments of what I took to be Spanish with a reference to San Diego, which I knew to be a seaport in California. Piecing all I heard together – 'shipping out', 'foreign parts', 'outside the law', I came to the conclusion that he was a fugitive from his home country.

I had not heard the 'all clear'. Nor did I hear the key turn in the lock. I was slumped on the floor near to the stove which had gone cold when I felt a hand on my shoulder. Sheer exhaustion had brought me down. And I had suffered the worst dream in my life. I had seen Marc Troska carried away in a blanket, Madame Beriot had certified him 'inanimé'. My number – 441 – had been called by a grotesque-looking Satanic character in a black uniform and with a pair of horns projecting from his head. I was tied hand and foot and put on a burning pyre. This fearful encounter with the spirit of evil would not be my last.

'On your feet, boy,' I heard a voice say. I came out of my stupor and peered through a veiled light to see Franz de Bruyne wearing a black homburg hat. The room seemed to be crowded with people. Shivering, I was helped on to my bunk and covered over with blankets. I wrapped my cold hands around the mug of hot acorn coffee Franz passed up to me. Grandmère Tauzin was down on her knees rekindling the stove. Beneath me, Madame Beriot was attending to Marc Troska. I heard her say to Franz: 'Il est plus mort que vif.'

A blunt remark – more dead than alive. Grandmère Tauzin's strong arms lifted the limp American out of his bunk and sat him in the armchair. He had to take nourishment, Madame Beriot said. Grandmère Tauzin spoon-fed him a bouillon soup. After a full mug had been induced down his throat, she washed him and he was put back to bed. And Corporal Laufer made a concession after Madame Beriot appealed to him; we could have enough wood and coal to keep the room at an even temperature, 'bien essentiel', she told him, to ward off complications and give the American a fair chance. It was surprising, the concern, care and attention, considering how often the extreme penalty was imposed on the Fort's male inmates.

Unashamedly, I ate an abundant breakfast – a bowl of 'bouillie', sweetened porridge with condensed milk, and several slices of toasted black bread spread with a mild margarine and orange marmalade. I drank tea for the first time since leaving the island; Franz petitioned around the building and brought in a packet of 'Maypole' which came in International Red Cross parcels, a quantity of Tate and Lyle sugar lumps and a brown teapot. Also – a highly valued acquisition to which Herman closed his one good eye – an unfranchised electric boiling-ring to be hidden away during the day and used only at night.

My mind and my time was fully occupied. Trumpet-tongued Grand-mère Tauzin – she seemed to have her hands in all kinds of tasks – was let in periodically to feed Marc Troska strong broth and to wash him, top to bottom. Whenever I felt the need, I was escorted to the communal lavatories and washroom. I paid a visit to the 'Bucklige', the hunchback, as Herman called Charlo the barber, cobbler and, more important I was to learn, a forger of keys. Charlo trimmed my hair, shaved off a stubble of beard and cleansed my face with a stringent medicated solution.

I came under Madame Beriot's critical scrutiny. She noted my height and my weight as the administration commanded. She looked in my eyes, down my throat, checked my teeth, pored over my finger-nails, pummelled my chest and tapped the nerves in my knees. At her insistence, I lowered my trousers; she took stock of my prick and turned over my balls with a narrow wooden instrument. I answered 'no Madame' when she asked if I had ever been inflicted with VD. She pronounced me sound.

I met Lutchez, a chubby character with a mischievous grin. Swiss-born, thirty-eight years old, a political journalist and linguist, Lutchez was charged with looking after the second-hand clothing store, abandoned small goods and chattels. He equipped me with underwear, a warm woollen shirt, a thick pullover, cord trousers of good quality and cut, and a pair of near-new rope-soled shoes.

I was neither bored nor idle. When I wasn't watching the lethargic Marc Troska – I had been instructed to pound at the door for assistance in an emergency – I was reading, thankful that the French language had been obligatory in my education, or I was attracted to the window where I would sit discreetly peering from behind a corner of the blackout blind at the women strolling the courtyard, my mind full of imagination.

Apart from the general issue of prepared food rations, base in quality, I received delicacies, generous contributions from better-off prisoners who were delivered provisions by relatives and friends outside. And I was not without visitors; Laufer and Weismann put their heads in occasionally, and Herman lingered with Franz de Bruyne to chat awhile. Franz told me of an offer, coming from Room 40, the same room from which the half-bottle of red wine had materialized on the evening of our admission, to take care of our laundry. With his customary wink, Franz said Room 40 was inhabited by some choice 'skirts'.

In the evenings after roll-call, if the screams of the air-raid sirens didn't pierce the stone walls of the building and plunge the rooms into darkness, I was entertained with music. Lying beneath the warmth of my blankets, I listened to the crooners and ballad-singers – 'les chanteurs et chanteuses de charme et des rues'. I slept easily, awakened only by Marc Troska's wandering mind which dragged on night after night, his family and the enigmatic Sylvia paramount in his ramblings.

I could take comfort; Madame Beriot said the American had turned the corner, he would get steadily better. This was heartening news, because, by all accounts, it was odds on that we were going to be room-mates in the Fort for some time and I looked forward to sharing his company in a responsive way, on this side of his grave.

Despite the inhibitions – the blackout blind, the locked door, no exercise and social exclusion – we were both fortunate to have come to a place without like or equal, often described as a heavenly refuge by those arriving from the tough prisons around Paris. After a period of solitary confinement, deprivation and oppression, Romainville offered compass-ion, good fellowship and affection. However, in our ignorance, it was easy to become complacent; in the ensuing weeks we were to learn the real reason for Romainville.

The month of January 1942 was coming to a close. Marc Troska was sitting up and taking notice. He had been nursed better with kid gloves; and no one was better pleased than Grandmère Tauzin to see him smile and poking fun. He had had a full measure of what he called 'that grizzled old mountain ox' scouring his ears and around his private parts with a wet flannel. He could feed himself and walk, if tottery at first, to the lavatory and washroom. And, as if to celebrate his deliverance, Oberleutnant Frederic Kaiser arrived with Corporal Weismann trailing at his heels and carrying two cardboard boxes.

Weismann barked out 'achtung', or 'attention', but the natty, good-looking Oberleutnant dismissed the normal protocol. 'Not the occasion,' he said with a wag of a hand. In a courteous manner, he commiserated with Marc Troska and, in compensation for his pains, pointed to the boxes with the emblem of the International Red Cross on the wrappings – 'All nice things to eat,' he said.

Compared to our first meeting at the Kommandantur, the Oberleut-nant was noticeably more relaxed; he sat himself down in the armchair and stayed long enough to drink a cup of tea, made 'diligently', he observed, 'as only the British can do'. He apologized for the restrictions imposed as 'necessary in the circumstances'. But, he remarked, Hauptmann Bruchenbach was not unyielding; he thought the order would come under review when next the Hauptmann carried out an inspection.

Time did not drag, the days seemed all too short. With Marc Troska fully restored, putting on weight and involved in our 'ménage à deux', it was essential to give and take. We were two full-blooded fellows with different personalities and from different backgrounds bound together by fate. He was older by six years and with a greater breadth of knowledge and experience; he had a good head for languages – French, German, Spanish and Italian. From the little I gleaned, I had no doubt that he was an adventurer, a globe-trotter, but he declared a preference for Paris as the place to hang his hat. And he was loyal to the French people; joining the resistance was not for thrills, but out of genuine affection for the country. When I touched on the subject of Sylvia and questioned his reason for abandoning his own country, he appeared startled; he was evasive and I guessed it was a private matter which he didn't want to talk about. Perhaps in time, I thought, he would draw me into his confidence on his own initiative.

Marc Troska taught me how to play poker. We were vain, spending time in front of an old cheval mirror and experimenting in dress sense, hair and moustache fads. We were both adept at the stove, frying potatoes to a crisp brown and Canadian bacon which came rolled tightly in a tin. We concocted stews, adding seasoning, herbs and meat extracts to give a nice flavour to the daily issue of uninteresting soup.

Hardly a day went by without Franz arriving with a gift from both sides of the building. We shared a stick of crusty white bread, a taste of real butter, a hard-boiled egg, sausage, honey cake or a mug of natural coffee; not infrequently, two servings of spaghetti, bolognaise or with an oil and garlic dressing, were accompanied by a half-bottle of wine. Franz made us familiar with the names of our benefactors; on occasion, he would slip us a note which contained encouragement, broad humour, flattery and endearment.

We were treated to many diversions. Madame Beriot, always formal, never smiling, made a daily round. Grandmère Tauzin brought us clean linen, swept the floor and passed over it with a damp mop. Sneaking from behind the blackout blind, we watched the men at recreation in the courtyard; they kicked a football and played boules. On the other side of the wire fence, muffled against the cold, the women strolled the perimeter, singly, in pairs and small groups. We estimated their ages, commented on their looks, their proportions and how they moved. There were those who sensed a hidden presence behind the blind; we

were often rewarded with a guarded wave of a hand and a kiss blown
from gloved finger-tips.

We shared periods of disquiet. Corporal Weismann's innuendo –
Romainville was not all 'Wein und Rosen' – was borne out when the
building sank into a strange silence. We heard no music, no singing;
voices were whispered and no one appeared in the courtyard. There was
a tell-tale sign of chagrin on Franz's face when he brought our rations in.
When pressed, he sighed and bemoaned the 'passing' of a 'comrade,' a
'chum' gone to Mont Valérien near Longchamp racecourse, removed by
the Gestapo. It was a casualty which left a shadow over the whole
building and touched on the soft spot of the corporals.

The show of grief having been seen out, normality returned to the
building, if only for the short-term. We missed little. There was another
pleasurable activity afoot to which we bent our ears. 'Le week-end' was
unhurried. One or more of the duty corporals had part or the whole of a
Saturday or Sunday at leisure. It was noteworthy that none of the
corporals slept in the building; after the evening roll-call they retired to
their beds in the military barrack-building outside the perimeter of the
barbed wire.

Our room, 26, was situated at the top of the staircase leading from the
ground floor, the staircase continuing to the upper floor of the men's
division. On the skirts of Room 26 was the main communicating door
to the women's division. Someone had a magical key – we heard it
turning in the lock and recognized the sharp creak of the hinges when
the door was opened. Women's voices, barely audible, girlish titters and
the patter of light feet on the staircase and along the corridor outside
proved that a cunning enterprise was flourishing.

Marc Troska tackled Franz at the first opportunity. 'What goes on
after hours, Franz? So the chicks come out to play?'

Franz was cagey. He winked. 'Keep a cool head. You might get lucky,'
was all he said.

The Key to the Door

With my head in the clouds, I was awakened to a gentle tapping at the
door. I sat up in my bunk and cocked an ear. A voice breathed out. 'Allo,
les gars! Are you sleeping?'

I reached out and switched on the light. Beneath, Marc Troska stirred.
I heard a faint rustle at the door. Looking down, I saw a small hand
appear under a gap, palm upward. The fingers wriggled. Roused, I
scrambled down to the floorboards, fell on my knees and touched the
brown hand as if it was godly. 'Not sleeping,' I called out weakly. I bent
my head and nuzzled my nose in the palm of the hand like an affectionate

dog. The hand was fragrant, a soupçon of lavender. Brazen, I licked each sensuous finger. The hand was retrieved.

'Le pauvre garçon!' a voice said sympathetically. 'Il a faim pour l'affection!' A moment of giggling, then the voice was projected through the keyhole. 'Allo! Méchant! Whose leeps eat my hand, eh?'

I pleaded guilty, apologized for my 'effronterie', and introduced myself. I asked her name. She replied: Lucy. 'Ah, from room forty,' I said. 'My laundry girl!' And I thanked her for all the good things she and her friends had sent us.

'C'est rien ... nothing,' she replied. 'We help each other when we can.' Tenderly, she asked: 'Is it tedious shut up all the time?'

'Bearable,' I answered. 'But it would be a treat to have one foot out of the door at this moment.'

'La patience!' Lucy said. 'Doors are made to open. Have confidence in Franz.'

'Franz tells me you are very pretty, Lucy,' I said.

Another voice replied. It belonged to Colette, one of Lucy's soul mates. She endorsed Franz's description of Lucy in glowing terms. 'Lucy is beautiful, une brunette, petite et mignonne. C'est une perle.'

I put an eye to the keyhole, wanting to catch a glimpse of the little 'pearl' for myself. But the electric light bulb hanging at the end of a flex over the stairwell was of the meanest wattage, all I saw was a wavering shadow.

At night, between the sheets, my mind was possessed by Lucy's image. During the short hours of daylight, I took many peeps into the courtyard hoping I might be compensated for my insomnia, but the few women who braved the cold winds were well-camouflaged in heavy coats, bonnets and mufflers. And I feared that Franz might come into the room one morning to break the news of Lucy's departure. The Fort's prisoner population was small and vulnerable to displacement without notice.

Our initiation into Romainville's clandestine night-life was not as imminent as we had hoped. Franz kept us briefed. The shaping of a piece of metal to fit our lock was the drawback, according to Charlo, the cobbler-barber and occasional locksmith. A pattern was elusive. Madame Beriot, we were told, was protective towards the women, well-aware of the after-hours frolics; her key was kept out of range of Charlo's prying eyes.

Herman, for the most part the relief guard for the building, was only in temporary possession of a key when on duty. Corporals Laufer and Weismann were shaved by the little hunchback on alternate days, their keys hung on a ring attached to their trouser belts hidden underneath their tunics. Weismann, the more slipshod of the pair, occasionally set his bunch down on the washstand before he sat back in the barber's chair; it was only then that Charlo could make a mental note of the intricacies in the teeth and prongs of the archaic instrument.

When Oberleutnant Frederic Kaiser next paid us a visit, Marc Troska put the question of exercise outdoors to him – 'a few rounds of the courtyard each day, Herr Oberleutnant'. The request was received sympathetically; Marc Troska was advised to prepare an appeal in writing to Hauptmann Bruchenbach, the Oberleutnant undertaking to deliver the text personally.

The Oberleutnant's visits became more frequent and, in time, informal. He enjoyed conversing in English, anticipated a cup of tea sweetened with condensed milk, a biscuit or a round of thin-cut toasted black bread spread with margarine and orange marmalade. I could see he was smitten by the American's good looks, and a sparkling personality which ebbed and flowed. When Marc Troska elected to call the Oberleutnant 'Freddy', which sounded more mellow than Frederic, the Oberleutnant was tickled pink and we adopted forenames all round ... 'but, please not within earshot of the Hauptmann,' he said.

Before the war, the Oberleutnant had been employed as a representative for a banking house in Frankfurt. He had made two trips to the west coast of America, combining business with pleasure from Los Angeles to San Francisco. Like me, he was enthralled by Marc Troska's descriptive reminiscences of historical landmarks, in particular the 'Mother Lode' country. In his schooldays, the cultural Oberleutnant had acquired an impressive knowledge of the great gold rush of 1849 and the ghost towns left in its wake.

Wells Fargo, tailraces, bedrocks and diggings aside, and forgetting his Hauptmann's bitter condemnation of American decadence, the Oberleutnant was all ears to Marc Troska's exposé of the more gaudy topographical locations of southern California; Sunset Boulevard, downtown seedy bars and clip-joints, good-time girls and nancy-boys; and liberal Hollywood, showy, extravagant, undisciplined and pleasantly wicked. The Oberleutnant was amused by the spice and loose talk; he laughed easily.

When questioned about his private life, Marc Troska hedged as I expected. He revealed that he had been born in New York; an only child, he went with his mother and father to live in the San Fernando Valley at the age of fourteen. His hobby, photography, turned into a profession in later years. His parents, he said, were both killed in an accident. He made no mention of Sylvia, and I wondered if his haunting memory of her was somehow linked to the tragedy of his mother and father. When the Oberleutnant asked him why he hadn't returned to his home when there had been ample warning that Paris was going to be occupied and

America would be drawn into the war, he shrugged his shoulders and said: 'I owed it to my friends not to run away.'

The Oberleutnant had no doubt as to who would emerge the victors in the war. He was not politically-minded, but his loyalty was to his country and Hitler and he saw the defeat of Germany as inconceivable. What concerned him, personally, was how long victory would be now that America had entered into the battle. Moreover, the thought of actual combat, being in the thick of things when he might be killed or maimed for life, alarmed him. Like 'everybody', he said, he didn't know what the next day had in store for him.

For the time being, the flamboyant Freddy Kaiser was sitting pretty. Paris, a city by which he had been captivated in halcyon days, was on the doorstep; he knew where to find the company and entertainment of his own choosing. And Romainville offered him many comforts and rewards, that equalled the advantage enjoyed by top-ranking officers installed in prestigious requisitioned Parisian houses and apartments. Freddy had a retinue of serfs; he had a soft spot for the energetic old grandmother Tauzin, she was his exclusive 'lavandière', daily washing his shirts and underwear. Freddy was coy about his 'undies'; nothing was put to dry in the open on the communal line, all the finishing touches were performed in an alcove behind the soup cauldrons in the cookhouse.

Charlo cut Freddy's fair hair. Another who was rewarded with gifts of bread and cigarettes was Max, a slight black-eyed Hungarian Jew who once flourished in business as a 'maître tailleur' and who boasted of having served his apprenticeship in London's Savile Row. In a rearranged room on the first floor, Max took care of Freddy's wardrobe of uniforms, hand-stitching buttons and insignia and pressing trousers to a knife-edge crease. The rewards which supplemented the ordinary rations were welcome to a man without relatives or friends on the outside; perhaps more important to Max, he had it in his head that as long as he continued to be of service to all the officers in the garrison, he would be spared the 'selections'.

Not all our visitors were made welcome. Hauptmann Bruchenbach's roving dogsbody, Lance-Corporal Gunther 'Biscuit' Klaus, the odious Billy Bunter of Romainville, had been on compassionate leave at the time of our arrival at the Fort. His home had been damaged in an aerial bombardment and his father injured by what the jumbo Klaus called terrorist flyers. As if seeking vengeance, he made his presence known immediately after his return to duty, charging into our room like a bull on the rampage. The command to 'aufstehen, nix parler, nix rauchen' in the presence of a German soldier spouted from his thick lips.

He had an insidious grin on his razor-nicked, doughy-like bespectacled face. Prudently, we stubbed out our cigarettes and stood to attention in silence.

Klaus towered above both of us, a Goliath on legs as thick as railway sleepers and with a girth as broad as a cart-horse's. Our eyes followed his movements, the floorboards creaked under his huge weight as he made an inspection. He disturbed our bedding, pried into our food cupboard, and ridiculed our pin-ups. His sour breath fanned our faces. In faltering French he accused us of being 'des saboteurs' and 'des criminels', and with some gratification, reminded us that tomorrow or the day after tomorrow could be our last day above ground.

Good tidings trod on the heels of the scaremongering Klaus. Corporal Laufer came to inform us that Hauptmann Bruchenbach had granted two short periods of exercise outdoors, fifteen minutes in the morning and the same amount of time in the afternoon. Laufer had orders to clear both sides of the courtyard to prevent over-familiarity with the other prisoners.

This was a tiny restriction! We felt like a pair of wild animals released from cramped cages to stretch their legs and sniff at the grass. Laufer allowed Max, the tailor, to collect our trousers for sponging and pressing, which he did for free as a special favour; and anticipating a female audience at the windows when we took our bow into the courtyard, we presented ourselves to Charlo who styled and shampooed our hair.

Before Corporal Weismann blew his whistle to clear the courtyard, he gave us a lecture with a mean look in his eyes. Don't forget, he said, we had to ignore the women, not speak to them or answer their questions. 'Compris? Nur promenade,' he warned.

We chorused: 'Jawohl, Herr Weismann. Bien compris.' Shaved, powdered and Brylcreemed, we followed Weismann down the stairs and walked into the crisp freshness of the morning, the courtyard ours for fifteen salubrious minutes. Heads bent, our shoes crunching into the gravel, we made wide turns of the arena, aware we were being scrutinized and analysed. After a few turns, from the furthermost point I sneaked a glance at the building. The women were bunched like dolls at the half-open windows; mischievously inclined, they gestured with their hands, hurrahed, flashed smiles and blew kisses.

A red-faced Weismann shook his fist up at the women. His authority seemed to lack drive, it had no effect in stemming the more venturous of suggestives meant for our ears. Half-smiling, Weismann parried at the women in whimsical French. They were 'chiennes en chaleur' with 'les langues pendues', bitches in heat with their tongues hanging out, 'pee-peeing' in their drawers.

The courtyard reverberated with loud laughter at the retorts that flew back in Weismann's face, the more brazen of the women letting everyone into the secret that she never wore 'them'. A voice from the men's division shouted: 'Mettre à l'épreuve! Let us see!' With that, the crowning touch fluttered out of a window in the shape of a large pair of black bloomers on the end of a broom handle.

When the easy-going Herman was designated to supervise our periods of exercise, the atmosphere was more relaxed. With each circuit of the courtyard, I cast my eyes up at the windows, the women, as they were and always would be, both an inspiration and objects of desire. At close range, I had a chance to study their faces. The variations were undisguised; those who had long been established in the Fort were serene, coiffured, rouged, decorated and brassy. Those recently taken from the streets without warning were reserved, red-eyed and anxious, still to come to terms with their confinement. The third classification, those transferred from sordid prison dungeons and counting their blessings, were conspicuous by their haggard looks, pale and blemished faces, and shorn and straggling hair.

Bursting to know, I said to Herman: 'Wo Lucy? Which one, Herman?'

He had the answer for me on the next round of the courtyard. The darkish girl in the white blouse at a window on the second floor with Colette. I shortened my step and walked close to the wire fence. I glanced up. A weak glimmer of winter sunlight reflected on the faces of the two young women to the right of the clock on the building. They sat at the open window, their arms folded over the sill. On my next round of the courtyard, I took a long, hard, penetrating look. Lucy was even more beautiful than I had bargained for. On the last lap, before our re-entry into the building, Lucy smiled down at me and pouted her lips. 'A bientôt!' I heard her call out.

I could not sleep thinking of Lucy. Like many horny young men who could temporarily put anxiety aside, I longed for the closeness and affection of a woman. But there were other effects which bedevilled sound sleep; wretched were the air-raid alarms, the ear-splitting screams of sirens and the incessant thump-thump of cannons. Bad dreams were not uncommon, though I seemed to be less tormented than Marc Troska by this burden.

There was the phenomenon of the howling dog in the early hours which chilled our nerves. High-pitched whines came from somewhere beyond the east walls of the ramparts, but seemed closer because of the echo. Evidently we were not alone in being moved by this uncanny disturbance; that something was amiss was plain on Corporal Weismann's face when he and Franz arrived with our breakfast. His customary chirpy 'guten Morgen' was grunted, and we missed the grin and wink from the Belgian which lent a welcome routine to the start of each new day.

Stress was impossible to bottle up. A sudden change in mood or temperament implied anxiety and worse; no news or bad news from home, sickness, death or an arrest in the family, a notice of deportation, the inevitable parting of lovers or unfaithfulness reached out to every-one. And there was the overhanging threat of multiple 'selections' which Marc Troska and I had yet to experience, a process which left everyone in tortured suspense.

'What's with the long face, Franz?' Marc Troska asked guardedly. Were we about to be told an item of news relating to one or both of us? Were we about to eat our last breakfast? Invariably, we became sus-picious, expecting the worst, bad news was on the agenda for everyone, it was simply a question of when.

It was Weismann who first hinted at the reason for gloom. Yawning, he said: 'Nix dormir, das Hund heulen.'

So the howling dog was at fault! Its cries and whines had kept half the garrison awake and unnerved the prisoners, and not for the first time. Weismann even knew the name of the dog, Bella, and described it as black with white spots. According to the corporal, Bella was bad news.

Ill-omened! The opinions were divided. Absurd superstition? A coincidence? Credible? Whilst we drank our coffee, Franz unfolded the story of the black-and-white dog. She had been the companion of one Fourquet, a whiskered old vagrant who had inhabited the neighbouring district of Bagnolet. Fourquet had been arrested for stealing German military equipment, nothing of great value, he told those curious to know, just a pair of boots, some socks and a greatcoat, all second-hand. Lodged in the Fort, Fourquet had only one concern: Bella, rescued from a rubbish-dump as a puppy. He was untiring in the stories he told about his four-legged friend ... her magical tricks, how her intelligence earned them a few pennies, and how she had fetched help when he broke a leg and blacked out. 'Une toutou dans un million,' he told his listeners.

That Fourquet would be released, no one disagreed. A petty crime in old age did not warrant more than a reprimand from the Military Tribunal. Meanwhile Fourquet thought that Bella could fend for herself for a short while, and as if to prove that she had not deserted him, one clear night he chanced to look up to the crown of the steps leading to the Kommandantur; there, he claimed until he became blue in the face, he saw his dog. Opening his window, he leaned out and called her name. Fourquet swore she answered back, barking several times before being disturbed by a patrolling guard.

The sceptics were unkind. 'Pauvre vieux! Sa chienne fantôme!' They screwed their fingers into the side of their heads; Fourquet was dim-sighted, somewhat hard of hearing, a bit of a 'coucou'. How could a dog enter the Fort at night when the only entrance was closed and guarded? A dog could not scale high walls. True, one heard dogs barking but the disturbance came from the rough ground on the other side of the ramparts.

The only other person who claimed to have seen a forbidden animal within the compound was Corporal Weismann. A dog had brushed past his legs one night, he insisted. He heard it panting; it growled and he remembered stumbling into the bushes bordering the steps. But Franz said Weismann's corroboration was unreliable. The corporal tended to hallucinate after a boozy night out in Montmartre and it wasn't the first time he had taken a tumble.

The leg-pullers had good reason to think again. After another tire-some night when the dog had given its encore, Fourquet's voice was heard to ring through the corridors long before roll-call. 'C'est elle, Bella! Bella!' he shouted. He shocked the entire building when he blurted out that his dog had come to express her grief for the reason that 'aujourd'hui, c'est moi pour le poteau,' he said calmly.

Fourquet's anticipation – his day for the stake – based on a dog's cries, produced a disturbing effect on the doom merchants. He was scolded and cold-shouldered, and Corporal Laufer threatened to lock him up in isolation if he persisted in roaming the corridors, offering a hand and embracing those he accosted. But Fourquet adopted a 'je m'en fiche' attitude, and got Charlo to cut his hair and trim his beard, handing over some of his tobacco as a reward for the service.

Fourquet ate two helpings of soup and all his bread ration at midday. He then lay down on his bunk for an hour as he was apt to do after a meal. He was in the middle of a game of chess with the whimsical language teacher, the Hungarian-born Professor Katz, another impover-ished nonconformist of no fixed abode but one with greater intelligence, when his number was called. Unruffled, Fourquet was loaded into a grey-green bus with seven other men to be whisked away to the most feared prison in all Paris – the hexagon-shaped fortress of Mont Valérien a few kilometres away at Nanterre – to face the firing-squad. In all the prison at Fort Mont Valérien accounted for some 7,000 executed men, several hundred of them from Romainville.

Had the incident been an isolated one, it could have been dismissed as a mere coincidence, but not even those steeped in the supernatural could explain why a dog – Fourquet's presumably – continued to cry period-ically in the early hours even after her master's departure, and Franz confessed that the elusive dog had prophesied tragedy on the same scale on two subsequent occasions.

So it was that the building was wrapped in tension. The familiar sounds our ears had become attuned to after each morning's roll-call were subdued. We missed the chirpy whistling, the spontaneous chants, the rap at the door and a cheery 'bonjour les gars' as the men passed to and fro outside in the corridor. When we went down into the courtyard for our first exercise of the day, the faces at the windows were noticeably sparse. Unfailing, Lucy and Colette were in place; they both waved their hands, but their smiles were somewhat burdened.

There were many prisoners, men and women, who had faced the stark reality of Romainville before. It wasn't all 'Wein und Rosen' as Corporal Weismann once warned us. And Franz left us in no doubt as to the procedure leading up to the 'selections'. It was a grave ceremony starting with the unheralded arrival of the grey-green autobus, the 'Leichenwagen' (hearse), each window flanked by a guard of the dreaded Schutzstaffel army group; next, thirty minutes of frightening suspense listening for one's number to be called. The luckless barely had time to light up a cigarette or shake the hand of his room-companion before making his exit.

As the clock approached the hour of three, we could start to breathe again, at least for the rest of the day, Franz said. The autobus had not been known to come after that time; nor did it operate on a Saturday, a Sunday or recognized holidays.

We watched the clock: every shift of the minute hand seemed an eternity. The deathly suspense and uncertainty curbed any desire for food. We voted to brew the remainder of our real coffee, and we savoured it with a lacing of cognac which the kindly Franz despatched to our room with the obliging Corporal Herman. Marc Troska resigned himself to a shave and a change of clothing. Chain-smoking, he sat down at the table to play solo-whist. I lay on my bunk with a French romantic novel which told the sob-story of a beautiful young heiress, daughter of a rich tyrant, in love with a boy from the servant classes. 'Papa' conspired to have the rascal flogged and transported to Devil's Island. After a couple of pages, I found it hard going, difficult to focus my mind on imaginative drama when I was enmeshed in the real thing.

I took a peep into the courtyard. The cold March wind stirred the tall weeds growing around the perimeter. Arm-in-arm, a couple of heavily-clothed women paced the circuit. This side, a trickle of men braved the elements. Professor Katz was easily recognizable by his stooping figure and odd garb, a lean, hawk-nosed elderly man, his hands deeply entrenched in the pockets of a long French military capote, and a flying-helmet, a relic of the First World War, protecting his balding head and jumbo-like ears. Beyond the perimeter, an unenthusiastic squad of soldiers were undergoing combat drill on their parade ground, charging with fixed bayonets at ridiculous straw and cardboard caricatures of British soldiers.

In the event, I wrote a letter to my mother. At first, I was stumped for words. I didn't want to appear dramatic or morbid, nor did I want her to think her son lacked courage to face an unpleasant end to his life. Briefly, I wrote:

Dear Mum,
I don't know if you'll ever get this letter. You must have wondered where I had gone. Never did I think I'd come to a place called Romainville, in Paris. But I'm with many good people, Mum. However, there's something you should know. I may, at any time, be sent to Mont Valérien, near Longchamp racecourse. I don't like to say this, Mum, but it's a prison where they shoot prisoners. I'm not too afraid. I'm told it's over very quick. Better than being run over and crushed by a double-decker bus, Mum, eh?

I think of you every day, Mum. My love to you and everybody in Beaumont.

The letter, written in pencil on a blank page torn from a book, was addressed and furled into a cardboard cylinder; together with all our desirable possessions, cigarettes, chocolate, tea, sugar, tinned goods and perfumed soap which Lucy had sent us, it was stashed in a niche beneath a loosened floorboard under the bunk; if both of us were earmarked for Mont Valérien, the items would be retrieved and distributed among those unprovided for, and my letter, hopefully, would find a new hiding place until, in the future, it might find its way to my mother in Jersey.

I was not brought up without any religion. Thanks and praise to God were recited first thing at school each morning. Once a year there was a church service to commemorate the dead of the 1914-18 war. Before going to bed at night, I went down on my knees with my sisters to say a short prayer. In the hour I attended Sunday school I was bored stiff. God was not my idol and I thought I could easily live without him.

Shamelessly, on this day of uncertainty when neurosis prevailed because of a bogey dog, I called on God to spare my life, if just for this once, so that I might snatch a sweet moment of time with Lucy, by whom I was well-favoured. The little I knew about this 'petite bijou' I gleaned from the canny Belgian, Franz. She was a young woman from a class he called 'le beau-monde', the gay and fashionable world, and 'bien aisée' (well-to-do). Bright and cultured, Lucy was born in Carcassonne of thoroughbred parents, a Spanish mother and an Italian father. Lucy's home was at Clermont-Ferrand and she had a property in Nice.

I was no stranger to Lucy's class of people, though far from having any intimate connection. On the island of Jersey, in the better seasons, I met their gleaming white yachts in St Helier's harbour when they docked from the continent and from further horizons. I touched my cap and lugged their baggage to chauffeur-driven limousines and up to their hotel rooms and hovered about for a tip. Weathered, stiff-necked nabobs; crocked-up, overcoloured wives; overweening mistresses; flighty young girls in trousers or shorts; and demanding young blades in blue blazers and white flannels.

I served them buttered scones and cream teas on the sidelines of tennis courts, and carried weighty trays and set them down on tables under coloured umbrellas on private beaches, waited upon the dinner tables, served cocktails, poured wine, listened to the gossip and cast a crafty eye at the girls' bulging, sun-tanned breasts and sniffed their teasing scent.

Class, or social standing in private life, mattered not in Romainville. Rich or poor, said Corporal Laufer, everyone was in the same boat, sharing the same fears and anxieties. All the bankers, stockbrokers, merchants, and land-owners of Paris were assembled in Romainville; anyone could see they were rich by the size of the blackmarket parcels delivered to the gate.

There were many engaging characters, men and women, lodged in the old Fort, some with affected mannerisms, adopted ranks, even titles. Counts, Barons, Baronesses, the genuine, the dubious and the bogus consorted amicably with politicians, judges, genuinely exalted persons and ordinary types: shop assistants, secretaries, labourers, prostitutes and habitual criminals. There were differences, political and domestic, rivalry, sharp tongues, teeth bared, and henpecks, but never serious enough to excite hate; on the whole, the fluctuating community existed in a spirit of camaraderie.

'If it's a crisis,' Franz warned, 'then you will hear Corporal Weismann blowing his whistle to clear the courtyard until he's blue in the face. Everybody will go to their rooms, shut the doors and wait.' Three o'clock had come and gone. Weismann's alert was hardly penetrating, unusually tame. We heard his heavy tread on the stairway. It was time for our period of exercise. The whole building heaved a sigh of relief, if only for another day.

An April Week-End

We entered the fourth month of the year. April's sun, though lacking in strength, was a bouquet after the winter's gelidity and rain. And the air was bracing when we took our exercise in the prime of the morning. The obstruction still covering the window did not cast a gloom over our spirits; we had come to a stage when we were quietly gloating, and for good reason.

It was a Saturday. The building seemed to purr with contentment, aroused by singing, music and laughter. A week-end to wind down and indulge in one's own game, ignoring the fact that a general 'selection', statistically, was long overdue. At breakfast time, Franz had waltzed into our room. Setting the tray down on the table, and winking at the gawping Herman, Franz passed over a cardboard communication designed as a heart; it was crayoned in bright colours and captioned: 'Une soirée de plaisir!' Incredibly, it was a witty and expressive invitation. 'Dress as you please.' With Herman looking over our shoulders, we laughed at a provocative sketch of a naked couple in a dancing pose. 'Musique et Cabaret,' we were informed. With girlish caution, the invitation was signed: La Brune et la Jaune.

Lucy and Colette. At last, the contretemps had been removed. A key to our door was safely in our hands. On the previous night, 'Bossu' Charlo had unceasingly laboured with his cutting tools at the lock. Silently, with nerves taut, we listened to the rasp of a file – gentle adjustments to the main part of a scrap of metal. There were countless probes into the eye of the lock; we heard Charlo's small grunts and curses … 'merde' … 'encore un peu' … 'diable' … 'un moment' … 'le voilà qui vient' … and, finally, the magical 'click'. The door was pushed open. Charlo's grinning face came into view. He raised his hat. He kissed the key. 'Avec mes compliments, Messieurs,' he said.

In the late afternoon, Herman looked in to shake our hands and say 'auf Wiedersehen'. He was off on a short leave to see his wife, Herta; hopefully, he said, clasping the palms of his hands together and offering up a prayer, to be given some good news of his soldier sons. Shutting our door and giving a precautionary turn of the key in the lock, he delved into a pocket of his jacket to show us the gift he was taking to his wife. He pulled out a crumpled but clean handkerchief; disentangling the four corners as a magician might to tease his audience, a rehearsal, no doubt, of a procedure intended to keep his Herta on tenterhooks before revealing the contents of a miniature box, he dazzled our eyes with a brilliant gem and, breaking into a grin, watched for our reaction.

'Prima Diamant! Wunderbar, Herman!' Marc Troska enthused. Did it cost a lot?

Herman shook his head. It had cost him 'nichts'. The diamond, one from a nest-egg which Franz had smuggled into the Fort, had been set into a gold ring by a Paris jeweller. The gift, Franz explained, was a worthwhile investment; Herman, a good German, had carried out many errands without seeking reward and closed his good eye to the illicit liaisons between the divisions.

Roll-call. Corporal Laufer put his head through the door and enquired: 'Alles gut?' We both nodded and reciprocated his 'bonsoir, schlaf wohl'. With Laufer out of the way, we made ready for the promised incursion into no-man's-land. Earlier, before going off on his regular binge into the dives of Montmartre, Corporal Weismann had allowed us a hot shower. Our faces were shaved to a velvety finish and our moustaches trimmed and edged. Our mode of dress had been studiously decided. The chubby, humorous Swiss 'intellekt' and wardrobe caretaker, Lutchez, found me a pair of beige corduroy trousers that might not have fitted so perfectly had they not shrunk from many washings. From a stockpile of garments, casual and formal wear, even regimentals, I chose a near-new, off-white, polo-neck jumper, white half-hose and a pair of quality soft leather moccasins. Marc Troska chose to dress like a pavement artist. His faded pink shirt was of a style worn by a flamenco dancer – crimped edging at the facing and bouffant sleeves. His trousers were Mediterranean blue, tight-fitting and a little short in the leg. A pair of canvas tennis shoes were freshened up with blanco-whitening and tied with laces of sisal string.

We were ready, waiting and sweet-smelling, but now that we were on the brink of our promised rendezvous we weren't wholly confident. It seemed incredible. Was someone really coming to tap at our door to escort us across into the divine sanctum of petticoats and skirts? Marc Troska was impatient. He kept pacing the room muttering 'all fucking crazy' and he pissed into the bucket every few minutes.

I was similarly affected by an attack of nerves. We filled the room with cigarette smoke. I looked in the mirror, combed my hair and revived my face with a dash of eau-de-cologne. Aircraft passed overhead. The sirens remained quiet. An alert would not impede the night's gambol, we had been assured; on the contrary, a blackout would be an advantage to those bent on breaking the rules. The fat ferret, Lance-Corporal 'Biscuit' Klaus, who had been known to pluck up enough courage to venture out of doors after dark to snoop around, turned cowardy-custard on hearing the sirens and the violent noises. The Oberleutnant, Freddy Kaiser, presented little or no problem at week-ends. His Saturday and Sunday evenings, through to the early hours, were spent in a club for officers in Paris among his own particular clan. Hauptmann Bruchenbach was unlikely to put a boot outside his front door after hours. He would be with a bottle, if not alone, in the company of hard-drinking officers of the garrison. Corporal Laufer was not a gallivanter. He was plagued by an ulcer and usually passed a peaceful hour playing a game of chess in his barrackroom with a drink to induce early sleep. Corporal Weismann, on the other hand, could prove a pest if he found himself short of funds, involuntarily returning to the Fort unduly early to seek out the insomniacs, the conversationalists and the gamblers who congregated until all hours in 'le Club', the communal room on the first floor furnished with tables and chairs and equipped with playing cards, dice and board games. Weismann might be hungry. He knew he could cadge a bite to eat and a mug of coffee.

The piss-bucket was almost half full when we heard the tap at our door. A voice called: 'Holà, les gars! Allez donc!' My hand trembling, I put the key in the lock and the door opened easily. Our caller we knew only by description and gossip. Corporal Weismann ridiculed him and called him all kinds of names. The 'verfluchten Araber' was a bluffer, a poser, a pimp, a pederast and a womanizer among other imputations.

Smiling broadly, a single gold tooth prominent among a pearly-white set in mint condition, the tall, handsome, dusky French-Arab, Khalid, greeted us warmly. Taking a couple of steps into the room and half-closing the door, he said, in the dual language commonly used: 'Messieurs, good evening. Je suis à votre service. If you are ready, I will conduct you to the harem.'

Khalid's manner was well-polished. I could see why Corporal Weismann curled a lip at the mere mention of his name. It was difficult not to break into a laugh. It was his appearance. His crinkly, jet-black hair was glossy and well-groomed, brushed back from the forehead. But it was the clothing that prompted Marc Troska to whistle through his teeth and remark: 'Well! That beats everything!'

His mode of dress *was* flamboyant. He wore a purple 'jaquette de smoking' with a black velvet collar and matching rolled lapels, and a white silk cravat; underneath, a cream-coloured pyjama suit; and his feet were encased in buff-coloured slip-ons, the uppers initialled in gold ornamental needlework with the letter K. Two long, brown fingers, the nails nicely manicured, grasped a black and gold cigarette holder. He cut a figure befitting an elegant drawing-room.

Khalid was not offended by Marc Troska's tease. Maintaining his attractive smile, he said, 'Ah, I know what you are thinking! But, chez la maison, I dress as I please. Here, au Fort, it makes little difference, I like to be natural, it is good for the morale and charms the women.'

Somewhat set at ease by Khalid's composure, we followed his instructions, each took a fork, a plate and a drinking glass. Locking the door, we
stepped out into the gloomy shadows of the stairwell. It was the first
time Marc Troska and I had been 'abroad' at night. One low-powered
electric-light bulb illuminated the way across the head of the stairs to the
door of the division. The heavy door was ajar. Khalid pushed it open and
the hinges creaked like the plaint of a frog. 'Christ Almighty!' Marc
Troska muttered.

Our seasoned guide led us along the hazy corridor; a few peculiar
figures flitted silently by, women in night attire with heavy shawls
around their shoulders to ward off the damp, biting chill in the air. Our
infiltration did not jolt or surprise them. 'Bravo!' a voice said in passing.
We were congratulated and bid: 'Amusez-vous bien, Messieurs.'

Room 40 was on the rear side of the building, half-way along the
corridor, almost opposite the day-room-cum-office of the corporals.
Khalid tapped lightly at the door and called out: 'Allo, c'est moi, Khalid
avec les invités.' My heart put on a burst of speed when I heard the door
being unlocked from inside. It opened. We were first met by a composite
of warm air, garlic, onions and Gauloises. I squinted through the haze.
The assembly of faces was not immediately discernible. The lighting in
the room had been reduced to a soft night-club glow, a red shade with a
broad band of white bobbles veiled the electric light bulb which hung on
a flex from the ceiling; in addition, two flickering candles reposed on a
chequered oilcloth covering a well-provisioned table.

A colourful gathering of people had turned out. Lutchez, sporting a
Ronald Colman moustache, his thick untidy hair tumbling over his
forehead, came to the front; clownish in dress, what he called his 'tenue
de soirée' was an ill-fitting, unmatched flannel pyjama jacket and trousers
and an old pair of furry slippers. But he was evidently the kingpin in the
building and put up a hand to still the chatter. 'Le silence, mes amis,' he
commanded. 'Before the introductions, une petite toast.'

The drinking glasses we had carried in were filled from a large
saucepan that gurgled gently on the backplate of a woodburning stove, a
concoction of red wine, cognac and a non-alcoholic additive to further
the distribution. Lutchez raised his glass high. Everyone followed suit.
'Salut la grande Britannique et les États-Unis!' and beaming: 'Welcome
to the party, my friends.'

I stood ready to hear a roll of a drum or a verse from a ceremonial
song. But from a script which, obviously, had been hatched up by the
witty Swiss and rehearsed beforehand, our hosts chorused: 'Bienvenus!
Welcome to the fucking-party!'

Lutchez quelled the laughter. In the moment of hush, his next words were directed towards Marc Troska and me. In a jocular vein, he explained that the 'landlord' would take a dim view of the breach in the 'tenancy' if it was brought to his notice ... an order to 'quit' would be unlikely, but a penalty would have to be paid. More seriously, Lutchez said that the volunteers placed at look-out posts were dependable, but one had to allow for the unexpected, at a given signal we had no more than two minutes to evacuate the women's division and return to our room and to our own beds. It was sound advice on how to preserve the illicit relationships.

The warming beverage quickly instilled me with the confidence I needed to meet a variety of people with 'savoir faire' – people with whom, in ordinary life, I might never have become intimately acquainted; this I saw as a privilege. In total, we were twelve in the room, six men and six women in the prime of life. My mind was so absorbed with the roguish company it did not dawn upon me to ask myself who might live and who might die.

I went through the pleasing ceremony of handshaking and cheek-embracing in the conventional manner to which I was becoming accustomed. Lucy put out a hand, the same delicate brown hand which she had squeezed under the gap at the base of our door. I reminded her. She laughed. 'Sois raisonnable,' she said, 'you may caress it but try not to *eat* it this time.'

I wanted to devour her whole, I was so magnetized by her fragrance. She was a mere slip, a figure accentuated by the garment she wore – nothing more it appeared than a green satin dress with a deep neckline and secured at the shoulders by thin straps. Her stockings were pure silk, reserved, she said uplifting a leg, 'pour les occasions spéciales'. When I finished poring over her, she tossed her head coquettishly and asked: 'Je te plais? Do you like what you see?'

God! Did she please me? I took a gulp from my second glass of 'punch' and munched on a biscuit spread with a liver paste. I wanted to tell her that she had the flawless beauty and polished style of the woman of my dreams. Lucy was my Hedy Lamarr. In truth, I was a naive youth where thoroughbred women were concerned; never before had I been motivated by a woman who generated such physical excitement into my bones. I was a beggar promised champagne and caviar. How could I answer Lucy? I remembered the times I had sat in a cheap cinema seat and marvelled at the suave and handsome screen-lover with the liquorice-stick accent, Charles Boyer, for his masterly manner and approach to his beautiful ladies. I answered Lucy's question whimsically, as 'Pépé le Moko' might have answered Miss Lamarr from the lines of a script. 'Of course, et bien sûr, chère fille! Vous êtes absolument ravissante et séduisante! Vraiment une ange!' Endearments in the French language sounded poetic and polished to me.

Lucy's brown eyes twinkled. Putting a hand to her heart she sighed 'ah … !' 'Pour un anglais c'est bien présenté,' she said. 'You have been reading romance, I think.'

I whispered in her ear. 'A dream, Lucy! You are not real! I am in the company of a beautiful phantom. I am very much afraid that you will disappear through the wall.'

'Absurd! I *am* real!' she stressed. She took both my hands and slipped them to the back of her waist. She stood on the toes of her high-heeled black patent shoes and took my head between the palms of her hands and kissed my lips. The kiss was unceasing. My head spun. She pressed her body firmly against my groin. 'Voilà,' she said, 'my soul is warm and alive.'

I hugged her. I was treated to the sweet smell of eau-de-cologne and rouge. I kissed her lips, her face, her neck and her silk-smooth shoulders. But then, she must have sensed the enormity of my want as she back-stepped. 'La patience, chéri,' she chided. 'In France … we take food first, after we do what we want. C'est bien comme ça.'

Water bubbled over the side of a large porringer and spat onto the stove's hotplate. Through a gush of steam, Franz de Bruyne called out: 'Aux assiettes, Mesdames et Messieurs.'

With glasses replenished, we all took seats. Partners sat on the bottom tiers of the two double bunks, on cushioned chairs and on the part-carpeted floor. We wished each other 'bon appétit' and we ate 'gourmand' – mounds of long spaghetti cords garnished with diced salami, finely chopped onions lightly fried and flavoured with spices; white crisp bread and pure butter, and a selection of cheeses; like the honey-cake, the real coffee and cigarettes that came after, all thanks to relatives and friends who made regular trips to the door of the Kommandantur.

In the intervals between feasting, with the conversation continuing at a low ebb, I glanced around me. It was difficult to believe that I was in captivity with the gravity of execution threatening. Room 40 was spacious and cosy. Apart from the intermittent flash of a searchlight penetrating through the moth-holes in the curtains hanging over the two windows, a distant scream of a siren and an occasional blink of the electric light bulb, nothing suggested hostility or danger. The four tenants sharing the amenities: Lucy; Colette, the long-limbed French-Hungarian dancer who had chosen Marc Troska for her lover; Gaby, a petite Hungarian with gypsy features, a 'chanteuse de ballade' and Khalid's tender passion; and Paulette, senior in age, a bubbly blonde Parisienne prostitute who was coupled to Lutchez, had combined their

feminine ingenuities to enhance the austerity of the room. The two
bunks were gaily curtained with salvaged material and the bedding
made snug with non-institutional blankets and sheets. Cushions were
scattered over the bedspreads. A child's plaything of the long past in the
form of a one-armed doll was perched on a pillow. The walls were
pasted with illustrations cut from art magazines and cover-pages from
Photoplay, *Motion Picture* and other Hollywood periodicals; a gallery of
'beaux gueules' showed their white teeth. Trinkets and mementos were
neatly arranged on a communal dressing-table: hairpins, brushes, ear-
rings, bracelets; filling the edges around the oval mirror was a photograph of a little boy in a sailor suit; leaning towards it, I read the
inscription: 'Christian à huit ans'. A 'glossy' of a top-hatted, tail-dressed,
long-legged Colette on stage in her professional heyday. One of 'Gaby
en cabaret, la nuit de Nöel: Brasserie Marius. Paris 1939'. Among the
privileged classes, a photo of Paulette as a playgirl in shorts, long
blonde hair blowing in the breeze under a peaked cap, sailing the
freedom of the Mediterranean at the wheel of a sleek-looking yacht:
'L'Hirondelle, St Tropez'. Lucy celebrating her 'Vingtième' birthday
with friends at the 'Regence Plaza, Paris'. And, of recent date, a photograph of Lucy's parents: 'Maman et Papa. Pour notre chère fille.
Courage petite.'

Between the windows, standing against the wall on an upended
sauerkraut barrel, was a bright display of paper flowers arranged in a
'pot de chambre'. The communal wardrobe, an open framework of steel
tubing cemented into a side wall with planed boards for overshelves,
accommodated a collection of clothing on hangers, winter and summer
wear, shoes, boots and slippers. Stretched overhead from wall to wall an
airing-line of plaited sisal string was festooned with ironed underwear.

'À la santé!' 'À la prochaine!' Good health and to the next time. Filled
with good cheer, we all vowed to meet and celebrate at Maxim's after
the war. Dreamy optimism! I put up a quick prayer. I wanted time to
stop. Snuggling up to Lucy I held her hand. The company had become
still, hypnotized by the tiny Gaby singing songs which brought a lump
to one's throat, the 'maladroit' violinist, Polish Baron Viktor Wladzimir, plucking quietly at an instrument which cried out for new strings.

I looked intently at the faces of my new-found friends, of about my
age and a good many years older, people, Lucy told me, who had
known pain and suffering. As a boy I had smarted with pain when I was
stung by a swarm of wasps whilst out in the fields blackberrying, when I
had a toothache, when I rode my bike into a wall and when my mother
lanced a carbuncle at the back of my neck with a hat-pin. All my bodily
discomforts had been within limits. Torment and torture I related to

the Chinese because, in my ignorance, I believed them to be the only race, apart from jungle savages, to practise cruel acts.

Gaby's pretty face bore the stub marks of cigarette burns on both cheeks, and an indentation from the blow of a truncheon was hidden under a fringe of dark hair which fell short of her eyebrows. Colette's left wrist had been wrenched and a finger was out of shape. Lucky it wasn't a leg, she said. Thérèse, 'la couturière' and Franz de Bruyne's companion, a stocky woman with bobbed hair turning grey, spoke with a grating sound in her throat; she was hard of hearing, frequently cupping a hand to an ear when spoken to. She had been near to death. At the fearsome Gestapo building, 9 Rue des Saussaies, a side street within a stone's throw of the immortal Champs-Élysées, Thérèse had been subjected to extreme violence, open-handed slaps to the face, kickings and deprivation of sleep. But what would forever remain imprinted on her mind was a noose being slipped over her neck, her weight twisting on the end of the rope and her eyeballs about to pop out of their sockets. There followed an agreeable sensation of floating peacefully on a cloud with 'le bon Dieu' calling her name. Thérèse was brought back to earth with a jolt. She blasted God for his trickery and cried herself blind.

Lucy, so far, had been spared the wrath of the Gestapo. So had Paulette, up to a point. Her life-style, however, underwent a dramatic upheaval soon after the Germans entered Paris. Maxim's, the Lido, the Côte d'Azur and Monte Carlo were pleasure grounds catering for all the sophisticated luxuries to which she had grown accustomed. The pampered extravagance ended with the Occupation.

Tragedy struck the family when Paulette was seventeen. Her mother died; her father was ailing, a legacy from the First World War when he was gassed; and a younger sister contracted consumption. Doctors and medicines were costly. Money was scarce in the house. Paulette wanted to see her father properly cared for in his decline, and she dreamed of sending her sister to Switzerland for treatment. Before her eighteenth birthday she made a bold decision. She took to the streets, first strolling a suburban district, then turning the corner and exploring the arcades of the Rue de Rivoli and richer pickings.

To be a habitual 'fille de joie' had not been Paulette's original intention. Treatment for her father and sister proved to be lengthier and more costly than first envisaged. After a year, there came a welcome reprieve from hanging about the avenues and boulevards; nicknamed 'Poupée', she became the protégée of a 'Papa riche' who lavished his affection and money on her and set her up in an apartment on the Place de la Madeleine. But the nice arrangement ended three years after its début; Paulette's patron died of a heart attack leaving the roof over her head for a short term, the furnishings, a collection of clothing from the best fashion houses but hardly a sou. Addicted to gracious living, Paulette returned to the open market but with a list of opulent acquaintances vying for her favours from which she could pick and choose.

Paulette's father being long dead, and her sister hanging on to life in a Swiss sanatorium out of harm's way, made the Occupation easier for her to withstand. Restrictions and tight rationing were in full evidence among the ordinary inhabitants, but for the German hierarchy, their collaborators and the new rich, champagne and caviare were still to be had at Paulette's favourite eating houses. However, Paulette was walking a tight-rope; officer ranks, Obersts of the Wehrmacht and Standarten-führers of the Schutzstaffeln, were duelling for the beautiful 'Poupée'. One, more thick-necked, proposed a relationship which alarmed her; hand-written, besotted messages arrived on her doorstep daily, delivered by a uniformed courier with a bunch of flowers. Paulette, treading warily, politely turned down invitations to social functions, the theatre and horse-racing. When a precious set of jewellery arrived, she shuddered to think how it came to be in the German officer's hands.

Nothing could induce Paulette to associate with a Boche. But the German was not the kind to be rebuffed. She was followed, in the streets and into restaurants; her private life became increasingly insecure. Then the crunch – she was abducted by the officer's driver and another accomplice. Blindfolded, she was driven to an apartment somewhere in the city. In her long, vulnerable profession she had adequately dealt with pests and many threatening events, but to embitter a pig-headed, high-ranking German officer was a different matter. She knew it was essential to keep her sangfroid.

A captive behind locked doors, Paulette first tried to humour her objectionable 'host'. But his hard drinking, lewdness and exhibitionism chilled her with fear. Never before had she been degraded or rough-handled. Actuated by impulse, she struck him in the face with a bottle. Blood spurting from his nose, she watched him slump to the floor. In that dreadful moment, Paulette knew she would have to abandon her pied-à-terre and all her worldly possessions and flee the city.

Paulette acted with all speed. She made her retreat through a window, dropping feet first on to soft ground. Unhurt, and guided by a cloudless night sky, she found herself walking across the near-deserted Pont-Neuf bridge over the river Seine. Challenged by a sentry, she calmly produced the 'passe-debout' with which she had been legitimately privileged. Allowed to pass unhindered, Paulette took a course in the direction of the Rue des Prouvaires and the sanctuary of the Poste de Police where she knew she would find a trusted friend.

With a new identity and a change of appearance, Paulette moved a hundred kilometres to the city of Orléans where she was enrolled into an underground organization. Relatively content and impressed by her new environment – hazardous at that – and her fellow-conspirators, she took on the role of cook and general help for those who were sent into the thick of the action. Her back-seat labour of love came to an abrupt end when the German police raided the premises and arrested the occupants.

The scars healed, Paulette could now laugh easily, but she often thought back to the comfortable apartment she had been forced to abandon just a few teasing kilometres away from the Fort; probably, she said ruefully, all her personal effects, particularly her treasured wardrobe of clothing, had been boxed and despatched to some 'Boche Frau'. Paulette's new wardrobe, far less lavish or extensive than the outfits born from the houses of 'Schiaparelli' and 'Chanel' – hand-me-downs bequeathed by those women leaving the Fort for parts only God knew where – had been remodelled by Thérèse who had spent all her working life as a needlewoman in haute couture.

Hearing much and missing nothing, I could see a remarkable resemblance to another Hollywood nymph who once had me panting in my seat in a cinema: Paulette was somewhat fuller in the face and figure than Jean Harlow, but she was blessed with the same doe eyes, the same chin, eyebrows plucked in a thin arch, and soft silky blonde hair brushed back from the forehead and falling in large coils over the ears.

Paulette's dress, her 'robe de cocktail', was daring, a startling red in colour with a scallop-shaped knee-length hem decorated with brilliant sequins: when she pitched forward, the frontage billowed out and showed her navel. 'De la maison Romainville', Lucy laughingly explained the design. 'You see, here, we are back to our adolescence,' she said earnestly. 'We dress up, paint our faces like dolls, share the lip-stick, the rouge and the scent ... pour l'esprit, a game we play; it is very important to laugh, to make jokes, to flirt, and when we are sad we weep and we grieve ... au caractère naturel.'

In the progress of time, my ears would hearken to many stories which might strain the credulity of the uninitiated. Baron Viktor Wladzimir and his childhood friend, Helena, both in their early fifties, had a poignant experience to relate. Pinched, hair cropped and patchy so that her ears stood out, Helena was unfussy about her mode of dress. Withdrawn, a twitchy woman who spoke only her native Polish and a few words of basic German and French, she was moulded to Viktor, hanging on to his every word; when he nodded or shook his head she did likewise without knowing what was being spoken about, and when he laughed she laughed with a hand covering her mouth, 'un poing Boche dans la bouche' (a German fist in the mouth) Viktor pointed out.

Born in neighbouring provincial villages, Viktor and Helena attended the same school. They might have married but for Viktor falling for a city girl. Helena bore the interloper no grudge; at the wedding she was the bridesmaid and the two women became firm friends. Then came the war, the German invasion and agitation. Helena, married to a veterinary, saw her husband arrested for giving aid to partisans. For seven long days she was forced to attend the place where his battered body hung, feet first, from a tree … a brutal warning to others with patriotic causes in mind.

Then came the twist of fate which brought Helena and Viktor closer together than they had ever been. Two young drunken SS soldiers adrift stumbled on Viktor's wife, Lydia, as she was coming across a meadow, having collected a young son from school. Viktor, working nearby on his farm, was alerted by the boy's screams. He jumped on his horse and galloped along a dirt-track. He first spotted the drab grey canvas top of a Kübelwagen above a hedgerow. That sighting alone pointed to something terrible. 'Then,' said Viktor, 'I saw her, Lydia, lying face down in the stream where I used to play as a boy. Sacrebleu! She was dead … drowned, strangled, I didn't know … but her blood was running with the water.'

Viktor heard laughing coming from a barn. He moved slowly, creeping up to the wide opening. He peered. The two were laid out, a bottle between them, the older a Hauptscharführer. Viktor retraced his steps. Searching the Kübelwagen, he found two pistols in their holsters. They were loaded. Viktor had thought of going to the house for his shotgun, it would have done more damage but he was afraid they might have left before he returned. The laughing stopped when the Germans saw Viktor, pistols in hand. The Hauptscharführer wanted to talk … '"Sprechen, sprechen, Polski, nix schiessen!" … he didn't know Lydia was my wife.'

Viktor felt nothing but hate. Two brutes had violated and killed the dearest possession in his life. It was a psychological moment to avenge the killing of his good friend, Ramon, Helena's husband. He fired at the younger one first, putting a bullet in the stomach and two more in the head. The Hauptscharführer was half-way up on his feet but fell back howling when Viktor aimed at his legs and finished him off with successive shots to the chest.

With the help of a trusted friend, Viktor carried the bodies to the Kübelwagen. At the farm, they dug a pit, pushed the small vehicle in, set it alight and covered the debris with manure. That accomplished, Viktor buried Lydia in a grave which he left unmarked and without informing the appropriate authority of her death. Viktor lost no time in hatching a plan. First, his son was sent to live with Viktor's sister in another province. Then, with Helena and on her own initiative, they were both spirited away by devious routes to Vendôme in France, 170 kilometres from Paris. Here they took refuge and were made welcome by Viktor's brother, Stefan, who had set up home in the region two years before the outbreak of war.

It was a move for the worse. Viktor readily admitted he had been impulsive, blaming himself for what he called 'un saut dans l'inconnu' (a leap into the unknown), implicating Helena when she could have remained in her own home with no harm done. He was pricked by conscience. Helena had suffered greatest after her arrest, a victim of Gestapo interrogation at their other shameful address, 74 avenue Foch, where screams floated almost nightly from the upper floor of the building into the neighbouring streets.

Franz, Viktor and Lutchez had been verbally abused and pushed around as a matter of course, nothing more serious. Khalid, who gave thanks to Allah, arrived in the Fort straight from his home without so much as 'une botte au derrière'. Generally, it was the women who bore the brunt of violence, and I would always be impressed by their complaisance and the joking way they compared their scars, their 'souvenirs de guerre'.

Professor Katz knocked at the door and entered the room. Shrouded in a heavy blanket, he had come to report to Lutchez and to collect a bowl of spaghetti and a couple of cigarettes, his reward as the controller of 'les guets', a group of volunteers who took up look-out duties for a consideration because they received nothing more than the standard ration of alimentation or because they were adventurous and took the opportunity to cock a snook at authority. Whatever the reason for keeping vigil at a window, the unions between the divisions would have long been annihilated without those who placed themselves at the Professor's disposal.

Rubbing his hands over the moderate heat of the stove, the Professor said: 'Quiet on all fronts, Lutchez.' With wistful eyes, he watched Lutchez scooping up the spaghetti from the pot with a large spoon and fork, and when the bowl reached the point of overflowing the Professor humbly thanked him with a gentle slap on the back. 'You're very good to me, Lutchez,' he said.

The Professor – an unofficially bestowed title, I assumed – was a likeable old man, eccentric, alert, unafraid, interesting and brilliant in languages. Some qualities, however, were not appreciated. He had the distinction of occupying a room to himself, not as a privilege but of necessity; his habits were slipshod, foul to his immediate neighbours; he slept in his bed undressed, was averse to showering, and would jump at the chance of an occasional chore whilst neglecting to clean his own room.

A nomad all his adult life, inhabiting the meanest quarters in Paris, pocketing pennies from poor students and earning a little more from irregular writings for journals, the Professor had dared to advocate his personal solution to Germany's national socialist doctrines, which he forecast would have a disastrous impact on the world unless stopped. With a biting wit, he claimed to have said: 'Hitler's Germany should be divided into portions, as a grocer would divide a whole cheese, and be shared among its neighbours.'

With Germans darkening the Paris street, the Professor – Jew written all over his face – was found a cell at the prison of Fresnes. Whether or not the Gestapo read or heard about his theory, he wasn't told, but they trampled his spectacles and his dentures suffered a similar fate. Because his dentures couldn't be replaced, the mastication of solid food presented a problem; the hard black bread, for example, had to be soaked overnight in a basin of acorn coffee. Spectacles were another matter and no longer a problem after his admission to Romainville; Dr Beriot stocked a selection of optical aids collected from prison mortuaries and execution chambers. Pince-nez, half-moons and even monocles were among various frames of all shapes and sizes displayed in a glass-fronted cabinet in the infirmary.

It was midnight when the Professor left the room; Viktor and Helena said 'bonne nuit' and 'Dieu vous préserve' and left at the same time. Lutchez put a finger up to his lips. 'En silence absolu, mes enfants,' he warned. Conversation had to be continued in mere whispers, one had to respect the neighbours and non-participants, a rule applicable to other nooks throughout the building where couples liaisoned. Besides, in the still of the early morning, boisterous and intoxicated voices coming from the wrong side of the division were liable to reach the ears of the guard patrolling the perimeter.

The room fell into near darkness, lit by one candle. Lutchez signalled, not unexpectedly, that it was time for a 'little shagging'. I had drunk a liberal amount of fortified wine and I was seeing through a haze, but I was clear-headed enough not to be ready to perform shoulder to shoulder. My modesty won me a reprieve. Lucy chucked me under the chin. 'Timid, eh?' She took my hand. 'Come,' she said, 'we go to your room.'

We slipped out of the room on tiptoe, along the eerie corridor and through the open communicating door. Lucy went in search of the Professor to brief him on our whereabouts. Room 26 had grown cold. In the dark, I rekindled the stove with paper and wood; with the flue wide open, the temperature had risen to a comfortable degree by the time Lucy stepped in.

Now that we were separated from the others, those erotic thoughts I had conjured up in my mind over the past weeks, since I first touched her hand, could be put into practice. I felt an excessive lust for my dreamboat and I told her so. 'Mon ange,' she cooed. 'À votre disposition. Do as you please with me,' she said. Everything about her inflamed me, the burr and eloquence of voice, her expression, her shape, and her lips which I kissed unremittingly, urged on by the question mark which hung around our necks.

Lucy's need was as urgent as mine, as unrestrained. She flicked her tongue out and played it over my face, about my throat, and plucked at the buttons of my shirt. I slipped the straps of her dress away from her shoulders and the bodice fell over her naked waist. I kneaded her plump breasts in the palms of my hands then suckled on the brown, swollen nipples. I lifted the skirt of her dress and traced my fingers between the folds of her backside, feeling, teasing and arousing the most vulnerable part.

My prick was muscle-bound inside my slacks, bursting to break through the flap of the flies. Lucy took up a fitting position, one leg on the floor, the other over the edge of the table. I felt the electrifying touch of her fingers as she gently pulled at my prick and freed it from the obstruction; in that instant, I was so aroused I came to grief.

Panting, I said: 'I botched it, Lucy. Je m'excuse, chérie.'

My embarrassment was brief. Lucy shrugged. She put me at ease. 'I understand,' she said. 'It is not a catastrophe, you are eager and strong.'

Physical strength, no; but I was eager to prove that I could please her to the full; there was still time before the Professor came knocking at the door. After the reparation of my faux pas, I dropped a chunk of wood into the bowl of the stove, reheated enough coffee for two cups, lit a cigarette to share, sat down with my arm around Lucy and, in a state of relaxation and quiet, pondered my next move.

I took my mattress and laid it out beneath the window. I undressed and stretched out on my back. Lucy took the cue; she dropped down on her knees and by inducement, hands and mouth, pumped up my lithe-ness until it was 'superbement énorme'. Still kneeling, she pulled the hem of her dress back over the curves of her hips. My hands reached out for her shoulders and she closed in, settling herself gently down on my stomach to make a faultless connection.

At that positive instant, the shaded electric light bulb went out without the usual warning. I didn't want total darkness, I wanted to look upon the fulfilment in Lucy's beautiful face, to cherish it in my memory for all time. I stretched out an arm, my fingers jerked at the ring-pull of the black-out blind and the roller pivoted and accelerated to the top of the window frame with a resounding whack.

Brilliant ribbons of light criss-crossed the sky, probing the clouds and reflecting the beams into all four corners of the room. Sirens wailed. Above our heads flew thunderous machines on their perilous course. Cannons fired and bombs erupted. The window rattled. But Lucy and I were bent on exploiting our golden moment; our ears deaf to the world, we were locked together in an earthy play.

Lucy shivered and snuggled her head into the pit of my shoulder. Her breasts heaved and I felt her heart pounding. Her dress lay open, torn, split at the seams. I reached for the blankets and covered her nakedness. 'I've ruined your dress, Lucy,' I said.

She sighed, from deep down. 'A dress can be replaced,' she replied. 'I have others for you to pull to pieces if you want.'

I upturned her head and kissed her eyes. They were wet. 'You're crying, Lucy!'

'Un petit chagrin, that is all,' she replied with a little sniff of the nose. 'I told you we women sometimes weeped. When I hear the aeroplanes passing, I am reminded that they have come across the water, just a teasing distance from the poison all France lives under.' Her voice faltered ... 'And there is Jean-Claude,' she said, grasping my hand tightly, 'my husband who escaped with De Gaulle to London ... le beau, fier Jean-Claude, Capitaine de l'armée de France, thirty-two years old. We were married just three years before the Germans arrived. We were happy, with true love. Now, when I think of him, I feel a little shame. He was the first man in my life – c'est vrai, honest truth – and when we became separated I promised myself there would be no other in my life even if the war was to last ten years. But loyalty and mode of conduct, as we all know, is held cheap in the Fort. When they lock you up in a cage with no one to talk to, nothing to see but the walls, not even a corner of the sky, and hearing nothing but keys ... keys ... and screams, you feel your mind is going crazy and you look to kill yourself. By chance, by accident – je ne sais pas – they bring you here where you can wash the dirt away from your body, look in a mirror and brush your hair and put on fresh clothing. You want to talk your head off and laugh. And when your eyes fall on the men you want to be a woman admired again. Right or wrong, "à tort ou à raison", as we women say, life is too uncertain, too ... '

It was the all clear. I jumped to my feet and pulled the blind down seconds before the electric-light was restored. There was enough coffee on a low heat for two more cups, acorn-flavoured but nicely sweet. Lucy lay curled, propped up against the wall under the window like a ragged doll, one black patent shoe sticking out from under the blankets, damp eyes peering wistfully through a tangle of hair and rouge smeared across her mouth like the sediment from a sandwich of jam.

She gave a sleepy smile. 'I look a mess, eh? Like I have been put through a ... how do you say "une essoreuse à linge?"'

'A wringer, Lucy,' I answered in good heart. That she was a married woman had occurred to me. Nothing so young and beautiful could have failed to excite the attention of all the world and its roués. It was of no consequence to me that she was wedded. We were both bound by time: allotted a time of death, perhaps a day away, a week, or a month? At length, our paths were bound to lead in different directions. I told Lucy that I'd be proud to be her 'grande passion' as long as she wished, depending of course on the 'will of heaven'.

'They will not send you to Mont Valérien, if that is what is in your mind. No, not a British subject.'

They were words which had been said to me before, meant to instil confidence. Some prisoners, knowing that their own backs were half-way against a wall, were always ready to lessen the strain of others who had misgivings. 'I have my doubts, Lucy,' I said. 'I'm a piddling nobody to the British government if that's what you mean, they'll not care a toss. My mother would ache for me. Of all her children scattered about, she worried most for me, her youngest son. She was clairvoyant; she read tea leaves in the bottom of a cup and lines on the palm of a hand; when she looked at a lighted candle she said she could see things as plain as the nose on her face when the flame was at its strongest. The signs she saw for me were never promising; I was too tall for my age, too thin, and too frail among other shortcomings; it was an open secret that I wouldn't make old bones.'

'I think nothing of fortune-telling,' Lucy asserted. 'It is stories from old wives. I was never one for being brave. When I was at school and did bad things, my mistress called me "petit démon". I would pretend to faint before she could put a hand on me. I remember the day when I saw blood on my clothing. I cried. I thought I was going to bleed and die like a poor animal in an abattoir. Dying is, as we say, "matière à réflexion". Here, one often asks, how will it come? With humiliation? With pain? Dying would not be so terrible if one could choose to die at home among family and friends.' Lucy's face broke into a smile. 'Paulette says if she goes to the *poteau* she will take down her drawers

and show them her backside. Me? Stick out my tongue if I don't
swallow it first.'

A gentle tap came at the door. Professor Katz poked his head
through. 'C'est l'heure pour se coucher,' he said quietly.

The bunk rocked. My bleary eyes opened. Instinctively, my two hands
grabbed at the raised sides of the bunk for fear of falling. The building
had been struck by a bomb. So I thought.

I had been in a deep, erotic sleep, bedazzled by beautiful, ridiculous
fantasies. I had seen the Fort transformed into a romantic, intemperate
castle in the sky, my bed a pink, delectable cloud besieged by gorgeous,
adulating nymphs in brilliant rainbow-coloured silken negligées. I
feasted, caroused and mated. Laufer and Weismann were my flunkies. I
saw the absurd Hauptmann Bruchenbach as a cringing beggar, scrambling on all fours for cigarette butts and licking the corks from discarded wine bottles. In a ballet skirt, Freddy Kaiser danced a graceful
minuet accompanied by Viktor Wladzimir playing his rejuvenated
violin. Even more farcical, a much-deflated 'Biscuit' Klaus was astride a
mountain of Red Cross parcels, shedding tears as he made a reluctant
distribution.

'Himmel! Schweinerei! Aufgestanden!' I was propelled back to earth
and came into collision with the morose Lance-Corporal foaming at the
mouth. Behind his rounded steel spectacles, his stony eyes stared into
my face. He yelled: 'L'appel, auf … auf!' Roll-call, Klaus said, turning
to a grinning Franz de Bruyne, called for a prisoner to be standing at
attention and fully dressed. Klaus nudged Marc Troska's lethargic body
with the toe of his boot. We, Klaus told Franz, were a useless pair of
swine doing nothing industrious to bring on tiredness yet had the
impertinence to stagnate in bed until ten in the morning.

Franz reminded the shirty Klaus that it was a Sunday, a 'Sonntag' for
rest, prayer and good-fellowship. Klaus turned on him with a curl of the
lip. 'Alle Scheisse, Franz!' Did that 'Jüdisch Schweinkopf, Churchill' care
what day of the week it was when he ordered his 'fliegende Banditen' to
Germany to kill civilians? 'Freundschaft? Mein Arsch!' Klaus growled.

We struggled into our clothing. Klaus snooped around the room,
sniffing like a bloodhound as was his custom. Would he find a clue? A
trace of Lucy's scent? After she left, I had been scrupulously careful,
doing as directed, opening windows in the darkness to expel any out-of-
place smells, washing the cups, burning the smudged cigarette ends,
sweeping the floor and going down on my aching limbs to fish in the
cracks and grooves on the floorboards for tell-tale hair-pins or alien
fibres in the manner of the sharp-eyed sleuth, Sherlock Holmes; and I

had folded the crumpled mess of clothing that Marc Troska had discarded, slapdash, before collapsing into his bed comatose.

The whole of a Sunday morning was devoted to religious worship from right and left and in a variety of competing tongues. Persistent were the prayers and hymns, in chorus and single-handed, with a sudden burst of weird chanting – mumbo-jumbo to my ears.

After the midday meal the courtyards thronged with strollers; sombre-suited men in brushed hats, tidy berets and polished boots dragged their steps around the perimeter in pairs and small cliques. Surprisingly, the habitual scruff, Professor Katz, given fair warning, graced the Sabbath with spit and polish, surfacing cleanly shaved and in a fresh shirt. Now that spring was with us and the climate less harsh, Franz de Bruyne interrupted his busy time table to join in a game of boules.

It was the women who attracted the whistles on a Sunday afternoon, treating their man of the hour to serenades and fond looks. The older ones paraded 'en grande tenue', plumed hats, two-piece costumes, smart shoes and, to no purpose, a handbag; the girls, prattlers in the majority, boisterous and showy, with a trend towards the national economy drive to save on materials, short skirts with broad waist belts, divided skirts reaching just below the knees, fitted breeches, half-hose and full stockings, high heeled shoes and high boots; top marks to those with pinched waists and lean legs.

Included out of this weekly window-dressing, Marc Troska and I were envious of the free-and-easy atmosphere. Soldiers from the garrison with time on their hands before guard duties stopped to hobnob with the prisoners through the barbed-wire fence; they chin-wagged, swapped brands in cigarettes, fooled around and made passes at the women. I, for one, could not believe that these pally, mostly middle-aged, grey-green uniformed conscripts would ever come to bear anyone ill will.

Behind the locked door of Room 26, the satisfaction of Sunday afternoons was the preparation of high-tea, depending on what was held on reserve in the larder. Thanks to our well-set-up friends, Lucy among them, with guardian angels outside the rampart walls, and thanks to the organization in Geneva renowned throughout the world for coming to the aid of those in need in times of war and disaster, our provisions met our choice of menu. Favoured was a tin of Crosse and Blackwell pilchards in tomato sauce, an abundance of sliced cooked potatoes fried in the day's ration of margarine, black bread thinly cut with pure butter, honey cake, and endless cups of liberally sweetened strong tea.

After four months in the Fort, we could easily identify callers by the knock at the door, those without authorization to enter wanting to converse through the keyhole. Granted 'carte-blanche', an unsmiling Dr

Beriot came into the room while we were seated at the table; she said 'bon appétit, Messieurs' and apologized for the untimely intrusion. She was about to withdraw, but Marc Troska took her by the arm and persuaded her to sit down in the armchair. Whilst others – with the exception of the Swiss, Lutchez – addressed her in the formal way to her face, 'Dr Beriot' or 'Madame Beriot', Marc Troska's manner was throw-away; it was plain 'Louise' or 'Ma chère Louise'.

'Louise' accepted a cup of tea, which was served to her with a saucer. A biscuit was rejected. She was 'sans uniforme'. It was the very first time we had seen her without the monotonous black and white striped turban which sometimes leaned over on her head. Her well-brushed red hair hung loosely on her shoulders. She looked a picture, bosomy in a green jumper with a pleated skirt in a matching colour; her silk stockings, the one flaw in her outfit, noticeably mended. Her looks, her bearing and shape belied her rumoured forty-five years.

Marc Troska went overboard in his praise of her beauty. I did not think she understood 'knock out'. When, in oily French, he called her 'charmante, absolument jolie' and, referring to her sense of dress, 'goût exquis' and her hair, 'fil d'or', he won a half-smile.

'Je vous dis un grand merci pour les compliments, Monsieur Troska,' she said firmly in her native tongue, which implied displeasure of some kind.

But, as I had guessed, she hadn't come looking for compliments – it was to rap both of us over the knuckles. And we both knew what for. Her sense of hearing was good, she said, and little missed her eyes. Though not entirely to blame, she conceded, we had yielded to temptation without giving a thought to the risks or the complications or the issues. Everyone would be punished, and the women would suffer the greatest if the 'bêtises' were uncovered. She had already given Khalid a piece of her mind; Franz de Bruyne had not escaped censure, but it was 'Lutchez, le chef de bande,' she thought the worst of – obstinate and irresponsible.

Louise Beriot stirred her tea and brooded on the matter which filled her mind, what she called 'rien que la passion folle'. She looked as if she might break into tears. The women, especially the younger ones, she lamented, were vulnerable, really stupid. Married women too! With children! From respectable homes! They were her responsibility; they came to her with their problems, to be comforted when they were low; they discussed their letters from home; they made plans for their return; a new carpet for the sitting-room, new curtains for the bedroom, new clothing for the children … simple things like that. The women were not all without hope or belief. Louise Beriot prescribed, encouraged and cautioned. The women listened; but 'malheureusement' they were not always heedful. 'Think!' she said. 'What of the risk to a pregnant woman transported to a labour camp in Germany or wherever? She would be isolated; her life and that of an unborn child threatened.'

I had no answer. I hung my head and bit on my lip. Marc Troska was at a loss for words. The lecture was unforeseen. No one had warned us. Louise Beriot persisted, admitting that she had ended one or two pregnancies to prevent recrimination from sources beyond the Hauptmann's office. This was undoubtedly morally questionable but a matter on which God only would pass judgement in time to come. There was a psychological moment when she had been tempted to appeal to Oberleutnant Kaiser; 'un cri de coeur'. She knew him as a reasonable and sympathetic man who would handle the affair by simply closing up the loopholes and without reporting to his Hauptmann. But she had second thoughts. She asked herself, how would she be appraised? A sneak? An informer? A spoilsport? She would be ostracized. Life within the Fort would have become imposssible.

Selection

'Le week-end', as it was called by both prisoners and custodians, had been all too preciously short. Monday was not the best day of the week. Firstly, it was 'le jour pour faire la lessive et nettoyage': chores to which everyone lent a hand. Rooms and corridors were swept and scrubbed, and mattresses turned and blankets aired over the window-sills. The building reeked with the odour of carbolic.

We, in Room 26, were spared the detail. A gang of three women, headed by the loud-mouthed Grandmère Tauzin, arrived armed with all the equipment. Whilst we watched from the confines of the corridor, the knockabout trio in their dust-caps and sackcloth aprons thumped the mattresses, beat the blankets with a cane, and freshened up the beds with clean linen.

More crucial to a Monday morning was the start to five long days of uncertainty and suspense, the niggling question of life or death or deportation always at the back of one's mind. Lutchez's somewhat unreliable assurances, 'at three o'clock in the afternoons we can unbend' and that 'Saturday, Sunday and a festive day' were time off for the firing-squad, were not entirely believed.

Louise Beriot's reasoning did not go down too well with Marc Troska. Without the women and the affection they offered of their own free will, the Fort would lose its novelty, he told her in melting words. No prison in Paris, not in the whole of France, was its equal, he said. 'We did not choose to come here, Louise, it was written in the stars. Think of the thousands in solitary who would give an eye and an arm to change places. This is only a temporary arrangement, perhaps a short run for many of us, Louise. One day we might return to Romainville, to look, to think, to laugh, and to cry.'

I listened, saying nothing, leaving the more subtle American to alleviate the woman's fears. She looked weary; she stood up and thanked us for the tea. Before she reached the door, Marc Troska gently detained her and kissed her on the side of the mouth. Caught off guard, for a second or two she remained rooted to the floorboards, seemingly numbed. Then one hand fell blindly on the door-latch, the other unearthed a handkerchief; she whimpered, and before she stepped out of the room, I saw her eyes fill with tears.

My second encounter with Lucy on the Sunday evening was curtailed because of Corporal Weismann's untimely return to the Fort from Montmartre. As ill luck would have it, he was not yet ready for his bed; he came into the building looking for company in the communal room among those indisposed to sleep. And Weismann was the bearer of some disturbing news.

I slept serenely after Lucy had departed the room 'à toute vitesse' until I was awakened by Marc Troska blundering around in the dark. He flicked at his lighter noisily and lit a cigarette. I squinted at the glow, and I was about to turn over and go back to sleep when he called: 'Are you awake?'

I yawned. 'I am now,' I said.

'It's that bloody dog again,' he complained. 'Howling like it's being leathered.'

I sat bolt upright in my bunk and strained my ears. Outside the window, the branches of the trees rustled in a tempered wind and my ears picked up the stamping of heavy boots on the machine-gun platform sited on the bank at the southern end of the building; other than that the early morning was calm. The howling of dogs in the dead of night was a frequent and disturbing event, in all probability throw-outs or strays searching for food. One only, shunning company, was at the root of the phobia.

'Was it Bella?' I asked.

'I wouldn't bet on her,' he answered edgily. 'Maybe I imagined it.'

I jumped down from my bed and put my overcoat across my shoulders. At the window, I lifted the blackout blind. It was not yet dawn. Lights were glowing in the garrison cookhouse and white wood-smoke was billowing out of a chimney pot. My eyes searched the shadowy line of the casements, the grass bank above and the length of the ramparts. I saw nothing and returned to the warmth of my blankets.

Almost everyone was susceptible to bad dreams, superstition and imagination. Aircraft sounds and violent bursts of gunfire were approved of. But rum noises coming from beyond the perimeter in the early hours jarred the nerves of the faint-hearted. The shifting of heavy metal containers and cauldrons in the quarter of the garrison cookhouse was often at fault; and the clatter of canteens could be taken for that of a machine-gun's mechanism. The strength of the noises and vibrations hinged on the prevailing atmospheric conditions, the echoes becoming trapped in the basin between the thick surrounding rampart walls. The clear voices of civilians passing by outside often floated over the walls.

Franz de Bruyne shrugged off the controversial subject of Bella when he arrived with our coffee accompanied by Corporal Weismann. People were too bothered by one dog. It was starting to get tiring. It was Weismann who broke the news. An assassination had been perpetrated on a German soldier in the city. It was 'seriös', Weismann said shaking his head indignantly. Franz butted in. 'Sorry, I told the blabber-mouth to keep it under his cap.' Weismann, blank-minded, held up the fingers of both hands and, gingerly, closed and opened them five times. 'Ein deutsche Soldat kaputt,' he said, 'fünfzig Zivilisten schiessen. Compris?'

Plain spoken! 'Is that the ratio?' I asked Franz. 'Fifty for one?'

'A low-grade soldier, yes. More for a senior man,' Franz acknowledged.

The killing of a German soldier was perhaps imprudent, certainly ill-starred. Some among us would shout 'bravo!' Lutchez, regardless, would say 'fucking good!' Marc Troska was noncommittal. I thought the price to pay was too high. The extenuating factor was that the fifty hostages selected for execution would be taken from all the prisons and places of detention in Paris.

Long faces were everywhere when we took our next exercise. The morning's sun was warming, men had their sleeves rolled up as they wielded brooms and mops. Professor Katz was being dutiful, standing on a step-ladder to wash and polish Louise Beriot's infirmary windows and to earn an extra crust. Max, the tailor, could be seen at his sewing-machine, and Charlo's scissors could be heard snipping at heads. Khalid, 'le fainéant' (the idle one), sat at an open window in a flamboyant shirt and neckerchief, musing, seemingly unconcerned, his elongated cigarette holder clenched between his sparkling white teeth. And Lutchez, the dodgy ballad-monger with a sparse portfolio of songs, went about his duties chanting in his usual monotonous tone:

Jack Dunn, son of a gun
Out in France one day,
Keeps fit, doing his bit,
Up to his eyes in shit.
Each night after the fight,
To pass the time away,
He sings this little song
and this is what he says …

It was time for 'le vieux sac à ouvrage' (the old work-bag), Grandmère Tauzin and her team of 'éplucheuses' (potato peelers), to clog their way to Franz de Bruyne's cookhouse to prepare a mountain of vegetables for the meal of the day. Lucy and Colette, in headscarfs, waved brooms out of a window and blew kisses before we returned to our room.

The street killing of a German soldier weighed on my mind, an unforeseen contingency which greatly added to our anxieties. Marc Troska agreed that we had no guarantee of immunity from execution. We both made provisions for it. The letter to my mother was brought up to date with little alteration to the text. Ready to cry, I told her the day, the month and that I was nearing my twenty-second birthday. I said I was well and with good friends in the same jam who gave me a great deal of courage.

We boxed our reserves, to be distributed if we fell to the 'selection'. Marc Troska calculated that if he was allowed to smoke on the journey to Mont Valérien he would need three cigarettes, two to smoke on the bus and one at the wall. Perhaps more at risk than I because of his Semitic heritage, he was remarkably composed. He whistled whilst shaving; he styled his moustache, oiled and brushed his hair. He dressed himself in a pink shirt, loosely knotted a white silk handkerchief around his neck, one which Colette had stitched for him, and squeezed his legs into a pair of blue 'drainpipes'. His face broke into a grin when he admired himself in the Cheval mirror. 'Just a thought,' he said, 'the bastards will mess it all up if they put a bag over my head.'

We were aware of the procedure – the telephone ringing in the custodians' office-dayroom, the shrilling of its bell greatly amplified by the silence within the building, followed immediately by the frantic urgency of a whistle being blown in the courtyard to warn everyone to go to their own rooms … to pray and perhaps to say their last goodbye.

Oberleutnant Freddy Kaiser would tell us how much his Hauptmann hated the whole grisly ritual, an 'unpleasant' and 'unavoidable' function of his office, 'wholly out of the Hauptmann's jurisdiction'. And the 'compassionate' Hauptmann was careful not to advise those to be depor-

ted or executed a moment too soon; a telephone call from Paris gave him
the names and numbers, and he knew approximately how long it took
the autobus to make the rounds of the prisons for the pick-up before
arriving in the Fort to complete the full load.

Following the protocol which ruled in the event of a 'selection', the
Hauptmann's active-duty, burnished steel-helmet was at the ready; this
fearsome piece of headgear lent six inches to the stunted man's height.
Rain or shine, the Hauptmann would stand at an open window, a cigarette burning between nicotine-stained fingers and a glass of schnapps at
hand, to listen for the whine of a heavy engine negotiating the steep,
narrow streets of Les Lilas. At a given signal, Freddy Kaiser, similarly
helmeted, would reach for the intercommunication instrument and warn
the duty corporals: 'Achtung! Die Schutzstaffelpolizei kommen sofort!'

Executions, Freddy confessed, left him demoralized. Like many of the
prisoners, male and female, Freddy had been at the Fort since its
inauguration into a place of detention for political hostages. In the
presence of his Hauptmann, Freddy was 'korrekt', wooden but polite. At
other times his rapport with the community was exemplary. That he
socialized with a clique, adopted first names, drank their tea and coffee
and accepted their biscuits, was best concealed from his Hauptmann.
Freddy had been known to grieve when someone with whom he had
been on a special footing had departed for Mont Valérien.

On this day, when Hauptmann Bruchenbach put down the telephone
receiver, he directed a finger to a name on the list: 'de Bruyne, Oberleutnant,' he said dolefully. Freddy blanched when he was advised to enlist a
new cook.

Franz de Bruyne had fired the cauldrons; the peelers were dismissed
after cleaning up; the women collected their midday meal of vegetable
soup; next came the half-dozen men elected to the duty, they were
queuing at the cookhouse door when Corporal Weismann blew a frantic
blast of his whistle. His voice was far-reaching: 'Achtung! Attention!
Prisonniers aux chambres! Schnell! Accélérez!' Weismann's command
was repeated up and down the corridors. Those men in the communal
room broke off their discourses, turned their playing-cards face down,
pushed back their chairs, shook hands and embraced.

Doors closed, one after another. An eerie silence followed; it was a
silence that reminded me of an Armistice day morning at school when
the pupils were summoned together at two minutes to eleven to stand
well-drilled and give their attention to the boom of the ceremonial
cannon, and to fasten their blinkered minds on the tragedies of the Great
War. I, for one, was unable to grasp the full horror of man's aggression
and callous indifference when waging war.

A floorboard creaked; a chair scraped; someone sneezed; someone coughed; something dropped; someone swore; someone grunted; someone farted; someone chuckled; someone retorted: 'Salaud!'

First, there was the rolling, grumbling whirr of a heavy engine; the wheels of the bus jolted over the flagging surface, under the arch and into the Fort. Then a sharp increase in the engine's revolutions before the downward grind through the gearbox to take the first bend in the narrow gradient of the unmade road; the thud of the wheels over the pot-holes and, finally, the squeal of the brake-linings as the lengthy vehicle crunched to a stop alongside the sentry-box trenching on the cookhouse where the soup cauldrons generated steam untended.

I lifted the blind a cautious inch or two, and went down on my knees so that I had a view of both courtyards and the steps leading into the basin from the Kommandantur. Corporal Weismann looked an uncomfortable figure, kicking at the gravel mid-ground, his helmet pulled down over his small pink ears, the leather strap tucked under the flab of his fleshy chin, and a rifle clumsily slung on his shoulder.

Hauptmann Bruchenbach came into view, his spidery, black-booted legs flea-hopping down each step. Towering alongside, broad-shouldered and soft-capped, stumped a Sturmbannführer with the twin silver flashes of the almighty SS on the collar of his tunic and miscell-aneous ribbons emblazoned on his chest, reflecting an achievement or two through defiance in some way or another. More graceful of step came the lean Freddy Kaiser, gripped by a sense of self-importance, a telltale bundle of documents held fast in his brown-gloved hand. 'Biscuit' Klaus trod his Goliath boots one careful step at a time, his helmet perched on his head like a thimble saddled to a pumpkin.

The heel-clicking and 'Heil Hitlers' heard from the assembly of junior SS officers and other ranks from the bus was a cue for the women to raise their voices in bold opposition. In unity, they stood at the windows and brandished their fists; they sang out strongly, so that their voices carried to the streets of Romainville; and the inhabitants, perhaps under cover or not counting the risk, bared their heads to the revolutionary hymn, the 'Marseillaise'.

Above, on the second floor, Franz de Bruyne, Viktor Wladzimir and Lutchez, all three sharing a spacious room, sat quietly at their regular places at the table. All were well-versed in the procedure. Franz, acting as he always did at a time of crisis, had changed from his working clothes to a brown, tailored, narrow-striped, three-piece suit. A brown homburg hat in a velvety material had been unpacked from its box, ready to be put on his head. Viktor's treasured roll-neck jumper had been knitted by Helena; beige breeches and brown riding boots completed the rig-out he had chosen just in case. Viktor's second love, the violin which his heart ached to master, was wrapped in newspaper in the hope of its finding a new home. Lutchez was unshaven, in roomy flannels, sockless and in slippers; 'Les balles de fusil,' he was heard to say, 'n'ont point de respect ni pour le décorum ni pour la mode.'

We downed the last of our cognac, two fiery measures nursed for the occasion. With my ears glued to the door, I listened, heart thumping, to the murmur of guttural voices and shifting feet, seemingly unhurried as they faltered and came to a pause midway and parallel, I easily judged, to the women's corridor. A door opened; an order, barely audible, was mouthed and, without delay – perhaps a fleeting moment to pick up one's holdall or backpack – small footsteps jog-trotted in the direction of the stairwell and into the courtyard, to be conducted on a second bus to the transit camp at Compiègne for deportation.

We were long-acquainted with the 'creak' of the communicating door. We had become endeared to it. On this occasion there was no 'intimate' connection. I went cold; 'they' were outside our door. I turned to Marc Troska. He was sitting at the table with a book, either engrossed in it or just making a show. Cigarette smoke leaked from his nostrils. I whispered: 'Stub it out.' He dropped the cigarette butt onto the floor and trod it flat.

Freddy Kaiser's voice came to our ears clearly. 'Zimmer 26, Herr Sturmbannführer. Der Engländer und der Amerikaner zusammen.' Hushed voices, a mocking laugh, a rustle of papers, and then an order to open up. The key grated in the lock; it turned with a loud click.

Christ almighty! Both of us? One, for sure. I bit on my tongue. This was the moment when I needed courage, even a mere token. To die a natural death in a bed and surrounded by family and friends, as Lucy said, was the right of every mother's son. To die with one's back to a wall, perhaps pinioned to a stake with a black hood over one's head, was too distressing to contemplate. And it was the harrowing preliminaries to an execution; dragged out, devious and unethical. How many times had I seen the ludicrous imitation on a cinema screen? Would I face the firing-squad and die gamely? Or would I go in the guise of Rocky Sullivan in *Angels with Dirty Faces*, who went to the electric-chair struggling, bleating and crying out for all the world to hear: 'I don't wanna die ... I don't wanna ... ' Marc Troska vowed to sing out the 'Battle Hymn of the Republic' before the command to fire.

I stood by the bunk, Marc Troska facing me. My shoulders were straight, my chin up, and my hands at my sides. I was first to come under the Sturmbannführer's scrutiny. He looked me up and down. My mind began to race. Christ! Was he gauging my height and my build for a

coffin? I moved my head sidelong; the cognac, which had done nothing
to lighten the strain, was still hot on my breath.

'Name und Nummer?' he asked.

I returned his look, and I answered with the utmost politeness as my
mother would have wanted me to. This man, a Major, struck me as a
different kettle of fish from the unforgotten little runt, Tostevin of the
Jersey police and his gangling tool, Ben Shenton, both of whom had
deserved contempt and abuse.

'Faramus, Herr Sturmbannführer. Schreiben F.A.R.A.M.U.S.
Nummer: Vier hundert, ein und vierzig,' I said without wavering.

'Wie alt?'

'Zwei und zwanzig ... Juli, Herr Sturmbannführer.' Would I be given
the thumbs down to my twenty-second birthday?

Freddy put a thin document into the hands of the Sturmbannführer.
'Jersey Insel geboren, Herr Sturmbannführer,' he said, referring to my
place of birth.

My document! Why mine? The Sturmbannführer scanned the particulars, throwing me sidelong glances. I was not yet out of the wood. I
watched him, trying to read his mind. His expression was deadpan.
What was it about this 'corps d'élite' that made even their brothers-in-
arms, the Wehrmacht, spit in the dust! Lutchez would say: 'Don't be
fooled by the uniform ... all that gild and garnish. Undress them and
what do you see? A bricklayer? A plumber? A gangster? Some jumped-
up cunt from the town hall? Me? I shit in their ugly faces!'

Freddy avoided my look of inquiry; a small gesture, a wink or a nudge,
might have put me out of my misery. Hauptmann Bruchenbach stood
two feet inside the room, his face told me nothing. 'Biscuit' Klaus's bulk
filled the door-frame, an insidious, deep-rooted grin on his balloon-like
face.

The weight off my shoulders, if only momentarily, it was the turn of
Marc Troska to come under scrutiny, 'der Amerikaner mit dem Polni-
schen Zuname, Herr Sturmbannführer,' Freddy asserted. To give him
credit, Freddy made no reference to Troska's half-Jewish lineage. Marc
answered all the questions put to him without batting an eyelid. At one
point, the Sturmbannführer chuckled when he fastened his eyes on our
pin-ups.

I was prepared to believe he had come to our room simply out of
curiosity. He glanced at our collection of books and chattels, and he
lifted the lid off our saucepan of cooked haricot beans, bacon and garnish
which stood impassive at the back of the stove; bending his head, he
took a deep sniff. 'Knoblauch, zu viel Knoblauch,' he said recoiling.

Obviously he had no stomach for garlic. He turned abruptly on his heels, saluted in a slipshod way, said 'Auf Wiedersehen,' and strode out of the room. What a relief! Good riddance, I muttered after the door closed. I had lived through several long minutes of suspicion, suspension, and funk, more than enough torment for my lifetime. We had been counted out, but neither of us had any reason to revel in our good fortune; the whole charade would be repeated over the months to come, a burden from which no one was exempt.

Who among us had been taken? Whose face would no longer be seen in the courtyards? We had yet to be told. Ironically, we were to profit by the misfortune of others. Soon after the departure of the buses, we were startled by Corporal Laufer's urgent footsteps. They stopped at the door. Laufer bustled in. 'Achtung!' he warned. 'Hauptmann Bruchenbach kommt sofort.'

Now what? Nonplussed, we stood to attention. Stirred by some motive, Bruchenbach toddled in, followed by a scowling Klaus carrying two Red Cross parcels. Klaus slammed them down unceremoniously on the table. 'Chacun son paquet,' Bruchenbach said – a windfall! They were motivated by conscience, was my guess.

A Red Cross parcel was worth more than its weight in gold. We both overplayed our gratitude, bowing, almost falling at Bruchenbach's boots like serfs. Pushing our luck, Marc Troska immediately stretched the Hauptmann's stroke of moral sensitivity; pointing to the black-out blind, he said that it was bad for the eyes. And, in what sounded like a fanciful voice, he drew the Hauptmann's attention to the unnatural light in the room which, after five months, was a strain, not to mention uneconomic. It would be a treat to wake up in the morning to see the sunrise, he said, and 'bei Nacht, Herr Hauptmann,' gaze up at the stars.

The room went quiet. Bruchenbach blinked through his thick spectacles at the obstruction. He brooded. Corporal Laufer, long in the face, gaped. Klaus looked daggers. Bruchenbach took three short steps to the window and parted the blind. It might have been the dismal emptiness of the courtyards that persuaded him to tug at the cord which set the roller spinning to the top of the window-frame.

At once, the four walls of the room shimmered to the play of the afternoon sun. Even our beggarly furnishings seemed to rejoice in the welcome relief. Again we thanked Bruchenbach. But, unlooked-for and off the Hauptmann's own bat, Corporal Laufer was instructed to hand over the key to our room. Bruchenbach, maintaining his good temper, flipped the key on to the table. We were free, he said, at liberty to circulate and associate with the other prisoners; one slip of the rules, he warned, would lead to the punishment cells and continuing restraint.

Corporal Laufer, last to leave the room, hesitated at the open door.

His face expressed emotion. 'Franz partir,' he said before retreating. And so, without so much as a handshake, the Belgian had gone to Mont Valérien. Despite our release into the community on parole, news of Franz's going to his execution left both of us depressed. Lucy was so right when she said that one's spirits often came under attack without warning.

Corporal Laufer had alerted Lutchez to our new conditions. When Lutchez, a weepy Viktor Wladzimir, and a grieving Khalid presented themselves, we were overwhelmed by their embraces, relieved to see we had scraped through the selection. The number of casualties to leave in one batch was higher than at any time before; nine men to Mont Valérien and five women to the rumoured unhealthy camp at Compiègne for deportation, it was widely believed, to a 'labour' camp. The cause of Khalid's heavy heart was the loss of his love, Gaby the singer from Room 40, now with an empty space.

Chivalrous to the end, Franz had gone with a smile on his face, a smile that would be sorely missed. He had taken measures beforehand as most prisoners did. Lutchez carried a full bottle of cognac which Franz had purposely put aside in the event of his death and, as was Franz's express wish, we raised full glasses and drank a toast to 'un brave ami' and those to die with him.

Franz bequeathed his personal effects to those he affectionately called 'clochards', hoboes in the community; his gold pocket-watch and a little money to Professor Katz; his tobacco and a cigarette-lighter to the hunchback, Charlo, whilst other derelicts benefited from Franz's store of provisions. Franz had not forgotten Room 26. He left a 'good luck' note wrapped around two diamonds, small specimens which, when sold, would keep Marc Troska and me with a loaded table for several weeks.

As after every tragic event, a temporary veto was put on music and amorous activity as a mark of respect. Special prayers were said in an over-crowded communal room with Laufer and Weismann, fully uniformed, in attendance. Louise Beriot, dressed in black, sat on a bench with the corporals. After the last hymn was sung, Lutchez, standing on a makeshift platform, addressed the community. Tactfully speaking in German for the benefit of the custodians, he told of the sympathy expressed by the pair for the departed. Neither 'Herr Laufer' nor 'Herr Weismann' were a part of the tyrannical administration that sent innocent people to their deaths; both were ordinary, decent soldiers, Lutchez said. It put us on the credit side when Laufer and Weismann bashfully stood up to a round of applause.

A Close Run Thing

Cut loose of our chains, Marc Troska and I took every advantage of our independence and nosed around our half of the building at will, fetching our coffee and rations from the cookhouse where a new cook, a Breton fisherman, was at work. We stood in line twice a day for roll-call, making new friends and finding new interests.

In the courtyard we learned to play boules; we kicked a football about, and joined in the free-for-all, the permissiveness and the banter between courtyards when authority was slack. On rainy days and after dark, our time was well occupied with card games and table-tennis; with half an ear, I listened to the political orators, the discussions and arguments often bordering on threats of a thrashing. Next to my periodical excursions into forbidden territory, I thrilled and fastened on to those professionals once employed in the entertainment industry; the Fort was rich with comics, impersonators, singers and musicians.

Herman came back from leave to learn of Franz de Bruyne's execution. Behind the locked door of our room, he broke down and sobbed. In a pocket he carried a note to Franz from his wife, Herta, thanking him for the gift of the diamond ring. One day, with God's help, she wrote, she hoped Franz would visit their home.

Everyone was advised against taking advantage of Herman's kindly disposition and his inattention to rules. Herman, well-balanced, first counselled Lutchez who made all the decisions, deciding what was important and what was of no consequence. Acting as postman or courier for the exclusive convenience of any individual was not done without Lutchez's permission and only if the delivery of a letter, or vice-versa, was a matter of life and death. The exchange of our two diamonds for money with a Paris dealer received Lutchez's early approval; within a few days our larder was stocked with blackmarket goods.

We were both enrolled into the labour force, Marc Troska to the enviable task of handyman in the garrison cookhouse with three other men-prisoners. At midday, he was fed a canteen of soup thick with potatoes, savoury dumplings and slivers of meat, returning in the late afternoon with left-overs, the scourings from the cauldrons, bread and vegetable trimmings that were welcomed into the communal pot.

Weeding, hoeing and raking gardens had been one of my many casual jobs as a boy after school hours. But I wasn't chosen to tend to the flowers and plants bordering the banks of the unmade road and the vegetable patch at the rear of the Kommandantur because I was versed in horticulture. The middle-aged guard, Alfred, a plasterer by trade, singled me out because he needed to improve his English. A pleasant-enough man, with cheeky optimism, Alfred expected Germany to take possession of England before the end of the year. Alfred's confidence brimmed over the top; 'mit gut English-speaking', as he put it to me, he would stand a chance of an administrative post, a 'Bürgermeister' no less.

Office of mayor? A pipe-dream! And it would be a small town in the west country of England which Alfred would choose to adopt for himself, his wife and three children. He showed me some cherished postcards of Devon and Cornwall collected when, as a young man with a bike, he toured the villages and hamlets with a brother. One postcard showed an old inn with a thatched roof where they had put up overnight, and he remembered the bedroom with the sloping floor reputed to be haunted by a gentleman ghost. Second to none was the thick, rich dairy cream and the 'Apfelmost' which he drank by the bucket. And, presumptuously, he thought my German might be good enough for him to give me a job as an interpreter after the war.

Whilst I poked about nature's earth, Alfred read aloud from an Edgar Wallace novel or from whatever reading matter in English was at hand, constantly calling for correct pronunciations and explanations. He was earnest, but his determination was often trying, if not boring. But gardening and tutoring was infinitely better than scrubbing out the military barrack-building and the lavatories. Besides there were compensations; with the arrival of warm summer weather we often sat in the sun to yawn or took a leisurely stroll around the banks of the ramparts to chat.

On a nice day little manual work was done. We would continue the lessons out of sight, sitting on the rampart wall high above the moat where I could see the white silhouette of the Sacré-Coeur in the distance. On the threshold, I would acknowledge the hands raised in greeting from passing civilians who retained an uneasy freedom.

When it rained, Alfred and I would convene to the woodshed, where, on some days, we would find Lutchez and Viktor Wladzimir splitting kindling. Lutchez, in his mischievous way, would clown around and instruct Alfred in infantile prose: 'The cow jumped over the moon' and 'The butler and her ladyship were caught shagging in the pantry.' Silly talk that brought on fits of laughter.

I was content with my workaday schedule; two and a half hours in the mornings, a bit less in the afternoons, five days a week. Alfred appreciated my company; each day he brought me a sandwich of sorts, fatty pork wedged between two slices of thick-cut black bread, a strong-smelling cheese and, in turn, a vile-looking 'Blutwurst' which I had no liking for.

On a black day, when the whistle warned of an emergency, I would down my tools and run at the double back to my room carrying with me Alfred's blessing.

Not a moment of my leisure time was ill-spent. Preparing the evening meal was a pleasure shared by Marc Troska and me. And we 'entertained' or were entertained; usually, it was Lutchez, Viktor Wladzimir and Khalid who found places at our table or for us at theirs. Menus were simple and adventurous within the limits of availability. Because of Marc Troska's cookhouse stint raw potatoes were plentiful, so we had potatoes 'sauté a l'oignon', 'au vapeur', 'au sauce de fromage'. There were stews on occasion, but not much meat. Haricot beans, bought on the blackmarket, were cooked in fat pork to taste or two scraps of greasy bacon from a tin. The tempting contents from Red Cross parcels, scarce because of 'Biscuit' Klaus's tendency to treat them as his own possessions and almost never distributed unbroken – one parcel shared by many – were eaten with great appreciation and discrimination. Apart from the twice daily issue of soup, not always palatable unless reconstituted, sauerkraut was generally available; again, this German cabbage, with a little 'savoir faire' appeared as an agreeable dish, hot or cold.

Sufficient food was generally the priority. There were always those prepared to barter their rations for tobacco or alcohol. With stomachs appeased and nerves tempered by stimulants, it was the women we looked to for a psychological cure; without these precious pearls life in the Fort would vegetate.

Among the women newcomers, replacing those gone for deportation, there were some choice bits. Some paraded pert, knowing; some were affected and stand-offish; some genteel; some naive, apprehensive, fearful.

Marc Troska, fancy-free after an amicable 'divorce' from the lovely dancer, Colette, was wooing a Dutch girl. Khalid, made a 'widower' by Gaby's going, was bunk-hopping. Swopping was becoming popular, much to the disgust of Louise Beriot. And, in full summer, the women were at their loveliest, craved after in thin frocks, in singlets, with breasts 'dégagé' and bouncy, in short skirts and shorts that uncovered their limbs.

With all the temptations, my allegiance to Lucy remained solid. Rarely did a day pass when she did not communicate with pencil and paper. No matter how short the note, childish or repetitive in words, if she even wrote 'I love you, mon ange,' my head would be put into a spin. And, on a clear field, when the administration was short-handed and lax, on a Friday, perhaps a Saturday or a Sunday evening, Lucy and I would be physically united.

A letter from home, with good or not so good news, was shared among the community. Too infrequently, a close relative would arrive at the Kommandantur armed with a permit to visit. It was said corruption at a high level procured the stamp of approval. It was thought a king's ransom might procure someone's freedom. Perhaps it was possible, but it had not been tested. Nothing and no one at the Paris headquarters, Lutchez would say, was trustworthy or had decent feelings; he wouldn't part with a penny to a Boche, not even for an evening out at the theatre.

I saw an expression of absolute joy on Lucy's face. From her court-yard, she fluttered an envelope up at my window. 'From Mama and Papa,' she cried out, 'des nouvelles extraordinaires.' Her mother wrote: 'Chère fille. Prendre ton mal en patience encore un peu de temps ... ' With God's help, Lucy's parents were planning to travel to Paris to pay her a visit; some good news, but not to raise false hopes, people with influence were negotiating for Lucy's release.

Lucy discounted the time it had taken the letter to reach her ... several weeks. A visit could come 'today, tomorrow, or the next day,' she said with high hopes. And if she was going to be released, did another two weeks or so matter after eighteen months of detention? Would I miss her? I wished for nothing more than to see her leave the Fort safe and unharmed, I told her. But I would be sick at heart without her presence.

Lucy was my pillow of support. My nights were often sleepless believing that she might be whisked away in secrecy. It would not be the first time that someone had gone missing overnight. Early mornings, mindless of the selfish motive, I would jump down from my bunk to lean out of the window to look for someone who would tell me Lucy was still in the Fort. Marc Troska would yawn. He thought I put too much emphasis on a single woman. It was wasted effort with no future, he said in a breath of pessimism.

I knew what he meant. We were both 'up for grabs', as he put it. Pro-posals came our way in the shape of 'billets-doux', little love-notes that passed freely from across the division. Some of the notes were straight to the point, saucy, descriptive and good for a laugh; some were wild and professed to know every trick; a minority, which stirred my feelings, came from those among the younger set who wrote of parents who enforced strict discipline; a traditional kiss on the cheeks, yes, 'mais jamais d'une manière émotive sur la bouche'.

Lucy knew about the notes. The women openly gossiped about their objects of fantasy. There were petty jealousies, some squabbling, some hair-pulling, some cat-spitting. Louise Beriot was always at hand to referee. A talk, a caution, and a hug and a kiss between rivals settled the differences; no one proved spiteful enough to expose the goings-on to the Kommandantur.

'It's your business, chéri,' Lucy said without fuss. 'But please tell me if you stop loving me.'

Marc Troska was not the only one who thought lives were too much in the balance to play a straight game. Whilst many, like Khalid, were devious and greedy, a few had it bad, talking of true love, a promise in an engagement, even marriage after the war. Among the earnest, there were airy-fairy 'marriages', the man referring to his partner as 'ma femme' and the woman to hers as 'mon mari'. Invariably, such attachments were broken off by mutual consent or came unstuck when the 'husband' went to Mont Valérien or the 'wife' was deported.

I had no plans to ditch Lucy for another love. Bodily pleasures apart, she had been kind and comforting, washing and ironing my laundry and spoiling me with gifts. She was the girl I always dreamed about; she made me feel manly and worldly-wise. I wanted her friendship and love to hold good on a permanent basis; the age difference, a few years, was of no consequence.

The cluster of trees outside our window was in full flourish, the foliage heavy enough to obscure our view of the scantily-dressed women in light hats soaking up the sun as they lay on blankets in their courtyard. Corporal Weismann spent many hours rubber-necking from his window, ogling the smooth, lean, uncovered legs with – Grandmère Tauzin wickedly said – a hand in his pocket. Lance Corporal Klaus was unimpressed; he was careful to give the women's contours and postures a wide berth, heedful of the verbal abuse that was often tossed in his face and alert to the threat, instigated by Weismann, of being grabbed and stripped of his trousers.

It was mid-August with long days of sunshine. The air was sweet-scented and the birds in full song. Wild flowers were growing in profusion between the coils of barbed-wire around the perimeter of the courtyards and on the grassy banks, an illusory garden of Eden with butterflies, bees and other winged insects hovering about and gathering the sugary juices.

Peace and quiet in temporary reign, it was the season for dreamy nostalgia, everyone remembering the good days long passed and having something to tell. Lutchez recalled his last boozy weekend before the occupation of Paris, tippling 'brut' in the balmy backwoods of Reims with the wife of a director 'de la maison Taittinger'. Khalid returning to the city of sorrow in a hurry, at the wheel of his snazzy Delage after spending two enchanting weeks with 'une mannequine superbe' at her

Cap-Ferrat villa and just in time to see the Germans put on a strutting parade with a brass band along his beloved Champs-Élysées.

Khalid was impressive, a 'bon vivant' who filled young heads with stories of his adventures. His style of living appealed to me; an apartment in the exclusive 'huitième' ward, a chalet at Chamonix, a fast car, a cheque-book, a tailor, and a retinue of beautiful women. A playboy! Or, as Paulette bluntly said, knowing him inside out, 'un maquereau de premier ordre'. A prosperous pimp! All that was necessary to prove oneself capable, Paulette said, was 'l'air de jeunesse, des beaux traits, une bonne tête, bonnes mannières, de bonne humeur, la confidence et l'impudence'. A full bag of tricks! I was half-way qualified; given the chance I might come out on top. Garrulous as he was about his private life, Khalid, like so many, was unwilling to talk about the reason for his arrest.

Opulent Grasse, above Cannes, was the bi-annual retreat for the well-to-do middle-aged friends in the clothing trade, Zobel and Weinberger, warm and fragrant bachelors whose only 'crime' was to be born Jews. Their only fear was separation; if they were destined to die, they prayed to be summoned together, a wish that would be granted at a fearsome place we were yet to learn about ... Buchenwald in Germany.

Professor Katz who had never known a time when he ranked high, was greeted with a bow and fussed over. The francs he had in his pockets at any one time wouldn't buy him a bus ticket to the Bois de Boulogne. On days of idleness, he had been happy to walk to the banks of the river Seine, to sit and watch the world go by and to picnic on bread and cheese.

Grandmère Tauzin spent a satisfying month each year on her brother's farm outside Dinan, Brittany. She looked after the grandchildren and helped with the harvest. Each Sunday a bus would take the family to the beach at St Malo. If there was anything she regretted it was the absence of the little children, their tears, their laughter, and their love. Ready and willing to talk about her arrest – it was no secret – she was proud to have been the brains behind the escape of her two sons to England. Hence her imprisonment as a hostage.

Holidays in foreign parts were not for those with empty purses, my mother said. People from all over paid good money to come to Jersey for their pleasures; what was good enough for them was good enough for us and we did not have to bear any cost. In a sense, my mother was right. She did have to watch the pennies, but we were blessed with natural riches; a beautiful, docile piece of land with free and wholesome air, long hours of sunshine, a temperate sea, safe beaches for children, caves to explore, and a countryside of trails, lush green meadows and fragrant orchards, all within easy reach.

Lucy 'commissioned' the roly-poly banker and amateur artist, Bernard, to paint my portrait in oils. A deal was made, three packs of 'Week End', the brand of mild cigarettes available at dear prices, but fast going out of stock on the blackmarket. Like a second-rate Adonis, I posed on a high stool in the courtyard, arms folded, stripped to the waist and brown as a berry, for a head and shoulders creation. From across the division, Lucy looked on admiringly, pleased with her investment, giving each masterly stroke of the brush an enthusiastic nod of approval.

Bernard worked diligently during the hours of sunlight. He insisted on realism; no half-smile, he needed to capture the shadows, a hint of apprehension, and perspiration. Lucy hoped Bernard would put the finishing touches to the canvas before her 'threatened' release so that she might carry the 'aide-mémoire' home. But if Bernard knew it was a race against time for another reason, he was undistracted. If one went by the law of averages, Bernard, a Jew, was next in line for Mont Valérien.

Room 26 became the central point for information, news, discussion, counselling and guidance, Lutchez invariably in the chair. Raymond Barrat, a wireless telegraphy technician from Fontainebleau, had built a receiving-set which he kept hidden in a niche in the roof-space. Only Raymond and Lutchez listened to the war bulletins coming from Berlin and London. Reading the official German newspapers and those from the collaborationist press that Herman brought in, and the unmentionable resistance news-sheets smuggled in by the patriotic dustman who drove his 'gazogène' – a lorry powered by wood – into the Fort twice weekly to collect the rubbish, the wily Lutchez pieced together and analysed the dispatches, announcements, distortions, propaganda and home truths. Had it not been for the folly of the Germans in attacking Russia and biting off more than they could chew, France and England would be deep in the shit, 'bien dans la merde', Lutchez said. We were over the moon to be told that Germany could not win the war. The question was, when would it end? No one, not even Lutchez, could hazard more than a guess.

It was not design, merely chance – perhaps boosted by a feeling of well-being and complacency in thinking that a Paris uprising and an Allied invasion were on the cards – that led me to cheat on Lucy. I was in good form, mentally and physically, and I did have a frequent lust for some of the pretty newcomers, but I managed to keep it down to no more than a wavering eye when they took to the sun in tormenting positions.

I had a sneaking envy of Marc Troska for having more than his fair share, bent on 'fucking himself into a grave', Lutchez said. What a way to go, I thought! And the American was seriously competing for Louise

Beriot's affections. Lutchez was at a loss to understand why when there was a surfeit of choice in other directions. The woman was attractive, Lutchez conceded, but pushing forty-six, old enough to be Marc Troska's mother. Not Lutchez's type; she was too lean, too straight-laced, too dictatorial, and she walked with a mince. Lutchez liked women with meat, well-rounded hips, plump breasts and a firm backside, 'comme Paulette'. In any event, he said, Marc Troska was wasting his time.

Khalid, the self-styled connoisseur of beautiful women, argued with Lutchez. Louise Beriot had a rare quality which only men of good taste would appreciate. Granted, she rarely smiled, but when she did her whole face radiated, not a wrinkle nor a blemish to be seen. She was elegant, delicate as a butterfly, and had shapely legs. Given the opportunity, Khalid would bed Louise Beriot for himself. And he was willing to bet his gold tooth that Louise Beriot would give Marc Troska the brush-off.

Whispers buzzing around implied that Louise Beriot had had the 'question' popped to her before. Despite Lutchez's uncomplimentary drivel, Lucy said that he had been first to try his hand. Whether 'une femme mariée' or 'non mariée' no one knew; Louise Beriot was tight-lipped about her private life. Corporal Weismann believed her to be a prisoner of importance; he opened and closed doors for her like a flunkey. Hauptmann Bruchenbach favoured her with a click of his heels. Freddy Kaiser valued her as if she was his beloved mother. And it was Corporal Laufer who spelled out the instructions to those, like Professor Katz, he appointed to fetch her coffee and rations. Each morning, a 'Zimmermädchen' arrived at the infirmary to clean the rooms and make Louise Beriot's bed, not the commonplace wooden bunk with slats, but a divan-bed with springs, a soft mattress and a headboard.

I would have bet on Marc Troska's chances. I knew more than most. All of a sudden he had become secretive and unreadable. I detected a gradual softening in Louise Beriot's attitude towards him. She took to visiting our room for no apparent reason, sitting down obediently, taking tea, and laughing at his wit. With me, she was still formal – 'Monsieur l'Anglais' or 'Monsieur Antoine'. Of old, it was a civil 'Monsieur Troska' or, when vexed, 'l'impudent Américain'. Now, with frequency but behind a closed door, it was plain 'Marc'. Moreover, something unprecedented which added to the intrigue, Louise Beriot had allowed herself to be persuaded to visit a hairdresser and beautician.

Herman's neglect of his duty had been a contributing factor to my act of gross infidelity. He had unlocked the communicating door on the ground floor at the hour assigned for collection of the evening soup.

Instead of keeping surveillance, noting the numbers passing through to the cookhouse and back as Laufer and Weismann would have done, Herman had wandered away in search of company in the communal room for the twenty or so minutes it took to complete the function.

I was last to leave the cookhouse, returning by the recognized path in the women's courtyard, hugging the wall of the building and turning into the open doorway and the broad stairwell. Turning left, I was about to step past the door of the shower-room when it opened. I stopped in my tracks. Steam surrounded a tall, slender figure wrapped in white towelling who emerged, long yellow hair wet and dishevelled, with beads of oily moisture punctuating her face and running down her legs.

Caught off-guard, she fluttered before giggling. 'Ah, là-là! What a time to catch me!'

Her expression of surprise was not meant to be an invitation as far as I could see. She was Marc Troska's first love, Colette. I kissed her damp cheeks, in the brotherly manner which I had often adopted before, and I paid her a compliment: 'Comme vous êtes magnifique!' I slipped my free hand around her waist and hugged her closer. I meant to go no further. But then I quickly became magnetized by the heat of her body; vibes penetrated through my shorts. I kissed her on the mouth, wildly. For several precious seconds we floundered in a state of indecision, my hand feeling under the towelling. I set the canteen of soup down and started to unbutton my flies.

Startled, she said: 'Not here! C'est impossible!' She bit her lip, turned her head and scanned the long length of the corridor.

'In the douche,' I said.

She put a finger to her lips. 'Non, c'est occupée,' she protested.

I picked up the canteen, took her by the hand and steered her to the stairwell. Her face frowned, then broke into a smile. 'Ah, ça!' she said. 'Comme c'est romantique! L'armoire de nettoyage!'

An old cliché, 'any port in a storm', came to mind. She needed no coaxing; she squeezed her way into the broom-cupboard, her shoulders wading through a collection of cleaning implements. She handed me a bucket which I upturned over the canteen to smother the spiralling vapour. With the door a few inches ajar, there was enough light to see clearly; the early evening sun streamed into the stairwell from the courtyard and pierced through a network of cracks and grooves in the old staircase and the wooden walls of the cupboard.

There was no time to engage in preliminaries. Colette sat, half-standing, on an empty sauerkraut barrel, the towelling at her feet. The smell of damp rags and carbolic was overmuch. My neck was crimped into my shoulders beneath the stairs, and my legs trembled and buckled under the exertion of trying to keep my feet in an advantageous position. I blundered, probed, slipped about, happened on, lost her, found her; and then, steadfast, she held on one-handed until I was completely spent.

Sweating profusely, I helped her to her feet. We stayed still, hearts pounding, until the footsteps over our heads receded. I was struck with a feeling of guilt, having submitted her to the crudity of a foul cupboard. I whispered my apology. She laughed softly. With a whimsical sigh, she said: 'Loving in a bed with silk sheets, music and champagne is the dream of every woman, chéri; but, if I am favoured, I promise you that I will never turn my nose up at a cupboard.' Eyes clouding, she kissed me. 'My guilt is greater,' she said. 'Lucy is my dear friend and she loves you. This place is another world ... deceiving, frightening, hopeless, sympathetic and friendly, I don't care if I never leave.'

I waited until she had gone, back to the shower-room to wash the dust from her hair and the dirt from her face. Cautiously, my ears pricked, I peeped into the stairwell. It was the slack period, nothing and no one stirred. The muscles in my legs had jellied. I picked up the canteen and set off. In the corridor, I spied Herman, about to turn the key in the lock of the communicating door. I called out: 'Hey, Herman! Ein Moment.' With second wind, I explained my delay: 'Konversation mit der Koch in der Küche, compris?' A downright lie, in slack German but easy to understand.

Herman nodded. 'Du letzt?' he asked.

'Ja, alles fini, Herman.' I mopped my brow with the back of my free hand. 'Der Sonne heiss,' I said veering past.

Herman squinted. 'Scheisse auf Kopf,' he said.

Shit on my head? My hand went up. I unpicked a cobweb from my hair and loosened a few grains of grit which drifted down to the stone floor. A spider's web, I said with a shrug.

Herman's good eye lowered. He pointed a finger. 'Gottverdammt, Knöpfe offen!'

The flap of my flies was wide open. Thinking quickly, I stammered an explanation. 'Schlafen, compris Herman?' I had been taking a nap on my bunk at the time of the soup collection, and my shorts had been pulled on in a hurry to get to the kitchen. It might have been the construction of my German which left him scratching his head and with his nose to the ground. With one foot poised on the first step leading up to my room, I turned to see him looking down at a patch of water outside the shower-room. Sleuth-like, he followed the trail of wet footprints to the door of the broom-cupboard.

Marc Troska had set the table by the time I returned to the room.

Sliced potatoes and two roundels of salami were sizzling in a pan over the burner of our electric-plate; he was too engrossed with the preparation of the meal to question my leaden feet. I had a mind to surprise him and shout: 'Hey, guess what! I've just this minute slap-banged Colette!' But no! I wasn't exactly cock-a-hoop. I needed to blot out the incident because of Lucy.

I half-expected it when Herman came bursting in. He ignored Marc Troska's greeting. Gaping at me, a clownish grin on his face, he swore good-humouredly. 'Donnerwetter! Dein Freund,' he said to Marc Troska and pointing to me, 'figging! Ich weiss gut! Unter dem Treppenhaus im Schrank. Jawohl!'

There was a stunned silence for a second or two. A puzzled look on his face, Marc Troska put down the skimmer and switched off the heat. 'What's this about you fucking in the cupboard under the staircase? At this time of the day?' He touched the canteen with the back of a hand. 'Soup's not all that hot!' he said.

Herman laid bare his discovery. It was futile to make a denial. Herman was a friend, he wasn't going to make out a report, nor would he blab to Laufer or Weismann. But I didn't want him to suspect Lucy as the other half in the shabby event; Herman admired Lucy, she was a fine lady, not the kind of woman to lower her dignity within the cramped confines of a stinking cupboard. And Colette deserved equal anonymity; Herman thought her warm-hearted and she showed concern, frequently enquiring about the well-being of Herman's two soldier sons and his wife, Herta.

I shook my head. 'Nicht Lucy,' I told Herman; I stressed it and left it at that.

Marc Troska had taken the count. I was desolate. Louise Beriot was with me, refusing everyone but the custodians admittance into the room. She had her own private grief, red-eyed for those snatched without a claim to be judged.

Half-way through the morning, Corporal Weismann's whistle had signalled an emergency. With sinking heart, I followed the well-tried course of action, downing my tools, shaking hands with a dispirited Alfred and trotting back to my room to change from my working clothes into something foppish; a clean rigout and a neat appearance was good policy in a psychological crisis.

We swallowed our Dutch courage and sat back to listen to the familiar pattern of man-made sounds, the garbled orders, the scraping of boots and the creaking of floorboards apparently designed to wreck one's nerves in advance. In the short interval, as always when I was exposed to the danger of a 'selection', my last thoughts were for my mother. Given a last wish, I would have told her how grateful I was for a kind and loving childhood, and how sorry I was for the times I tried her patience and made her cry when she was so weary with hardship and from hard work. Trivia flashed through my mind; a bloody nose after running into a stone wall on my tricycle when I was five; scrumping and making a clean get-away, every little boy's dream; broken windows pinned on *my* head and an irate villager shouting harsh words at my mother, 'C'est votre petit vilain à tort,' which invariably led to the puffed-up parish 'connétable' putting me through the third degree; the very first time I tasted strawberries and fresh cream, pinched from a bowl in a hotel dining-room; my name engraved in my school's black book for one and all to see. Someone, looking through the archives and putting a finger on my case history, might say: 'I wonder what happened to *him?*'

'Tür aufmachen!' It was an order we'd heard a few times before, often no more than an itch to stick their nose in. 'Gefangenen, Achtung!' Freddy Kaiser yelped. The SS character this time was one rank below the normal predator, a Hauptsturmführer; when he faced me his large close-cropped head and wide ears blotted out our pin up of Dorothy Lamour in a grass skirt on the opposite wall. I stared into an unshapely face, by far the ugliest I had seen. Loose neck flesh hung down over the collar of his jacket. His nose, with yawning nostrils sprouting hairs, was bent at an angle, and his jaw was square and coarse. Anyone stone-blind would have sensed the evil in this fish-eyed SS man who caused my lips to twitch.

Which one was the American half-Jew? I was of no material interest to the man; he moved two steps sideways and breathed into Marc Troska's face. I did not dare look at my room-mate. The abuse levelled at him because of his parentage was too painful to bear. He stood firm and said nothing. Freddy Kaiser and Hauptmann Bruchenbach stood shamefaced at the open door, restraining their anger at the Hauptsturmführer's outpourings. Bruchenbach was known for his mischievous disposition towards Jews, but merely in a tiresome way and only when under the influence of drink, never with this aggression bordering on violence.

The Hauptsturmführer's hatred for Jews, especially if they were of American origin, was undisguised. His order to Marc Troska, 'ausfall, du halb-Jude, Autobus ... schnell!' chilled me to the bone. It was done in an instant. Marc Troska spurted out of the room, his plimsolls slithering along the length of the corridor to the women's staircase, to melt away in the courtyard before boarding the bus for Mont Valérien. Freddy Kaiser, ashen-faced, was the last to leave the room. At the door he paused and looked back over his shoulder; he opened his mouth to say something, thought better of it and quietly closed the door behind him.

I turned the key in the lock. Tears came to me easily. I would sorely miss Marc Troska. I couldn't claim to have a deep insight into his character, my knowledge of him amounted to very little. He was enigmatic, impenetrable, incommunicable and, as Louise Beriot was to admit, 'persistant, frauduleux, amusant, toujours le théâtre'. No one could have wished for a more compatible companion.

Louise Beriot made a pot of tea. I was left with the unenviable task of folding up Marc Troska's bedding, bundling up his clothing and disposing of the knick-knacks he had collected over the months. He had listed some bequests; a coiled, gold-plated tie-pin for Viktor Wladzimir; a silver fountain-pen for Khalid; a tortoiseshell comb for Lutchez; a cigarette-lighter for Max, the tailor; cigarettes for Professor Katz; a tablet of scented soap for Herman which, no doubt, would find its way to Herta, his wife; lastly, a letter, folded and gummed down.

The possibility of named beneficiaries falling to selections at any one time was taken into consideration; therefore, substitute names were included on the lists. Herman came in with the names of those removed and a half-bottle of schnapps, foul stuff to my taste which, taken at a gulp, was nevertheless calming. Seven men had gone, an all-Jewish contingent – among them, Bernard the banker and amateur artist; elderly Marcel, an advocate, and one who did occasional 'look-out' duty; Michel Jacobsen, a nineteen-year-old medical student who pursued his education on the risky side of the building; Willi Blumenson, a placid Dutch librarian; Frizell, a middle-aged 'cambrioleur acrobate' whose speculative profession had brought him down to the ground with a crash; and 'Colonel' Vattier, a bulbous-nosed 'vétérinaire' and gambler.

Lucy sent me a note of commiseration via Herman. When Louise Beriot left me, I was glad for the company of Lutchez, Viktor Wladzimir and Khalid; others streamed in to express their sympathy. Laufer and Weismann stopped by and were offered a drink; surprisingly, Weismann, usually on the take, chipped in with a litre of rough wine which went down well on top of the schnapps.

Late that afternoon we were still drinking, exchanging glances, not saying much, thinking a great deal, mental images forming of a wooded hill and the hexagon-shaped Fortress of Mont Valérien which so often haunted our sleep. It was Corporal Weismann who pulled us out of our reveries with his frantic shouting. He burst in on us with his braces hanging down over his trousers and in stockinged feet. He had difficulty with his speech. My first thoughts were that he had been drinking hard, fallen asleep and dreamed something scary. He clutched at the side of the bunk and slurred in my face. 'Sofort … tout de suite … Oberleutnant Kaiser kommen … Amerikaner mit!'

Lutchez told Weismann to keep calm and gently pushed him into the armchair. Khalid made a face and screwed a forefinger into the side of his head. It was unlike Khalid to be rude to Weismann under his nose. Told he was a 'soûlard' and 'fou comme un bouc', Weismann went into a tizzy. He narrowed his eyes; he had been drinking, yes, but he was neither a drunkard nor stupid like a goat, he snapped at Khalid. He had heard 'très bien'. The Oberleutnant had telephoned to say he was on his way down, 'avec l'Américain … Troska!'

Sensational news! We did not swallow it whole. Corporal Laufer, better adjusted than his crapulent colleague, was not in the building to corroborate the facts. True or false, Weismann's report spread like wildfire. Windows were thrown open and all eyes focused upon the crown of the hill leading from the Kommandantur. Daylight was fading, long shadows hung down over the steps, and there was a chilly damp lingering about the late autumn air. I built up the fire with wood and coal. No man had ever returned from Mont Valérien; if Marc Troska had been resurrected he'd need to be warm.

For once, Weismann had been badly maligned. Freddy Kaiser's springy, black-booted steps first came into view, and no one could mistake the pink shirt and the white silk handkerchief tied loosely around Marc Troska's neck. Gasps of disbelief greeted the sight of his hands raised above his head like a conquering hero returning home.

Freddy turned a blind eye to the embraces from the women crowding the courtyard, the stairwell and the corridor. Marc Troska's tired-looking face was smeared red and he flagged as he crossed the division, grasping outstretched hands before sinking prostrate into the armchair to swallow a stiff measure of cognac which some good soul had foraged for him.

A bad joke, Freddy confided to a crowded room. The American had not officially been listed. And he was anxious for everyone to know that such mindless conduct was not condoned by Hauptmann Bruchenbach. We must all understand that, however junior in rank, an officer of the 'Schutzstaffeln' could not be censured or remonstrated with; to have challenged the Hauptsturmführer at the time might have ended in real grief.

Marc Troska came to the same conclusion. He had been introduced to the programme of events at Mont Valérien, and if there was to be another time he would be more sure of himself when he went and would laugh in the shadow of the Devil's lair. He was surprised, he said, at his self-possession on the journey. As well as those taken from Romainville, others filled the bus, taken from city prisons. Every man was resigned to his fate, like lambs going to slaughter, not even a 'baa'. With an equal number of heavily armed SS guards taking up the window seats there was no escape. And there were those who treated what was to come coldly, even making light of their last hour.

Frizell, the 'cat' burglar, complained to the nervous 'con de chauffeur', the civilian driver who was unsure of the road and was turning too far to the north. 'Prends le chemin en ligne direct, imbécile,' he shouted. Frizell wanted to take a last look at the Eiffel Tower; as a young man it had been his ambition to climb the lofty structure, but at four hundred metres off the ground he could never find the nerve; besides, what was there to steal 'tout en haut'?

At the Gare du Nord, Marcel the advocate pointed to the building where he first started work as a junior clerk; nothing had altered structurally so far as he could see, the same brown-coloured paint coated the street door and the boot scraper was still firmly embedded in the base of the wall. Paris wasn't resplendent or gay any more, everyone agreed; swastikas were flying from hotels and public buildings, collaborationist posters still desecrated walls, wooden signs in the German language pointed in every direction, red and white sentry boxes and concrete pillboxes were sprouting everywhere, and the pavements and cafés were crowded with ugly uniforms; only the women were beautiful, perhaps paler and more pinched than anyone had seen before, but when they saw the bus with their fellow-countrymen almost eclipsed by broad shoulders and steel helmets they waved and blew kisses. That warm acknowledge-ment all across the city had a tonic effect on everybody, Marc Troska said.

'Colonel' Vattier got his last wish. The bus skirted Longchamp racecourse where, 'dans les jours de bonheur', he had lost a few shirts, but when in luck's way he celebrated with champagne and caviare. Reflecting on those sentimental days, he had never been a bad loser, he told Marc.

The chatter and the banter stopped when the guards buttoned up their tunics and snuffed out their cigarettes as the bus climbed the narrow wooded gradient to the door of Mont Valérien. Inside the quadrangle, the men were ordered out. Bernard tripped and lost a sabot; two guards played football with it. Formed into two lines, an ailing man with a breathing problem reported he had left his throat pump on the bus.

The place was squalid and there was a smell of bad eggs in the air. Men shivered standing in the cold; they rubbed their hands and stamped their feet. There was no panic, just quiet resignation, some heads bent in prayer, some raised aloft to a grey sky. Ten were taken at a time.

'I was in the last batch with Bernard, young Michel Jacobsen and Frizell. When it came to our turn, an Untersturmführer stopped me in my tracks, a big grin all over his face, he pointed to a black Citroën car and told me to get in. I was being returned to Romainville, he said. I had been put through what he called "die Probe", a rehearsal or experiment; next time, I wouldn't be so *glücklich*, he promised. All of a sudden, I wanted to scream. I felt like a quitter. Bernard called out, "Cheerio, Marc." I had a second or two to look back. Young Michel blew me kisses and shouted: "Envoyez un gros baiser à Madeleine de la chambre 51." Back numbers now, memories will grow dim. Will their names ever be written in the good book? I'll remember them; I'll never rid the volleys of gunfire from my head.'

The Last Christmas

Christmas was within sight. Marc Troska had recovered from his ordeal: he had had two weeks to uncoil; less boisterous, going about his early morning routine of outdoor exercises in a half-hearted way, and with recurring nightmares. Although it was not generally known, Louise Beriot had played a part in healing his condition. There was no doubt in my mind, the acquaintance had blossomed; had I one, I would have bet a Red Cross parcel they were love-making.

My affair with Colette had gone undetected. An opportunity for a second encounter presented itself. Poor Lucy required dental treatment at the internment camp of St Denis, where the dentistry was fully equipped for complex surgery, under the care of British and American internees. This meant an overnight stay for Lucy. Caddishly, I enticed Colette to a vacant room on the top floor where we spent a late evening together.

I became steeped in treachery, steadily and cunningly pulling away from my allegiance to Lucy. Her declaration of love for me, I wanted to keep very much intact; but Colette had whetted my appetite for irregular partners, I sought to do the rounds like Khalid and other free-agents whose affairs were without compromise. Now that the long winter nights were upon us, Khalid looked for a new diversion, inviting some of the bolder men and women to a room on the top floor on a share one, share all basis. I was offered membership of this exclusive group, but after a trial run the venture was abandoned; Lutchez said it had proved too wild, too risky.

Marc Troska was only mildly curious about our new neighbours, given a room one short step across the division. Pretty French-Polish sisters, Danuta and Zofia would go on record as the two youngest prisoners among the women – 'just children from an infant school' were the commiserating words spoken by one from a crowd of window watchers when the girls first came into view by way of the unmade road, commonly known as 'la porte de derrière'. Each girl carried a small suitcase; they were identically dressed: floppy-brimmed hats, white mufflers, dark jackets and skirts, long black stockings and sturdy shoes. From a bourgeois family, each wore the insignia of German hate and prejudice – the yellow Star of David.

Models of virtue, the girls were shy of the reception awaiting them. We all wondered about each other, and frequently asked what offence had been done, the whys and the wherefores. 'Parce que nous sommes Juives' was a good enough reason; Jews were at risk in the home as well as on the streets. By chance, they had come to Romainville direct, thus escaping the web of Gestapo, interrogation, rape and incarceration at the squalid wooden ex-army barracks, which made up the 'Jewish camp' six kilometres away at Drancy. That was the gateway to Auschwitz and Mauthausen and the gas chambers which were an essential part in the programme of extermination at these camps that was, as yet, unknown to the men and women of Romainville.

Danuta and Zofia, suffering the common disease of home-sickness to which almost everyone was prone in early days, found many shoulders to cry on. Older women, who were themselves mothers of sixteen- and seventeen-year-old daughters and who had known the anguish of brutally enforced family displacement, were easily moved to pity. Fuss and tenderness, and a first letter from home with the well-employed assurance that everything was being done to secure an early release, helped to dry the tears and soothe the heavy hearts of the two girls.

Louise Beriot showed her concern for the sisters for another reason. They were no more than 'bébés', wet behind the ears, she warned the younger men obsessed with wenching. There were many interesting and more worthwhile pastimes than fishing for the girls' favours; one could learn a language, shorthand, art, chess, even receive political instruction if the mind was so inclined. But, it was asked, to what purpose? One's path pointed to Mont Valérien; better to enjoy one's last days on earth in the company of a woman when the choice of a partner was so easily accomplished.

At first I contented myself with a nod of the head from my open window to theirs and the natural pleasantries of 'bonjour Mesdemoiselles', how are you? Passing the time of day, providing it was brief and not misemployed, was usually tolerated by the custodians. After a while, under cover of darkness, I could hold a cosy conversation with the younger of the two, Zofia, and, by stretching out an arm, touch her finger-tips.

Danuta, a student of music like her sister, was drawn to Marc Troska; they had something in common – Polish fathers; moreover, he could tell Danuta about the city of San Francisco where her uncle, 'Mikal, le frère de Papa', lived with his American-born wife. And Danuta, who spoke only a few basic words of English, wanted to know if Monsieur Troska would assist in a wider learning of the language.

But when I put forward the overture, I received a shake of the head. One student of English was acceptable, not two, Marc Troska said, referring to the occasional hour when Alfred came to the room on an exceptionally wet or hard frosty day. There were a couple of women capable of teaching Danuta English, he said. 'The thought of pencil and paper, verbs and nouns or whatever, "je suis – I am," and " the pen of my aunt", would send me up the fucking wall.' Danuta's innocence did nothing to excite his attention; and 'Papa's' line of business – he was an undertaker – was a bad omen as far as he was concerned.

Striking up a warmer friendship with the dimple-cheeked Zofia went by degrees and stealth. A tap at her door after hours to whisper a 'goodnight, sleep well' or to deliver a little benevolence, two mugs of cocoa and a couple of slices of toasted black bread, was to put my two feet into the room. Flitting kisses would be my reward. Like two puppies taking first sniffs outdoors, the girls gradually gained confidence. They got into the swing of daily routines, sharing in the chores and, with sharp ears, took an interest in the mature goings-on, wanting to learn about fashions, hair styles and make-up.

Danuta, the more well-developed of the two, was first to break loose from their severe style of clothing; after experimenting, she emerged with flair, pretty accessories and the prevailing hair-do – short at the back of the neck, sweeping sides and a straight fringe. We could see Khalid making a discreet play for Danuta's attention. We were all well-acquainted with the crafty ways he employed to attract a woman new to the Fort whom he hungered after, choosing a time when he had the courtyard to himself so that he could parade his handsome charms free of competition. The women, watching from the windows, would sigh, blow kisses and call out: 'Mais comme il est beau!' The men, not behaving as Khalid would wish, teased him with cat and dog noises. And he was always on guard against Corporal Weismann's foul tongue; Weismann's 'Pigalle' jargon was enough to send him cringing back into the building.

Both girls were endowed with a gift for music; Danuta had been receiving tuition in the viola and Zofia in the violin. Framed diplomas were hanging on a wall of the sitting-room at home, and to back up the claim, Zofia borrowed Viktor Wladzimir's newly-restrung violin. Her choice of composition was out of my depth; but for those, including Freddy Kaiser, with a good ear for musical skill, Zofia passed the test with flying colours. This led Louise Beriot to petition Hauptmann Bruchenbach; the elder sister, she told him, needed to continue with her studies, would he permit Danuta's viola to be delivered from her home to the Fort? Bruchenbach was not altogether unsympathetic to the request, he admitted to a liking for stringed instruments, but it was a tall order; besides, 'la maison', he said, was already well-furnished with instruments, the Fort was not meant to be a place for entertainment.

'But no, Lucy!' I said with a show of indignation. There was nothing one could call 'au grand sérieux' between Zofia and me, I told her when she called me to account. Just being polite, exchanging a few pleasantries, that was about it, I said. Not quite the truth. I had sown the seeds and made positive headway in my calculation, once sneaking into her room in the dead of night with the young 'macaroni' Stefano, a play-acting Italian to whom Danuta was drawn. We spent a half-hour whispering, holding hands and kissing tamely.

Lucy was clearly upset by the hearsay. She stayed out of sight in her room for several days before sending me a note. With tears in her eyes, she wrote she had not been herself – there had been no news from her parents, nothing in the post and she felt completely abandoned. 'La mélancolie, chéri!' She feared my love for her was on the wane; she saw all our plans crumbling.

'La maladie de Romainville.' Love was an essential part of life in the Fort; death came a poor second. Broken romances, broken hearts were many, infidelity making a great contribution; it was the women who suffered the more disturbing and emotional traumas when they saw their lovers and sometimes their husbands going to Mont Valérien.

Men and women were inspired with foolish passions and made turtle-dove pledges, by word of mouth and written down on paper – 'I love you forever' and 'don't forget me after the war' were common, senti-mental terms blotting out home responsibilities, loving husbands and pining wives and children. 'Engagements' were in fashion, symbolized by rings created from bone, another sideline of Charlo's which earned him cigarettes.

Lucy was at her happiest planning for her new life and mine; rarely did she mention her husband or what role he might play in due course. She dazzled me with her designs; 'we' would make Paris our home, with a terrace or a garden somewhere central and close to friends; and, of course, for the long week-ends and holidays, an apartment or a villa on the Mediterranean coast.

Her shopping list was extravagant and endless: new furniture and fittings for two dwellings, a motor-car of my own choice, and Khalid would introduce me to the best tailor and shirtmaker in the whole of Paris. Inwardly, I smiled. 'I'm counting the cost, Lucy,' I said. 'What bank will I have to rob? When I left Jersey I had seven shillings saved up in the Post Office, enough to buy one good cigar. I come from a working-class family, my mother had to scrub hard to make ends meet, and she still lives in an old cottage without gas or electricity and with running water a mile away. Me, Lucy? I was on the Parish. I did odd jobs. I've no prospects!'

Lucy's big brown eyes widened. She smiled and she stroked my bottom. 'Then you are poor in money,' she said mischievously.

'Poor as a church mouse,' I replied. 'But,' I said, 'money and possessions are not everything, coming out from here alive is more important.'

She glowed. 'Of course, chéri! But you don't understand! I have plenty of money of my own, dans une banque Suisse. Enough for us both, chéri!'

I made a face, feigning shock. 'Lucy! That's shameful!' I tutted. 'Wouldn't that make me a "grippe-sou" or a "maquereau" like Khalid?'

'Mais non! Khalid is a good fellow, a good mixer who lives off many women. You,' she said softening her voice, 'would be different, "mon homme marqué personnel". C'est bien compris?'

I understood well. If that was what Lucy wanted and if it was to be, I had nothing against being paired with her. She went on to tell me of her plans. She was going into business with Thérèse, the couturier and friend of the late Franz de Bruyne, together with Paulette who vowed to give up her former lifestyle to marry Lutchez. Thérèse, Lucy said, was brilliant with pen and paper and scissors, sketching and designing creations which she filed away in a box; all three women agreed that fashion after the war would be foremost in the minds of women who had been denied the amenities of milliners and dressmakers for so long. My ears buzzed with majestic-sounding names like Schiaparelli, Lucien Lelong and Madame Worth. Who they actually were I didn't know.

The fort was full of people with starry-eyed ideals for after the war. Perhaps Charlo's was the most far-fetched. He was going to set up a brothel 'pour les gens au-dessous de la moyenne'. A house of living dolls, no man above the height of five feet would be permitted entry. The proportions of the rooms, furniture and beds would be in keeping, under-sized ... 'Like the pricks of the patrons,' Lutchez scoffed.

'La Maison Romainville.' That was the ingenious trademark Lucy agreed upon. I asked her: 'Where would I fit in?' A man would be needed about the house, she said; I would be installed as a director with my own office and a salary if I wished. I laughed out loud. I pictured myself fitted out in striped trousers and a black jacket with a carnation in the buttonhole, perhaps meandering around with my hands behind my back in a sweet-scented salon filled with gorgeous women. It *was* comical when I thought back to the days when I had been hard pressed, forced to empty dustbins and sweep horse-shit on the public roads.

Lucy asked what I thought. I had come a long way in a short time since my deportation from Jersey. I had grown self-confident. I was learning about the cultural things in life, at home among people who had once moved in high circles, some with 'handles' to their names and of a rank that I had been taught to treat with respect as a boy. Now they sought my company, gave me the glad hand and linked arms in a turn of the courtyard. We shared a lofty optimism; making plans, however hare-brained, and having faith in one's own salvation, however improbable, was essential to one's sanity and morale. Yes, I told Lucy, I wished for nothing more than to be a part of her life to the end of time.

I was sincere in my sentiments, but Lucy's plans were scattered to the winds by my deceit. Herman strode into the room with an unhappy look on his face, carrying my laundry as I had sent it to Lucy, crumpled and unwashed. He guessed why Lucy was angry. 'Ich weiss warum,' he said to a grinning Marc Troska. 'Er mit Jungfer, Zofia, figging ich glaube.'

That I had 'figged' Zofia, as Herman crudely put it, had not gone untalked about. She had been seen entering my room in her night-clothing, enough evidence for most. Seducing Zofia had not been a walkover; coaxing her to take the first bold step across and into the men's division had been a trial. 'Papa' had written; 'Conduisez-vous bien, mes filles,' do nothing to endanger your release. And 'Papa' would be furious if he knew his daughters had taken to painting their faces with rouge and sipping at a small glass of watered wine.

When Zofia saw the gallery of pin-ups and some of the more outrage-ous magazine cut-outs of scantily-dressed girls, especially Marc Troska's favourite of a stark-naked Negress with big glossy breasts and red nipples, she giggled and said: 'Scandaleux!' If 'Papa' knew, he would go and lie down on his bed of pain. Her uncle Mikal had written about Americans being 'démonstratif' and a little 'démonté'. Neither she nor Danuta had ever seen illustrations of that nature pasted up on the walls; nor had they ever been to a cinema. Papa always kept a tight rein; he allowed them to see lantern-slides of far-off places but nothing that might disgust or corrupt. Even the music they were taught was in the best of taste.

Zofia's tiny fists clenched and she trembled when I pulled the skirt of her nightdress over her hips. Her naked backside was smooth as silk to my hands. She was small and snug; she winced and a tear rolled down onto a dimpled cheek. She looked up into my eyes and stuttered ... 'un bébé? ... si cela peut se faire.'

I was taken aback. I asked her if she had been listening to Maria Baranbanov. Lucy had known about the attractive Russian-Swiss even before Maria had communicated with me. 'I do not know how you will answer,' Lucy had said, 'the poor girl has her head in the clouds; please be sympathetic but careful, Maria is suicidal.' Maria had tried to kill herself. A tall girl, Maria was sickly-looking and walking on crutches when she arrived in the Fort from the Jewish camp at Drancy where the shifting of Jews to Germany never stopped. She had avoided a transport, if only temporarily, by throwing herself from a high window, breaking both legs on hitting the ground. Now having recovered, the nagging thought remained with her; would she be returning to the squalor of Drancy or would she be forced to leave the Fort direct for a German labour camp? Whichever, the prospects were too frightening for Maria to contemplate.

Maria's communication was written in a combination of two languages, English and French. She addressed me as 'Cher ami.' She first asked to be excused for her 'effronterie'. She feared her plea for help might be seen as the 'wandering of the mind'. She was honest; but, as she admitted, 'non héroique'. Before embarking on the crux of the matter, she wrote about her childhood, describing the very first school she attended at Annecy. She had a pony called Domino, very old now, who pulled the buggy to and from infant school when she was five years old. Domino was nearing the end of his life and would be grieving; the pony, several dogs and cats, had been left in the care of an old servant. Maria yearned to be with them.

Her mother and father had taken refuge in Switzerland; and 'Micha, mon bien-aimé', her fiancé, was in hiding. Micha was thirty, nine years older than Maria. Yes, they had slept together, because of love for each other, and they planned to marry. But, I was assured, there had never been anyone else and she had not been molested by the Germans.

Micha was a strong and wise man. He would choose to see Maria alive and well even if it meant taking what some people might think a 'gross' step to avoid deportation to a German labour camp. At Drancy there had been talk of exclusive Jewish camps established for a most disturbing purpose. 'Papa Baranbanov' would be of the same mind as Micha; if I would help her, 'Papa, un homme très riche', would reward me well after the war. 'You are British,' Maria wrote; the Germans do not hate the British. I would be a survivor, she believed. Would I make her pregnant?

She would claim her pregnancy was from a British union, thus securing her objective.

Maria's reasoning was idiotic. The contents of the letter were too critical for me to answer without proper advice, Lutchez said. The poor girl needed a psychoanalyst. I was attracted to her, but was advised to string her along, play for time; meanwhile, Louise Beriot agreed to take Maria under her wing and try to implant into her troubled mind that Jews were in no more danger than those of any other race or religion. We did not know then of the enormous crimes being perpetrated against selected races across the whole of Europe.

Christmas week. Incredibly, a festive occasion was promised! Hauptmann Bruchenbach received a small delegation of women at his residence, Louise Beriot the spokeswoman. She could use her graceful charms to advantage and the Hauptmann was susceptible to her as to no other. She appealed to reason; the prisoners deserved a little extra consideration when the new year predicted bitter changes. Bluntly, she asked how many among us would see another Christmas?

Bruchenbach guessed what Lousie Beriot was implying. His own future was in doubt. His moods were unpredictable, drunk or sober. He was going through a thin time, Freddy Kaiser revealed. The Hauptmann, he said, needed a lengthy furlough, rarely did he leave the Fort for more than an evening. In all truth, it wasn't a matter of absolute dedication to his command, he was living in almost as much uncertainty as the prisoners. A thousand officers rendered invalids at the Russian front were ready to jump into Bruchenbach's feathered bed. The Hauptmann was neither old enough nor sufficiently unfit to be disqualified from active service.

There was another reason for Bruchenbach's uneasiness, shared by Freddy Kaiser and the garrison. There was the ongoing talk of a Paris uprising; the name Henri Tanguy was on everybody's lips. Those who knew of him said he was a fearless thirty-four year old activist, a Breton communist resistance leader who went by the name of 'Colonel Rol'. All Paris was looking to the skies for a drop of weapons, one heard. Given the ammunition, two million resolute Parisians were ready to do battle under the leadership of the popular 'Colonel'. And, an added concern for our captors, thousands of prisoners in the tough city jails promised to wreak a terrible revenge on the enemy; the river Seine, Lutchez said, would run with blood – 'le sang des Allemands'.

Meeting with the women, Bruchenbach took the opportunity to defend his office. He was an officer of the Wehrmacht, responsible only for the domestic management of the prisoners. He admitted there were injustices; he did not agree with them, but to cross swords with the Schutzstaffel would only aggravate that authority and attract their attention.

'Bien sûr, Monsieur le Capitaine!' The delegation of women understood and could speak on behalf of all the prisoners. 'Monsieur le Capitaine' was not responsible for the deportation or the executions; absolutely everyone agreed that Monsieur was 'un homme sensible et sympathique', which would be credited to 'Monsieur' when liberation came.

Bruchenbach warmed to the assurance, Louise Beriot said. He opened a bottle of wine and personally poured out four glasses. He passed cigarettes around and spent half an hour in good-humoured banter before giving Corporal Laufer instructions.

'Jawohl.' We could put up Christmas decorations.

'Jawohl.' We could have a communal meal.

'Jawohl.' We could have a concert.

'Jawohl.' We could have a distribution of Red Cross parcels.

Lucy was not talking to me. I sent her a note and waited a few hours for a reply. None came. I knocked at her door after hours and called out through the keyhole: 'Lucy, it's me with my fingers crossed.'

After a moment or two I heard her reply. 'Fiche-moi la paix,' she said.

'I'm sorry Lucy ... avec beaucoup de regrets. What can I do to make up?'

'Faire une petite promenade ... au loin!'

Take a little walk ... over a long distance! I heard laughter. I got up off my knees and retreated with my tail between my legs to my room to commiserate with myself. I felt down in the dumps. I would miss Lucy's love, her blown kisses, the little hand waves from her courtyard, and the red mouth impressions on the tails of my shirts which were returned to me after careful washing and ironing.

I wasn't put off by Lucy's snub. Her pride had been hurt but I sought to renew her friendship. I composed a long letter and asked her not to let a little indiscretion come between us; time was too short, too precious, I wrote; I reminded her of our plans and went overboard, in all sincerity, in my praises. 'You, my dearest Lucy, are the beautiful fantasy of my youth, the alluring Hedy Lamarr who planted butterflies in my stomach, set my heart thumping, my knees tingling and caused me sleepless nights. You, "chère amante", are that exquisite dream come true; "je suis malade d'amour pour toi", please ... please don't condemn me to bear the rest of my life, short as it may be, in your bad graces.' With the letter, I sent her a Christmas gift of a fancy holder filled with her favourite colour of rouge powder which Herman had scoured Paris for and purchased at a price which exhausted my financial resources and put me in debt. The letter was unanswered but the rouge was not returned. I was pleased.

Lucy, her nose high in the air whenever she passed me, took on the role of set-dresser. I had half a mind to grab her and put her across my knee. Granted free passage across the division, she transformed the men's communal room into the likeness of a bistro with shaded lights and small tables covered with red-chequered cloths. Home-made multi-coloured paper chains were strung from wall to wall. Lucy seemed composed, the promise of a visit from her parents and her release temporarily forgotten in all the industrious activity afoot; labour, by hand and the sewing-machine, was non-stop; women were snipping at old newspapers, pasting the sections and turning them into face masks and comical hats; and cast off materials were being stitched and made into dresses. Women were going about in curlers and protecting new hair-dos with dust-caps.

It was a gay atmosphere, free from care, no one giving a thought to deportations or executions. Food was to be pooled and a menu planned. Cards were designed for inviting special guests, including the Haupt-mann. The handsome Lucien Paradis, the tender-hearted 'pédéraste' who mourned his loss of liberty in frequent bouts of crying and who at forty had a great fear of old age, for once was uncomplaining; he was in the thick of things, prancing about the corridors as if he had suddenly been endowed with new energy. Appointed 'le maître de cérémonie', Lucien was drawing up a programme and holding auditions. At the Christmas Day show this music-hall artiste and female impersonator blackened his face and mimicked golden-skinned Josephine Baker, the 'toast' of Paris; and sang in the sentimental style of the Corsican-born heart-throb, Tino Rossi. Not long afterwards Paradis was deported to Buchenwald Concentration Camp. Mentally ill, he was put to work in a stone quarry and was crushed to death by a runaway truck in November 1943.

Excitement was at fever pitch. It was Christmas Eve. Good news for Herman. He came into the room beaming. Marc Troska was at his work in the garrison cookhouse. Herman grasped my hand. 'Wunderbar!' he whooped. 'Wilhelm und Alex wohl, Frankreich kommen,' he said. A letter from his sons told Herman that they were being rested from the Russian front to a unit at Abbeville, no more than 160 kilometres from Paris. Herman, overjoyed, wiped away a tear and set down on the table a large bottle of schnapps which he had hidden in a deep pocket of his greatcoat. 'Zelebrieren,' Herman said.

It was mid-afternoon. Corporal Laufer unlocked the communicating doors on all floors. Providing room doors were left wide open and one conducted oneself in an upright manner it was come and go as one pleased. And Lutchez passed on an order; no cupboard love; no slap and tickle; one was on trust; one had to consider those of a certain age let out of harness to socialize with their opposite numbers.

Maria Baranbanov, dressed in a blue frock with white collar, white cuffs and white buttons, came to the room accompanied by Louise Beriot. Both women looked radiant. The setting was warm and snug, the red heat from the woodburning stove staved off the wintriness outside the window. On the table was a light tea of thin-cut fish paste sandwiches and Osborne biscuits. Louise Beriot was purring, her green eyes giving Marc Troska fond looks. Their entanglement was no longer a secret and, under our breath, it was three cheers.

When communicating a matter of urgency Corporal Weismann went about it rumbustiously, his voice could be heard at long range. He burst into the room like a tornado with his rifle slung over his shoulder. 'Nach Kommandantur,' he yelled in my face. 'Tout de suite!'

The order came to me like a kick in the stomach. 'Warum?' I asked, choking on a sandwich.

Weismann didn't know why. He had taken a message on the telephone from 'nach oben'. He had been ordered to escort me 'up the hill'.

I had only seconds to prepare. For what? I pulled on the white woollen hat Lucy had knitted me. Marc Troska wrapped a sheet of newspaper around the remaining sandwiches and stuffed them into a pocket of my Harris tweed overcoat together with a bar of hard chocolate and a handful of cigarettes. There was barely time to shake hands. Lutchez, tipped off, met me at the door and walked with me to the end of the corridor. He was as baffled as I was. 'It's only Thursday, Lutchez,' I said. 'Men do go to Mont Valérien singly as you well know.'

A tearful Lucy waited at the bottom of the staircase. She threw her arms around me; Weismann allowed her emotions to go unchallenged. 'Be brave, chéri,' she cried in my face. 'I had no right to be angry. I'm sorry ... plein de regrets ... I love you, chéri ... I love you ... !'

Lucy's whimpering voice echoed to the gate. Shivering, I turned up my coat collar. Weismann walked briskly; I followed in his wake, stepping round the mud-filled potholes in the unmade road. We said nothing; Weismann was almost as tense as I was, he knew what was going through my mind. We approached the crown of the hill; the first ominous sign to look for was a black Citroën car flying a swastika pennant. My eyes turned to the darkening sky, and I gave a moment's thought to the letter hidden under the floorboards, there had been no time to add a postscript to my mother. Gravel crunching under his heavy

boots, Weismann broke the silence. 'Nix Polizei … alles gut,' he said, as
if the load had been taken off *his* mind.

So far, so good! But what if the Citroën was on its way! The genteel
silver-haired steward, Gustave, was waiting at the door. Before allowing
us to step on to the tiles in the hallway, he pointed to the mat and told
me sternly to wipe my shoes, as I remembered him doing before.

We both wiped our feet. Weismann asked, in a whisper: 'Was gibt,
Gustave?'

Gustave put up a wrinkled finger to his lips. Ignoring the question, he
turned to me; stroking my backside, he whispered in my ear: 'Hauptmann gutmitig, nix Angst, compris?'

Bruchenbach in a good mood! No need for me to fear! I could have
kissed the old fairy. He knocked gingerly at Bruchenbach's door. The
smell of Virginia tobacco was strong. Bruchenbach stood in part-mufti,
in slippers, a pullover, and warming the seat of his breeches against the
crackling heat of a log fire, a cigarette burning between his lips and a full
glass at hand. Seated, pensive, was Freddy Kaiser.

Bruchenbach looked straight into my face. With a twist of a smile, he
said: 'Merry Christmas to you,' a greeting which, evidently, he had
practised beforehand. It was unusually cordial of him; I thought to
myself, surely to goodness no German could be so hard of heart as to
wish me the compliments of the season before imparting bad news. 'And
to you, Herr Hauptmann,' I answered.

He pointed to the other armchair and invited me to sit down. He dealt
patiently with Weismann, telling him to ease his rigid stance, put his rifle
aside and find a seat. Bruchenbach filled two glasses with red wine,
passed one to me and the other to Weismann. With a cigarette apiece,
Weismann and I jumped to our feet when Bruchenbach raised his glass
to mark the occasion with a toast. 'Für Deutschland! Prosit!' he called.

I could have blown a raspberry; diplomacy was my best course and I
joined in the reply with my fingers crossed. Weismann carried his
enthusiasm to excess, adding a 'Heil Hitler' which caused a stony silence
before Bruchenbach scowled and muttered 'Arschloch' under his breath.
He appeared to be in no hurry to make the reason for my summons
known to me; it didn't occur to me that it might have been motivated
simply by goodwill. I speculated whilst he gabbled away in his own
language and in tortuous English and French. Was I about to be
transferred to the internment camp at St Denis? Quite apart from being
worried about keeping my skin whole, I wasn't drawn to that sanctum.
Was I about to be released and returned to Jersey? Unlikely.

Bruchenbach turned to a large book of maps lying on his desk. He
opened it at a marker and said 'Nordengland. Compris?'

ABOVE LEFT: *Anthony Faramus's birthplace: Les Marais Cottage, Beaumont Hill. His mother is standing outside the door*

ABOVE RIGHT: *The Forum Cinema, St Helier, Jersey*

RIGHT: *German gun emplacement on the Jersey coast*

OPPOSITE: *Entrance to the Fort de Romainville, Les Lilas, Paris, used by the Germans to hold political prisoners under sentence of death*

ABOVE: *The courtyard in front of the prison building was divided by a length of chicken wire, with men to the left and women to the right. Faramus's room was just under the clock; that of Danuta and Sofia was immediately to its right*

RIGHT: *Stairs from the ground floor to Room 26. On the left is the coal bunker door through which women were smuggled*

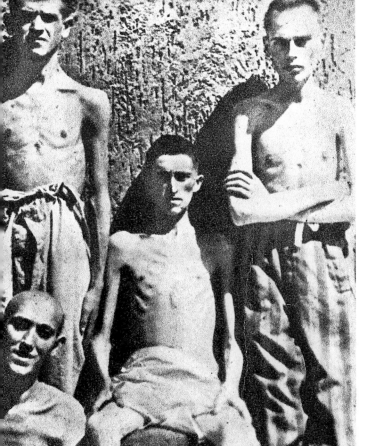

ABOVE: *The* Appel Platz *during roll call at Buchenwald*

LEFT: *An illegal photograph of malnourished prisoners in Buchenwald. Faramus is on the right: No (E) 42324*

OPPOSITE ABOVE: *The first glimpse of Mauthausen concentration camp*

OPPOSITE BELOW: *New arrivals in the reception area at Mauthausen*

OPPOSITE ABOVE: *Prominent Nazis visiting Mauthausen. From second on left to right: Colonel Franz Ziereis (Camp Commandant), Heinrich Himmler, August Eigruber (Gauleiter of Linz) and behind him on the right Captain Georg Bachmayer (Deputy Commandant)*

OPPOSITE BELOW: *Mauthausen. The Austrian escaper Hans Bonarewitz is led to the gallows by the camp orchestra*

LEFT: *The death steps at Mauthausen, up which the prisoners carried blocks of stone weighing up to sixty pounds*

BELOW: *The quarry at Mauthausen*

ABOVE: *Tony and Mary courting on Hampstead Heath*

LEFT: *Anthony Faramus as a POW in* The Colditz Story

I leaned over and saw where he was pointing a finger. 'Manchester Stadt,' I said.

His finger moved fourteen kilometres north. What did I know about the town of Rochdale? I sank back in the chair. I was puzzled. Was he playing at some kind of geographical conundrum? I knew Rochdale to be the birthplace of the Co-operative Society to which my mother paid dues at the rate of sixpence a week. Useless information which I passed on.

'Rochdale industriell!' Bruchenbach blurted. 'Baumwolle Fabrik! Gummi Fabrik! Compris?'

'Cotton and rubber factories,' I told Freddy, who looked ill at ease.

Bruchenbach refilled the glasses. Freddy rationed himself to one glass. Bruchenbach asked: Did I know anyone living in Rochdale? Anyone 'speziell'?

I shook my head. Why, I wondered, should he be interested in such an unearthly place? I thought ... wait! Did the Germans attach some material importance to the Lancashire town? I, like others in captivity, had an abnormal tendency towards suspicion, often ridiculous. Was I being quizzed for a military reason? I took it for granted German intelligence knew that Rochdale produced war materials. Were they thinking I knew someone of importance, like a British government official with an address in the town, so that they might send the Luftwaffe to bomb the place? I said to Bruchenbach: 'Ehrlich, cross my heart, Herr Hauptmann, ich wissen nicht Person auskommen von Rochdale.'

Bruchenbach gave me a blank look. He pressed. I had to know someone living in Rochdale. He offered me a clue. 'Une femme', a lady 'bien connue' to me. He touched his forehead. 'Denken,' he said.

I did, I thought hard. I rattled my brains as if my life depended on a correct answer. I glanced at Freddy. He was unreadable, bored by the charade. Suddenly, it dawned on me. I fell about laughing. I clapped my hands. 'Ich wissen jetzt, Herr Hauptmann! Der Frau, Gracie Fields!'

Bruchenbach frowned. He looked nettled. Evidently it wasn't *her*. He turned to Freddy. 'Wer?' he asked of the Oberleutnant.

Freddy didn't know 'who'. Thinking the name might produce some interest, I wrote it down in large letters. 'The singer!' I said to Freddy. 'La chanteuse célèbre, Rochdale geboren,' I told the Hauptmann. Alcoholically infused, I dared to sing the opening lyrics of 'I'm sitting on top of the world'. Then, in German: 'Ich sitzen auf Spitze von die Welt'. After a refrain, Weismann called: 'Bravo!' Freddy grinned. Bruchenbach wasn't enraptured.

I said to Freddy: 'My mother played that song on a record till the cows came home. That screeching voice was enough to make a fucking parson swear.' I bullshitted a story. 'Gracie was the rage of all England; she once entertained royalty and the deutsch minister, Herr von Ribbentrop, at Buckingham Palace; she was invited to sing in Berlin, before Herr Hitler. Das true, Herr Hauptmann,' I said.

Bruchenbach said 'Scheisse' and spat into the fire. After refilling his glass, he asked: Did I know a 'Frau Leach?'

'Nicht savvy, Frau Leach, Herr Hauptmann,' I answered.

Bruchenbach bellowed impatiently. 'Deine Schwester, Rochdale habiter, Gottverdammt!'

My sister! At last the riddle was unravelling. Freddy went to a cupboard and took out a large opened parcel. 'It's for you,' he said. 'With a letter.'

My best Christmas ever! By what magical process of postal communication between two countries at war, I asked myself, had my eldest sister discovered my whereabouts? Through a maze of channels, my mother in Jersey and the good offices of the Red Cross in London and Switzerland. I was no longer a missing person.

My vivacious sister, who had been evacuated to England from Jersey on the last boat out, was now Mrs Leach, domiciled at number 16 Allotment Street, Freehold, Rochdale, which she described as a 'two up and two down', and a bicycle ride to the lavatory. Not much of a place but the wedding was 'posh', a reception with a buffet and champagne at the Flying Horse in the town square. The letter went on:

Wish you had been here. I had two lovely bridesmaids, Jill, a cinema usherette, (you'd do all right in her back row … ha ha) and Betty (right up your street) who works on the perfumery counter at Boots the chemists. I showed them your photograph, the one taken with that Jaguar sports car you sometimes hired for a Sunday afternoon. However you managed (you know what) in the back seat I don't know. Anyway, they went potty over you and hope to see you in Rochdale soon … by goom. (They talk funny here.) Jill sent you the scented soap. Betty the face tonic. Mum is all right. Don't worry about her. She couldn't imagine what had happened to you. It was a week before she found out, she says. She went to the town hall and saw that nasty bit of work, you know the one who pinched you for joy-riding. He told her. He made her cry. He had the nerve to say he had done her a favour. A proper load of scallywags there. I'm sure Mum could have said more in the letter she wrote me. Anyhow, trust you to find a way to get to Paris, eh! Keep your pecker up. Knowing you I think you will, given half the

chance, ha ha. Those froggies are hot stuff. I'll do my best to send
you another parcel before long. They reckon the post takes up to
three months. The packet of 400 Senior Service is from your
brother-in-law, Len. (I'm not sure if I've done the right thing. I was
caught on the hop. He's a bit of an old woman.) My neighbours
have been good. The tins of corned beef come from Harold, the fat
butcher on the corner of the street. I expect I'll have to pay him in
kind, ha ha. The jumper was hand-knitted for Len by his darling
mother. It will look better on you. The bottle of brandy is from my
friend, Florrie; she's the landlady at my local pub. The cake I baked,
it's got the taste of sherry. I know how much you like cake with
fruit. It's in a tin, so it should stay fresh for six months ...

My sister enclosed the official letter which the Red Cross had written
to her ... 'We are pleased to inform you that your brother has been traced
to the Fort de Romainville, Les Lilas, Paris. His number is 441. We have
written to his mother in Jersey. We will undertake to direct any correspondence through the recognized channels; however, we have to tell you
that your brother is listed a 'political detainee' and, regretfully, we cannot
assist as otherwise stated ... '

The meaning was clear. I was not a prisoner-of-war, nor did I come
under the protection of the much-talked-about Geneva Convention,
though some thought it had latterly been extended to cover the
treatment of civilians in wartime. If this was the case, then the agreement
was obviously worthless. But I was in no mood to dwell on man's bad
faith and treachery. It was a time for celebration, I said to Bruchenbach.
Inspired with hope, I pulled the cork from the neck of the brandy bottle.

More than an hour had elapsed since I had left the building. I guessed
there would be some consternation. The communal dinner would have
been prepared and ready to serve. The cabaret would follow. Everyone
was looking to Weismann for news. But Weismann had not returned to
the building. Lucy grew worried. She went to see Lutchez. Lutchez
called Herman, left to hold the reins in Corporal Laufer's absence.
Herman was instructed to put his nose to the ground. His first port of
call was the barrack-building; he knew Weismann to be empty-headed at
times, Weismann might have returned to his quarters without warning,
to wash and change. Herman peeked into Weismann's locker; Weismann's stepping-out uniform was hanging in place and his best pair of
boots stowed on a shelf.

Herman then climbed the steps and walked to the guardhouse at the
entrance to the Fort. He drew another blank. 'Nein,' the duty-guard told
him, the 'Engländer' had not passed through the gate. Neither had

Weismann. 'Nein,' neither the Gestapo nor the Feldgendarmerie had paid a call. From the guardhouse, Herman focused his good eye across the driveway to the Kommandantur. The building was in total darkness, there wasn't a glimmer of light to be seen behind the shuttered windows.

Herman pondered. He then picked his way towards the building, his boots crunching into the loose gravel. Halfway, he stopped; he couldn't think of a legitimate excuse to call at the front door. Gustave, he well knew, was an unusual, unpredictable man who didn't like to be disturbed unnecessarily. Herman was tempted to skirt around the building to the rear where the fat ass Klaus was quartered. But this meant stepping over a narrow, uneven path dotted with broken paving stones bordered by rockery, a blind and perilous expedition in the pitchy shadows. The chicken-hearted Klaus would be struck by fright and raise the alarm at any disquiet; he'd heard stories of the underground movement penetrating military dwellings on throat-cutting incursions.

Herman, at the point of backing away, inched his way to the first window of Bruchenbach's office. Crouching low, he listened. 'Gottverdammt!' He cupped a hand to his ear. 'Lachen und singen,' he muttered under his breath. 'Nein!' He wasn't mistaken, he told Lutchez when he reported back. 'Betrunken!' he said. 'Jawohl, der Engländer auch!'

I managed to stagger to my feet when Gustave shook my shoulders. Weismann was in a stupor. Freddy was curled up in the armchair asleep, and Bruchenbach's head rested on his desk. Klaus came in to help Gustave toss Weismann and me out through the front door; my departure, unlike my reception, was without sentiment, an outraged Klaus called us 'faul Schweine' and dared to put a boot to my backside.

'You didn't make it back unaided,' an amused Marc Troska said when I awakened in the warmth of my bunk. It was late in the morning of Christmas Day, I suffered only the after-effects of the impromptu soirée with Bruchenbach and the liberation of Florrie's bottle of brandy: nothing worse than a headache and a squeamish stomach. The patrolling guard had stumbled on two bodies laid out in the shrubbery bordering the unmade road. Herman answered the call for help with two stretchers and bearers. Carried to the showers, Weismann and I were stripped, bathed and rubbed down; revived, we were removed to our beds. For my part, the pangs of the binge were a rewarding conclusion to an evening which had started out on a note of despair.

Christmas evening. Trestle-tables were laid with an abundance of food; better-off relatives and friends had entrusted blackmarket restaurants with the kind of fare we would soon only dream about. And poorer relations tightened their belts over the holiday, arriving at the guardhouse with ready-cooked meals in casseroles, crocks and mess tins.

After the tables had been cleared away, the programme of events went smoothly, according to plan. The uninvited, unwanted, ever-watchful Klaus was quickly disposed of. He was treated to a generous portion of chocolate pudding which had been doctored with a laxative; an enraged Gustave later reported that the sickly lance corporal's bowels had erupted, causing a stink in every part of the house.

Hauptmann Bruchenbach surpassed himself in good manners when he took his seat for the cabaret accompanied by the garrison commander, both moderately sober. They showed their appreciation for the professionalism of the performers, laughing at the clowning and applauding each act. Bruchenbach called for an 'encore' before the duo of strings left the stage: Zofia with Viktor Wladzimir's violin and Danuta playing a cello which Herman had borrowed from a fellow soldier gone on Christmas leave. The sisters, dressed in identical costumes stitched for the occasion – short white pinafore dresses with puffed sleeves, white hose and black slippers – looked like nymphs out of a book of fairy tales. How instrumental Romainville had been in transforming the sisters' characteristics in only a short time. From pining and spotless maidens, they had developed into sensual maturity. But the unholy joy into which they had been inveigled was coming to an end; their young lives were doomed to the gas chambers of Auschwitz, an ugly place in far away Southern Poland. And for us all, it would be the last Christmas in the Fort; for the great majority, the last Christmas anywhere.

Caring Friends

The new year was programmed for mishaps and great sorrow. It was an ill wind which blew across the courtyard. Each morning, looking through a window streaming with condensation, I saw an overcast sky and heavy clouds low over the ramparts. Continuous rain flooded the well-trodden trails circling the courtyards, only the resolute ventured outdoors under umbrellas and in mackintoshes. Room 26, however, was invariably warm, a skeleton-key to the custodians' coal bunker at the foot of our staircase provided a balanced supply of fuel for our stove. One gratifying thing was that Klaus's bulk had slipped on ice, and he was laid up with a fractured leg.

With gardening at a standstill, I took to the woodshed with Alfred where he continued with his English learning seated in front of a brazier. I grew to be appreciative of Alfred's gift of sandwiches. Marc Troska and I were temporarily without funds; prices of blackmarket food, drink, and cigarettes were exorbitant and biting at the pockets and purses of those with ready cash. Marius Vernet, a fifty-year-old banknote forger was experimenting with makeshift materials, on the lookout for top quality equipment that might escape the notice of the blackmarketeers.

Danuta was shedding tears for gallant Stefano, shot through the head by a scoundrel of a veteran work-party guard, Corporal Vetter. Lance Corporal Klaus, back on his two feet again, had seen the young Italian planting a kiss on Danuta in the women's stairwell after returning from the cookhouse. This merited forty-eight hours in solitary confinement on bread and water, Klaus told Laufer. To appease the fat oaf, Laufer agreed; and Stefano, carrying his bedding, cheerfully climbed the stairs to a punishment cell on the top floor. On his second day, Stefano peered through the bars of his open window overlooking the unmade road to clown at a passing work-party. Vetter, thinking the fingers-to-nose gesticulation was meant for him, raised his rifle and pulled the trigger. When Stefano was seen to fall back, everyone thought he was feigning a hit. A shocked Louise Beriot said he had died instantaneously, 'meurtre avec préméditation', she told Bruchenbach. The Hauptmann, too, was affected, perhaps not so much by the violent death of one Italian, but Louise Beriot's charge of wilful murder would have to be reported to his superiors in Paris; this would lead to some paper work, some aggravation, and an investigation which he could well do without. Corporal Vetter was convicted by a military tribunal for 'Totschlag' (manslaughter). Sentenced to just 14 days imprisonment, Vetter was returned to the Fort for a brief period before being transferred to an active duty unit.

It was a Saturday. The alarm bells were ringing. Social plans for the evening were in ruin, not only for the prisoners but also for the custodians. We had been promised a clear run of the building; Corporal Weismann, talking loud and big, had shacked up with a new female, the purest thing in all Paris if he was to be believed. Corporal Laufer, ulcer permitting, was scheduled to leave the Fort with a party from the garrison, Klaus included, for a 'soldaten Konzert' in the city. The building would be left in the capable hands of Herman who would take the evening roll-call before retiring to his barrack-room.

Pierre Serge 'verschwand', vanished into thin air. I was one in the workparty of four detailed to the entrance, to clean and scrub the reception post and guard's rest-room. With me was the work-shy Khalid in kid-gloves to protect his soft hands; the belly-aching, decaying Lucien Paradis; and Pierre Serge Choumoff, a quiet, unassuming, pipe-smoking young man somewhat aloof to the pranks and the risqué diversions which men of his age sought with barely a pause. Some thought he was over-religious and 'un peu maboul', a bit cracked. If anything, Pierre Serge was slick, cunning and plucky.

'Biscuit' Klaus was in a tizzy, thinking that the missing man had somehow sneaked back into the building unnoticed. Stomping the corridors and throwing doors open, he clashed with Weismann; Klaus was the pig's head if he thought the missing Choumoff had returned to the building without an escort, he, Weismann, would have been the first to know. After every nook and cranny was searched, the casemates in the thickness of the old walls, the disused stables, the woodshed and the clump of woodland, 'der Gefangene, Pierre Serge Choumoff' was officially posted a 'Fluchtling'.

There was no reason to celebrate the escape. Feelings were mixed, a minority holding the opinion that it was a matter of 'sauve qui peut'. If family reprisals were not threatened then 'bravo, très bien!' Some condemned the runaway for a callous indifference to those left behind to face the music; it was generally accepted that some penalty of a mild nature would be imposed by Bruchenbach, but a far worse penalty was feared from the authority in Paris.

Behind closed doors – only those with essential duties to the garrison were allowed out – we waited for the bubble to burst. Freddy Kaiser was angrier than I had ever seen him before; one 'stupid fellow', he said, had put his fellow-men and the Kommandantur at risk. The generous privileges granted to the prisoners were in jeopardy, Freddy warned. The authority in Paris had to be advised that the matter had not been dismissed without some effective imposition; hopefully, when they were advised it would be the end of the matter.

Louise Beriot, on behalf of the women, and Lutchez representing the men, agreed to the conditions put forward. All prisoners, other than those on essential work, would remain confined to their rooms for three days; there would be no restrictions on the use of the washroom or lavatories; the communal rooms and the courtyards would be out of bounds; and parcels delivered to the gate-house would be withheld. What we had not bargained for, those who had been with Pierre Serge at the time of his escape would be isolated in the punishment cells for the period.*

* Mathematician, scientific author and engineer, Pierre Serge Choumoff was born in Paris, 1921. An active member of the resistance movement, he was first imprisoned in the city's Cherche-Midi jail before his transfer to Romainville. He made his escape over the rampart wall behind the guard's rest-room where he was at work, dropping into the dry moat unseen to slip away into the streets of Les Lilas. Shortly afterwards, he was recaptured and transported to the concentration camp of Gusen (No 15014) and then a few kilometres away to the Mother Camp, Mauthausen, Upper Austria.

A survivor, Pierre Serge was evacuated from Mauthausen by the International Red Cross on 19 May 1945 and was returned to Paris eleven days later. Without much delay, he returned to Austria with a mission to research the complex of the infamous Mauthausen Concentration Camp and its gas-chambers.

We did not know whether Pierre Serge's escape had anything to do with the 'selection' soon after. It was Professor Katz's birthday, and thanks to Lucy, who had received some money from her parents, Room 26 was financially stable and able to clink glasses with a hero. A giant greeting card had been designed and signatures collected. Max contributed a couple of hours of his time to the alteration of a navy-blue suit to fit a lean frame; and Lutchez supplied the accessories, a near-new shirt, a tie and a pair of craftsman-made shoes. Charlo cut the professor's hair and shaved him. Never had he looked so gentlemanly.

There were six place-settings on the table in Room 26. Lutchez, whose idea it was, said the occasion was well-merited, a reward for 'unselfish devotion' to the duty of look-out. Khalid, Viktor Wladzimir, Marc Troska and I applauded that tribute. At a given signal – a knock on the wall – Zofia played 'Happy Birthday' on the violin and we sang 'For He's a Jolly Good Fellow'. Overwhelmed by the attention, the Professor had a cry; where, in all the world, he asked would he find so many caring friends.

After we had finished eating, we trooped along to the communal room for a concert. Pride of place was reserved, three cushioned chairs, one for Louise Beriot, one for the Professor, and the other waiting for Freddy Kaiser who had promised his patronage. Freddy was behind time when he left the Kommandantur. Sheltering under an umbrella from the pouring rain, he stopped to listen half-way down the steps. He could hear a concertina and Lucien Paradis singing 'Il pleut sur la route'. He thought the song appropriate for the inclement weather. As he reached the bottom of the steps, he was startled by a rumbling noise. Music and song became muffled. Freddy recognized the noise of heavy engines but of a greater resonance than at any time before. He climbed back up the steps two at a time, to see a canvas-topped Kübelwagen preceding three buses sweep past in a flurry of spray. Masked headlamps at full power, the convoy negotiated the unmade road and pulled up with a squeal of brakes close to the casemate at the north of the building. Freddy sprinted back to the Kommandantur.

In the smoke-filled communal room, Lutchez shouted: 'Éteins la lumière!' The room, suddenly plunged into darkness, went into a frozen silence. Shadowy figures scrambled to the windows and peered through the blackout blinds. The sky was pitch black, unmarked by any ribbon of searchlight. The rumpus was not caused by low-flying aircraft as we first suspected. Watchful eyes saw a fused together brightness at the bend of the unmade road; powerful engines whined, gear-boxes grated and headlamps deflected shuttered beams of light across a sea of bewildered

faces. 'Merde!' an uneasy voice was heard to say. 'C'est ça les autobus! Un
… deux … et le troisième!'

Three buses! Bad news! And so late in the evening? Ordered to our
rooms, I stood in the darkness at the open window to listen to a
profusion of guttural voices at sixes and sevens. Arc lamps played over
the area between the women's courtyard and the cookhouse. The blackout blind down and the light switched on, Marc Troska sat in the
armchair to read. Unlike the great majority, he had no ties. I aired the
deposit of miscellanea meant for my mother. There was little I could add
without being repetitive, except to add the date and to emphasize the
gravity of the happening: 'worse than at any time before, Mum, and so
soon after Christmas'.

Corporal Weismann later came in to enlighten us. He had been
drinking but he was coherent. He slumped down in a chair and I lit a
cigarette for him. 'Blutbad!' he spluttered. 'Ein ganz Blutbad!'

A bloodbath! Marc Troska put his book aside. We were both shaken
by Weismann's insensitivity of expression. Rankled, I asked: 'Was für
Blutbad, Herr Weismann?'

Weismann was well informed. He had recognized the Hauptscharführer in charge of the SS guards, a 'dumm Scheiss' who frequented the
drinking clubs in Montmartre. The sergeant told him there were ninety
prisoners being held overnight in the casemates, made up of Spanish and
French communists from the prisons of Paris with a few Jews from
Drancy camp. A further ten men from Romainville were scheduled to
join them at daybreak for Mont Valérien. Weismann didn't know who.

Herman made a welcome appearance. He was long-faced. He brought
us a swallow of schnapps in a flask and a note from Lucy for me. She was
praying for me, she wrote. Nothing in her heart had changed, nor would
it ever turn upside down, she vowed. Her sentiments cheered me.

Zofia, we heard, had picked up the violin which, tragically, was on the
point of becoming her property. Strings muted, she played 'Chanson
tempête' for Marc Troska who had drilled her in the song. Lying on his
bunk, he sang the lyrics but not without a tremor in his voice.

It was comforting to see Louise Beriot. Her visit was not unexpected.
She looked tired to the point of collapse, flitting about the floors of the
building inspiring courage in those most affected by the immensity of
the crime to come. I thought it was her wish to snatch a few moments of
privacy with Marc Troska; in stockinged feet, I left the room quietly,
closed the door and, stealthily, climbed the stairs to the second floor and
slipped into Lutchez's room.

Lutchez was in pyjamas with a blanket draped around his shoulders.
He was at the table with Viktor Wladzimir playing chess. Khalid was

picking at his long finger-nails, giving them a treatment with a file and a buffer. Words stuck in their throats. Whenever danger breathed down his neck, Viktor was another who was meticulous about his choice of clothing; he favoured a dashing pair of cream-coloured cavalry-breeches, a high-necked black jumper which Helena had knitted him for Christmas, a hacking-jacket and brown high boots polished to a lustre. He looked every inch a fighter.

Viktor had put his affairs in order. We were all victims of habits at such times of peril; shaking hands, embracing, and saying 'adieu, mon vieux, juste en cas' was a harrowing ritual. Tucked between books on a shelf was the familiar manilla envelope for Helena. On the third finger of Viktor's left hand was a bone ring with the letters V and H intertwined. In a cardboard box were small items of sentimental value which Viktor had labelled and assigned. His violin which had often been out of favour when he played it would remain with Zofia until it would qualify for yet another successor.

I dozed in my bunk fully dressed; sound sleep was out of the question. Marc Troska brewed endless cups of our bona fide coffee. Word for word, 'gloom and misery' were everywhere. Rain lashed the window. Air-raid sirens screamed. Guns thundered. From the casemates came loud cheering and fiery songs. Long before dawn, we shaved and washed. Marc Troska cooked a breakfast of fried potatoes and fat bacon which stuck in our throats.

At first light, things started to stir within the building; all the familiar jarring human sounds were being enacted, heavy, dragging footsteps, doors opening and shutting, stunted dialogue, sounds that conveyed intimidation and which have remained recorded in my mind for all time. Looking down into the women's courtyard, I saw a yawning Corporal Weismann toing and froing on guard, his breath heavy on a frost-laden air, and it crossed my mind how much more miserable it was to go to one's death on a cold morning.

Engines warmed up; two of the buses departed with fist-clenching and chanting martyrs, the third bus being delayed because of a mechanical fault. An hour later it left. On board was Viktor Wladzimir; the good loser, Charlo, and his crack-brained vision of a brothel for midgets; and, among seven others taken from the building, our wireless engineer, Raymond Barrat from Fontainebleau.

Viktor's departure left Helena, his childhood friend to whom he had promised marriage, without the vital pillar of support which maintained her proper mind. Helena's welfare had always been a matter of constant concern to him. He told Lutchez, many times, he feared Helena would do herself harm if he went to Mont Valérien. Louise Beriot climbed the stairs to Helena's room on the second landing to break the sad news and to deliver Viktor's letter.

Helena did not have to be told Viktor had gone to his execution. She had looked out from her window when the reactivated bus turned painfully slowly around the corner of the building. Like many onlookers at the rear windows, she had seen Viktor's upturned face and a hand held high in a last farewell. The three women found her seated at her table with a book of prayers. She was dressed in outdoor clothing, a long grey overcoat with a seedy astrakhan collar and cuffs, a black felt hat pulled down over her head, and stout leather shoes. Her room was clean and tidy, as it always was. But, as if a shift had been anticipated, an old fabric-framed suitcase, filled to bursting, was sited conveniently by the door. Her bedding had been folded; arranged on the mattress was her sewing-box, a new-made patchwork cushion cover, paper flowers, books and a pair of Viktor's socks newly darned.

Helena asked to be left alone. She had no wish for anyone to sit around the table to share her grief. She exchanged embraces with the three women and then they quietly evacuated the room. Louise Beriot went to see Lutchez, he had been closest to Viktor. Lutchez expected the worst. He was not cold-hearted; but, he said, if Helena planned to do away with her own life then allow her to, 'à tort ou à raison'. To alert the Kommandantur would result in Helena's isolation in a cell under lock and key where she would quickly lose her sanity. Lutchez would not be party to that extremity. What was the alternative? A physically frail woman, Helena's inevitable deportation to a German labour camp would kill her cruelly. To allow Helena's wish was the kindest concession, Lutchez said.

To commit suicide was one's right; it was not cowardice, as I would come to see, but a desperate act to end the cruelty and torture one was forced to endure and to stick one's tongue out at one's personal enemy. Helena died soon after dusk, a few hours after Viktor had gone to the wall. It was Corporal Laufer who raised the alarm. We heard him shouting: 'Die Frau, Helena. Selbstmord!' Flapping his arms, he rushed into our room and told Marc Troska and me to come quick. With Lutchez and Khalid at our heels, we crossed the division, shoving past weeping women in the corridor and down the staircase into the darkened courtyard to the rear of the building. Here, seen by the light of Laufer's torch, was Helena's frail body, huddled against the wall like a broken doll. 'Dead' groaned Laufer. He pointed the beam of his torch up at an open window. She had jumped to her death.

A short note left on Helena's table said 'adieu' and 'auf Wiedersehen'. She thanked her friends for the good understanding she had been shown and hoped no one would be troubled by her decision. Her coffin arrived on the tailgate of Marcel Allard's refuse lorry, jammed in between galvanized bins. It was as light as a kite; it looked like a stretched orange box; the wood was thin and joined by glue and rusted nails, and the lid was distorted and secured with thick wire. After the interior was rid of small animal droppings, the box was scrubbed with hot water and carbolic soap and left to dry in the heat of the cookhouse.

In place, Helena looked at peace. The bruising on her face had been masked by powder and rouge; her hair had been washed and brushed and her frame clothed in a white nightdress. The 'hearse' was makeshift; the head, tail and side panels had been removed from the handcart and the platform was covered by a red carpet runner. Between her cold hands, Helena held a bouquet of paper flowers.

In a co-operative mood, Hauptmann Bruchenbach gave consent to a cortège of eight, four men and four women. Marc Troska and I took the shafts of the cart whilst Lutchez and Khalid put their weight to the rear. Louise Beriot, Lucy, Paulette and Colette followed in the wake and Weismann and Herman were assigned as the escorts. The steel-rimmed wheels crushed into the gravel and jolted over the rain-filled potholes in the unmade road on the slow climb to the Kommandantur. The windows thronged with men and women, tearful and openly weeping. At the half-way mark, the guard mounting the machine-gun platform turned and saluted and soldiers passing came to attention until the cortège disappeared over the hill, nice gestures which would have pleased Viktor.

Hauptmann Bruchenbach and Freddy Kaiser stood stiffly at the open door of the Kommandantur. Parked alongside was a small military truck with a uniformed driver and an attendant. The coffin was gently lifted on board; salutes were exchanged and we stood in a group to watch the truck fade out of sight into the streets of Les Lilas, carrying Helena's body to a place unknown.

'Partie avec la dignité, malgré tout,' Louise Beriot remarked.

Lutchez asked: 'Is it not the right of everyone to leave this world with wholesome respect?'

Due respect, even a modest container and a decent place of burial, would be denied to millions.

Grandmère Tauzin was unwell but wouldn't admit to failing health. The old lady was worn out, Louise Beriot said. It was time for her to sit quietly with her sewing and knitting instead of carrying on with her many tasks, in the cookhouse, washing and ironing for Freddy and, 'allons donc!' . . . flitting about the draughty corridors at night keeping watch.

She pooh-poohed all the advice. She had been out of sorts before, nothing that had kept her down for more than a day. 'Bah!' She had a little wind in the tubes, that was all; her heartbeat had always been irregular, 'en retard, en avance'; did it matter as long as the heart worked? But Louise Beriot was duly anxious; the old lady's illness needed to be treated in a hospital and it was for Hauptmann Bruchenbach to decide if a transfer was within his jurisdiction. Grandmère Tauzin was obstinate, she wouldn't allow herself to be moved even if offered the opportunity, she made it known. If 'le bon Dieu' decided to terminate her life, then let it be in the Fort among friends.

It was April 1943, 'le mois le plus charmant', Lucien Paradis said wringing his hands. In his heart, he treasured the spring before the war; the flowers showing their colours in the Tuileries gardens, the crowded pavement cafés, the social scene, the influence of fashions, gay and gorgeous clothing for all to see in shop windows, a stroll with one's best friend along the banks of the Seine before dinner at 'Chez Augusta' on the cranky side of the town . . . all the enchantment of living which Lucy promised and which I was storing in the depths of my mind.

For the second time, I was able to see the trees outside my window bursting into bud. Small birds were happily singing and flitting from sill to sill for crumbs of bread, mere morsels which one day I would see men squabble over and fight to the death for. Despite the pleasant change of season and some ground for hope, we were living on a seesaw, one day up and the next down. Our custodians themselves were ill at ease. All manner of news was filtering into the Fort, brought in by an influx of newcomers from city prisons and from those snatched off the streets.

The optimists were in a majority. They pinned their chances of survival on a rescue from the air with the help of the armies of the underground movement. Lutchez – everyone looked to the Swiss when it was a question of morale – was open-minded; the time was ripe for an air-drop, he said; there would be a few thousand civilian casualties, some devastation to the most beautiful city in the world, but the Germans would be routed. And those versed in military strategy agreed.

Would we see the billowing canopies of the rumoured parachutists falling from the sky over Paris? Some thought not. And if we did, the Germans would slaughter every man and woman held in captivity at the very first sighting. One had to be prepared to do battle, Lutchez said, not that he feared violence from the garrison; according to Herman, who would be the first to surrender his gun, the soldiers had little or no stomach to shoot down civilians, they were good family men, not cold-blooded like the SS.

Rumours of another kind were troubling Laufer and Weismann.

There was talk of marching orders for the whole garrison, with certain exemptions, to active duty on the battle front. Laufer could be sitting pretty with his chronic stomach complaint; so could Herman with his one good eye, but Weismann was huffed, his medical examination had passed him 'gesund'. Down in the dumps, he told Lutchez it might be the Russian front. He suffered from varicose veins and poor blood circulation; the Arctic conditions would kill him if the 'figging Russkies' didn't get him first. Weismann had heard the Russians didn't take prisoners. He'd gladly give himself up to the British, the sooner the better, he said.

Freddy Kaiser, too, was going through a thin time. He was young and fit; there was no reason why his position couldn't be filled by an older man, someone incapacitated. He didn't have the temperament to shoot at anyone, never had he had cause to remove his pistol from its holster. He was a softie, he said; he wouldn't put a heel on a spider, he even disapproved of Klaus setting mousetraps. God only knew what his mother would do if he was sent to Russia, he groaned.

With many things hanging in the balance, one noticed a mellowing in Laufer's and Weismann's attitude; Weismann, in particular, thinking that the British might yet arrive in time to extract him from the 'Scheisse', was watching his p's and q's, not raising his voice insufferably and addressing those he habitually maligned with a show of respect. Hard to believe it was 'Monsieur Khalid' and not the 'figging Araber'. Professor Katz, too, was spared Weismann's bitter tongue; it was no longer 'das alt Arschloch' but 'der Professor'.

To be 'agréable' or 'gentil' to the prisoners was catching. Marc Troska was returning from the military cookhouse each afternoon with a bonus of bread, potatoes and flavourful left-over soup donated by the cook-sergeant. Soldiers were tipping the room and dormitory cleaners with bread and sausage. It was noticeable that a sullen 'Biscuit' Klaus was saying 'bonjour', and after Lutchez threatened to have his 'Hoden' cut off when the British arrived, the wretched lance-corporal made a distribution of Red Cross parcels.

One could not openly flout the rules on fraternization, but providing one did not come to a dead stop at the courtyard division, Laufer and Weismann now ignored the subtle chit-chat which crossed back and forth. Herman, already biased towards our side, took to informing on his fellow-custodians' movements for after hours. This proved helpful when planning social get-togethers with one's woman, ideally on a Saturday or a Sunday afternoon of tranquillity when Laufer usually retired early to his barrack-room for a sleep and the more active Weismann set off to Montmartre on a binge.

With Herman in sole charge of the building, hobnobbing with the card and chess players, and a look-out or two at the windows, Lucy and I climbed the short flight of twisting stairs, passed the nook which housed the clock's mechanism to the 'grenier', the vast attic space which stretched the entire length of the building. Here, in one of the many open stalls, we looked out of the fanlight window over the rooftops of Les Lilas to the white dome of the distant Sacré-Coeur. And we were both filled with a yearning for our freedom.

'It is all there for you and me to share and enjoy, chéri,' Lucy said in a whisper. 'The Arc de Triomphe, the Tour Eiffel and the river, all the places you want to see ... perhaps tomorrow, the next ... who knows? Paris will soon come to full life again; this house will be a memento of great sadness and mixed blessings.' Ready to cry, she asked: 'What is it you will want to do first, chéri?'

'Walk with you along the Champs-Élysées, hand-in-hand and without a care in the world. Then bring you back here when I will go down on my hands and knees in gratitude for the generous friendship shown to me and for your love, Lucy.'

'Oh! Then it must be, for our friends who have gone and must never be forgotten. Do you think they will come ... the British?' she asked in a voice which lacked faith.

I stood by Lutchez's thoughts, perhaps leaning more to the dark side, not trusting some miracle-maker in London or wherever for my way out. My desire for freedom, like everyone of my age, in the best years of our lives, was urgent. Three years had already been spent in forcible restraint; would the war last another three as many predicted? I wanted to have faith in the Allies. I wanted to think they cared for all those distressed, those gone to Mont Valérien and those trembling in the balance. But I listened – as I would listen again in time to come – to those among us skilled in politics, government and war. My mind boggled at the deep sense of dissatisfaction levelled at those 'idiots à Londres' directing the war from 'le confort de leurs fauteuils et leurs pavillons de golf'. These 'crétins', do they really care about you and me? And I was alarmed by some of the opinions aired. An incursion on Paris by air was feasible but what of the consequences 'politiquement?' It would lead to a powerful Communist take-over of the city and, eventually, the control of all France. Is that what you want, 'mon vieux'? I, for one, didn't care if the Communists, the Gaullists, the Allies or whoever took over the country; the squabbling of governments and political parties seemed not to be in the best interests of the many thousands awaiting execution and deportation.

The Beginning of the End

It was my birthday. I was twenty-three. No cause for celebration. Lucy sent me a chocolate cake which I set aside. A calamity! I was going to die of a dreadful disease. So I believed. I was 'hors de service', bedridden almost, wibble-wabbling about the room to use the piss-bucket in burning pain. Khalid was amused, putting it around that my 'levier de commande', my joy-stick was 'kaputt'. And, in his usual crude way, Weismann was telling the women that I was down with the clap, my 'machine-outil' was wilting and about to 'tomber de fatigue'.

No laughing matter! I was suffering discomfort and fright. Unaware that I had been bitten and infected by an insect which had flown in through the open window during the night, I jumped down from my bunk to prepare for roll-call only to feel a strange leaden heaviness in between my legs. On inspection, my eyes bulged, I became rooted to the floorboards. My prick was huge, swollen to three times its normal size.

Marc Troska peeked. His jaw dropped. 'God almighty!' he gasped.

Corporal Laufer looked. 'Ach, du lieber Himmel!' he said. 'Der Vampir!'

I retorted: 'Malade! Krank!' I needed an urgent medical opinion, 'ein medizinisch Meinung', I told Laufer.

'Tout de suite,' Laufer agreed. 'Madame Beriot bringen.'

'Nein,' I protested. There was an able male doctor among the prisoners, I told Laufer; he could diagnose my problem and perhaps suggest a remedy.

But Laufer was adamant. Only Louise Beriot, no one else, had the Hauptmann's authority to tend to those reporting sick. What was my objection? Was I bashful? Was my 'ding' so special? 'Bah!' Laufer scoffed. 'Madame Beriot' had seen many hundred – 'lang, dick und klein'.

A solution of warm water and iodine unbent my legs after a week. I was fit and ready to function again. And things were stirring within the Fort. The garrison, one could see, was being drilled as never before. Grey-headed old stagers among the soldiers, flat-footed and knobbly-kneed, and with full back-packs, were slithering along the ground in the heat of the sun, climbing over obstacles and charging at cardboard silhouettes with bayonets drawn.

The prisoner population was on the increase, with more men and women arriving than leaving. Empty rooms were being made ready for those coming from the city prisons and straight off the streets. Among the former were young men long deprived of the tender essentials, they cast sheep's eyes at the girls, staggered by the fact that such divine creatures were still in existence. The smooth system of communication and association which had been in operation from the outset was now threatened by hot-headedness and horny desire.

Grandmère Tauzin was close to death. She had been moved to a room on the ground floor where, in her last days, she could look on the courtyards and acknowledge the salutes from the men. A retinue of 'nurses' attended to her every need; they washed her, fed her and lit her cigarettes. Her voice, which lost little of its strength to the end, would be heard calling to Zofia in the room above for a piece of her favourite music. And Lucien Paradis was on call to sing ballads.

Louise Beriot begged Hauptmann Bruchenbach to allow the men to cross the division to pay their last respects. Bruchenbach nodded; he gave notice to Laufer; 'die Grossmutter' could receive anyone she asked for by name. Fading, she was still full of wit and unafraid. She joked about 'la boîte', the plywood coffin which would be arriving to carry her off. If it was anything like Helena's, 'd'occasion', second-hand, she wanted it treated before she was laid out. And 'soyez tranquille' she whispered in Lutchez's ear, from her new home in seventh heaven she promised to stay on the 'qui-vive'; nothing would miss her eyes.

Her gnarled old face was ash-coloured and the thin form of her frame made little impression under the blankets, but when I bent my head to kiss her for the last time I saw the familiar glint in her eyes. She took my hand, a feeble grip, 'Mon vieux, Antoine,' she croaked, 'vive la Grande-Bretagne.' Then she put my hand into Lucy's. 'Marchez ensemble,' to the end, she said. Her head rolled on the pillow to Marc Troska standing on the other side of the bed. She had a special affection for the American. 'Marcello, mon beau gar,' she said reaching out with a hand to stroke his face, 'grâce à Dieu pour les Américains.'

My eyes clouding, I whispered 'adieu Grandmère,' and as I slipped out of the room I caught a glimpse of her black surgical boot consigned to the stone floor. That night I experienced a dreadful dream. I saw a mountain of discarded footwear and walking apparatus, conventional and grotesque, boots and shoes, clogs, leg-irons and crutches. Naked beings with missing limbs were clamouring and clambering up the huge stockpile searching and rummaging through.

Room 26 was made ready to receive an additional prisoner, an illustrious person. Two scrubbing women arrived with cleaning tools to wash the floor and walls and to air our bedding, even the odd flea had to be flushed out and liquidated by order. A proper bed was installed, one with springs and two mattresses, fitting for a fine gentleman, a 'Herzog', Corporal Weismann let on: a Duke. And Weismann found a near-new 'pot de chambre' in white enamel with a matching lid, solely for the 'Herzog' to piss in.

It was a red-carpet entry for our new guest. Windows crowded, we watched the slimly-built man in a belted raincoat and trilby hat coming from over the hill. Freddy Kaiser steered him down the steps, chivalrously sharing his umbrella under a light fall of rain. Behind, blowing like a rhinoceros, came the reluctant porter, Klaus, with a large valise gripped in each hand. Freddy, full of chat and with time to spare, stopped half-way down to indicate with a sweeping finger the building and its attachments, much as a property agent might do with a prospective buyer: 'As you can see, the main residence, not of so much historical interest as the surrounding walls, but with fifty or so rooms of varied proportions on three floors; to the right of the courtyard the servants' quarters, stables and garages; in all, some five acres with a splendid view of the Sacré-Coeur … '!

No one could deny the distinguishing traits of a well-bred man. He was handsome, in his early fifties, slim of build, medium height, straight shoulders, dark hair grey-flecked and well-groomed, a neat moustache and nice hands. Max, the tailor with an eye for quality material and cut, was to say the man's navy-blue suit was the work of a craftsman, as were the black leather shoes on his feet. After making his acquaintance, I was inspired to write on the newcomer to my mother:

Dear Mum,

Bringing you up to-date. It's August, the weather is fine and warm. I'm keeping all right, as I hope you are there with all the problems of the Occupation.

It's getting a bit cramped in here now. Guess what? We've got a new room-mate. A true-blue Duke. He's from Chile, that's in South America, the Duke of Andia. He speaks perfect English, a bit of a namby-pamby to look at but a decent-enough chap when you get to know him.

He's got a good eye for the women. I think we'll get along fine. Things are humming here. I can expect a move before long. Where? Anybody's guess.

My love as always.

Room 26, Khalid said, had been blessed 'avec un type inoffensif et vraiment bizarre'. Only 'un valet de chambre' could have packed the Duke's valises in such an orderly manner, Khalid said, poring over effects which he gallantly admitted surpassed his own flowery wardrobe. It was like watching a magician pulling out surprises from a bottomless chest. I counted more than a dozen beautiful shirts, collar-attached and collar separate, 'd'une maison bien connue', Khalid whispered in my ear. There were neck-ties and cravats in contrasting colours, socks by the bundle, jackets and trousers for town and for country. It wasn't the delicate daintiness of the Duke's underwear embroided with initials which provoked titters, it was apparel like a startling red Japanese kimono with a horned animal motif blowing flames, a pair of cream-coloured flannels and a pair of chequered plus-fours. Hiding a smile, Khalid said: 'Monsieur le Duc, malheureusement ici il n'y a pas un terrain de golf.'

We had hit the jack-pot in Room 26. From the start Marc Troska and I had shared everything in the way of food, cigarettes and alcohol as they were available. Andy, as we came to call the Duke, readily accepted the invitation into our commune. His 'porte-monnaie' was loaded with banknotes in French and Swiss currency. Turning out his pockets, he brought to light a gold toothpick, a gold fountain-pen and two golden guineas; his watch was also a valuable commodity. We were now shareholders in an El Dorado, good fortune at a time when funds were depleted and a larder reduced to little more than bare rations. Armed with a list Herman went shopping.

Lutchez, playful with the Duke, invariably made a small bow and addressed him as 'your Grace'. When Lutchez asked him if he fancied a woman, 'une jolie petite chatte', the Duke replied without batting an eyelid: 'Bless my soul! Is it possible?'

Lutchez had just the woman in mind for the approving Andy, one who, among others, had already put in a bid. She was a sophisticated piece, an Italian, supposedly a Countess. She was attractive, kept herself well-dressed; slim skirts, blouses and shirts. She gave her age as thirty-five. Lucy said she was more than forty. It was a woman's prerogative to be untruthful about her origins and her age when romantically-inclined, Lutchez said.

'Countess' Valentina was introduced to the Duke of Andia on the night of Lutchez's engagement party.

The majority of attachments were ill-fated or mere passing fancies with a quick turnover of partners, but the bond between Lutchez and Paulette had been one of fidelity since they had been brought together in the Fort two years before. Neither had been married. Lutchez said he had always been too busy, too travelled to think of settling down in one place and with responsibilities. He knew all there was to know about Paulette's less than virtuous past life; it bothered him not at all. With a separation threatening, he made no secret of his love for Paulette; and blushing for once, he couldn't bring himself to propose a marriage in spoken words. With the help of the Duke, Lutchez composed a letter.

Paulette expressed her joy by bursting into tears, Lucy said. She had been propositioned before, more times than she could remember, by insolvents, by roués and by the genuinely kind like the 'papa-riche' with whom she once cohabited. She had never met anyone like Lutchez. He was brave, clever, witty, 'un peu excentrique'; she knew little about his background, 'un journaliste politique' who moved about and lived in hotels; and he wasn't particularly handsome, a round boyish face with sparkling eyes which women admired. She saw faults, but no man was perfect. He went over the top with politics, smoked too much, did no body exercises, dressed indifferently and whistled tunelessly; for all that, she loved him, she couldn't imagine her future without Lutchez.

Lutchez was on the receiving end of handshakes and backslaps. He was smartly turned out for the get-together in Room 26. Max had taken pains to alter a suit to Lutchez's shape and size, and he had been presented with a new shirt and cravat from the Duke's bottom-drawer. Herman hired a 'vélo-taxi' to carry back blackmarket food and drink, smuggling the parcels into the building after darkness on the night before.

It was a full house, a company of ten assembled for the ceremony. Apart from the man and woman of the hour, there was the ambitious 'Countess' Valentina and the receptive Duke; Colette partnered by Khalid. Louise Beriot, not counting the risk for once, and no longer hiding her involvement with Marc Troska behind a curtain of pretence, held his hand for all to see and cradled her head on his shoulder; Lucy and me, drawn even closer together for fear of what was to come.

We drank several toasts. A little 'fou', and with tormenting thoughts, we stood quiet and listened to Zofia playing 'J'attendrai' on her violin. When Professor Katz knocked on the door and announced, apologetically, that it was 'l'heure du couvre-feu', we all joined hands and, in hushed tones, sang the Marseillaise. It was the swan-song. There would be no more formal occasions. It was 'le commencement de la fin'.

'Auf wiedersehen' to Laufer and Weismann. Laufer complained that he had not escaped the draft despite his chronic complaint. We all gathered together in the communal room to bid them farewell. Both were emotionally affected by a flattering tribute spoken by Lutchez; they would be remembered as two ordinary German soldiers who had carried out their duties in a decent and humane way. We were all gripped by sadness and regret at their departure, particularly when Herman informed Lutchez that the replacements were two 'hard heads'.

The acceptable Alfred, the aspiring 'mayor' of an English country village, was on his way with a long face. He came to shake my hand and wish me 'good luck'. I would miss his whopping sandwiches. He presented me with a bottle of schnapps, in appreciation of my friendship and patience over the long months we had consorted together. I was truly touched. I thought to myself, what a remarkable contrast to my fellow-countrymen in the Jersey island jail who lorded over their prisoners with callous indifference!

Feldwebel (Sergeant) Kroll was a lanky, thin and leathery-faced Berliner with a black moustache modelled on that of his Führer's. Kroll's colleague, Corporal Bremer, an oily, pint-sized individual with an insidious grin on his clean-shaven face, had been detected listening at doors and peering through keyholes from his debut, shabby behaviour typical of 'Biscuit' Klaus who had evaded the call to active duty and had reverted to his former obnoxious self now that the threat of an invasion had passed.

To counteract the snoop, Bremer, one could stuff paper into keyholes and put up a resistance to undue interference in matters which had been approved by Hauptmann Bruchenbach; neither Kroll nor Bremer approved of the easy-going customs and habits, there was too much clubbability, too many opportunities; the men could do their own washing and who had heard of ironing in a prison?

Kroll, like Bremer, had been recruited from a criminal institution in Germany. The Hauptmann had had no voice in the choice, Freddy confided. Freddy himself didn't think well of the pair, but he had to remain neutral as long as they carried out their duties without inciting a revolt. There was nothing to be done about Bremer's prowling about the corridors at all hours of the night. Kroll, quick to notice how the rules were being flouted after Bremer reported chit-chat and gestures bouncing across the division from the windows and the courtyards, became obsessed with overhauling the system throughout the building. Kroll confined the women to their rooms for the time it took the men detailed to the cookhouse to collect the rations. And it was all too easy for the men to communicate with the women in the communal lavatory, the low brick outbuilding with rows of squat cubicles and an imaginary boundary at the midpoint of the structure which had never been breached. From his own observations, Kroll said that the 'Scheiss-haus' was more of a social club. The remedy was to build a wall up to the ceiling half-way along.

Herman did not escape Kroll's fault-finding. Herman was idle, lax and made himself at home with the prisoners, playing cards, drinking their good coffee and accepting their cigarettes. Herman would be better employed in a hospital for old women. And Kroll had an even lower opinion of 'Biscuit' Klaus; the useless fat donkey spent too much time locked in the Red Cross parcel store.

We had come to an impasse, Lutchez said. Our long run of luck was at an end. The key to the communicating door was no longer of any use. Professor Katz disbanded his group of look-outs; instinct had told the industrious Kroll that all was not 'korrekt' after he and Bremer retired to their barrack-room for the night. Henceforth, Kroll made it known, he and Bremer would take it in turns to sleep on the bed in their office each night. And, as an added precaution, Bremer fitted sliding-bolts to each of the three communicating doors.

When Kroll proposed a curfew behind locked room doors with lights out two hours after the last roll-call each evening, there were rumblings of dissent from both sides of the division. With Lutchez interpreting – neither Kroll nor Bremer spoke French except for 'oui-ing' and 'non-ing' – Louise Beriot told Kroll that the prisoners had to have normal access to the lavatories at all times; there were those who suffered from incontinence; others, like newcomers, were sensitive to a change of diet, diarrhoea was prevalent. 'Le sergent' was impertinent to expect the women to resort to receptacles, she angrily said.

Kroll replied that he was more concerned with discipline and security, a job which he had been appointed to do as he saw fit. 'Ein tausend' pots and buckets were in use day and night in the prison where he had come from; if the smell got up our noses then we could throw open the windows. But Kroll reckoned without the pluck of the women. A group 'en colère' stormed into his office. If Kroll carried out his threat, they spelled out, the first full bucket would be over his head, 'un shampoo avec la pisse et la merde, Monsieur le sergent.'

A prickly situation was looming; Freddy Kaiser was drawn into the dispute. Freddy thought Kroll's proposition unpleasant and unworkable. All too politely, he told Kroll that Louise Beriot was responsible to the Kommandant for 'die Hygiene'; buckets were only to be used in emergencies and with Dr Beriot's approval. The threat removed, Kroll looked at the other means to whittle down the privileges we had previously enjoyed. Never before had we seen the punishment cells fully occupied; men and women were given a minimum of forty-eight hours on bread and water for small misdemeanours. This proved no hardship; Lutchez had duplicate keys, one for the door which led into a short corridor, the other opened the four cells, two on either side of the building.

Herman, never failing, passed Lucy a note. In it, I said that I would no longer be sending her my washing, we had to play down our association; Bremer was slick, pairing off couples by watching their behaviour in the courtyards from his office-window – the nodders, the hand-signallers and the strolling 'troubadours' who composed their own lyrics and sang messages over the fence in a language Bremer didn't understand. From now on, I told Lucy, a get-together would be 'par hasard', by chance.

'L'existence sans une femme et l'amour' was unacceptable. Lengthy and total blackouts came as a blessing to the horniest of young men who risked crawling under the wire in the courtyard to snatch a few throbbing minutes with a partner up against the wall of the building, undistracted by the scream of sirens and gun-fire or the reflection from probing searchlights.

I saw another way, which I wanted to think more dignified; in any case, less of a risk. It meant bringing Lutchez and Khalid into the plot. The custodian's coal-bunker at the foot of the stairs had supplied our stove with fuel filched in sensible quantities throughout the past winter. I had a duplicate key to the door. The exterior door, I remembered, was simply secured by a sliding bolt. The door opened inwards. Women regularly passed by on their way to the lavatory and the washing-lines, singly, in pairs, and in small groups.

Lutchez was intrigued. Together, we investigated. Looking out of a window above the entrance into the bunker we saw only one minor liability. At the northern end of the building, perched high on the bank some sixty feet or more beyond the cookhouse and in a direct line with the path taken by the women, was a guard on a machine-gun platform. We watched his habits at a time when women were to-ing and fro-ing. Like all guards at a four-hour standstill, he was bored. We saw his blindspots. He paced back and forth. Lit a cigarette. Looked at aeroplanes flying overhead. Chattered with a passing colleague. Called to a woman and made conversation. To divert the guard's attention for the briefest of seconds presented no difficulties so that a woman could slip away from a group into the bunker and up the stairs. The procedure for making an exit would operate in reverse.

Room 26 had the best access to the bunker; and the system operated smoothly, with little or no risk in the failing light and when the bolts were heard to slide into place on all three communicating doors. It was a team effort, half a dozen proven men and women with sealed lips taking turns, the 'Countess' Valentina and the Duke among them.

It was fortunate that the stock of coal was thin on the floor; incoming 'guests' did not have to clamber over the pyramid I had seen in the winter months. A carpet of cardboard was laid down to avoid leaving a trail of black footprints in the stairwell and on the stairs. Professor Katz played a worthy part; at first light he could be seen searching with his hawk-like eyes for tell-tale particles of coal which might have been picked up on the sole of a slipper and dislodged on the staircase.

Meanwhile, another approach to the women came unexpectedly on offer. It was a free-for-all. A load-bearing joist in a dormitory-room on the second floor of the women's division was found to be in urgent need of repair. Two elderly masons from the neighbourhood were contracted by a constructional engineer to carry out the work. This necessitated boring a sizeable hole through the dormitory ceiling parallel to a chimney-breast and out into the attic space. At the end of each working day, the men covered the hole with a tarpaulin against the draught and hanging dust.

Had Kroll and Bremer meticulously inspected the length of the attic, they might have realized the opportunity for a liaison the hole in the dormitory ceiling presented. It was straightforward; a short climb by way of the stairs behind the clock's mechanism, the removal of the tarpaulin, and the hauling up of a chain of women on the end of a rope. With so many couples cavorting openly, the more modest taking to the seclusion of the stalls, rules were strictly enforced; no boisterous play, chatter muted, 'défense de fumer absolument'. The flame of a lighter and the glow of a cigarette at night would have leaked signals out through the skylights and the fractures in the old roof tiles.

Lutchez sought my help. Newly arrested, Georg Marquand, a police officer and resistance leader, was looking for a means to escape. It was imperative, Lutchez said, a matter of life or death to many patriots. My many strolls around the ramparts with Alfred had pin-pointed one or two practical outlets. The question of retaliatory measures if Georg went missing, as in the case of Pierre Serge Choumoff, was of little consequence. Our days, even hours in the Fort were numbered, Lutchez was convinced.

I sketched a plan for Georg. There were just two requirements. A rope we had: the one which had been successfully employed hauling up women from the dormitory over four weeks was in store. It was essential for Georg to be included in the cleaning party detailed on a Saturday to scrub out the garrison barrack building. Not a problem when most men ducked this chore.

Did I want to go with Georg? The invitation was tempting. As I knew, the prospect of getting clean away was good; most mornings a bank of heavy mist obscured the ramparts and the scrubland beyond the dry moat. Georg had a contact within walking distance where we could lie low before moving elsewhere within the city. Joining the resistance movement was another incentive, a risky venture but perhaps less perilous than what lay ahead. Trusted newcomers, like Georg, were telling about the labour camps in Germany and Austria for which the majority of us, men and women, were destined. There was work for the fit, gruelling work with scant rations and with fearful living conditions, but for the sick and old, there was no hope; under one's breath, and for the first time, there was talk about gas chambers.

But, like many with families at home, I would be exposing my mother to grave risk if I went missing. The police on Jersey island, either military or States civil police working in association with the Germans, would be certain to take her into custody, even deport her. That was the last thing I wanted on my conscience.

Orders from Hauptmann Bruchenbach put paid to Georg Marquand's well-laid plans. 'Les instructions directement de Paris,' Freddy Kaiser said wearily. Henceforth, all outdoor work-parties were confined to the building. Freddy read from a long list. But for a small number of exceptions, men and women, it was total exodus and imminent. Khalid was bewildered. Freddy couldn't tell him why his name and number weren't on the list. Could it be that he was marked for Mont Valérien?

The women were going first. They stood in ragged lines in the courtyard to be counted and checked by Kroll and Bremer, the mean corporal coming under some foul language and abuse which caused loud laughter. On the ground were the carry-alls and small suitcases threatening to burst, knotted bundles of clothing and cardboard boxes packed with food. Outside the gate three buses waited.

The weather was mild, but the women were heavily clad, mackintoshes over greatcoats, hooded cloaks, trousers, knickerbockers, leggings, top-boots and strong shoes. Around some waists were rolled blankets secured by sisal string and spare footwear was strung around some necks; all the protective clothing needed to combat the climate of freezing terror they were going to meet with in the days ahead.

Everything Lucy and I could think of had been turned over in our minds and had been said. Smuggled into Room 26 with Paulette and 'Countess' Valentina on the last night, Lucy had cried like a child in my arms. Poor Lucy, let down by promises which offered little chance of materializing, she hadn't heard from her parents for many months. No word from my sister in Rochdale since I was taken by surprise the Christmas before; nothing from my mother in Jersey. We guessed that letters were at the mercy of indifferent German postal communications and parcels vulnerable to thieves.

Lucy promised to be brave. She was in good health and strong of mind, a quality of importance to stand the test of endurance. And she was going in good company, with Paulette, Colette and Thérèse. Moreover, she was going knowing that I loved her and that our parting might be only for a short duration; we would be brought together, she said, in a world without resentment, without anger and without fear. 'Is that too much to ask for, chéri?' she asked.

I shook my head, lost in thought. After a long silence, I said: 'It's what ought to be, Lucy.' Who was I to judge on the aftermath of the war? I remembered in a cinema in 1938 watching on news-reel the gullible British Prime Minister, Neville Chamberlain, stepping down from an aeroplane on his return from Germany after meeting with 'Herr Hitler'. The trusting man waved a piece of paper at the camera and cheerfully announced: 'Peace in our time.' The audience clapped and hurrahed. I applauded with them, not really knowing what it was all about. Now better informed, I went along with Lutchez, who said: 'Don't be fooled, when this war is over you won't have far to go to find another, there will be neither peace nor justice in the world.'

Singing the Marseillaise at the top of their voices, the women climbed into the waiting buses. The men called from the windows: 'Courage et la confiance!' 'Adieu!' 'À bientôt!' 'Bon voyage!'

Large suitcases were 'verboten'. My luggage was a cardboard box, filled with small items for hygiene and food-stuffs. Heeding a warning from the women, the men dressed warmly. I wore my Harris tweed overcoat which smelt of camphor, two thick jumpers underneath, a wool vest next to my skin, long underpants and long woollen hose.

Louise Beriot came to our room. She embraced the Duke and me. She was emotional. With mixed feelings, I took a last look at the room which had been my lodging for nigh on two years, then, with the Duke, moved to the communal room, leaving Louise Beriot to spend the last few minutes alone with Marc Troska.

I said 'auf wiedersehen' to a weepy Herman. I would miss him. I wished him well. He was one German who had served the community kindly. 'Au revoir, Khalid.' Unhappy Khalid, all his close friends abandoning him at a stroke. There was one thing to cheer him up – he, alone, held the key to the coal-bunker; given the opportunity he would put it to good use.

We filed into the courtyard. At a trestle-table, 'Biscuit' Klaus doled out a day's ration of bread and cheese to each departing man. He flinched at the abuse. Standing firm, Hauptmann Bruchenbach gave each man a curt nod of the head; had he offered me his hand I would have taken it, one could accuse him of stupidity but not of wickedness. Freddy Kaiser stood with his head bowed, the previous evening he had paid the building a courtesy visit. He was a sadder man but not wiser; actuated by a love for his country, he stubbornly refused to believe that Germany was about to receive a good hiding.

The buses filled to capacity, we set off on the first leg to Germany and the little known. We skirted the city in slow convoy, passing through the industrial town of St Denis where I had undergone a period of solitary confinement, then on to a place called Senlis, the half-way mark to Compiègne. I was seated with Marc Troska; come what may, we were resolved to go hand in hand; our friendship had long been sealed, only an irreversible tragedy would part us. In the seat behind, as different as

chalk from cheese, sat the Duke and the Professor as talkative as parrots
in the English language. Opposite, sat Max nursing his precious box of
needles, cotton and scissors on his knees. Perhaps Max was thinking that
his craft might give him a further lease of life. Lutchez was engaged in an
earnest conversation with an uneasy-looking Georg Marquand who
would be keeping watch for a means to escape.

Passers-by waved hands at the ill-favoured procession. Young girls
blew kisses and old men touched their caps at the sight of the faces
peering through the closed windows. But our guards were something
else, beefy and flint-faced SS soldiers; they silenced our ready retorts to
the natives with verbal threats and pointed their machine-pistols, hostile
gestures to which we were unaccustomed. The oppressive conduct of
these special soldiers was insignificant compared with what was in the
offing. No one expected the equal of Romainville at Compiègne, we
were all prepared for a strict regime comparable to the prisons of Paris
under German control, but not for anything to warrant the construction
of a great monument outside the gates of the camp after the war in
memory of the 53,000 men, women and children who died uncared for
within, or who were deported and murdered.

Not the appetizing aroma of a highly seasoned pot-au-feu which had
been the speciality of individual cuisines at Romainville, but a smell of
utter repugnance wafted up my nostrils as I marched into the camp's vast
quadrangle, the size of three football pitches. I was horror-stricken,
caught off guard like everyone else. I stepped over a dragging gully of
mucus, bladder fluid, vomit and blood. Prisoners were hanging about
friendless, in twos and in groups; many were thin, sick-looking, ready to
drop. At one point, corpses were stockpiled awaiting collection.

Hut 3 was raised off the ground, perched on concrete stumps. The
accommodation, one large dormitory and a small annex which served as
a latrine, was without furnishings except for the bare necessities, two-
and three-tier bunks to sleep some one hundred men, a few trestle-tables,
forms and stools. The room was without lighting or heating; three
windows facing the quadrangle had paint-blackened glass.

There were no pillows to the bunks. I laid my head in the crook of my
arm to sleep. The two thin blankets were full of holes and foul smelling.
Like everyone else, I lay fully clothed, my personal things tucked
between my legs to counteract the sneak-thieves we had been warned
about who prowled around in the dead of night. The room was already
partly occupied by men from the prisons of Paris before our arrival
from Romainville and, as we were quick to learn, there was a ready-
market for commodities of every description, tobacco being the prime
target.

Sleep was hard to come by. It was cold. I blinked in the intermittent brightness of the searchlights directed in an arc at the huts. Harsh sounds were many: hawking lungs, grunts, sobs, screams coming from outside, killer-dogs on the loose sniffing at the door. The traffic to the latrine was constant. One had to step warily in the darkness, the floor was thick with slime, the plumbing clanged, and the wash-basins and pans leaked, were cracked and blocked.

At reveille, just after first light, I was glad to get out of my bunk. I ached like never before; my mouth was sour, my face and hands filthy and my body sore from scratching. We formed a queue to receive a mug of ersatz coffee and a portion of hard black bread. The coffee, like the soup we were later to collect, was thin and lukewarm. By day, the door was left unlocked and we were given the freedom of the quadrangle, watched closely by a ring of guards in tall towers and others patrolling the area.

The women's camp was well-segregated. It was impossible to recognize any individual or group from a distance. But, late on the second day, a message from a source known only to Georg Marquand confirmed that the women from Romainville were still there, due to leave on the next transport out. And I was to learn more from Georg before the zero hour, a man who was accomplished at underhand scheming and, like many of his breed, indifferent to danger. And I was paying attention to those who had some practical experience of the journey from Compiègne's marshalling yards to Buchenwald in Germany, men recaptured after escaping. More than two thousand prisoners were herded into twenty cattle trucks. Suffocation would account for a great loss of life in the first hour. Shock, death from heart failure and from other causes would reduce the numbers in each truck by half before the terminal was reached three to five days later. Among those arriving in one piece, some would have reached the point of insanity. The prospect was daunting.

'Sauve qui peut!' It was neck or nothing. Breaking out of the truck would be the least of the difficulties: the dangerous moments would be before and after, immediately before departure and at the moment of flight. Damage to military property was sabotage, a capital offence. Hardly a deterrent to desperate men. There was the moral issue: the sick and the cripples, and those too old to jump would be abandoned to guards schooled in brutality. Dissenters, those who might put up a resistance and sound the alarm, would be silenced, I was told. 'Tout ensemble', it was a matter for one's conscience.

I was one of a select few drawn into Georg Marquand's plan. Lutchez took me aside. That I would be putting my mother at risk by taking to my heels was now invalidated, he said. Like everyone else, I was a prisoner in transit, unregistered, 'ohne Name, ohne Nummer'. For all the administration cared about me I could be one of the many corpses collected twice daily for disposal. This assertion eased my mind.

We were into the early hours of the morning, the dawning of the big move, five days after leaving the divine comforts of Romainville. In Hut 3, men were cat-napping, restless, and talking in whispers. Here and there a cigarette glowed in the darkness. Having snatched some sleep earlier on, I was now vigilant, watching the crouching, shadowy figure of Georg Marquand down on his knees at the door. He, too, was tense, waiting to receive a colleague from the women's camp, the first phase in his elaborate plan. How, and by what means, would she be transported the three hundred metres across the neck of the quadrangle to Hut 3, avoiding the prowling dogs? And for what reason? That was a matter no one should concern themselves with, Georg said. All he asked of those closely allied to the plot was complete reticence; no greetings, no questions, no curiosity.

I was 'tooled-up'. In the waistband of my trousers a steel blade with small teeth was concealed; others had been entrusted with jemmies and boring tools, all of which had been bought with tobacco and food. Lying on my bunk, I evaluated my chances. Escapes en route were frequent. Many were bungled. To fail meant a violent death, at best a whipping. I wondered what I was letting myself in for. It all seemed so unreal, like an adventurous drama staged for the cinema screen, the leading characters and the bit-players sweating it out and taking instructions from the director, Georg Marquand, before going into action; and the exterior role-players with pretend machine-pistols depicting the enemy in uniforms hired from a theatrical costumier. And, at the end of the day, with no blood spilled, the company coming together in the pub around the corner for drinks and a laugh.

The activity coming from the marshalling yards rang true. The grating clunk and squeals of moving wheels set my teeth on edge; engines shunted and whistles blew. It was still dark outside when I heard a dog growl at the door. A guttural curse, a short pause, and then the door opened. A faint glimmer of light streaked into the corner of the room before vanishing in a breath. The woman, a slight figure dressed in black, had been safely delivered.

It was the next stage in which one needed 'le sangfroid', Georg said. The huts would be called out into the quadrangle by numbers, the prisoners ordered to leave in single file to a point designated for body searches. The guards would exercise some discretion, picking and choosing from an estimated two thousand men and women. The first twenty out from Hut 3 would come under the protection of a Hauptscharführer, a fat, short man, Georg said. A faux pas by anyone would mean sudden death.

It was dawn. A hazy light penetrated through the painted glass in the windows. Georg took a roll-call. Each man he called answered 'ici'. I took my place in the line, at number six. Georg was at the head; behind, his protégée whose identity and involvement would remain a mystery. She looked no more than eighteen years of age, and she could easily pass for one of the many youths among us, short hair under a cap, pale of face, and shabbily dressed. Lutchez was at number three; Marc Troska at number four; in front of me the placid Professor; behind me, the Duke putting on a brave face; coming next, Max the tailor lamenting the loss of his sewing-box, confiscated at the time of entry into the camp.

A loudspeaker crackled. It carried its menacing message over and over again to every corner and with increasing pitch. 'Achtung! Achtung! Gefangenen nach Transportieren. Mach fertig! Mach schnell!' The order, hysterically delivered, was repeated in French.

There came a sustained blowing of whistles, barking of dogs and cracking of whips. 'Surtout la calme,' Georg called over his shoulder. A tight line snaked around the wall of the hut and between the rows of bunks. Lifeless forms could be seen under the blankets of some bunks. The night had taken its toll.

'Baracke drei! Aus! Aus!' The door was flung open. Keep calm, I said to myself; look for the sergeant, stout and short as the man had been described. The long line shuffled forward, small step by small step out into the damp cold. The man was easily identified. He stood out deliberately obtrusive. Behind the handkerchief he held up to his nose, he shouted: 'Schnell, vite, schnell!' He indicated with a hand. 'Rühren, rühren!'

Get a move on! Georg quickly followed the direction, thus bypassing the trestle tables where random body-searches were in operation. We were halted in a zone staked out with tall open fencing, within calling distance of the women filing past four abreast. I turned my eyes away. I didn't want to see Lucy amongst this bedraggled crowd. I wanted to remember her as I had last seen her, beautiful and brimming with health, not pitted against beefy matronly guards who threatened and taunted.

Three hundred women having embarked into the first three trucks, the whistles blew for the men. The columns moved off at a shuffling pace, frequently coming to a halt for the laggards, the infirm and the cripples to catch up, helped by guards wielding their fists and their rubber truncheons. I glanced back. Stretcher-bearers and prisoner-orderlies pushing hand-carts were at the rear, carrying the legless and paralytic. The quadrangle suggested a field in the wake of a battle with bodies cut down; strewn clothing, baggage, boots and shoes littered the ground. It was the longest slog over the shortest distance I had ever endured.

'Quarante Hommes ou Huit Chevaux.' Forty men or eight horses were the fading words stencilled on the outside of the trucks. The counting stopped only when two and a half times the recommended human maximum was reached. With the doors closed, the degree of heat generated inside was at the fever mark. Wedged shoulder to shoulder, we were all over-burdened with clothing. Air came from a small aperture set high in only one corner, benefiting the few standing in front. A thin layer of straw was scattered over the wooden floor; and, at the centre, an oil drum serving as a latrine filled a space for four men.

My body was clamped in a human vice. Everything about me ached. My arms and legs were trapped. My vision was blurred. My dank hair hung down over my face and sweat dribbled into my mouth. I, like everyone else, had a raging thirst. Water, there was none. We were not yet underway, but the straw under my feet was already a quagmire of diarrhoea and vomit which caused additional distress to the few who lay helplessly trapped on the floor. We had been thrown into a restless mobile grave.

At a snail's pace, the twenty heavily-laden trucks pulled away from the marshalling yards and out into the country. The wheels rolling, our faces were fanned by currents of air coming through chinks in the wooden walls, and rainwater trickled through the roof on to our heads and into our upturned mouths. The relief, if only temporary, appeased the arid throats of the weepers and the grousers.

Thirst assailed us all, causing fright and mental derangement. One man harped on his past occupation brewing beer; another, a *viticulteur*, spoke about his wine cellar. This caused torment and outbursts of anger. From somewhere in the lurid gauze of light, Georg Marquand's voice was heard to call 'à l'ordre!' We had to make elbow and legroom, he said. To grapple with the dead, or those presumed to be without life, proved to be a trial of strength and macabre manoeuvre. Fatalities were passed over our heads and stacked parallel to one end wall shoulder high, held fast by a broad barrier of backs.

I could now move my arms and exercise the cramped muscles in my legs by lifting one foot at a time. It was near darkness before the bickering petered out. Stress and extreme fatigue had sapped our resilience and there were those who were half-asleep on their feet. But for a few dissenting voices, everyone rallied to Georg Marquand's call for support. It was crucial, to clear a space at the centre. This was carried out by shifting the empty oil drum, turning it upside down for two men to sit on and taking a backward step by exerting pressure on one's neighbour.

Those who said they were familiar with the region agreed that the convoy was travelling on the Soissons-Reims line, in all probability pulling towards Metz. The wheels were turning slowly, with frequent holdups because of priority traffic and air-raid alarms. At this rate of progress, it could take more than two days to reach Metz; in the interim, we could expect repeated tours of inspection, damage to the truck would be noticed, with disastrous results. Calculations of speed, distance and time, meant breaking out in the early hours of the morning before reaching the city of Reims, some ninety kilometres from Compiègne, and one hundred and fifty from Paris, for which many among us hoped to aim. And there was another reason to make every minute count; escape, or an attempt, did not exclude other trucks ahead and behind. The point was not disputed, it was first out, first away.

Lutchez and others had taken note on boarding. Our truck was number eight from the engine, well-sited. From one to twenty, there were six elevated observation posts; guards armed with heavy machine-guns had an uninterrupted view of the rooftops, and by leaning sidelong they could see the doors, easily managed at a bend in the track; but whilst the convoy was on the move, the guards could not see the underframes.

For my own part, I did not favour leaving through a hole in the floorboards, the clearance beneath could not be trusted when on the move; I had a vision of being speared or crushed by some ingenious contraption fitted to the underframe. My preference was the sliding door, a more delicate operation; precision was crucial when gouging out a hole no bigger than a fist without disturbing the outer skin until the very last moment, immediately before an arm and a hand reached out to lift the retaining pin from its eye.

Georg Marquand made the decision to assail both outlets simultaneously. Tools were called for and gathered. By the feeble light of a shaded stub of candle, men took turns to bore, pick and lever, the splitting of wood had the sound-effects of exploding fire-crackers. When stationary in pitch darkness, flashes of torch-light could be seen oscillating outside, heavy boots crunching into stone-chips brought on a nervous silence; even those plagued by respiratory disorders suppressed their wheezes, snorts, heaves and coughs. Startling, too, were the fists thumping at the doors and the foul-mouthed curses and threats invoked upon us.

The convoy, rolling, sluggish, jolting, and clattering over points at intersections, was buffeted by strong winds. Rain teemed through the roof like through a colander, saturating clothing already filthy with urine and other human deposits. My overcoat was besmirched, as were my hands, my face and my hair. But the seasonal wind and rain were a blessing, the foul air was tempered by it and each of us collected enough water to cool our throats. Hellish in the heat of the summer, I imagined.

I longed to lie down, if not to sleep, to sprawl and ease the pressing weight off my legs, I was so bone-weary. It was the rainwater running into my eyes and over my face that kept me aware of the men at work. Fixed in my mind and repeated to myself over and over again were Georg Marquand's instructions. 'Courez à toute vitesse comme un lièvre.' At the word 'go', run like a hare. Don't look back. Don't wait for friends. Aim for cover, woods, spinneys and outbuildings. Keep away from the main roads. Lie low at first light. 'Mettez en garde,' Georg said. One must be careful whom one approached. There were collaborators as well as patriots.

Having evaded the initial danger, dodging machine-gun bullets, I would be hard to catch. As a youth at school, I had shaped up well at athletics; the hop, skip and jump and the short sprint had seen me up in front, but the 'cross-country' had been my speciality, and I was confident, despite the weariness I felt, that fear and my long legs would lend me wings.

What then? If not with Marc Troska I would be left with my own decisions. I would have to find the safest way to Paris. How? Along out-of-the-way roads and in the hours of darkness. Perhaps five nights of jogging. How would I eat, drink and clean myself? I didn't know. Before leaving Romainville, Khalid had given me the address of a friend who could be trusted, a café in the Rue Berger. The Duke, who insisted he was strong enough to make the attempt, said I could go with him. He knew of someone living on the outskirts of Reims, if he could get to a telephone he would have help. Professor Katz intended to stay put, he was too old to take to his heels; besides, he said, his face would give him away, no one would mistake him for anything but a Jew. He was prepared to 'face the music' with Max.

Lutchez's voice came over clearly. It expressed triumph. 'We have a hole big enough to shit through,' he said. I looked. Marc Troska was down on his knees, a probing hand through a yawning puncture in the floorboards. But their excitement was short-lived. Marc Troska's fingers touched cold steel, a thick net had been secured to the underframe and we had no cutting device with which to get to grips with such a cunning obstacle. Nothing had been gained but a draught of cold air and, as Lutchez quipped, a hole which could function as a latrine.

Now we were jittery. Was the pin in the eye securing the doors loose fitting? Had the guards learned a lesson from past breakouts and made the doors impregnable? We were about to find out. The thin outer shell of the saucer-shaped hollow in one door panel was, as yet, unbroken.

With a rag wrapped around a fist, Georg punched hard. The shell split cleanly and flew out on the wind. He put a hand through, then the arm. Everyone gagged and tightly strained, Georg was heard to say: 'J'ai la main dessus le pivot.'

'He's got his hand to the pin,' I whispered to the Duke.

'C'est libre, Georg?' Lutchez was heard to ask.

The silence which followed the crucial question was agonizing. If the pin was secure we were damned. I gave a thought to Lucy, up front in one of the first three trucks, perhaps dead or at the point of death. Every truck would be stricken with fatalities. It would be intolerable suffering for the women. No doubt there was a wicked policy to get rid of great numbers of prisoners before the end of the journey because it was expedient.

My thoughts were interrupted by the answer which came. 'Oui,' Georg said. 'Bien en main!'

'Tout va bien,' Lutchez called out.

Cheers were faint. I said to the Duke: 'Thank Christ! Georg has the pin in his hand.'

A hard pull at the doors and they scraped open, first a few inches, enough for us to see ragged clouds above the tall trees. The wind had sobered down, the rain had stopped, but the moon was unfavourable. I made ready to take off. I hesitated before discarding my overcoat, now an encumbrance since it had become wet through. There was some shoving, elbowing and shouldering, those who were staying forced to give way to those intending to make a break for it when Georg gave the order.

I was bunched in against the side wall, two metres away from the doors. There was hardly a sound within the truck. The dull pitch of the wheels was all one could hear above Georg's critical commentary. 'Ça marche la vitesse,' he was heard to say. The speed was opportune. But we were travelling in a zone of high walls and warehouses, or steep banks with no cover, and the moon was playing 'cache-cache' with the clouds. Georg was looking for a flat surface, thickets, dipping fields and coverts.

Loud piercing screams suddenly reached our ears. Machine-guns loosened off. The convoy came to a stop as if the engine had hit a steel wall head-on. The stack of corpses tumbled adrift like wet sandbags. It was bedlam. Men were crushed and bruised. My nose bloodied, I disentangled myself from the imbroglio. There were empty spaces, the doors were wide open but I fell back. A pall of smoke hung in the air, men raced by panic-stricken, and bullets ricocheted. A powerful torchlight scanned the interior. A pistol, aimed indiscriminately, was discharged. A howl, a whimper, a grunt, a curse. Cringing, I was possessed by a dreadful fear. All my brave resolutions seemed to have deserted me at a stroke. Guards swarmed around the truck with torches and swinging lanterns. Cursing, they whipped those standing out onto a slaggy side track. I wanted to be shot rather than beaten to death or hanged. We were ordered to undress. We stood naked.

I could see it all now. Arc-lamps sizzled under sodden trees, shedding light on a bloody carnage. Bodies lay spread-eagled on the rugged surface, between wheels and buffers where they had floundered; others had been cut down by machine-gun bullets on a rising bank, some having slithered down on the greasy surface clutching tufts of weeds in their hands. A number of recaptured men were being subjected to a special process – garrotting from low hanging branches of a tree. Marc Troska, I was stunned to see, was among them. Truck number 5 – it had triggered off the chaos in its reckless haste to beat all others in a breakout – was on fire; guards and prisoners were dousing the flames; and, farther down the line, there was another unholy mêlée.

Guards vented their fury on our naked bodies, beating our remnants back into the truck with whips and rubber truncheons. The doors securely battened down, it was dawn before the convoy rumbled on again. As far as one could judge, from the original one hundred or so men and one girl, thirty were living but not all undamaged, thirty-six lay dead and the remaining were missing.

Apart from bruises and a nose bleed I was unscathed. Max had a bullet in a leg, above the knee. Another bullet had grazed the Professor's temple and he had a black eye. The Duke had a sprained foot, otherwise he was unhurt. Lutchez had been beaten about the head and had lost a tooth. Others complained of injuries, some painful, some tolerable. The cold attacked us all.

I was reunited with my overcoat. The corpses were stripped of clothing above the waist; vests, shirts, pullovers, waistcoats and jackets were found to be dry and reasonably free from dirt. There was enough to go round. And one could substitute sleeved undergarments for long drawers. When the corpses were stacked at one end, we had freedom of movement. The clutter, wet straw and human deposits, was flushed through the hole in the floor.

The days were long, the nights even longer. The convoy made its mournful way with torturing slowness. Another day. Again we scrutinized one another and it seemed that for each of the three days we had been in transit each had aged ten years. Men who were middle-aged now looked senile; young men looked middle-aged, with deep sunken lines in what had been smooth; youthful faces were now the faces of idiots, lit only with despondency, dejection and utter despair. I felt as if all my life was but a remote dream of the distant past; so long ago, it seemed, had I been a young man with enthusiasm and vitality. I realized that it is not only time that ages.

The torturing pangs of thirst returned. How long could we endure it again? I began to have hallucinations. I saw myself as a boy again, given a few pennies by my mother to buy an ice-cream or a bottle of soda-pop. Oh, for a jug of cold water! Here I was , in my early twenties, suffering a thirst which no man could bear for long, lying comatose on the foul floor of a cattle truck in the company of dead men. Why? What had I done to merit this wickedness? What had my friend Marc Troska done to justify a cruel hanging? I looked at the Professor, old enough to be my grand-father, he had confronted death with courage and dignity; here he was now, still standing upright, righteous and undaunted.

Did the rest of the world know how the Germans were treating people like us? Would I ever be able to convince anyone of the brutalities, if I survived? What was the purpose of it all? What driving force impelled the Germans to go to such lengths of cruelty? I had already seen enough to fill my memory. More, and even worse, was to come.

Gaunt and isolated, composed of innumerable barrack-like huts in dreary formation, line after line, the concentration camp of Buchenwald looked, I imagine, something like a Klondike shanty-town. It stood sloping from the main entrance gate, down to as far as a weary, hollowed eye could see, the surrounding country bare, bleak and brown, sparse trees dotted here and there.

The camp was divided into two parts: the Small Camp (Kleine Lager) and the Big Camp (Grosse Lager). The Small Camp was the quarantine zone, mainly for the new arrivals, to prevent the spreading of diseases to those living in the two-storey Blocks of the Big Camp who had been inoculated and passed as 'gesund'.

I shared a wide wooden bunk with nine others, sleeping on bare boards, each issued with a thin blanket which was weighed down with fleas and lice, vomit and blood. We slept sardine-like, overwhelmed by the smell of human excreta and diseased bodies, with crawling things constantly gorging on the flesh of skulls, legs, arms and testicles. Throughout the long nights, voices cried out in hunger, in fear, in pain, or from a blow of an unneighbourly fist. Some men still had the strength for strife and scraps.

Daily, long before dawn, pugnacious room helps, motivated by extra rations, would roughly waken those fortunate enough to be sleeping, 'encouraging' them with a hail of blows from a stick to the buttocks or a brutal attack in the ribs with any weapon that came to hand. We were then paraded in the streets outside for the routine roll-call, streets that were no more than levelled mud surfaces which, after a heavy downpour of rain, became quagmires, slimy with body filth, blood and phlegm from diseased throats and lungs.

Icy winds assailed our bony frames as they howled down the bare alleys of the camp; there was nowhere to escape from them, no sheltered corner to huddle in for a little warmth and protection. Each roll-call claimed its victims; they broke ranks in a frenzy, propelling themselves with outstretched arms up against the electrified fence or were brought down by keen-eyed sentries who instantly opened fire on anyone coming within a short distance. A greater number silently expired where they stood. And when it was all over, ten thousand souls were left to wander aimlessly up and down, forbidden to return to their bunks till almost dusk.

In the middle of the day, long queues formed up for half a pint of tepid swede soup and a piece of mouldy black bread. This was the signal for friction, jostling, squabbling, wrestling, blows. Here madness swiftly overtook sound minds; hunger rapidly reduced men to savagery; monstrous acts were committed for the acquisition of a mere ounce of bread. Many of the weaker men were robbed of their rations.

After several weeks, I caught up with Lutchez. I had some difficulty in recognizing him. He had shrivelled. He had aged. Hadn't we all! His eyes were puffy, bruised, his shorn hair turned grey. Yet, for all that, he managed a mocking laugh. In a choking voice, he chanted: 'Jack Dunn, son of a fucking gun, up to his eyes in shit! What would they say in Leicester Square about this, eh?' I wondered what my poor mother would say.

Lutchez had lost none of his bravado. Belly-aching about communism was going to cost him his life. He wouldn't take a warning. The Communist 'prominenten', in the main German, Austrian and Polish criminals of a callous breed, well fed and well clothed and sharing some of the amenities of our SS guards, were strange, willing associates of evil who had a sort of unofficial, delegated power, and were unrestricted in their methods of enforcing their rule, as I was to see with even more ferocity in a place called Mauthausen. It seemed to me that illiteracy and savagery, with a little insanity thrown in, were the special qualifications necessary to gain such exalted positions.

Lutchez and I came upon the Duke. Surprisingly, he was bearing up well; bony, somewhat short of breath, he walked unfaltering, determined to stay the course. Sad Lucien Paradis was wallowing in self-pity. He was being transferred to the Big Camp; picked out to work in the stone quarry, his days were numbered and he knew it. His 'gai, cher' Paris was uppermost in his cracked mind as he pitifully sobbed at memories of old haunts and old friends. Near-suicidal, he threatened to walk up to the electric barbed wire. No one would stop him. He was just one more whose number was up.

I was fortunate, with a reserve of strength. But there was a long way to go. Put to work, my daily chore was conveying human filth to the primitive and unhygienic cesspools. Bedraggled, emaciated forms, teams of four, one to each shaft of a wooden box that was weighty enough when unladen, struggled in the mud and slime, bearing insanitary loads to the dumps. It was even worse when we were forced to climb down into the latrines – deep pits dug in the ground, a stout pole serving as a seat, another for a back rest – to lift out the bodies that had toppled over, submerged and eventually drowned in the muck which dyed our hands, legs and feet.

Eventually, with some hundreds of others, I was selected for transfer to a subsidiary camp, either Dora where bombs were manufactured or the petrol processing plants of Zeitz and Merseburg, to which normally only Jews were despatched. Either spelled disaster. At both, it was rumoured, prisoners were slave driven to the extreme limit of human and physical endurance.

On the eve of our departure, we lined up for an injection; male quacks, themselves prisoners, in grubby white jackets and with grubbier hands, jabbed questionable needles into our arms. Each man was issued with a jacket and trousers of thin blue and grey striped ersatz material, a cotton shirt and a pair of wooden-sole shoes with canvas uppers. This frail foot-gear was named by the French 'claquette', because of the smacking sound each made on the hard ground.

In the early hours of the night, my whole body throbbed. In pain, I tossed about, forced to the floor for fear of exasperating my bedfellows. My first thought was the liquid which had been pumped into my bloodstream. Had I been deliberately, perhaps fatally, poisoned? We had heard of one sinister method of death-dealing, by injecting vitriols, even milk, into prisoners selected for medical research.

It was some relief when the symptoms were diagnosed as pneumonia. The Block chief reluctantly removed me from the list of the doomed. The discomfort and pain tolerable, I was allowed to stay in the sick enclosure, where I was given a bunk to myself. I could only drink soup and that went down the hard way; my bread ration was thrown to the vultures who stubbornly besieged my sick bed.

Passed 'gesund', I was spared the ordeal of labouring at the cesspools, 'der Abort-Kommando', I was transferred to the Big Camp, lodged in a two-storey block, number 38, where the 'amenities' were somewhat better. We had access to running water, urinals and pans with and without wooden seats, cracked, stained and leaking – yet better than the primitive bogs. Paper? There was none. It was a punishable offence to use any material which caused blockages. Diarrhoea and dysentry plagued us all.

I had a bunk to myself, on a third tier. Two thin blankets instead of one. Queues for food rations were generally orderly, rarely a squabble or a fight. Militant factions were speedily dealt with, heavy-handedly. Thieves were hauled before a 'court' of Block-chiefs. Flogged unmercifully by bullying room assistants, persistent miscreants were strangled on the end of a short rope.

There was less violence to be seen in the maze of streets compared to the endless embroilments in the Small Camp, because the majority of prisoners were on outside labour details and not at a loose end. The camp police, privileged prisoners with normal haircuts, and dressed warmly and smartly in semi-uniforms, were always in evidence, on the look-out for the work-shy who had no business to be in their Blocks or hanging around the streets during the day. Except for the very sick with passes and those who had duties within the camp, every man worked beyond the perimeter. After dawn roll-call on the vast Appel Platz and immediately before the long columns marched out through the main gate, many artful dodgers mixed with the exempt to slip past the police cordons and find hiding places, but the severe penalties did not make it an attractive risk.

Never did we arrive at our places of work with our numbers intact. Each day, the long march depleted our ranks. Some, their hearts too tired to go on, dropped in their tracks; others, the dodderers and would-be scarperers, met their end by a bullet or were battered with rifle-butts. The return journey never passed without a fatal incident.

Sheer will-power kept me moving. On arrival at our destination, each man was issued with a pick or a shovel. We dug trenches, cleared debris from bomb damage, and repaired roads, watched over by some of the worst guards, illiterate, uncouth, unstable Ukrainians of the SS who goaded in particular the Jehovah's Witnesses and the homosexuals – the 'Mauves' and 'Pinks' according to the distinguishing coloured patches sewn onto their jackets and trousers. Children, often mere toddlers, from around the neighbourhood, were pests, pelting stones, hurling abuse at what they called 'Vogelscheuche' (scarecrows).

Each day we struggled on against our many adversaries – brutality, hunger, insanity and the elements among them; the freezing winds were cruel, it was always raining, varying from mild drizzles to heavy down-pours. The half-hour break we got in the middle of the day only tended to aggravate our condition, it was purely a short lull to appease the stomachs of the guards and Kapos – food was not for us. Each day brought fresh faces and replacements to my working party.

Back in the camp came the dreaded roll-call, immediately after the issue of the basic food rations which were wolfed down with all speed. And it was everyone to the Appel Platz without exception, the infirm, the crippled and the legless, who were carried on stretchers. Every ounce of strength was summoned up – it was a common sight to see a man crawling on his belly – so as not to lag behind, for we did not relish the cudgelling from our guards. And the band played on, portly, well-dressed musicians with string, brass and wind instruments executing a waltz or a lively tango rhythm whilst breathless, half-frozen souls frothed at the mouth, puked blood into the dirt, keeled over and died.

When the band stopped playing, a deadly hush filled the air. Not a stir from the multitude, no twitch of an eye, no chatter. Then came the 'Voice' from the loudspeaker. Snarling, chilling to the ears, it commanded:

'Ruhe!' Now, even the guards were temporarily still. A short pause, then: 'Mitzen ab!' Hats off as a respectful salute to the German nation.

Keen-eyed, the tellers took stock along the ranks, meticulously checking the numbers; every muscle in my body taut, unable to relax, I shifted my gaze only when the danger had passed. But would there be a recount? And a second, stretching into the late evening, perhaps into the early morning? Very likely if just one man was unaccounted for. A runaway? The Poles were good – or bad – at absconding, top of the list. The penalty was no deterrent.

The gallows once in place (a crude, portable contraption half the size of a goal-post with a hanging noose to the crossbar and a stool beneath), thirty thousand pairs of eyes were ordered to watch the gruesome ceremony. Outside the barbed wire, there was a different kind of audience on the terraces – off-duty guards, their wives, their children and the odd hanger-on out for thrills.

The star-turn, already blooded, was led in from the gaping jaws of the gate, surmounted by the rampant Prussian eagle, apt symbol of the German nation – a bird of prey. As he passed beneath this emblem, he was excused the obligatory salute, since his hands were tied behind his back. Strong arms hoisted him onto the stool. No resistance, no cringing, just calm resignation. The noose, a short frail rope, was placed over his shaven head. The loudspeaker crackled. The 'Voice' spoke in the tones of a schoolmaster. It lectured on the 'Schwein' who attempted to abandon his 'Kameraden', a stupid deed, 'nicht nachbarlich' (unneighbourly). The address, from an oft-repeated script, altered in one breath from patronizing to a tone of frenzy. We were all 'Dreck' (filth) the Voice screamed, deserving of the same 'Medizin' as our friend about to meet with the devil.

The drum-major raised his knobbled sticks and beat out a reverberatory sound. A shiny black boot kicked out at the stool. The body jerked, it pirouetted, twisting slowly at the end of the rope. Death came painfully slowly. Who was this martyr? A peasant? A bourgeois? An aristocrat? Did it matter? Did anyone care?

Night after long night, I lay in my bunk turning a deaf ear to broken men whimpering under the blankets – from sickness, from hunger, from cold, and from fear, men who were delirious and demented and who had become automata. I relived the sweet past, safe and sound with my good mother and father and free from evil. We were poor in terms of money but with a wealth of affection, never cold or hungry. A full belly. My mother's stews and dumplings. Her bread-and-butter puddings. Huge mounds of dough baked in the old brick oven which turned out hot and crusty bread.

It seemed as if Romainville was nothing more than an incredible dream of the past. I missed the freshness, the purity, the laughter, the comradeship; even Corporal Laufer's belly-aching and Weismann's sharp tongue would now be music to my ears. And what would Haupt-mann Bruchenbach – 'ich bin kein Nazi' – think about those he blamed for all the ills in the world, the targets for hostile feeling and great hate ... Jews? Would the sour little man be forever haunted, seeing their vulner-able hordes – endless, unresisting lines – being driven like sheep to the slaughter sheds of Auschwitz and Mauthausen? The 'dove' Freddy Kaiser, that gentleman of Germans, would have been horrified.

Lutchez had gone missing. There was a report that he had been murdered. I wasn't surprised. He was incorrigible, a man obsessed with taking on the communist overlords among us. Broken Lucien Paradis was sick, suffering the torments of the quarry where death would come cruelly. The Duke of Andia was skin and bone, suffering from malnut-rition and dementia handing out his food rations under pressure from marauding thugs. He would soon die here in Buchenwald, in August 1944. And what of the pretty things, dear Lucy, Paulette, Colette? Had these frail women survived the journey from Compiègne when strong men had broken down and come to grief?

I came across a number of British subjects dotted around the camp. In Block 16, twenty captured Allied agents were segregated, all doomed for execution in ones and twos. I recognized men from my native island, some I had known in the Jersey jail; Irish· subjects who had picked drunken brawls with German soldiers and served a couple of months' imprisonment imposed by the civil court before being deported as 'undesirables'; there were English conscientious objectors sent from the mainland before the Occupation to work the harvest who had refused employment on military projects; and I spotted the middle-aged Stanley Green, a well-known islander, and an 'ee-by-goom' Lancashire lad with the unlikely name of 'Chelsea'. Few would survive.

Stanley Green was formerly the manager of West's Cinema, which once stood on the corner of Peter Street and Bath Street, St Helier. A well-respected man who habitually stood in the foyer of the cinema to

greet the pick of the patrons, immaculate in full evening dress, he was
arrested and deported together with Clifford (Canon) Cohu for building
a wireless transmitter which was operated from the top of St Saviour's
Church. Canon Cohu was found guilty of plotting to spread BBC news;
sentenced to three years' imprisonment, he was transported from Jersey
island to Spergau concentration camp from where he never returned.

I reminded Stanley how once, when I paid fourpence for a seat in the
front row of his cinema, he cuffed me around the ears for creeping up
into the expensive row after the lights dimmed. Despite suffering terribly
from malnutrition, eczema and dysentery, Stanley managed a smile.

Buchenwald was liberated early in April 1945. Stanley was returned to
Jersey; a broken man, he died after a long illness, aged 74.

Sidney Green, son of Stanley, is a printer at Peel Terrace, St Saviour's.
He is naturally bitter. 'My father and Canon Cohu,' he insists, 'were
shopped by two islanders who were rewarded with 2000 Marks' (about
£200).

Sidney knows of others who were treacherous and responsible for
men like the Canon going to their deaths. Why were none brought to
trial after the war? Why, for that matter, were no Germans serving on the
island and known to have committed war crimes arrested and tried?

There was a desperate need by the British government of the day to see
all the British Channel Islands' wartime record in an unblemished light.
To have acknowledged the full horror of what went on in the tiny island
of Alderney and the cruelty and murder inflicted on east European slave
labourers and the countless deaths on the fortifications around the
coastline of Jersey and, in particular, in the tunnels of the German
Underground Hospital in the valley of St Peter under the TODT labour
organization and the Jersey States Labour Board, would have been to
destroy this rosy view.

It was the first day of August 1944. A day for joy. The Allied armies were
firmly established in France. Coming to our rescue? The weather was
sunny, warm to our skinny frames. I was excused work, recovering from
scarlet fever. Stripped to the waist, I joined three others, Dutch and
French acquaintances, to have my picture taken. A Dutchman working
in the effects store had come upon a camera with film. I stood, unsmiling, against a huge tree, unaware that the possession of photographic
equipment carried the death penalty.

Later, my attention was drawn to a heavy drone of aircraft somewhere
up in the bright, cloudless sky. Several formations of American bombers
on their way to attack military installations at Magdeburg or Jena,
one heard. A grand sight. I lolled about, greedily absorbing the sun,

impatiently waiting for the planes to return. They came, their numbers intact, it seemed. Steadily they approached the camp. Three or four peeled away and flew low over the camp to drop bomb after bomb. Only two small devices landed inside, one at the door of the crematorium, the other destroying an empty workshop.

The raid lasted only for a few enjoyable minutes, giving pleasure to the living, if not to the dead and wounded, many hundreds of prisoners and guards alike. Every available prisoner was ordered to assist in extinguishing the fires in the guards' quarters, administration offices and factories, and to help carry the dead to the crematorium. The German hierarchy had no respect even for their own casualties; once dead, they were fit only for the scrap-heap, to be buried in pits alongside their slaves or to fuel the flames in the incinerators.

With others of my detail, I picked my way through smoke and debris, through torn and dismembered bodies, searching for prisoners who might be saved, blind to the SS guards writhing in their agony, who screamed out 'helfen, bitte helfen' with bloody hands outstretched. Blistering feet, bandaged feet, shod feet, stepped gingerly aside. Opportunists, wily, insensible, revengeful, spat on, stamped on, kicked out, and seized on cigarettes, tobacco, watches and rings. Was this looting? Was it inhuman? Did I care?

The shadow of winter was quickly closing in on Buchenwald. The few trees were being stripped of their leaves by the cold, blustering winds, offering their bare, blackened boughs to the elements, whistling and howling through every crack and aperture of our frigid, wretched hovels, mercilessly attacking our rag-clad bodies. And to add to all the miseries, large imports were overspilling the Blocks.

Forlorn, I sat on a bench in 'Stube' A, a room occupied mainly by our 'betters', the Block-chief and his entourage of thugs; foremen and those working in prime jobs. Strange yoke-fellows some of these, German and Austrian long-termers among them, who wanted their freedom but not at the cost of Hitler's defeat.

What was I doing in this unholy hole, comparatively warm and with cooking smells? I was under strict orders not to leave the building. Within the hour, someone was going to determine my fate. I had committed an unpardonable sin. The day before, a freezing cold morning, at my place of work – 'Kommando das Grab' (communal graves) – I had momentarily set aside my shovel to blow into my numbed hands and fingers. I had not seen the approach of the SS Warrant Officer. Failing to acknowledge the man's presence and not coming to attention and removing my cap from my head until he had passed by was one crime, the interruption of my work without permission was another. I was punched and booted; worse, my number: (E) 42324 was noted in his book of reports.

I had been an inmate long enough to know the dreaded meaning. To avoid punishing reprisals, one adhered strictly to the rules, even a minor breach held the most fearful consequences – freezing to death; perhaps more kindly, a pistol shot in the back of the neck; more ceremonious and spine-chilling, the ancient Spanish mode of hanging – garrotting.

Standing with two Britishers at roll-call, I said in a low voice: 'My number was taken today.'

The tall, gangling Christopher Burney asked: 'Hell! What did you do?' through the side of his mouth.

'Unhöflich,' I answered.

Burney sniffed. 'Showing disrespect, eh?'*

'I get my number taken once in a while, it doesn't mean a lot,' Martin Perkins said.

Gallant, young Martin Perkins, small of stature, gentle by nature, yet with all the tough characteristics in my mental picture of a secret service agent.

With fellow-feeling, Perkins was trying to ease the tension within me.† Now, as I waited in the lonely emptiness of 'Stube' A, I knew for certain it was my last day in Buchenwald. My small space in a shared locker of 'Stube' C had been cleared of my drinking-mug, tin bowl and spoon, and my bunk had been allocated to a prisoner from the quarantine camp. I was left with nothing but the clothing given to me almost one year before and which had long become firmly joined to my body.

Watching me closely from his little domain – a curtained-off recess at one end of the room – was the Block-chief; his ears, too, were pricked to the raucous 'Voice' sporadically spouting commands by way of the loud-speaker system hooked up overhead. It was his responsibility to see that I responded to my number immediately it was called. As if I didn't already know the procedure, he had primed me with the course to take, the quickest way to the main gate, at the double, 'schnell wie der Wind', and cap in hand.

The eerie command came over loud and clear. No name. No nationality. Just the number: 'zwei und vierzig tausend ... drei hundert ... vier und zwanzig ... zu Tor rapportieren ... los.' I was on my feet and out of the door before the command faded away; half-sprinting, stumbling, I zig-zagged my way among the many Blocks and up the rising ground. The thin soles of my open toed boots squelched in the mud and rivulets of sewage flowing down the rutted street. Wheezing and panting, I came to a stop with jellying legs at the tall granite wall to the left of the main gate. Following the routine, I spread my feet and inclined my body inwards, the tip of my nose making contact with the roughly-hewn stone. Riveted, I waited.

Often during my years in captivity, I had come close to a violent death. I had pulled through many diseases which had proved fatal to strong and weak alike. Currently, I was suffering the common complaint of malnutrition. Unless those faceless mortals sitting in judgement had ruled that I

---

* Christopher Burney, then aged 25. An officer with Special Operations Executive (SOE). Captured in France. Survived. Author of: *The Dungeon Democrat; Solitary Confinement; Descent from Ararat*. Last known to be living in Normandy, France, as a recluse.

† Lieutenant Martin Perkins (Maurice Pertschuk) SOE. Aged 21. A poet, humorist and prankster. Executed in Buchenwald, late 1944.

would die this day, I would be left with no more than a few months, perhaps weeks, on this side of the grave.

Dying was not simple in Buchenwald. To slip quietly away into an eternal sleep was a common craving – but forbidden by our sub-human captors. I had long been prepared to accept my death in an acceptable manner – a shot in the back of the neck was reasonably quick and clean, with little time for pain. But to die slowly, cruelly by torture as I had seen, filled every man with morbid anxiety and made one's flesh creep.

Some sad examples of man's extreme wickedness were preserved a mere one hundred yards away from where I stood. Behind my back on the edge of the 'Appel Platz' was a long narrow single-storeyed building, the 'Wissenschaft' (medical scientific) Block. I had been one of the few permitted to glance around the dreadful place. A Dutch acquaintance, working there as a clerk, assured me it would be safe to show me around on a chosen day. 'You won't believe it until you see for yourself,' he said. 'When you get back home you'll have a story to tell.'

In a borrowed white cotton coat, I was smuggled in. No sooner had I stepped into this repository of infamy than I wanted to make a hurried exit. What dreadful exhibits! The shelves along the four walls of a large room were packed with parts from human bodies; I looked at heads sliced vertically and neatly, pickled in glass vats; faces clean-shaven and with stubbles of beard, eyes seemingly alive. In jars, balloon-glasses, punch-bowls and carboys were human innards and outward parts: hearts, livers, lungs, rectums, breasts, wombs, penises and vaginas, all meticulously labelled with ages and dates. And I shuddered to think how the victims died at the hands of the dissectors – medical students and scientists from Pathological and Biological Institutes.

I could die disregarded, from weakness and exposure where I stood. A hand on my left shoulder would mean the short walk to the 'schiessen' shed or death by some other devilish means; a turn to the right was anyone's guess. Whichever way did not bode well.

Behind me passed a procession of flat-carts and barrows loaded with corpses on the way to the incinerator. The acrid smoke from the squat chimney wafted up my nostrils and brought tears to my eyes. I longed to cuff away the irritant, blow my nose, scratch myself, shift my feet. I could piss in my trousers, except that the rules and watching eyes said: 'rühren nicht' – no moving.

Earlier in the morning, Yeo-Thomas had said, shaking my hand: 'Look, old boy, we're all going to bite the dust; whatever happens, spit at the bastards and shout out "God save the King." Nothing to it.'*

* Wing-Commander Yeo-Thomas. SOE code-name 'White Rabbit'. Survived Buchenwald. Changed identity with dead French prisoner and cheated the executioner.

I wasn't particularly attached to the British monarchy. My dear old mum would have said: 'For Christ's sake don't be rude to them, Son. Take your hands out of your pockets, call them Sir and say you're sorry.'

I had time to think of my head schoolmaster, Mr Gale, a heavy-handed disciplinarian. He had little love for me. My school-days at St Brelade's were not happy ones. I preferred to work manually, to do odd jobs to supplement my father's meagre wages. I was a glutton for corporal punishment. Caning had little effect, it was the shillings and pence that mattered most to a family living with tight purse strings.

Mr Gale instilled a feeling of inferiority in me. Because of my height, he would ask, 'Is it cold up there?' My ears were 'big enough to swing on'. I was all skin and bone, 'like a match with the wood scraped off'. I was held in contempt, called 'Faramouse', sometimes 'Shovel' after Chevalier, my father's surname; a 'little bastard', I was. Confused, I wasn't to know that my mother and father, the best of parents, lived together in what people called 'sin'.

At fourteen, on the day I left school, I was warned by Mr Gale: 'You'll never make good.' I stuck my fingers to my nose and ran. If he could see me now, he might have said 'You had it coming to you.' I heard myself muttering: 'You win, Sir! I'm standing in the corner. What's going to be the medicine? Not six of the best and a sore arse for a week, I bet.'

Heavy boots approached, long awkward strides crunching into the gravel. I pissed myself. Held my ground. I could have turned and run, to throw myself against the tall wall of barbed-wire to be electrocuted like others. A grunt, I felt a sharp tug at the sleeve of my coat – 'rechts', I shuffled forward, three paces ahead of the guard, one hand clutching at the waist of my sagging trousers heavy with piss and diarrhoea, my eyes clouded by cold tears and my nose oozing mucus. I passed through the wide gate, performed the ritual salute and, on order, scrambled onto the tail-gate of a canvas-topped truck standing with its engine idling on the road dubbed the 'Karacho,' slang for full speed ahead. Keep on the move. No loafing. Constant warnings to work-parties leaving the camp.

A grinding of the gears and the truck moved away. I squatted on the steel-sheeted floor, my guard sat on a cushion of empty sacks. The wheels jolted over pot-holes and bumped over debris; men at labour, shovelling and shifting rubble, moved aside and took a quick breather as the truck weaved by.

The road was flanked on one side by symmetrical buildings under repair, on the other side by blackened woods with fractured trees festooned with strips of clothing; fat carrion birds were squawking and tearing at bits of charred human remains dangling from burnt branches – trophies from the bombing of the Gustloff Arms Works and the DKW factories. [DKW stood for 'Deutsche Kraftwagen-Werke' – this was an engineering company that made motor-cars, among other things. At Buchenwald DKW was employing slave labour to produce armaments.]

The driver turned at a road junction signposted 'Weimar. Bahnhof Zwei Kilometer.' Without much interest, I had been briefed by a writer of German history that Weimar was a cultural centre in the eighteenth and nineteenth centuries, hallowed by Goethe, Bach, Liszt and other persons of note. I was not yet aware of a vast hinterland of German towns and villages blighted by sites even more squalid, sinister and heinous. Was it possible that there was a place worse than Buchenwald?

It seemed as if I was destined for yet another journey into the dark unknown. At Weimar station, I was conducted through the entrance into a spacious 'Wartesaal' thronging with military personnel and civilians. My tramp-like appearance was hardly a matter for curiosity, the German people were well-acquainted with 'Vogelscheuche'. Where before, in the heaven of Romainville, young girls and women had been attracted to me, girls now stepped aside, their noses in the air. Not surprising. I had seen my reflection in a mirror. I looked a goof; my hair was shorn close to the sides of my head, leaving a tuft in the middle; my jaw was slack, my eyes hollow, I missed an upper tooth, my clothing was encrusted with filth and I smelt.

Hidden away from the public at large, I was allowed to sit behind a stack of crates. Looking through the slats, I could see two podgy women in green overalls ladling out of bowls of steaming soup to an orderly queue. I noted the faces, pinched, tallowed, flat and unsmiling. Had the German people lost confidence in their war? Was the tide about to turn? Would Hitler's wonder weapon which we had heard so much about surface in time to drive back the Allied armies reported to be battling for Cologne?

'Engländer, ja?'

The question startled me. My guard's words were the first communicated to me. They were an odd bunch, our guards, with two sides to their temperaments; on their own they could be reasonable, chatty, even concerned; in a bunch, sullen, spiteful, dangerous and murderous. I answered the question with a nod of my head.

'Haben sie Hunger?'

A fatuous question! My bread ration, normally issued at reveille, had been withheld by the Block-chief; food was not to be wasted on men about to die or departing the camp. Again I nodded.

'Hier warten,' he said, leaving me unattended. I watched him through the open slats, a big man with the rank of sergeant. He went in front of the food queue, picked up two slices of black bread, thrust a bowl under the soup ladle and returned. A tense moment, I thought he was about to torment me; he held the bowl chest high, stirred the contents with a spoon whilst his eyes glanced around and about. Satisfied he had not attracted notice, he put the bread and bowl into my outstretched hands and turned his broad back on me. He muttered something about having his throat slit if some busybody reported him.

The transfer passed quickly. I was hustled into a 'Polizeiwagen' attached to public railway coaches. A narrow corridor, shoulder-width, led me to a one-man cell already occupied by two others, both young men, both in a similar unclean state and affected with respiratory and skin diseases.

We shook hands; despite the cramped space, I was welcomed and offered the half-moon-shaped wooden seat which was attached by brackets to a panel, one meant to fit a very small backside. Nicolas from Paris introduced himself as a medical student; the other, Barnado from Milan, a bank clerk. There were no language barriers, both were fluent in English and we all spoke French. We knew nothing of our destination.

The train moved along the tracks slowly and with spasmodic jolts, rarely more than at a snail's pace with frequent halts when air-raid sirens screamed. Alternating seating arrangements – two standing upright shoulder to shoulder – we were enclosed in a furnace-like heat with only one small aperture above our heads, insufficient for proper ventilation. Perspiration ran into my eyes and down my neck; only once on the journey did we receive a few minutes' relief when the door was opened and, one at a time, we were allowed access to the lavatory and drinking water which was tainted brown and tasted foul.

After endless claustrophobic hours on into the night, we detrained in the city of Leipzig; some seventy men and women, many showing stress, were marshalled into pairs and marched through dark and deserted streets to a prison. Here, in small groups, we were led away by burly trustees to a stone-built outhouse. After removing our clothing, a steaming water-hose was played on our bodies and a high-powered jet disintegrated the solidified matter that had clung to our flesh like limpets to a rock, and the fragments were washed down a drain.

Somewhat restored, we were unexpectedly handed clean clothing, fed bread and soup and bedded down on mattresses in a warm corridor for the remaining hours of the night. When the first light streamed in through the barred windows, a sharp blast from a whistle brought the sleepers to their feet. As anticipated, Leipzig was just one stage of the journey; now, we learned, our next stop was to be Dresden.

We formed a line to receive a mug of thin gruel and a wedge of dry bread with a short stick of rancid 'Wurst'. The march to the station was made through crowded streets along the centre of the thoroughfare. The column was hardly a novelty or an attraction to the population hurrying to their places of work.

Our reception at Dresden, a city as yet untouched by the ravages of war, was significantly less than sympathetic. Its title to grandeur was sadly undermined by its medieval prison and torture chambers and the base and cruel jailers to whom we were introduced. First, everybody was systematically searched; pockets, mouths, even rectums came under careful inspection for hidden pieces of jewellery. The slapping and punching were true to type.

Having escaped the scrutineer unscathed, I groped my way along a badly-lit, well-trodden, flint-flagged passage reeking of damp, the light trailing to a dark shadow with every advancing foot until, further on, I came to a veiled light from an electric bulb set overhead in a grilled aperture; then narrow twisting steps and I was plunged into abysmal darkness to trip over prostrate bodies of men and women sunk in wretchedness.

The black hole, full to the hatches, cramped one's movement; any change of position, a shift of an arm or leg, was a trial and inflamed tempers. Throughout the night I lay inert where I had fallen, listening to the wrangling, the cursing and the weeping.

Dawn, and a thin streak of light coming through a window with small squares of toughened glass thinly coated with black paint revealed a scene that could have been created by Victor Hugo, a cast of 'les misérables' caged in a humid dungeon, befuddled, bruised and bleeding, kneeling, squatting and laid out on a floor sodden with body filth and blood.

Guards stepped on cringing men and women, prodding with the toes of boots, selecting the ablest and unbeaten for transportation and ignoring the lifeless. Having passed the crude audition – by giving a grunt in response to a thump in the chest and a kick in the groin – I was led to a quadrangle, lined up and marched out of the prison, unfed and unwatered.

Two abreast, the long column snaked its way along streets of baroque buildings and – commented someone still lively-minded enough to miss nothing – stores housing fine pottery and works of art. A bridge over the river Elbe and we arrived at a siding; before boarding the train and taking up my place in a cell, I looked back and cursed the city to extinction. Had I foreseen the fury and havoc about to be unleashed on it and its inhabitants from the air, I would have clapped my hands and cried with joy.

Once again, Nicolas, Barnado and I shared the space in the cell. Except for swollen ankles, a cut lip and body bruises, I was without injury. Nicolas sported a black eye and was feverish; Barnado limped and had a sprained wrist. No one had escaped the gloved fist or the steel-toed boot, not even the women.

We were physically spent, spoke little or not at all and politely kept to the seating arrangement. Our destination had been made known: we were on our way to another country – Czechoslovakia. For what reason? No one knew. But it was common knowledge that the Germans were obsessed with shifting their prisoners to and fro over long distances and at great cost in time and manpower.

On arriving in the city of Prague we were taken by surprise. It was a startling reversal from the reception committee in Dresden. Conducted to a wooden barrack building at the station, we were received by a small unit of elderly Wehrmacht soldiers who quietly murmured at our dishevelled and sickly appearance. They demonstrated kindness and tolerance beyond belief! Motherly women in neat overalls dished up bowls of goulash-like soup, bread and sweetened ersatz coffee. The food, more than sufficient, and the hearts of gold set my veins atingle so that even my skin seemed to share in the celebration. Prisoners, perhaps thinking that their nightmares had, at long last, ground to a halt, talked their heads off. Laughing and crying, they were full of gratitude and fell at the knees of the bun-haired women who held their hands and ministered to their wounds.

It was impossible not to shed tears. A rosy-cheeked woman with greying hair who reminded me of my mother put a comforting arm around my shoulders. 'Stärke und Mut' (strength and courage) for a little while longer; the war was almost at an end, no more than a month and I would be free to return home, she said. They were tender words, sharing the grief; but her evaluation of events and her prediction were sadly miscalculated, eight more punishing months were yet to be endured. Millions were destined to die. I was yet to witness a huge slaughter of life far beyond one's imagination, far greater than the horror of Buchenwald.

No more than a stop for breath. In the huge prison of Pankras, a large assembly arriving from many countries asked questions and were fed answers, some inaccurate, some insensitive, some truthful. Few had ever heard the name Mauthausen; those who had described it as a village on the Danube, twenty kilometres from Linz, in Upper Austria. Those who might have had some practical experience of camp Mauthausen were tight-lipped, perhaps with good reason; to have let out the truth about the sector of land behind that village in the back of beyond, a place designed and built for one purpose only, that of exterminating Germany's opponents regardless of political conviction, race or religion

– children not excepted – would have been to strike morbid fear into
people totally oblivious of the evil in store. And I was just one among
two thousand heading for the purgatory of Mauthausen.

It took all morning and early afternoon to fill the railway coaches with
'passengers' who arrived in groups from Pankras prison and elsewhere, a
miscellaneous humanity of men, women, children and infants in arms
seized and abducted directly from their homes, the city-dwellers standing out from the country people, together with those hauled out from
mental hospitals and crèches.

Some families, sound in wind and limb, turned out well; they carried
suitcases, cardboard boxes, panniers and backpacks; the men were
inflated with winter clothing, garment over garment, trilby and
homburg hats, stout boots and leggings; their women were heavy in
furs, padded coats, woolly hats, brogue shoes and high boots; and the
children were well-protected from the bitter cold in knickerbockers,
bloomers, gaiters, bonnets and mittens. Those less prosperous and down
at heel carried little, wore little and shivered in the wind. A headcount of
two thousand five hundred was ticked off as they climbed into the
coaches. Less than a quarter of that number would actually see
Mauthausen camp.

There was ample room to stretch out, even walk about. I shared a
space in a compartment with Nicolas and Barnado, thankful for a seat of
slatted-wood to myself. Our stay in Pankras prison, though brief, had
given us time to patch up our wounds. The guards, of the older
Wehrmacht brigade and less inclined to mete out the violence of their SS
counterparts, had fed us soup and bread twice a day; they had allowed
proper washing and distributed clean clothing into the bargain. Apart
from minor bodily discomforts – diarrhoea, skin rashes and nits and lice
which we had long learned to accommodate – we three were reasonably
rested, with youth on our side and sufficient strength of mind to resist the
inevitable hell lying ahead on which many had been briefed at Pankras.

For all that there was a remarkable calm throughout the carriages.
Those who had joined the convoy at the railway sidings were unaware of
the real danger. Many had been told that they were going to a new
settlement to work on construction, at farming or in their own trade, or
to a retreat if they were incapable of labour because of weakness or old
age; these superfluous groups were what the regime labelled 'nutzlos',
useless people 'taking bread from good German mouths'.

The carriage was comfortably warm. Some people played chess, read
from books and Bibles or engaged in earnest conversation. Infants
sucked contentedly on flush breasts or struggled with spent-looking

breasts. Some toddlers were fed a milky oatmeal from flasks whilst others made do with dry crusts. And those children with vitality, angelic and wide-eyed, played a game of 'cache-cache' in the aisle and under the seats watched by a guard at either end with dead-pan faces. The feeble and the senile seemed dazed and indifferent; and the very old people, grey-bearded men and white-haired women with shrivelled faces and wandering wits, stared at the roof open-mouthed or slept soundly.

Nicolas flirted with a young, bosomy, French-speaking Czech nurse who had been arrested with two of her patients only some hours before. His racy manner, fresh smile and romantic poetry entertained her and diffused the strain of her sudden loss of freedom. There were many girls looking for attention from the younger men, girls with blemished looks, skin diseases, tremors, general ill-health, and victims of assault who had spent many months in detention and isolation. These girls, some no more than half-grown, originated from several eastern countries, from cities and rural regions. Few, if any, would live to see the morning.

Our guards, somewhat reluctant veterans recruited from administrative posts to replace the younger, more forceful and virile SS who habitually rode with the convoys, were alert to a revolt or an escape. Either was feasible. There were those among us with strength enough to tackle our two guards. But the odds against coming out best were less than even. Apart from the incapacitated and the vulnerable who would be abandoned to inevitable reprisals, runaways would have to face the fierce and cruel elements; looking through the windows, one could see nothing but overhanging black clouds, a vast unfriendly and unsheltered no-man's-land buried in deep snow and whipped up by a howling gale. No human being lacking food and protective clothing could survive more than a very short time in a temperature well below freezing point.

The journey was dragging and not without hazards. Whilst several sick and old people cried out for attention, able-bodied men in the first carriages were called out and directed onto the tracks to shovel away snowdrifts in the path of the engine. This was a frequent occurrence. Some men were reported to have escaped, but the time and trouble and risk to the guards of carrying out a search meant that they did not bother. If anyone wanted to commit suicide, said the guards, they weren't going to get in the way.

We were called to order. A senior guard came into the carriage and addressed us with questionable politeness – 'Damen' and 'Herren'. Playfully ruffling the head of a child romping around his legs, he told us that the end of the journey was approaching; we had fifteen minutes to 'mach fertig'. At the station, Mauthausen, we would receive hot soup and a warm bed. Beaming, he walked the length of the carriage, stopping here and there to wish people 'auf wiedersehen' and 'viel Glück'. Some, in ignorance, responded to his slippery sentiments with a hearty 'danke' and a praise to heaven.

That we could expect to be treated to a hot meal and a warm bed was absurd. The announcement was nothing but a callous ploy to suppress alarm and panic – a warning and a signal to the experienced that we were about to meet with a scene of great annihilation.

Chess sets were folded. Men stood up and stretched their legs. Yawning children were dressed and their toys put away. Precious possessions were packed into bags and tied into manageable bundles. Women spent precious seconds brushing and combing their hair. Voices were raised in a babble of languages. Husbands kissed their wives and hugged their children. Strangers shook hands and called for God's protection.

The women and children were required to disembark first; the cripples and the feeble to remain seated, and those who had passed away, mercifully spared from further suffering. On our feet, in single file along the aisle, we waited for the wheels to grind to a halt. Now stationary, the coach hung suspended high over the river Danube; looking through a window, I could see swirling fog straggling the water and enveloping the banks. The wheels rolled slowly forward, a few metres at a time, stopping and restarting in violent jerks, until I could see a crescent-shaped haze of light over a bridgehead.

Step by step, I eased my way onward; behind me came Nicolas and Barnado. About to take my turn and touch down on to the track, I was startled by the sound of a single pistol-shot like that from a starting-gun which in happier times cleared the way to a test of pace and endurance in a sporting event. But in this unequal, ill-fated and drawn-out contest there would be no winners.

My feet found the ground. More shooting, the unmistakable sound of rapid fire from machine-pistols. Whines, screams, cries, curses. Something ugly and fearsome was being unleashed in the front lines. I stumbled in the dark, now looking for a means of escape. There was none. The coaches were surrounded by psychopathic guards with the dreaded twin silver flashes of the SS on their tunic collars. I had seen chaos and panic before, at Compiègne in France and on the journey to Buchenwald – ferocious dogs snarling and snapping, guards striking out with fists, boots and whips indiscriminately – but never did I expect to see such a system of terror tactics deployed against cripples, old people and little children.

The station was shrouded in a freezing fog. Flares and arc-lamps lit up a wide tract in a smoky phosphorescence. Many prisoners were driven by shock and hysteria to run the gauntlet of guns and whips; they broke away, turned round and jumped in the river. Half-blinded by the fluid forming in my eyes and running down my face, I tripped over the rails, discarded baggage and fallen bodies; crazed, paralysed, voiceless and stuttering men and women struggled to get up off their knees, hands reached out begging for help. 'Helfen, bitte helfen!' they pleaded. Children, quaking with cold, stumbled around aimlessly, crying, screaming and calling for 'Mama' and 'Papa'. Guards snatched infants from their mothers' arms and tossed them aside like porters who deliberately display a lack of responsibility in handling packages labelled: WITH CARE. I once read: 'Even in past times of savagery, the most brutish of barbarians were not devoid of human spark for they usually spared the infants. This could not be said of a regime that devoured the most precious ones who roused the greatest pity – innocent children.'

The station platform was stacked high with naked dead, evidently from an earlier transport as the bodies were congealed like carcases of frozen mutton. The clothing had been removed by a selective squad of prisoners already established in the camp; they went about their work with ghoulish zeal, not caring if their victims still had a breath of life. Their rewards were foodstuffs and tobacco found among the possessions; all items of value were collected by an overseer and taken to the coffers of the reigning authority.

Now, formed into a ragged and bewildered column, helped by the ever-flaying whips, the bloodied remnants were moved off. Bodies, dead and scarcely alive, and a great volume of clothing, luggage, boots, shoes, sticks, crutches, irons and artificial limbs were strewn over a wide area, on top of coaches, impaled on barbed-wire and hanging from trees.

Shuffling, limping, cringing, hammered, bleeding and wailing, the column was guided by lanterns and torches along the road bounding the Danube. Like battered whimpering puppies, children clung to the skirts of women, their mothers and their adopted mothers. Behind came the farm-wagons and four-wheeled carts with civilians at the reins of thin, tired-looking horses – 'Droschken' or 'taxis', said our guards scornfully – hired by the camp's administration to carry those too tired to make the journey on foot.

The fog thickening, I could see no sign of inhabitants as we passed through the village, just the dark outline of a long row of buildings to the right of the river. But one could sense a hidden presence behind locked doors and closed shutters, residents who were unable to see what was passing under their noses could easily hear. They knew what was going on.

Under pressure and continuous harassment, our numbers were depleted with every metre advanced along the narrow corridor;

prisoners dropped prostrate or were struck down to perish at the wayside. There was a halt for re-grouping. A short, twisting, slippery gradient, a high bank on one side, a deep ditch overlooked by a clump of bracken and tall trees on the other – a gravepit for the sluggards and the flounderers, convulsed, wild-eyed, bruised, bawling, half-naked and barefooted loose children among them, breaking though a bank of fog in their ones and twos.

A few minutes to piece myself together. One more corner to turn. I still retained all my clothing, but I was chilled to the bone. I counted myself among the fortunate; except for lacerations to my face and hands and a gash to my right thigh, I had escaped the brunt of the violence. Nicolas had a limp and a sprained wrist; Barnado was bleeding from the head and nose, nothing more; injuries of little consequence in comparison to the profusion of crushed bones, whip cuts, dog bites and bullet wounds.

It was difficult to hold fast to one's feet on the icy incline. I struggled forwards on all fours only to slither rearward when frantic hands grabbed my ankles. Mercifully, we were spared the whips, the guards were digging their own toes into the ground and finding it more manageable to walk backwards. At long last, and with the column drastically pruned, we came to level terrain bounded by dense woodland and outspreading snow-covered fields. A glassy skyline beyond, an elongated grey solid shape on rising ground and in half-light came into being; little talked about, only half-understood, I was looking at a huge, hideous blot, a dead-end on a portion of Austrian land, an architectural creation of extreme wickedness, 'Das Konzentrationslager, Mauthausen'.

PART 2

Mauthausen was to leave scars: the war was to end, but only after many years did I feel able to return there. Even then, as I have related, my original intention was not to visit the camp. Mary did not at first want me to go there at all, even though our holiday had brought us to Austria, and I knew that I owed it to my wife not to inist on it. Only Mary, with her long-standing tolerance, understood my temperament. Few women could have lived unflinchingly with the variation in my moods, but Mary had coped with the mess I was in after the war. It was she who had confronted the reality of what had happened to me. Most people, perhaps understandably, did not want to know about the nightmares which had gone on in Europe. They wanted the war to be over, and for there to be business as usual. Feeling that my problems were very much my own, I steered clear of marriage for more than eight years after Mauthausen. I didn't think it right to impose my problems on a wife. I was happy to be in the company of women for the briefest of unions whilst living independently.

My reintroduction into civilization fell somewhat short of my expectations. Incredibly, there were times when I regretted my return. Flown to England courtesy of the American army, who treated me liberally, with compassionate understanding and without counting the cost of a boarder in their hands, I quickly became exasperated by British officialdom; first, when I was abruptly removed from a friendly cottage-type hospital in the peace and quiet of the countryside to a large institution for incurables and the terminally ill.

'Be grateful,' I was told, 'it's far better than the place you've been at, by all accounts'. It was put to me straightforwardly and I understood. Unable to procure the longed-for privacy and medical care for lack of pounds, shillings and pence, I was obliged to accept charity. I was fed three times a day, bathed and given a book to read. I was not ungrateful, but I was tired of the bedlam and the emotional disturbances of unfortunate people on every side of me. I had some physical discomfort, a loss of power in my legs, but I was neither neurotic nor mentally unbalanced.

I had not informed my mother or any member of my family of my return from the grave. My intention had been first to rehabilitate myself, to put back the five stones I had lost and to see my hair grow to its normal thickness and length. The institution with its system of rigid rules did not help me to improve. I did not believe the inmates were ever meant to be let loose on the streets, and I resolved to extricate myself from the trap. I made an urgent appeal to my sister, the wartime evacuee from Jersey island to Rochdale in Lancashire.

I was tied down to an invalid carriage, a ridiculous 'granny' Bath-chair with two large wheels at the back of the basketwork chassis and a small one at the front steered by a long rod with a T-shaped handle. But I was able to move to a warm and loving pied-à-terre with neighbours, run-of-the-mill Rochdale people like the corner grocer and baker, brightening up my days. 'You need fattening up, lad, those daft buggers at Welfare will give you nowt, not even the skin off a bloody rice pudding, they won't.' Young cotton mill girls were an inspiration too, knocking at my sister's street door and bringing me hard-to-come-by eggs and fruit, and pies baked by 'Mum'. They offered to wheel me out to the park and, after a while, made passes and aroused my passions, breathing fresh life into me with the kind of kisses I hadn't experienced since leaving Romainville.

But it was those 'buggers' at Welfare, the 'gauleiters' of bumbledom who gave me the hump. The to-ing and fro-ing, the waiting in line, the form-filling, the fatuous questions, all for a pint of milk, a loaf of bread, a jar of malt extract and a pittance in a warrant to be cashed at the post office, not enough to cover what my sister was paying out.

Perseverance and strength of will put my wheel-chair up 'for sale'. I took to a pair of crutches, an event ruled unrealistic three months before, and, before my first Christmas of liberty, I was standing on my two feet unaided.

1946, intended to be a year of high hopes and long-dreamed-of independence, was to prove a stumbling-block to my ambitions. Walking, and with new energy, I could no longer make demands on my sister's loving devotion without making a contribution to the house-keeping; she had troubles of her own, three young children to clothe and feed and a wayward husband. I went about looking for work; alas, I hadn't expected to be frowned down and have doors shut in my face; I wasn't asking for a position of cardinal importance, just any work of an honest nature.

Who had been my previous employer?

Did I have references?

Had I been in the services?

No, Sir! I had not been a soldier or in that line. No, Sir! I had no references. If I may explain, Sir, my last place of employment was in Jersey, the war and all that ...

What doing?

Hotel work, Sir.

Catering, eh? When was that?

Er ... some time back, Sir. Summer of 'forty, thereabouts.

... Are you trying to tell me you've not been employed since?

I haven't been exactly idle, Sir. I've done the odd day digging trenches, mending roads, stuff like that. Not by choice, Sir! Sort of conscripted labour.

Where? What do you mean?

In camps, Sir. If I may explain ...

I became angry with myself for being spinelessly submissive, for crawling and trying to prove myself worthy of a trial to 'guvnors' sitting there smugly. There were times when I wanted to reply to the thumbs down with 'Bollocks, stick the job up your fat arse, matey.' But giving lip was short sighted in a town which was not all that big.

A lucky break came, sadly of a very short duration. The Rochdale postmaster was a more congenial fellow. 'Start tomorrow,' he said. 'We'll ask the authority in Jersey to send on a character reference.'

Sorting letters wasn't the career I wanted on a permanent basis but it was an opening. However, any hope that the postmaster might overlook the need to delve into my past was dashed by an urgent call to his office. He was apologetic, but answerable to Head Office. My old adversaries of the Jersey police had decreed me a person unfit to be employed where the Royal Mail was at risk.

More angry than bitter, I travelled the ten miles to Manchester and came upon a vacancy at the Queen's Hotel for a hall-porter. References, it appeared, were not obligatory, more important was an undertaking to share my tips with the head-porter. This compromise suited my purpose; the remuneration was not the priority, not for the time being, I was fed and happy to be in work.

Destiny struck me yet another blow. The hotel manager, a pompous man with a pretty daughter, was, I soon discovered, neurotically affected by the sight of uniformed American army personnel frequenting the guests' lounge and reading-room and wandering around the bedroom corridors at all hours. White and of high rank he could tolerate, but those 'darkies' lounging in the plush chairs and sofas and drinking with 'tarts' in the bar he found 'highly objectionable'.

Taking me aside, he said it was my job to evict them as discreetly as possible. The order was offensive. Tens of thousands owed their lives

and freedom to the American army; white and black soldiers alike had
made huge sacrifices for a common good, regardless of race or colour.
Had it not been for our American allies, I told the man, it would have
been men in German uniforms strutting around the rooms and corridors
of his hotel and making a play for his daughter.

Back on the streets and idle, I was befriended by a lady publican with
free access to the bar. Drinking seemed to blot out the teething troubles I
was experiencing in achieving any advancement. Between binges, I kept
telling myself that brushing away all obstacles and making good was but
a short step away.

The life of a 'roué', although enticing to a young man of my age who
had missed out on the companionship and the romantic love of women,
was fraught with danger in a small community. Seducing girls – the
prettiest were to be found behind 'cosmetics' in Boots the chemist – with
over-protective fathers was dicey enough; but an affair with an attractive
and voluptuous young officer in the Women's Auxiliary Air Force whose
husband was serving in the military police overseas risked causing a
scandal, perhaps a thrashing or worse.

'The husband's a major,' my sister said. 'He stands at six feet six, an
athlete, plays rugby, too.'

'Make yourself scarce before he comes on leave,' was fair advice. A
last fling around the town, a night on the tiles, tears and then, with
my sister's blessing and a few pounds in my pocket, I boarded a
London-bound train from Manchester, not without feeling that I was
alienating myself from kindly people who, despite my having achieved
notoriety within the circles of purity, wished me luck and good
health.

I was relieved to find a compartment to myself where the workings of
my mind would go uninterrupted by idle chatter from fellow travellers. I
needed room to think hard. I could have returned to my home in Jersey
where my mother eagerly awaited me, but I had already warned her that
I would not be able to live at ease with an administration responsible for
injustices and contributing to war crimes.

I knew my most immediate want, and that was to go to Paris and seek
to put into effect the pledge I made to Lucy and, if she was alive, to bring
into existence the wild and intoxicating images we had built into our
restless minds. But until I came into funds, Lucy, Paris and the odd and
wonderful friends of the Romainville era lay far over the horizon, out of
my reach.

With all my worldly possessions packed into one small case I walked
through Euston Station's vast shell and out into the streets. Where to
now? That was the question I put to myself as I drifted along without

any definite aim. I had the advantage of the weather. It was midsummer. I glanced at the passers-by, all going on their way seemingly with some purpose in life. The cafés and public-houses were thronged and inviting on a warm evening; courting couples were seated at pavement tables under coloured umbrellas in lively conversation and canoodling. I stopped and bought a glass of lemonade-shandy and sat among the unpaired pint drinkers to eat the cheese and tomato sandwich that had travelled in my pocket all the way from Rochdale.

Refreshed, I followed a sign pointing to Tottenham Court Road, Charing Cross Road and Leicester Square, the hub of the metropolis. There were long queues outside the cinemas and theatres; from a vast hoarding, Humphrey Bogart looked down over Piccadilly with a smoking pistol in his hand; and on the corner of Haymarket another presentation, a documentary-short asked: 'Hitler Lives?'

Sweating buskers were scooping up pennies thrown by people marking time in the queues; a wild-looking bearded gospeller preached on the depravity of human nature to a heckling audience; a ragged sandwich-boarded stroller predicted the end of the world; taxis honked; swanky cars cruised around the statue of Eros; and pretty tarts loitering on street corners were leggy, busty and not for me. It was a mysterious, loony, kinky, erotic, roisterous city full of suspicions. I had not come to stay.

The appetizing smells wafting out of kitchen ventilators in Soho restaurants were inviting. I had to be frugal. The little money in my pocket would stretch to a room in a cheap bed and breakfast house for no more than two nights. I was reasonably confident of finding a hotel that would give me a live-in job. And I was neither a picker nor a chooser.

Again, it was the long gap in my life that bunkered my chances, even for the most servile of work. I resorted to untruths and deception. 'Yes, Sir, I have some military service, now back on civvy street, Sir. I know about catering work, Sir. My references? In the post, Sir.' Hatched-up stories granted me a short respite. I washed dishes, ate left-overs and rested my head, usually on a primitive contraption in a damp basement next to the drains.

I had learned to have self-control, but I could not bear with the rigmarole found in the plush hotels of Mayfair and Park Lane. The humiliation and bullying to which the low grades were subjected by the head men, invariably of German or Italian origin, before the start of work each morning smacked too closely of a régime of the past: the roll-call, straight ranks, 'cut the cackle', a deathly hush; the inspection, finger-nails, shirt-cuffs, collar, back of ears, breath, hair and shoes.

Empty pockets. Penniless, I was a vagrant, sleeping under the stars on a bench beside the Thames at Westminster and on the grass in the Royal Parks. When morning came, the grass was fresh and green. I could smell the flowers, watch the birds and listen to their songs. Nothing had grown in the filth of Mauthausen, not a weed, and the birds, judging wisely, had avoided the place.

I was not hungry. The restaurants of Soho provided me with all the food I needed from the pig bins outside their back doors, provisions which I would have considered 'table d'hôte' in Mauthausen; yesterday's bread rolls, potatoes baked and boiled, vegetables and fruit. Back on my pitch, wherever I chose, I took breakfast and dinner in a deck-chair under the shade of a tree or in a shelter protected from a raw wind and watched an unbalanced world go by.

In the late autumn and with winter coming on, my daytime hangout was a warm public library or museum. Before dossing down for the night in the waiting-room of a mainline railway station I was drawn to cinemas, gaining entry through back doors. War films I watched two and three times around and quietly cheered when the enemy was skittled to the ground. These violent celluloid spectaculars fired my imagination; watching the play-acting, the destruction and the blood spilled was all too realistically manufactured. I was transfixed, almost intoxicated and thirsting for more.

Watching films depicting warlike aggression became an obsession and played havoc with the concepts in my mind. Without company, and now perhaps an unsociable person, I began to think aloud, to talk to myself and to laugh in my sleeve. I was aware of people staring at me and giving me a wide berth as they passed by. I troubled no one, nor did I interfere with anyone's peace and quiet; except, perhaps, and not intentionally, those delegated to authority who seemed to go out of their way to harass me at every opportunity.

Falling foul of the constabulary patrolling London's streets, I was forcefully taken by the arm and marched to police cells at Bow Street, Savile Row and Marylebone. In the mornings, unwashed, unshaved and tousled, I followed habitual drunks and prostitutes into the dock. Magistrates peered at me with distaste; the dialogue between 'His Honour' and the arresting constable was much of a monotonous muchness:

'Wandering abroad, your Honour. Of no fixed address.'

'Loitering with intent, your Worship. Attempted to abscond on the way to the police station. Stamped on my foot, he did.'

'Charge of indecency, your Honour. Seen to urinate behind a bus shelter. Gave a false name, said he was Fritz Goering, son of Hermann, your Honour.'

'Habitual vagrancy, your Worship. Of no fixed address. The prisoner was abusive, called me a c-u-n-t and said Hitler was a better f-u-c-k-i-n-g man than you'll ever be.'

'So, he's known to the Courts, is he, Constable?'

'Yes, Sir. Jersey born. Known to the police on that island, your Honour. Several convictions. Deported from the island in 1941, under a cloud I understand, your Honour. Incarcerated in some internment camp in France from what I can gather.'

I winced at the inexactitudes put forward but, in every case, held my tongue and kept my mouth shut. Pay five shillings, ten, twenty. I could not pay. Seven days, fourteen, one month, I could do and did. Taken in a black Maria, I became familiar with places like Wormwood Scrubs and Brixton jail, to mix with people who were compatible and with whom I could easily communicate, not all out-and-out scoundrels or evildoers, but good people oppressed, misjudged and stamped on by guardians of the law in blue uniforms, in wing-collars and with wigs.

Remanded 'in custody for a medical report', I was stripped naked, handed a nightshirt and put to bed in a dormitory with others — crackpots and those suspected of having a screw or two loose. Men in white coats noted my habits, washed and shaved me, accompanied me to the lavatory and, at feeding times, refused me a knife and fork.

I clowned, poked fun at the attendants and made an exhibition of myself, speaking in Germanic gibberish, and replying to orders with a hand raised outwards and a 'Heil Hitler', which did not amuse those watching over me.

Under escort, I was taken to the psychological department at St George's Hospital to see a head-shrinker who was a Jew and had experience in treating soldiers suffering from mental ailments caused by the traumas of battle. I was somewhat out of his sphere, he admitted. He was friendly, understanding, even sympathetic. But, studying my prison report, it wasn't favourable. I had been uncooperative, abusive, and my behaviour had been irrational, he said.

I was clear-headed and canny, realizing I could be declared certifiable with a stroke of a pen. My mode of behaviour, I explained, was one way of getting back at authority; I had been harassed, intimidated and disciplined by bigots for too long; perhaps I was 'odd', but my mind was perfectly sound; those who had judged me otherwise were bloody-minded and power-drunk, I said without mincing words.

Given a cup of tea and a sandwich, I was then put on show for a panel of students, young men and women. They sat on chairs two rows deep and gaped at me as if I were a freak or a 'something' from another planet. Pencil and paper to hand, they grilled me on the subject of concentration camps. Did I have bad dreams? Could I describe them? What was life like within the camps? Did I actually see people killed? How many? In what manner? How did I come to be a survivor? One eager beaver wanted to know about the details of the gas chamber at Mauthausen, down to the construction, the dimensions and the capacity.

I answered the simple but pointless questions patiently, and in a few short words. Pressed to enlarge, give a blow-by-blow account, I prickled and showed my resentment at being used as a guinea-pig. This displeased the group and frustrated their curiosity or their studies. My obstinacy, I was told, was not helping to solve my problem.

Returned to prison, I spent one night in my hospital bed, a further two in an ordinary cell and was then, to my astonishment, set loose back on the streets to pursue my nomad existence, sleeping rough and feeding as before, on restaurant kitchen-waste which I found more inviting and less monotonous than the prison swill.

A turning point was presented to me out of the blue. I came across a Canadian whom I had met in Wormwood Scrubs who said he had fought the war with the army in Europe. Down on his luck, he had gone into what he described as the 'field of entertainment', busking at a pitch near the Lyceum Theatre shared alternately by magicians, quick-sketch-artists, escapologists and aspiring poets.

My new-found friend's act was bizarre and out of the ordinary. He 'swallowed' razor-blades, chewed on glass and fastened the folds of his stomach flesh with large safety-pins. His derring-do drew the crowds – passers-by, sightseers and theatre-goers. My function was to pick up the coins thrown into the arena whilst keeping an eye open for plodding police.

With an occasional matinée and two regular performances in the evening, the rake-off allowed us to eat regularly with an occasional beer; at night we shared a private cubicle with two beds in a better-than-average doss-house where, for three extra pence, we had the use of a washroom with hot water, soap and a towel.

Our amicable partnership, was destined not to last. 'Canada' – I never learned his name – was not a well man; on the downward path, he had respiratory troubles, his lungs wheezed and his cough came in fits and starts. Inevitably, the number of performances was reduced to one nightly until the final curtain fell and he collapsed, haemorrhaging from the mouth, at the foot of the statue of Sir Henry Irving.

Watched by a sympathetic audience that dipped deeper into pockets than usual, suspecting a razor-blade had severed a vital artery, the prostrate Canadian was removed to hospital by ambulance. Accompanying him on the journey, I waited in a corridor for news, but not really expecting to be told of his demise. A nurse brought me a brown paper bag filled with possessions expressly bequeathed to me; a purse with several one pound notes and silver coins, a half-guinea piece, his wrist-watch, a tie-pin that proved to be gold, his fountain-pen and his silver ring.

This windfall, regrettable in its origin, would be put to good account. I disposed of the valuable items. Had my late friend known to what worthy cause the extra money would be put he would have given me the 'thumbs up'. First I made some purchases: a suit in an outfitter's in the Charing Cross Road, a shirt, a tie and a pair of suede shoes, all second-hand and of good quality. At Waterloo Station, I had a shave, a trim-up and a shampoo in the barber's shop. I was a man rejuvenated.

Cock-a-hoop, confident and prudent, I hitched a ride to the coast. Just a short stretch of water, a couple of hours of sailing, separated me from France. In my excitement, I had not given a thought to a piece of paper endorsed with a signature of authority allowing me to leave England. This impasse was easily overcome; a couple of drinks with a French seaman who listened to an emotional tale and my pining for Paris and ten shillings in his pocket got me on board his ship.

Paris

'Cherchez la femme.' Three words that I had oft-times repeated. Landing at Calais, I quickly became intoxicated by the tangs and tones of the country closest to my heart. The air was thick with garlic and Gauloises. I wanted to skip along the cobbled streets, I was so full of joy. I had an urge to shake hands with everybody and anybody and shout out 'Vive la France!' And I was just that much closer to Lucy. Was it four years, or was it five since we were parted?

I hitched a ride to Arras; another lift in a van carrying a load of spicy 'alimentation' took me all the way to Paris. On the road, we weaved through the city of Compiègne, passing the gates of the former transit camp that had claimed a huge loss of lives – my stepping stone to Germany and Buchenwald. I wanted to say to the driver: 'Slow down a bit, mon vieux, d'you know about this place?' But the man's foot was hard down on the accelerator, in a hurry to get to the depot and unload. A woman and a 'good table' awaited him.

Munching on a stick of new bread with Camembert cheese, I tried to engage the man on the matter of my objective. His answer was to shrug his shoulders; Paris, he said, was a vast place to look for someone at random after so many years. He was no help, too intent on preaching about the country's economy, political unrest and the strikes for workers' improvements. 'Demandez des nouvelles au poste de police,' he said as he wished me luck and set me down on the Pont Neuf bridge.

A piece of advice I was unlikely to take up. I shouted out 'bien des remerciements' and stopped to gaze down into the rippling waters of the Seine before crossing the bridge to the Rue de Rivoli. People darted by, hurrying from shopping and their places of work in the early evening. Clutching my one small suitcase, I squeezed through the dense traffic and ambled along the back streets of Les Halles. 'Where now?' I asked myself.

I stopped to linger in a bar, trying not to look out of place. I ordered a glass of red wine and ate a hard-boiled egg. I felt exhilarated by my surroundings. The place was alive; dolled-up girls, dandy-looking men, the ridiculous and the pretentious, cast much in the same mould I was privileged to meet in Romainville, were full of chatter. I listened to the banter, the wit, the vulgarity and, draining my second glass of 'rouge', laughed with the company.

I was directed to a 'pension' in the Rue des Halles, a tall narrow building with green paint peeling away from the window shutters and small washing hanging out over the window-sills. It was what I could afford in the way of accommodation. Despite its seedy-looking appearance, the place proved to be friendly and cheerful – no questions were asked. A small room in the attic was cheap and clean; it suited my purpose down to the ground.

I slept soundly. In the morning, after a hot shower, I descended into the breakfast room to be served a large cup of good coffee and freshly-baked croissants. Optimistic, 'avec la joie de vivre', I deliberated over my best course of action. My cash at hand would perhaps allow me three weeks to find Lucy or a clue to her whereabouts, a few days longer if I was to make every sou work hard.

But how best to go about my all-important mission in this strange city? All the memoranda which I had written down with Lucy's help had been confiscated at Compiègne camp before leaving for Germany. Little or nothing remained in my head, except I remembered saying over Lucy's tears, as if it were only yesterday: 'I will find you, my darling, even if I have to tramp every street, every boulevard, and every avenue.'

'Look for Paulette if you can't find me, I will never be far from her,' Lucy told me. I had only a vague recollection of Paulette living at a good address near to the Champs-Élysées, on an avenue beginning with the letter M. The proprietor lent me a street map. I found the avenues, Montaigne, Marigny, and Miromesnil all stretching over a great length; it would take me a lifetime to knock at every door and ask about an attractive blonde of forty or more called Paulette, known too by the pet name 'Poupée'. Another problem: Paulette had feared that her apartment would be taken over by some top-ranking German; she had sworn that nothing would induce her to return to a home made unclean.

There were others I might bump into. The playboy, Khalid, would greet me like a long-lost brother; he would help, even support me if need be. I could depend on Louise Beriot – she would want to be told about Marc Troska. Colette, with whom I had a fleeting and memorable affair, might still be dancing in night-clubs. Of course, I was assuming they were all alive.

Undaunted, I first walked the fashionable districts, the Rue de Rivoli, the Champs-Élysées and the gardens of the Tuileries where Lucy had formerly spent many hours of her leisure time. In the evenings, into the late hours, I rubbed shoulders with the smart set, peering into restaurants, the foyers of hotels, and I stood outside theatres and under the soft lights of night-haunts. I watched cruising limousines, smart roadsters and taxicabs taking on and setting down their fares. I stared at faces, at bill-boards, asked questions of commissionaires and stage-door keepers. I drew nothing, 'rien de rien'.

After spending a week and a good number of francs around the artistic quarter of Montmartre and imbibing cheap wine in sleazy clubs I was coming to the end of my resources. Lying in bed after another tiring and fruitless day, I was rapt in thought, wondering if I could get a menial job without credentials; the French were more tolerant and less likely to insist on detail providing one worked well. It was that or a reluctant return to England in much the same way as I had come to Paris.

I was brain-fagged, about to fall asleep when a knock came at the door. It was a timid knock, a woman's touch. I sat up, switched the bedside lamp on and called out 'entrez'.

My visitor opened the door, first put her head through and asked to be excused for her 'effronterie'. I recognized her as one of the young tarts I had seen coming and going. She was a pretty thing with lean legs and blonde hennaed hair short-cropped. She said a chirpy 'allo' and set down a bottle of red wine and two glasses on a side-table. She thought I was looking 'triste' and wanting company.

I could see it wasn't a cheap bottle of wine. I put a hand up and stopped her from pulling the cork. 'Wait!' I said. 'Pas si vite!' I was abrupt, to the point. I told her that I couldn't afford either the wine or her services, 'même pas pour un sou'.

She put her hands on her hips, gave a pained look and pouted her lips. 'Ah, dites donc!' she hissed. I had some 'front' to think she had come to do 'le business'. And on the cheap! It was purely a gesture coming from the heart, 'rien que'. She'd heard that I had come to Paris on some blind

venture. I was looking down in the mouth and she wondered if she could
help.

I quickly apologized. I was tired and a little melancholy, I admitted.
She nodded and smiled. 'It's not grave,' she said in English. She took the
bottle and grasped it between her knees. The cork came out with a loud
'plop'.

I needed to talk. She sat down on the edge of the bed and listened. I
told her about my mission without going into the story at length.
Paulette, if she could be located, was the best lead, I said. I described her
as I had known her at Romainville, down to the last detail. And
somewhat tactfully, putting Paulette's known vocation in a nice way,
'Elle était une fille de joie dans les meilleurs cercles, avec le surnom
"Poupée",' I said.

The girl puffed. 'Une véritable princesse! A ritzy tart, eh,' she said in
English.

Romainville meant nothing to Simone. During the Occupation, she
lived with her parents in Orléans. As a very young girl she had been in
the thick of things, the family uprooted, a brother imprisoned and an
uncle deported to Germany never to return. She remembered how very
close she had come to being raped by the retreating Germans after the
liberation of Paris and because of this, and other reasons related to the
Occupation, her door was closed to all that was 'Boche'.

Simone recognized the importance attached to my search for
Paulette's whereabouts. She knew one or two women who 'worked' the
prime districts, 'des femmes de la classe champagne et caviar', she
quipped. There was just a chance something or someone would turn up
by asking around.

My flagging spirits were re-kindled. Simone offered her help in more
ways than one and, without a sense of shame, I gratefully accepted. I
became a 'maquereau', a kept man for want of a better phrase. She was
twenty-one and I was pushing twenty-nine. She paid my rent, bought
me food and was generous with her affections. She was my companion
and guide to Paris as Lucy had intended to be. Hand in hand, we took
strolls along the river banks, sat in the wondrous setting of the Tuileries
gardens, climbed the Eiffel Tower and drank 'thé à l'anglaise' among the
'beau monde' in a café on the Champs-Élysées. Visiting the Sacré-Coeur,
a lump came to my throat; the magnificent monument had been a
sparkling beacon on the horizon whenever Lucy and I sneaked up to the
vast attic under the roof of the building in Romainville to gaze out of a
skylight window in dreamy expectation.

In old Montmartre, I was reminded of the incorrigible custodian,
Corporal Weismann, who spent most of his off-duty hours wolfing up

the trollops in the seedy clubs and, as was his habit, returning to the Fort three sheets to the wind to give Marc Troska and me a blown-up account, curves and all, of the beautiful girls he'd 'figged'. Sitting at a table in a cellar with Simone among a collection of oddbodies, cranks, tarts and 'pansies' in unconventional dress, I had a feeling that the ghost of Weismann was breathing down my neck. Nevertheless, I was having a carefree time, singing at the top of my voice to accordion music, chatting across tables littered with bottles, glasses and spilling ashtrays; through thick yellowish Gauloise smoke I watched the dancers on the cramped floor – poker-faced, clean-shaven and bearded men with stationary feet but restless hips – and I wondered where all these natives, 'gens de peu', had hung out in the dark days of the Occupation.

Three months passed. Nothing had developed. I talked to many people who had been incarcerated in the prisons of Paris, and found two had spent a day and night in Romainville immediately before the German evacuation. They were of no help. I tried a bureau set up to trace missing persons without valid names and former addresses – many prisoners adopted aliases for good reasons. Even the trusted Louise Beriot was 'une personne inconnue' – the result was negative. I recognized no one from the albums of photographs I was shown.

Simone didn't appear to be making any progress. But I became suspicious that she wasn't trying. She had grown complacent with our arrangement, talking about looking for better accommodation where we might live 'en ménage'. She had come to address me in terms of genuine affection – 'ma pomme d'amour' and 'mon chou-fleur'. She even intimated marriage and a wish to give up her profession for work with a little dignity, like a job as a secretary or receptionist.

I was wary. I did not want her hurt. Living together without the ties of marriage was acceptable to me, but not indefinitely. I was fond of her; she was attractive, charming, stylish, and with a good sense of humour. Her chosen way of life did not trouble me; indeed, I was more than grateful for it. But Lucy was the one closest to my heart and I had to determine whether she was alive or dead.

Unexpectedly, I was struck with a real cause for concern. Try as I might, I couldn't shake off the fear that I was sickening: the stairs to my room were getting more difficult to climb without pausing for breath; I had dizzy bouts, little desire for food, sleep did not come easily and when I awakened I was bathed in sweat. And I had an irritable cough.

'Rien que la grippe, chéri,' Simone said. I feared it was more than flu. I was put in mind of the thousands of concentration camp survivors who were struck down with fatal diseases that had lain dormant over the years. Left alone when Simone went about her business, I was morbidly

struck with the thought that I was not long for this world. I could not
burden Simone with my problem. I had it in mind to make my adieus by
letter and take off, during her absence, for Jersey to be with my mother
and sisters to live out my final days. Sunk in gloom, I even thought about
a burial place, not for the first time; given the choice, I would ask to be
buried among friends in the garden of silence at camp Mauthausen, from
where an inner voice often told me I had no proper claim to have left.

Simone was watchful. She arranged with the kindly 'patron' to put me
in a room on the ground floor. She pampered me, fed me delicacies and
prescribed a 'curative' drink each night before an early to bed routine. I
took things easier; more outings in the fresh air of the Tuileries gardens,
visits to exhibitions and museums, less time spent in smoke-filled dens.
But I had yet to pay homage at Romainville, a mere six kilometres away.
Simone expressed her wish to accompany me but I elected to wait until I
found someone who had the right to share in my fond, but often soured,
memories of that unique period in my prime.

Then came the first piece of news I did not want to hear. It was almost
a year since, unauthorized, I had set foot in France. Simone was slow to
tell me for fear of impairing my moderate recovery. Khalid was dead,
shot in some feud less than two years after his release from Romainville.
What tragic irony! For days I hung about brooding, thinking of the
handsome, gold-toothed, French-Arab who often vied good-
humouredly with Marc Troska for the pick of the women of the Fort and
who first led me to Lucy. Louise Beriot was also dead. The priggish
'imprenable' who eventually capitulated to the charms of Marc Troska
had been employed at the SS research institute at Schloss Mittersill in
Austria. She died on her return to Paris.

It was the appropriate time for what Simone called 'une petite distract-
ion'. With the month of August came 'les grandes vacances'. The whole
of Paris, it seemed, was shutting up shop and taking off for the seaside.
Simone shopped for new clothes; she bought me an informal rig-out,
light-coloured flannels, short-sleeved shirts, a navy-blue blazer, deck-
shoes and a pair of bathing-trunks, this an item I hadn't worn since the
last balmy days of June 1940 on the beach at Beaumont before the
German encroachment, a beach, like all others on the island, that was to
be posted 'Verboten'.

Before leaving on the six-hundred-kilometre journey by train to Cap-
Ferrat, near Bordeaux on the Atlantic coast, Simone put a wad of
banknotes into my hand. It was a great deal of money, much more than I
had ever handled. It crossed my mind, for a moment or two, that the
money was what was termed by the guardians of morality the 'wages of
sin'. I had never once questioned Simone's affairs, nor did she ever

discuss them with me. It was an agreeable understanding. Chance had brought us together, a blessing for me; without her love, without her generosity and her untiring patience I might have been picked up dying in some Paris gutter. Thinking back, my very preservation, it seemed, I owed to women. It was the brave women of Romainville, women from all classes and of all make-ups, the virtuous and those with human weaknesses, who formed a strong bond of friendship with one another, who put inspiration into the men, who cried and mourned with and for us, who entertained us and who made us laugh. It was the women who enhanced and beautified what was, in other respects, a forbidding place. It was Lena, a young Czech prisoner-nurse who did duty in the SS military hospital in camp Mauthausen, who sustained me with sufficient food, at great risk, to eke out the last vital days before the liberation; and it was my caring sister in Rochdale who came to my rescue at a time when my brain was in danger of clouding.

A whole month in the sunshine with bracing sea air was a shot in both arms. I came back to Paris full of zest, anxious to resume my search for that elusive face in the crowds. My health was on the mend, or so I thought, and my confidence was restored. I was satisfied, given time, I would find and recognize one mortal in the frenzied metropolis who had come away from the Fort alive.

It was Simone who broke the news. Not with the enthusiasm I would have wished. I was not to burst into a song and dance, the information gathered came from an indirect source, she warned. I could see she'd be better pleased if the news proved erroneous; her breasts heaved and she was ready to cry. Someone answering my description – a blonde, attractive, elegant, fortyish and, to give credence, with the nick-name 'Poupée' – had been traced to an address across the river near to the Quai de Grenelle in the fifteenth district.

I came out of the shower and started to dress. 'What does she do?' I asked Simone tentatively.

'Comme métier?'

'Yes, like work.'

She lowered her eyes. She sighed. 'Like me. La même chose.'

That was the answer I hoped I wouldn't hear. It implied disappointment, even worse. Paulette had promised many times never to return to her former life of laxity. She and Lucy had planned to set up in business together; they guessed the world of 'haute couture' would boom after the years when women had been impoverished and forced to improvise with inferior and cast-off materials. I had been invited to take part in that dreamy enterprise. Something untoward had happened!

With mixed feelings, I walked into the street with Simone to await a taxi. Flustered, she clutched my arm. 'Reviens comme tu veux,' she said, eyes flowing with tears.

We stood on the pavement. 'Soyez tranquille,' I said, taking her in my arms. 'I'll come back.'

I climbed into the back seat of the taxi. She put her head through the open window and I kissed her. The taxi drew away. 'Sois prévenu,' she called. 'Paulette, si c'est elle, a une blessure.'

Paulette with a wound or an injury! That was something I was unprepared for. Should I have been surprised? Few could claim to have come away from a concentration camp completely unscathed. Chronic bad health, missing limbs, disfigurement, obsessional fears and mental instability were all common complaints.

The driver pulled up in a quiet tree-lined street, outside a three-storey apartment building with narrow shaded balconies from which greenery hung. At first glance, the building had an air of privilege about it. Setting my feet down on to a cobbled pavement, I paid the driver and pushed open a pair of tall ornamental gates embellished with gilt paint, walked under a striped awning and along a narrow path neatly bordered with late autumn flowers. Trembling with emotion, I stopped at a white-painted door, ran a comb through my hair, adjusted my tie and pulled at a black handle that said 'Sonner'.

Broken footsteps approached. The door was opened by a part-uniformed concierge, with his own 'blessure', I was quick to notice, a surgical boot to his left leg. I said: 'Monsieur, bonjour,' gave him my name and inquired about 'Mademoiselle Paulette'.

He nodded, wrinkled his brow and scratched his chin. For one awful moment I thought I had come on a fool's errand. He looked me up and down and then blurted: 'Tiens, tiens! Monsieur! L'Anglais de Romain-ville!' And all in one breath, whilst I waited on the scrubbed doorstep, he told me what he had learned from 'Mademoiselle Paulette' over the years. He fell about me as if I were his long lost son, shaking my hand and embracing my cheeks. 'S'il vous plaît,' he said stepping smartly aside, 'soyez le bienvenu.'

I walked into a broad black and white tiled hallway. The concierge, Henri, pointed a finger to a staircase that curled upwards to a minstrel gallery. 'Au premier étage,' he said. The apartment to the right with a view of the river. He glanced at his pocket watch. 'Mademoiselle Paulette' wasn't due back for another hour. She would call down the moment she came in, as she usually did. 'Ah, mon vieux!' he said grinning widely. Paulette was going to faint from surprise when she saw me.

In the meantime, I was invited to meet Henri's wife, Ginette, a stout, jovial-looking woman. In their small cluttered basement rooms, I was greeted with more affectionate favours and praise. 'Incroyable!' she kept repeating. How many times, she asked of her husband, had she sat down with Paulette to mull over 'l'époque passée de Romainville?' What memories, eh! Was I well? I looked thin. I needed some fat on my bones.

Henri pulled the cork from a bottle of red wine, demonstrating that it was a good 'marque' by putting the label under my nose. I needed a drink. I wanted to put a couple of questions to Henri, but he drifted into a graphic account of his wartime exploits with the resistance movement. On the eve of the liberation of Paris, he took on the Panzers; he pointed to his surgical boot, half of his foot had been blown off, a small price to pay 'pour la délivrance', he said with an air of bravado.

I listened politely. Then, seizing the opportune moment when he took a pause from reminiscing to refill my glass, I asked: 'Paulette est de bonne santé?'

He nodded. 'Bien, malgré tout,' he replied.

Well, in spite of … ? I didn't press it. And I dreaded putting the next question to him. 'Et, Lucy, Monsieur?'

I winced even before the answer came. Henri's wife put a comforting arm around my shoulders. This gesture, in itself, was enough to tell me the worst. 'Morte, mon petit,' Ginette said quietly. 'En Autriche.'

Dead in Austria. For a long minute there was silence in the room. I gulped my wine. I needed to get intoxicated to blunt the sting. I cried as I had not done in an age. All my hopes shattered at one stroke. I had to own up to myself, to Henri and his wife, that there was always a doubt at the back of my mind. Did I really expect Lucy, so vulnerable, so delicate and warm-hearted a young woman, to hold out to the torments that struck down even the very strongest and fearless of men?

Later I heard Lucy's story from Paulette. She had been first put to work in a cartridge factory at Hirtenberg. She was transferred to an outdoor commando at Amstetten in the depth of winter, 1945, where she did heavy labour on railroad construction. She died two days before the liberation of Mauthausen, some eighteen months after our separation.

It was the voice that brought me out of my drugged numbness, the glass of cognac which Henri had placed in my hand was empty. The tone of the voice, melodious, was unmistakable even after the years since she last kissed me and said 'au revoir, it will not be for long' before we were dispersed north to the transit camp at Compiègne to prepare ourselves for a journey into obscurity.

'Descends,' Henri called up the stairs.

She came down, light-footed. 'Qu'est-ce que c'est, Henri?' she asked. 'Vous avez l'air méchant!'

'Surprise, un cadeau de loin,' Henri said.

A 'present' from a long way! At that instant she could not see me. I was standing on her blind side, a pink patch covered the 'blessure' to an eye, a thin scar trickled from under, passed over the cheek and stopped short of the upper lip. Despite that, she was Paulette, perhaps thinner, but shapely, beautiful and voluptuous.

I called softly, simply, 'Chérie! Paulette!'

Startled, she turned her blonde head in my direction. She stared at me open mouthed, momentarily confused. Then she let fall a bag of shopping and threw herself into my open arms. Trembling, she buried her face in my chest. She burst into tears, choking on words. 'Dieu merci,' she cried, 'not one day, not one hour has passed by when I have not thought about you … et Lutchez … et les autres … '

'You don't have to tell me about Lucy,' I said. 'I know from Ginette.' Her hold on me tightened. I knew she was bracing herself for news of Lutchez yet, after so long, she must have guessed he had vanished off the face of the earth like the countless thousands. She might have been thinking of that immortal night when, with Lutchez, Lucy, Colette and Louise Beriot among others, she came to Room 26 to toast a promise of marriage to the Swiss; and I remembered her warm praise of Lutchez, word for word almost: 'Un chic type, assez beau, au coeur intrépide, sympathique, un blagueur et fort en gueule … c'est surtout l'homme dont j'ai besoin.' And it was the first time I had seen Lutchez blush.

'Fort en gueule!' Three words that were relevant. It was Lutchez's 'strong mouth' which killed him, I wanted to say. 'Il est mort,' I said quietly, 'murdered in Buchenwald by the Communists.'

She sighed, deeply. 'Poor Lutchez, lui et sa politique,' she whimpered. She looked up. 'He might have had a change of heart, me with a blind side to my face,' she said meekly.

I shook my head. 'No, not Lutchez. He was constant; he would have been no less proud of you … '

She kissed me on the mouth. 'Lucy would have been happy to think we have been brought together,' she said faintly. 'She loved you, to the last breath.'

A taxi set us down in the narrow elevated cobbled streets of Les Lilas. Arm in arm, Paulette and I walked through the arched entrance to the ancient crumbling Fort. We were received by a 'poilu' wearing a light-brown uniform who saluted and conducted us to the commanding officer's residence, walking between the neat row of trees and exactly following the path which I and a very sick Marc Troska had taken one wintry day in the closing month of 1941.

In what was once Hauptmann Bruchenbach's comfortable office, we were warmly greeted by 'Monsieur le Commandant', whose only resemblance, rank apart, to his German predecessor was his heavily nicotine-stained fingers. Gone, I was quick to notice, was the Teutonic order and cleanliness. The air in the room was stagnant, several packets of Gauloises littered a cluttered desk; gone were the rich window curtains, the hide armchairs and the escritoire; where once a brilliant chandelier of crystal reeds dominated the centre of the ceiling a naked electric light bulb hung down on the end of a long flex; only the fitted carpet remained as a memento of Bruchenbach's reign, the royal-blue pile somewhat threadbare, wine-stained and pitted with cigarette burns. I gave a thought to Hauptmann Bruchenbach, who might have had time before running away to crate the pieces of furniture and fittings to send back home and enjoy in his retirement. I knew that before the Germans left the city the Gestapo ordered the execution of the eleven prisoners remaining in Romainville.

The Commandant glanced at the 'permis de visite' issued and signed by a higher authority. We shook hands. I could see he was enchanted by Paulette's elegant individualism; he was over-courteous, bowing to her almost, and he pulled up his chair, first dusting the seat with a brush of a hand before inviting her to sit on it. Hauptmann Bruchenbach, had he been watching, would have been sick. Could the Commandant assign one of his officers to guide us around? Paulette politely declined the offer – we would find our own way and in our own time, she replied.

We took the back route to the building, 'l'entrée de service' as it was sometimes known; the 'unmade' road was smooth to walk on, the potholes and the deep wheel-ruts caused by the heavily-laden Paris buses employed to take prisoners on their last ride to Mont Valérien had long been filled and levelled out.

Passing the sloping grass bank beneath the rampart wall where I once did 'Garten' duty under the supervision of my benevolent 'learning-to-speak-English' guard, I stopped to call up: 'Hello, Alfred! How are you today! Are we going to hoe the weeds? The cow jumped over the moon. Did you bring me a "Schweinefleisch" sandwich, my good man?' Hard luck, Alfred, I said under my breath, you never did become the 'Bürgermeister' of an English country village. I could have told you, Alfred.

We stopped at the rear of the building, at the spot where broken-hearted Polish Helena fell to her death. Paulette pulled her skirt up over her knees, knelt down and kissed the ground. Rounding the corner, we took a peep into the lean-to which served as a cookhouse and said a 'bonjour' to the ghost of Franz de Bruyne, the Belgian diamond merchant turned 'chef de cuisine' who went to Mont Valérien. The soup cauldrons were rusting, the long trestle-table where the party of 'éplu-cheuses' sat nattering whilst cleaning and chopping vegetables was thick with dead flies and fungus, but the knife scarrings and indentations were well-preserved.

The courtyard appeared larger without the perimeter of barbed-wire and the fence which divided the men from the women. Only a ring of weeds remained to remind us of the boundary. Inside, the building was a vast empty shell with all its intestines removed; thick dust, grime and wind-blown leaves littered the ground-floor hallway. Beneath the stairs leading to the first floor of the women's division, I opened the door to the cleaning cupboard where, and not without a feeling of guilt, I seized on the Godgiven opportunity to seduce the lovely Colette. The brooms, mops and buckets were gone – but not the cobwebs and spiders, nor the upturned sauerkraut barrel where Colette had sat to spread out her long limbs. Colette, the French-Hungarian cabaret dancer whose ambition was to see her name in lights went to Auschwitz Concentration Camp in Southern Poland, where she disappeared. I said nothing to Paulette about our randy liaison.

The 'infamous' communicating door, midway along the first floor, was ajar, a soft wind was whistling the long length of the corridor across the men's division. Paulette gingerly pushed open the door of Room 40, 'la chambre de Lucy', as everybody, including our custodians, referred to it, as if the room was a hallowed place. Inside, we stood silently; the room, once filled with laughter and song, too often with tears, had become a place of deep sorrow; the structure of piping fixed to one wall which served as a communal wardrobe had pulled away from the crumbling mortar, and the airing-line of plaited sisal string which I had often seen festooned with delicate lingerie was hanging down in two frayed lengths from its hooks. Paulette stooped – her keen eye had detected a sliver of metal caught up in a groove of the floorboards. Her long, shapely, red fingernails locked on to a hair-pin. She nestled it in the palm of a hand as if she had hit upon a precious gem before stowing it away in her purse. 'Comme c'est triste,' she whispered.

Across the division, we came to Room 26, the hotbed of intrigue and opportunism where Marc Troska and I were billeted, later to be joined by the anglophile Chilean, Duc d'Andia, who was to die in Buchenwald with a sick mind. The room had seen a more recent occupant, a pseudo-marble linoleum covered the old floorboards and a rusting steel filing-cabinet stood empty with its drawers open. The woodburning stove which had kept us warm during the long winter months and cooked our hotchpots and fricassées had been removed, but the scorch marks from the flue pipe still streaked the wall. Here then, on many clandestine evenings and nights, encompassed by doubt and suspicion, Lucy and I were entangled, two idealists inflamed with passion, dreaming and stretching our imaginations with little prospect of success.

A few steps on brought us to 'le Club', the men's communal room and the centre for learning, debate, political harangue, games, entertainment and occasional religious services. The room was stacked to the ceiling with the furniture and fittings from other rooms and dormitories; tables, chairs, clothing, photographs in broken frames, shoes, boots, hair brushes, combs, pots, pans and a great deal of paraphernalia that would remain unclaimed.

We climbed the dusty stairs to the second floor, to the four small punishment cells – 'les Cachots'. In one, where my amorous activities were halted by a short period of discipline and restraint, my initials were still scored on the wall above the window. In the vast attic – reached by a short flight of narrow twisting steps behind the mechanism of the clock, the centrepiece on the front face of the building above Room 26 – where couples lay, heads together, and indulged in love-making on long unthreatened week-ends, larking about and swapping partners, we stood at the same skylight-window through which Lucy and I often shared an inspiring view of Les Lilas' chimney-pots and the Sacré-Coeur behind.

Our tour of the sadly neglected building at an end, we took time to sit on a bench in the wintry sunshine of the courtyard, deep in our own private thoughts. I turned up my coat collar, sank my chin into my chest and closed my eyes. I listened, my eyes missing nothing in the dead light. Voices, sounds, vibrations, tremors, rhythms. 'Grandmère' Tauzin's bawdy laughter; Viktor Wladzimir's ailing violin; Corporal Weismann's lashing tongue; Lucien Paradis' tremulous song; Lutchez wrangling; clunk of boule striking boule. Lucy strolling. Lucy blowing kisses. Corporal Laufer watchful; Herman inattentive; Colette skipping; Marc Troska sweating, keeping fit; Professor Katz, meandering, nose dripping, always cold, always hungry. A droning sound; a danger signal; heavy wheels on gravel; the shadow of death; a Paris bus; scurrying footsteps; slamming doors; the silence of a grave. Who would be missed? Who would be mourned?

I was very sick, on the threshold of my epitaph. In compulsory isolation, up six flights of stairs in a darkened box-room of a cheap boarding-house in London's West Kensington, I lay in a bed of sweat, listless, heaving and coughing. I saw no one, heard nothing but passing traffic and a frequent knock at the ceiling of the room below from a faceless neighbour disturbed by my nightmares.

A tap at the door told me that a meal was on the mat outside for me to collect. I wanted only water, not food. I left my bed only to drag myself to the lavatory and back, a gruelling effort. And I was a bad risk to the other tenants. The landlady, understandably impatient for me to leave after six unprofitable weeks, had badgered the health people to have me removed from her premises; thus I was awaiting an ambulance or a hearse. Which came first was of little account. My body was wracked with tuberculosis.

Moreover, I was sick at heart. Tragedy had struck with a vengeance, not once but twice since meeting up with Paulette. Our relationship, sadly all too short, had been a happy and an exciting one and it had developed into a platonic love for each other. Inseparable almost, we spent long week-ends in the country, longer periods in the South of France fraternizing with the 'right' people, frequenting night spots, dining in plush restaurants and achieving many of the highlights Lucy and I had planned.

Between times, I dropped in on Simone, perhaps all too infrequently. I had no intention of losing sight of her. Simone was exceptional, someone to whom I was greatly indebted. Besides, her company and the circle she mixed with, down to earth characters living with easy minds, with desires unfulfilled but unrepining, were people to my liking. But Simone could not wholly accept my involvement with Paulette, a woman more than ten years my senior; it was 'rien qu'une liaison de la conscience', she said. Slowly, Simone sank into a world of her own; her roguish sparkle and ready wit which was a distinctive feature in her make-up faded away.

All the time I was living in a fool's paradise, loving two women and kidding myself that the general state of my health was sound when I was going downhill. And I watched Paulette's health taking a backward step; those bugs which had lain dormant were awake and on the move. First it was a cold and a few days confined to a warm bed. Then she was treated for an infection of the lungs. Tuberculosis, the greatest threat to concentration camp victims, finally killed her.

Distraught, and with the same lingering disease, I wrote a letter to Simone, intending to leave it with the concierge at her tiny apartment on the Boulevard St Michel as I was passing through on my regretted departure for England. The man looked at me full in the face then dropped his eyes, a symptom which, over the years, I had come to recognize as a bad omen. 'Simone!' he said. Didn't I know? 'La pauvre fille, elle s'est suicidée,' he told me.

Simone was found drowned in the river Seine.

I had been blessed with more than the proverbial nine lives of a cat, 'unvilling to die' said my Austrian Jewish refugee doctor when I reported to him after ten months of hospitalization and convalescence in the

Surrey countryside. Let off the lead to fend for myself, I was under-powered, missing a lung, several ribs and one or two non-essentials. I was given a warning, 'nix smoking, nix trinken, und nix vimmen'. Smoking was a habit I had long given up; strong alcohol I could easily pass by; but 'no women' was an unacceptable imposition.

I had been pronounced reasonably fit and was promised an average length of life if I resisted all temptations. I was comfortably housed, at an address in fashionable Chelsea where artists, actors, models, and young girls claiming to be debutantes were my neighbours. And I had no immediate money worries. Henri, the concierge at the apartment build-ing where I had lived with Paulette, had been in touch with me whilst I was in hospital. Paulette had made provision for me, generous to the end, considering she had few assets and little invested capital, preferring to enjoy the high-life.

My landlady was a genial Yorkshire woman who had lost her only son in the war, and I put her in mind of him. She placed me in a room on the ground floor to spare me the strain of climbing stairs; she discounted my rent and provided me with a diet of my own choosing. Three times a week I received a visit from a young therapist assigned to me by my sympathetic Austrian doctor. I was taught how best to breathe and how to perform gentle physical exercises which gradually led to better func-tioning.

Day by day I was putting on flesh; except for the occasional destruc-tive dream which left me drained and from which I often woke up at the door of my room, I was in good health and had idle hours to spend settling old scores. It had always been my resolution to expose those British Channel Islanders in Jersey who were responsible for causing innocent people to be deported to concentration camps and to their deaths. Now, with a settled address and a nice feeling of respectability, I put into preparation that moral obligation, first writing to my mother to inform her of my intention.

My mother had lived through the Occupation. Despite the shortage of food, she had often secretly passed provisions to East European slave labourers. Her reply was prompt, a cautionary letter. 'Be on your guard, Son,' she wrote. 'Those Boche bootlickers still rule the roost, you'll burn your fingers.' I knew what she meant. I knew who and what I was taking on. Despite the years of upset because of the German occupation, only a few hapless women, victims of fate nick-named 'Jerry-bags' owing to their familiarity towards German soldiers, had come under contempt and hostility; not one word of reproach had been levelled against the real opportunists and collaborators still in States government.

Jersey island was ruled by a group which was established by tradition,

among them honorary police officers, Centeniers and Vingteniers –
wealthy farmers and wealthier businessmen in the main – who carried
warrant cards which gave them a sense of grandeur and power. Before
the war, discrimination was prevalent, 'la classe ouvrière' was not invited
to contend for a place in the island's government; wealth and social rank
were absolute priorities to becoming a States senator or deputy; and
there was prejudice based upon race and religion, especially in the
schools, where children were not taught to respect all humankind; black
people, seen only in 'jungle' films, never in the flesh, were known as
nig-nogs, golliwogs and cannibals; Jews were known as Fagins, shysters
and bogeymen; the Irish were picked on as were objectors to military
service sent from the mainland of England to work. Bigoted States laws
disbarred Jews, Catholics and Freethinkers from holding the office of
Jurat (Magistrate).

First, I wrote a letter to the Attorney-General on Jersey island, Mr
Duret-Aubin, a bulky, oppressive predominant authority, informing
him that I was alive and well and ready to answer to the outstanding
charge 'that you were at large after the hour of curfew in contravention
of the laws as laid down by the German military forces in Occupation',
and reminding him of the £1 bail money deposited at the time of my
arrest by 'British Jersey police'. I offered an excuse for having failed to
answer to the charge at the time appointed: 'regrettably detained
abroad'.

There was no bite. I wrote again. I was in dispute with my conscience,
I said. First, I wanted to confess to a serious incident, one of homicide
when I drove a stolen military vehicle into a group of German soldiers in
the vicinity of Plemont in the north of the island. Second, I wanted to
clear up the matter of the burglary at the Bailiff's house at St Aubin's
when he was dispossessed of a quantity of contraband goods. And, I
wrote, there were other matters that needed to be considered.

Even after the long lapse in time, I thought that the Jersey authorities
would be cornered into making enquiries. My arrest would give me the
opportunity to expose the treachery of certain high-powered individuals
in open court. This second letter remained ignored.

I persisted. I addressed an envelope to the arch-traitor himself, Centenier A. Tostevin, alias 'Herr Doktor Goebbels'. I challenged the police-
inspector to answer allegations of his collaboration with the enemy in
Occupation, reminding the man of the damning evidence in a document
giving the names of the informers which the German Military Tribunal
had handed to me after my conviction for spreading propaganda material in the shape of newsletters dropped on the island by the Royal Air
Force.

The document, frail and yellowing but perfectly legible, had been in my mother's safe-keeping over the years. Printed in the German language, among other special points it told of my arrest by 'Jersey-Insel Polizei', the place, 'die Grand Hotel, West Park', on information, 'Auskunft', from 'Centenier A. Tostevin and Detective Constable B. Shenton.'

Back came a reply, not from the addressee but from a legal representative of the accused, threatening me with a civil court action for 'defamation'. It left me unconcerned, I had no property or capital at risk. I wrote back and repeated my charges. I threatened to go to the newspapers but, as I should have guessed, nothing resulted.

I had one last course of action. Send the document with all the particulars to the Home Office, I was advised. Though enjoying a self-governing position, it was explained, Jersey was allied to the British crown; therefore, justice in Whitehall was absolute. This I was naive enough to believe.

There came a knock at my door. It was my landlady. Her face beamed. 'Two gentlemen to see you,' she whispered.

Two unsmiling, burly-looking men dressed in grey suits and trilby hats, one clean-shaven, the other with a clipped moustache and carrying a briefcase, unmistakably engaged in 'plot and intrigue', strode into the room. I was respectful, bid them 'Good afternoon, gentlemen,' and looked for a handshake. None came. I stood firm. 'You're from the Home Office, about my complaint, I presume.'

The older of the two, the one with the briefcase, replied: 'As a result of your communication pertaining to Jersey.'

'Cut-and-dried, a bit of an eye-opener, eh?' I ventured to say.

They declined my invitation to sit down. 'Short of time,' the clean-shaven one said, looking at his watch.

'Look here!' said briefcase. 'I'm not going to beat about the bush; we've seen the correspondence; we've interviewed the people in Jersey you named; the document proves nothing; in fact, your allegations are completely without foundation ... malicious, I would say.'

I was stung. For a second I looked at them in silence. 'Malicious, eh!' I said angrily. 'Are you telling me that those bastards are going to get away with murder? Scot-free!'

Briefcase said in a controlled voice: 'Those people in Jersey went about their duties under extremely difficult circumstances ... correctly ... what one might call ... correct collaboration.' And nastily, he blurted out: 'See here! A word of caution, the authority in Jersey is willing to pigeonhole your imputations on account of your time spent in German prisons, brought about by your own misdoings. Our advice is to leave well alone. Is that clear?'

Seeing red, I pulled the door open. 'Out!' I shouted stepping aside. I followed them into the hall. 'Arseholes!' I called down. 'What were you two doing in the war? Picking your noses, eh?'

Briefcase turned on his heel at the open front door. 'Your tongue,' he hissed, 'could get you into hot water. You've got a criminal record, it wouldn't take a lot to put you away...'

'Fuck off, take your dummy with you,' I said, slamming the door on them.

My landlady was standing in the hall, looking apprehensive with a tray in her hands laden with a pot of tea and buttered scones. 'What was all that about?' she asked. 'Someone flying off the handle?'

I apologized for my language. 'Sorry you were put to the trouble. Tea would have been wasted on the likes of those two,' I said bitterly. 'So much for British justice!'

She sat down with me and poured tea into two of the cups. 'Is there nothing more you can do?' she asked after I had enlightened her.

I was at a loss to know. My mother would have echoed 'briefcase's' advice. 'Laissez faire,' she would have said. 'I had a good friend in Romainville,' I told my landlady, 'name of Lutchez. He was alert and quick of mind. He would have taken me aside and put me wise. "Politics!" he would have said. "No matter what country, it's much the same. Meddle with the Establishment, get up their noses and they'll rub you out." No one, nothing could scare Lutchez,' I said. 'It was the political system which silenced him.'

'But it couldn't happen here, not in this country,' my landlady protested.

'I wouldn't bet on it now,' I said.

Melodramatic as it seemed, I didn't want to be found dead in a ditch. Better to shelve the matter for the time being, I decided; I was about to take off for Southport to work as a roaming beach photographer for the summer season and the prospect was exciting: good pay, full board in a guest house on the seafront, fresh air which my doctor-friend recommended, and all the fun and games one could expect in a popular Lancashire resort.

I was at full steam; having only one functional lung did not lessen my energy to any great extent; I could play ball, swim, dance and have affairs with women in the normal way. There was just one serious problem to my tranquillity; although I went to bed pleasantly exhausted, I had no resistance to recurring nightmares, hearing voices and screams; distorted images besieged me; the Devil himself paid me visits and hostile forces hunted me down. I felt the pain from bullets; I was hanged, decapitated, gassed, drowned and dispatched in a myriad ways.

Sometimes I went sleep-walking. Picked up by the police, I found myself in a courtroom. 'Found wandering abroad, your Honour. The defendant was seen to be lurking suspiciously in shop-doorways dressed in pyjamas. When apprehended, he struggled violently and uttered abusive language.'

'Was he drunk?'

'No, your Honour. He did not appear to be under the influence of alcohol.'

Remanded in custody for police and medical reports, I was taken to a prison in Manchester, ironically just twelve miles from my sister's home in Rochdale. But I had no intention of worrying her with my predicament, it was a matter for me alone to explain and resolve.

In solitary confinement, I stared at four blank walls for a week. I was used to prison cells; they were all alike, bare of furnishings except for a raised wide wooden plank and a stained and foul-smelling mattress to sleep on. Badly cooked food, pulpy stuff measured out in a mess-tin, was pushed through a hatch in the door; a frequent and watchful eye peered through a Judas hole, and I heard nothing but jarring voices, the slamming of heavy doors and the jangling of keys – everything designed to wound the self-respect of guilty and innocent alike, a sad reflection on authority's unchristian attitude towards the underdog.

The examining doctor was starchy, an old hand at inquiring into abnormalities and emotional disturbances. I answered each question in an unruffled way, not wanting to show resentment or provoke a reason for prolonged detention. And I gave him the name of my doctor-friend in London's Chelsea, the one man who understood my symptoms and might be able to release me from my jailers. To my surprise the police-examiner agreed to make a telephone call to Chelsea instead of going through the lengthy procedure of letter-writing.

I listened to the exchange of dialogue; my doctor's thick Austrian accent was comforting to my ears. 'Nein, nein!' my doctor vehemently protested. 'Mein patient nicht crazy.' Nor was I a danger to anyone, I heard him say. I was simply reacting to a condition common to many victims of concentration camps, 'von dat vill mit heem be für alles time vielleicht'. There came an exchange of medical claptrap. Treatment by psychiatry? 'Nein, dat vill nicht verk.' Treatment by hypnotherapy? 'Nein, der experiment vill nicht helfen.' What then? 'Nix ... nutting!'

Nor was imprisonment a remedy, it was advised ... and his advice was heeded. Within twenty-four hours I was released, freed from judiciary and public examination. 'Go back to London, Southport's air doesn't agree with you,' the police-doctor suggested. He wouldn't guarantee me immunity from a repeat performance. But my rent at the guest house had been paid in advance, I had another three weeks in which to puzzle over my future and I had no wish to abandon the company of a pretty nurse who worked in a hospital nearby; besides, nine days spent within a prison cell had left me drained of colour.

Each night, when I alone occupied my bed, I took a precautionary measure. I first locked the bedroom door and put the key away in a drawer. That wasn't all. I then lay back on the bed between the sheets, shackled an ankle with stout cord and looped the slack end around a leg of the underframe. This ingenious contraption, though cumbersome, served me well for the remainder of the summer season.

London

On my return to London, I rented a bed-sitter in a Notting Hill Gate rooming-house filled with single people engaged in a variety of bizarre professions. Without much ado, I was introduced into the whimsical world of the 'film extra' or 'crowd artiste', as the more fastidious in the calling preferred to call those aspiring to stardom.

This was a somewhat precarious career, but it took me no time at all to get into the swing of things. Enthusiasm was the requirement, not talent; ironically, I was cast into a spate of films depicting war games, first as a yeoman in a medieval battle-scene on the studio's back-lot, shooting arrows from the turrets of a tower and screaming at the top of my voice in 'bloody' hand-to-hand combat. I saw 'active service' in the Army, Navy and Air Force, 'landing in Normandy on D-day' some-where near Gerrards Cross, in Buckinghamshire, firing blank rounds from a sub-machine gun at grey-green costumed figures retreating over the sand-dunes. As a 'submariner' I helped to send U-boats to their graves; and from the plywood cockpit of a 'Spitfire' poised ten feet above the studio floor, I was a dashing, dead-pan fighter-pilot downing Messerschmitts. I became obsessed with the character of an assassin in secret service missions and fighting a war underground with the 'Maquis' in 'German occupied country' convenient to Pinewood Studios.

Cast as a common soldier in the Crimean war, a walking casualty 'blooded-up', I was waiting in line one day for the legendary nurse, Flor-ence Nightingale. At the going-rate in terms of extra remuneration for grimacing and groaning, I was making a serious contribution in front of the camera and for sound-effects when something within the wall of my chest snapped. Instantly, I became disorientated and stumbled haem-orrhaging from the mouth among the 'dead' and 'dying'. Now a genuine stretcher-case, attended to by a genuine nurse attached to the studio, I was conveyed to London's Brompton Hospital where I lay inactive for three months.

My doctor shook his head when I reported back to him. 'Gottverdammt!' he said tutting. 'Leef off playing Soldaten!' My blood pressure was out of step, it was time to give up the rough and tumble of acting at imaginary wars; if I insisted on 'verking in die movies', I had to cast about for something less demanding, 'sumzing mit comedy und romance'.

But I was not in a position to pick and choose my parts; anything and everything was acceptable to members kept in the background of a cranky industry. Whilst not earning a great deal of money, it was an existence which suited me in more ways than one; I had leisure time, intoxicating friends, bubbly girls, the 'gorblimey' and the priggish, existentialists and nymphomaniacs. My mother once warned me that I'd never make 'old bones'. So be it! I was thirty-two, more than seven years had passed since Mauthausen; I would be more than grateful for a few more irresponsible years before finally burning myself out.

Mary, just twenty-three, born on the Isle of Dogs, and a mature student of acting came into the picture. The luck of the draw for me; we spent several days as a couple 'cruising' on a 'ship' at Elstree studios. Several films later, we became inseparable, and whilst any thought of marriage had previously been furthest from my mind I felt that I was backsliding. But, I asked myself, was it right for a drifter like me to propose to a virtuous, sensitive and trusting young girl, a lover of poetry and good music, whose future, unwedded, promised prosperity? I was of the fifth sign of the Zodiac, a Leo brought up in the Church of England; Mary an Aries and of the Catholic faith, but according to our Stars we were of the same element ... fire! Differences of religion and age were not a barrier to true love; six months after our first meeting we were married at Kensington Registry Office.

Though unequal – Mary's scale of pay and earnings surpassed mine – we pooled our monies and rented a bijou apartment in Bayswater within a stone's throw of Kensington Gardens, furnished it second-hand and, into the bargain, took on the responsibility of a dog and two cats. We were a happy family.

For many weeks I bore a sense of guilt. Before our marriage, I failed to own up to my shortcomings. The scars on my body I could fob off as souvenirs of war, but my bouts of insomnia and unconscious weeping and whimpering left Mary suspicious and led her to ask questions. Finally, I unburdened myself, omitting nothing. My disclosures led to no ill-feeling; Mary put her arms around me and said: 'You should have told me before, then I could have helped you sooner.'

Mary proved to be a ministering angel. Over the months and into the years we were drawn together even closer. Whilst I could not claim sound sleep or sweet dreams – not a day passed without thinking of the holocaust – I had a clean bill of health. Every so often I was attracted, as if by a gigantic magnet to which I had no power of resistance, to Paris. My lone trips, about which Mary held some reservations, left me with an easy peace of mind. However, I was saddened to see that the street and the quaint boarding-house where I had taken shelter and met Simone had suffered from the property developers; Paulette's old apartment-building had been bulldozed to make way for an ultra-modern block, and there were plans for reform at the Fort de Romainville.

I was obsessed with war memorials, museums and reminders of the Occupation, sitting for hours in a bistro drinking an apéritif with someone of similar emotional sentiments. Perhaps it was the individual mementos which held me spellbound; I stood on street corners to gaze up at the plaques screwed to the buildings honouring, among many others who died defiantly, 'Jean-Pierre, un citoyen et patriote qui est tombé ici pour la France.' I challenged young passers-by. 'Hey,' I said, pointing a finger up at a plaque, 'vous savez quelque chose de ce brave type?' A shrug of the shoulders, a 'rien, Monsieur', and they hurried away. The older generation, understandably, tended to be informative, some pontificating on a waste of a life, 'et pourquoi?'

After five years of happy marriage, stability, and well-being, I was dealt another rotten hand of cards. Elected to the twelve-man executive committee of the Film Artistes' Association, I quickly became the odd man out. It seemed to me that people of all ages, particularly the young with stars in their eyes, were encouraged to join the union largely to produce membership fees and kick-backs from photographic agents recommended for 'glamour' mug and body shots. In an up and down industry, few were ever to see the inside of a studio or go before a movie camera. Cubicles in one or two labour exchanges were marked out for disillusioned 'film extras' signing on.

Denouncing the union, I went on record as 'unbrotherly.' My past history was delved into by a police-officer attached to Scotland Yard, and a delegate from the union travelled to Jersey to interrogate my mother. Subsequently, I was expelled under the rarely-exercised rule that no one with a criminal record could become or retain membership of the union.

My expulsion was 'against the law of natural justice,' ruled Judge Melford Stevenson in the High Court. Not so, said two of the three Appeal Court judges at a later hearing, the Master of the Rolls, Lord Denning dissenting. One prickly judge, Diplock, remarked that where studio dressing rooms were concerned, artistes' belongings had to be safeguarded from the light-fingered. Five Law Lords chanted: 'And so say all of us.'

Without Mary's support, I might have shown my resentment of illiberal views in a belligerent manner. Barred from studios for life, we talked over the future with cool heads, coming to the conclusion that the time had come to go in search of new pastures. We sold our home, packed our bags and emigrated.

California

We were living in southern California with our menagerie of animals. With a climate of blue skies, long days of brilliant sunshine and invigorating nights, Palm Springs was a Shangri-la, an oasis of hot springs, spas, palm trees, citrus groves and snow-capped mountains, clean and sweet-smelling, a million miles from England's damp, often depressing weather and the Siberian winters of Buchenwald and Mauthausen.

In a large home on wheels with all the modern comforts and amenities of a villa in a garden setting, rich with colour, we had settled among humble and friendly natives.

I had no difficulty in finding employment. The question, 'Have you references?' was of secondary importance. 'Can you do a good job?' was what mattered. After a brief spell working in a hotel, I was recruited by a domestic agency to the role of chauffeur-butler to one of the wealthiest, crankiest of women in southern California. I had the qualifications for this lofty position – commonsense, bearing and tact; and I had acquired the basic training on the studio floor and played to the gallery in the *Importance of Being Earnest* as Lane, the butler for the overpowering Lady Bracknell.

At the wheel of a gleaming white Cadillac 'Limousine de Ville' fitted with air-conditioning and push-button electrics, and impeccably attired in a tailor-made, blue, tropical uniform-suit, I conducted and assisted 'my lady', an affected middle-aged woman of Italian origin with a trim figure but an unhappy face, hither and thither: to 'Countess Irene's' for hydro and physiotherapy and organic facial treatment, to Zaks for shopping before pecking at a luncheon of green salad and fresh fruit at the exclusive Racquet Club, thirty minutes precisely in the clover-shaped jacuzzi back at the house; next, a repose; when awakened, a hair-do, make-up, manicure and pedicure by visiting wizards, followed by a change from silk kimono into 'something voguish' from a Beverly Hills couturière, a cocktail with the week-ending 'le Roys' from Bel Air before a candlelit dinner on the patio under the twinkling stars at the palatial home of the Van Heusens. A typical day!

'My new man, all the way from London, England, you know! Cute, don't you think?' The formal introductions and the raggings, bordering on the suggestive, were not unlike those scripted for a top-drawer domestic comedy. Hovering on the touchlines I learned to smile in my sleeve at the party gossip. Women talked much of marriage and divorce, boasted about great amounts of alimony, showed concern and impatience for their wayward children, praised their doctors and, as though they were a collector's piece, unveiled the new 'pet' in their lives.

The men pow-wowed on the state of the almighty dollar, which took precedence over ulcers, the size of tits and the shape of legs and bums and who was 'screwing' who. About World War Two they knew 'all' the answers. About General MacArthur, and the great naval victories in the Pacific. Pearl Harbor? 'That was something ... God-damned Nips!' Hiroshima and Nagasaki? 'It was owed to the little bastards!' The war in Europe? 'Well man, we sure got you British out of a mess!'

I longed to take the flagwaggers aside and say: 'Look here, you Yanks hesitated long enough before giving a helping hand, and I could tell you a story or two about some gutsy men and women who died unhonoured and unmissed, stories that would make your blood curdle.' In the main they were amiable-enough, easy-going natives loaded with inherited wealth, outnumbered by the 'nouveau-riche' immigrant boorish film producers fortunate to have escaped the wrath of Nazism, smug movie-stars and starlets, land developers, brokers, canned-food merchants, politicians, impostors and freeloaders.

Empty stomachs had taken the greatest toll of life in the camps. Prisoners cried themselves blind with hunger, were at one another's throats and killed their neighbours for a crust of bread. Food I had learned to regard with gratitude; now I was living in a land of excess, of extravagance, of gluttony, of careless and uneconomic management, and of great waste. Knowing all there was to know about the great privation in other parts of the world, I was feeding my pets and those of my neighbours on discarded steaks, chicken and turkey breasts, and fresh salmon.

'My lady' was making overtures, cultivating me as more of a confidant than a servant. She addressed me by my Christian name and spared me the discomfort of my cap and gloves at the wheel of the car when she took to the front passenger seat; my uniform-suit was released to a charity shop and replaced by informal wear of my own choice, the accounts debited to a string of credit cards. Frequently, I was invited to take a place at a luncheon or dinner table in restaurants.

Plans were made to go to Europe on an extensive visit. Did I want to go by air or by ocean liner? What car did I want? A Mercedes? A

Rolls-Royce? Such an adventurous offer I might have been tempted to accept years before when scruples were not for consideration. I came to feel a twinge of sadness for ageing divorcees and widows beyond renovation, women weighted with wealth, bitchy, friendly, without true love, and lonely.

After a year in the desert, I hitched our mobile home to the Lincoln convertible and moved to the San Fernando Valley. Hollywood was on the threshold. Our intention was to explore the historic north portion of California, the heart of the Mother Lode country and the Sierras, places which my room-mate at Romainville, Marc Troska, had brought to life by stories to which I and Oberleutnant Freddy Kaiser had listened enthralled. It was hard to believe that I was on the point of exploring this legendary land for myself.

Then our plans were laid aside for the time being. A chance meeting with an old acquaintance from the film, *Colditz Story*, Bryan Forbes, who had achieved fame as a director and author, led me to a long-term contract with Columbia Studios playing a 'starving' and 'emaciated' prisoner-of-war in an epic called *King Rat*.

As a consequence, we searched for an apartment to rent in the Valley, not an easy objective with animals in the family. We came across an ideal garage conversion affording two bedrooms, a large sitting-room, bathroom, kitchen, small garden and privacy at a moderate rent.

Gingerly, I put it to the landlord: 'D'you mind animals?'

'How many?'

'Two cats and an Alsatian dog, all the way from England.'

'You gotta be nuts,' he said, 'bringing animals thousands of miles when we've got enough in this part of the world.' He pondered. 'Tell you what,' he said, 'd'you mind Jewish prayer meetings and hymn-singing on Sunday mornings, maybe once in the week?'

'It won't bother us or the animals,' I said.

I was getting a touch of the star treatment, being chauffeur-driven to a location fifty miles north of Hollywood, to a purpose-built encampment of bamboo and coconut-matting thronging with a cast of 'extras' recruited from Chinese and Japanese eating-houses and speakeasies. Mary, meanwhile, had joined a theatre company and, ironically, was cast in a play called *Oh, What a Lovely War* at the University of California.

My mind enlivened and fully occupied, with new friends and new interests and with Mary at hand or within reach, I could now discuss the holocaust with former concentration camp inmates without breaking into a cold sweat. European Jewish immigrants were often visibly scarred by crudely tattooed numbers on their forearms which they laid bare with a strange sense of pride, with long untreated ulcers which had eaten deep into the flesh and left a shrinkage on the surface of the skin, with lost limbs, with blind eyes, hardness of hearing and speech defects. These were some of the scapegoats of war, of political hatred and inhumanity, who had chosen to eke out their remaining days in a situation of remedial comfort, free from trouble and anxiety but not always from pain.

With filming at an end, I turned to more secure employment, easy to come by for British aliens not averse to 'domestic service'. I registered with a Beverly Hills agency specializing in hiring flunkies to the nabobs of Hollywood, better known as the 'fruit and nut cakes' of the movie world. What a glut was up for grabs! After a brief and disastrous encounter with a hypochondriac and a megalomaniac, I was introduced to an affable enough crackpot, a native of Bristol, England, Archibald Leach, alias Cary Grant. The world's women saw him as the perfect man, a divine hero, the male animal of their erotic dreams. Grant's script-writers characterized him as 'light-hearted, romantic, roguish, sportive'. His English housekeeper described Grant in three short words, 'mean, moody, moany'.

Mr 'Grint' or 'Grunt', as he was innocently named by admirers on foreign locations, lived in a run-down bachelor's bungalow tucked away in the exclusive hills overlooking West Hollywood. It was hardly the palatial home of a multi-millionaire movie star which his adoring fans envisaged. Saucepans and buckets caught the seasonal rainwater dripping through a ramshackle roof; damp yellowing walls were hung with paintings by leading impressionists; windows were hungry for a coat of paint; sun-beds were unreliable; only the guard-dog used the swimming-pool; and the cabins, where chosen 'things' of beauty, vamps and sirens, once peeled off to change into bathing suits or prepared to plunge nude for the former laird, the eccentric and frenzied Howard Hughes, were infested with vermin.

Grant had need for neither chauffeur nor butler, just a man to see to his dated wardrobe, his depreciating Rolls-Royce, unsolicited mail, personal shopping, and his headaches. As a bachelor without trustworthy friends, a stay-at-home person who viewed the world through the magic of television, he was uninteresting, unobjectionable, pampered, bored, boring and not the ideal employer. The closest he had been to war and battle was when he was put into the uniform of a submarine commander in the adventure movie *Destination Tokyo*. 'Up periscope ... Down periscope.' The threat of a nuclear war, with his life and his valuable possessions and property put at risk, was something else to worry about.

When 'poor old Cary' relinquished his independence for the ump-teenth time and, reluctantly it seemed to me, went to the altar in the gaming desert city of Las Vegas to marry a young woman, a state of martial law was declared within the household even before the confetti had been vacuumed away. The day-to-day activities of Grant and his personnel were drastically transformed. Whereas before it had been a routine of pottering about, a drive to the office at Universal Studios for no other reason but to put in an appearance, and periods of complete leisure and pleasure when the boss was away, life became disagreeable, disturbing and turbulent. The time had come for me to abandon the sinking ship and take to the life-boat.

The ups and downs of my experiences were common to the vast majority of Hollywood households where domestic servants are subjected to the tantrums of affluent and quirky employers. But living within this bizarre environment for more than four years left Mary and I with no regrets, nothing but happy memories and a wealth of new friends. There was still one more adventure in store, that of driving more than three thousand miles on the scenic route to New York, where we boarded a ship, bringing with us a menagerie of animals which included lovable Gumper, Grant's unwanted Alsatian 'guard' dog, bound for Europe and the well-earned vacation which was to lead me back to Austria and Mauthausen.

It was dawn. Low heavy clouds unleashed a steady fall of snow to add to the misery as we waited to be initiated into yet another place of torment. The main reception and dispersal area where the SS had their garages was already choked with many thousands of new arrivals admitted earlier, hundreds lying dead or dying from low body temperature or wounds. The vast area was overlooked on all four sides by thick rampart walls made of stone, with cat-walks. There was a small round observation tower to the left of the entrance, another, tall and square, to the right and policed by guards armed with machine-pistols and hand-grenades. Straight ahead, high on the north rampart wall, was a small purpose-built granite balcony with a commanding view of the hinterland and the long approach road to the camp, tailored to accommodate one person, SS Standartenführer (Colonel) Franz Ziereis, the Kommandant. Forty years of age, Ziereis was reputed to be the most evil of all concentration camp controllers. In the early days, his twisted mind converted a van into a mobile gas-chamber, to speed up the killing, which he often operated himself. It was used mostly to convey mentally-ill patients from hospitals and institutions. Occasionally, he would present himself to new arrivals from his lofty perch and make threatening gestures, pointing to the tall crematorium chimney which endlessly belched black acrid smoke.

There were visible gaps among the great assembly where bodies had slumped to the frozen ground. The distress was immense, the biting cold played havoc with the old people and those badly clothed and near-naked. My reserve of strength all but spent, I willed myself to stand unbowed. Arms thrashing, teeth chattering, I rambled: 'For Christ's sake keep to your feet … look alive!' I heeded my own advice, if feebly, stepping sideways, forwards and then backwards with small leaden steps, as if trying to get to grips with a clog-dance.

The rat-tat of machine-guns from beyond the rampart walls fused with the loud wailing and wringing of hands as senior guards, Untersturm-führers and Hauptscharführers (Second Lieutenants and Warrant

Officers), fleshy, brutish, pugilistic types, moved among the multitude wielding their truncheons and peering into faces. It was the terrifying process of selection, separation and elimination. Jews, as always, were first to be auditioned. Italians, with their dark traits, trembled in the balance, those who vehemently claimed they were 'nicht Jüdisch' came under suspicion and were not always given the benefit of the doubt. Second choice for hate were uniformed Russian officers who were grouped into a unit for attention of a special order; likewise, the 'nutzlos,' the useless – the very old, the chronically sick and the disabled – were quickly disposed of.

It was the warm water that brought me back to a conscious state. I found myself squatting naked on a wet concrete floor under a communal shower-head and in a wallow of slime, froth and diarrhoea. The hair on my bruised body had been shorn to the skin by a quack 'friseur' plying electric clippers and a cut-throat razor. Hosed free of filth, the next stage of my initiation into the camp was the disinfection room, where a stinging solution of black liquid was daubed over my head and applied to my private parts.

Still naked, I was moved to a glory hole densely packed with youths and older men similarly plucked and suffering from skin lesions and bleeding ulcers, Nicolas and Barnado among them. In sweltering fever-heat we queued for drinking water, a measured ladle of thin swede soup and a slice of black bread. This consideration, small as it was, and the cleansing of our bodies, was an indication that our lives were to be spared, at least for the time being.

We were allowed to rest. We slept, anaesthetized to the intermittent firing of machine-guns and loud screaming, signs of a great slaughter of the unwanted in progress. Unlike at Buchenwald, where murder was unhurried, killing in Mauthausen was an industry maintained at full speed.

Goaded by 'trusties' who barked their orders and drove us by the pressure of kicks and sticks, we crossed, twenty at at a time, to the clothing store on the main street. There was no choice, we accepted what was handed out with good grace. If it was too large or too small, one dared not show discontent. Strips of rags were issued to cover the feet and I received a pair of 'claquettes' manufactured from wood and canvas. The life of these open-toed sandles was short, yet, invariably, they out-lived the wearers.

In a black jacket which hung loosely over my spare frame and in trousers with legs which stopped short of my ankles, I made my way to the 'politisch Büro' to be interrogated by 'Sekretäre' prisoner-trusties, German, Austrian and Czech nationals chosen for their administrative abilities and knowledge of languages, a more moderate version of the feared 'prominenten' who lorded over the common herd and played on one's nerves.

The procedure was straightforward: name, country of origin, age, religion, trade and political tendency. Remembering how the few British and American subjects in Buchenwald camp were held in contempt by the 'Green' criminal element and by some of the more odious 'Reds' who held a commanding influence in the internal administration of that camp, I decided to register myself as a Frenchman to escape attention and curiosity.

I took my place at a trestle-table, sitting upright and with my cap in hand as the system demanded. My interviewer, a man in his late thirties, smartly dressed in a white polo-neck jumper and a navy-blue seaman's jacket and with all his hair neatly in place, barely gave me a glance. His lack of interest showed on his sufficiently-fed face; dealing with the humble masses had become a grindstone.

I answered his first question promptly and in the language he asked it, German.

'Nationalität, französisch.'

He looked up from his alphabetical register sharply. 'Eh bien!' he snapped. 'Parlez en français. C'est entendu?'

I answered tactfully and politely. 'Pardon, Monsieur. Bien entendu.'

'Votre age?'

'Vingt-quatre, Monsieur.'

'Nom de famille?'

I was ready with the answer, giving my father's surname, not my birth-name, to which I added his Christian name. 'Chevalier, Monsieur. Prénom, Charles.'

'Ou né?'

'En France, Monsieur.'

His pen poised in mid-air, he looked up impatiently. 'La ville, nom de dieu!'

'Monsieur, excusez! La ville? Ah, oui! … St Malo.' It was the French coastal town, a popular pre-war resort for day-trippers from the Channel Islands. That much I knew.

'Zone? Région?'

The question stumped me. I was unsure. Was the town of Saint Malo in Normandy or Brittany? Was it that important, I asked myself? The man was a Czech. Did he know? Did he care? I plumped for Normandy. 'La Normandie, Monsieur,' I replied after a moment's hesitation.

'Vous êtes sûr? Absolument?'

I confessed that I wasn't absolutely certain. Geography, I told him, was not my best subject at school. A lame excuse when I was trying to pass myself off as a native of the town. He seemed to be bent on making a song and dance about it. He pushed back his chair and my eyes followed him across the room. He buttonholed a colleague, conversed briefly and then returned to the table.

'La Grande Bretagne!' he retorted. And, in perfect English, he said, 'St Malo, my friend, is in Brittany. You are no more French than I am German. You see, I suspected your accent. I was a teacher of English and French in Prague. Tell me, why do you want to pass yourself off as a Frenchman?'

I explained the reason, to which he gave some hard thought. At present, I was bluntly informed, there were no other known British subjects in the camp; eleven had been executed two weeks previously. It was hardly the news I wanted to hear. Less brusque in manner, he said the choice was mine; he could register me as a French national but, in his opinion, to no advantage. On balance, it was better to stay 'British'. However, I could expect no favours except to be granted immunity from the quarantine camp. For this I praised heaven. I had experienced a period of quarantine in Buchenwald. Row upon row of wooden huts set in a quagmire of mud and raw sewage, a place for the damned, infected with deadly diseases left unattended, where revenge, punishment and murder among prisoners was predominant. Quarantine in Mauthausen, I was to learn, was no better.

I was assigned to Block 12 and given a bed in the upper tier of a three-storey bunk. The wooden hut was a replica of those in Buchenwald – two divisions, each accommodating some two hundred males, rooms A and B, and a small ante-room in the centre providing primitive washing and lavatory facilities; a circular stone basin with many taps delivered fetid water for drinking, and the room served as a temporary mortuary for the overnight dead.

My first impression of the camp was the marked difference from Buchenwald, not in custom, behaviour patterns, prisoner-committee rule or general management – although these were alarmingly worse in Mauthausen – but in size and composition. It was much smaller, more compact, and with less than half the number of prisoners. A plot of short side streets of gravelly rutted earth was arranged between rows of identical wooden huts and led off the broad main street, the 'Appelplatz'. This was the principal site which boasted the most feared building of all, a two-storeyed granite-built prison housing macabre instruments of torture and execution, a gas-chamber to accommodate sixty or more persons, four brick-built crematory ovens, a post-mortem chamber, a cellar for garrotting or killing by shooting and, on the upper floor, 36 tiny interrogation cells, all a mere fifty paces from Block 12.

By the main entrance gate stood the Wailing Wall, so named because of the cries of men tethered by the hands and feet to bull rings embedded in it. It was built of granite, about twenty feet long and eight feet high, and was topped with five strands of high-voltage barbed wire.

Intimidation, corruption, brutality and immorality all had their places as in Buchenwald, only to a more outrageous degree. Block 12 was 'governed' by Spanish 'prominenten', a small unit of long-serving prisoners with varied temperaments and political leanings who held their own courts and punished with a hard hand those who dared to complain or challenge their authority, not stopping short of flogging and murder.

The 'Blockälteste' (Block-chief) had a licence to plunder, at the expense of the ordinary prisoner. Food rations arriving at the Block were distributed from behind a closed curtain by appointed 'whips', usually cronies of the same nationality as the Block-chief, first setting aside more than enough for themselves, cheating on the bread by cutting slices from the allocated portions, nobbling the margarine and scooping up the vegetable content from the bottom of the soup drums. Room A had the advantage of a wood-burning stove, but it was out of bounds to the ordinary prisoner. Nightly, a 'cuisine' came into operation, the smell of bread toasting and the sizzle of vegetables frying was tormenting to hungry bellies.

Almost all Block-chiefs and their principal assistants were openly and shamelessly immoral. Each had a 'valet', a good-looking Polish or Russian boy from ten to fourteen years of age. These 'Lieblinge' or 'fleurettes' were devoted to their masters. They were well-nourished, sharing in the plunder of rations, and warmly clothed. Having easily submitted themselves to an unnatural relationship, they had been converted, perhaps willingly or perhaps through fear, to a life that would leave its stigma on them forever – if they were fortunate enough to number among the survivors. These boys, indoctrinated by their pervert tin-gods, were often dangerous; they would not hesitate to act as stool-pigeons, or hit and kick out at men old enough to be their great-grandfathers.

Kissing and cuddling was conducted openly with the intention of showing off. The more lurid activity was performed behind a wall of blankets and was not always pleasurable, to judge by some of the tear-jerking ordeals the boys underwent. Try as they did to please and satisfy, these young conscripts were not indispensable, the market was flushed with new consignments arriving daily, the procurers always on the lookout for sound and wholesome stock as they came in through the gate. The great majority of youths delivered to the camp were hardened to incarceration, they were no more than walking bones, diseased and unemployable; they, along with the 'old' loves, found themselves consigned to the scrap heap to await extermination.

Prisoners in general, therefore, were faced with two hostile factions, the tyrannical SS administration on the outside and the abominable clannish prisoner-prominenten deputizing on the inside. In overall charge was the 'Lagerführer' (Camp chief) and his second-in-command, both appointed by the Kommandant. These lickspittles, dressed in semi-military uniforms, policed the streets. On coming upon them, we were coerced into showing respect by standing aside and touching our forelocks. Another vicious breed of inmate was the 'Kapo' (prisoner foreman). As at Buchenwald they were particularly cruel to the humble band of Jehovah's Witnesses (Mauves) and the homosexuals (Pinks). Kapos selected Catholic priests for some of the more unpleasant tasks in a vain attempt to break their spirits; shovelling away mounds of excreta from the outdoor latrines and working as hodmen in the most feared detail of all – the granite quarries where a legion of slaves was crushed and beaten into the ground.

Whilst there was some brotherliness among the prisoners – the brave Catholic priests did their utmost to promote tolerance and decent feeling in a colony plagued by fear, despair, disease and hunger, suffering greatly themselves because they dared to show concern – animosity was obvious everywhere. There was mistrust, envy, and violent conflict. Nationalities and political differences clashed. The disgraced Italians, seen as slippery turncoats, sought sympathy but nobody loved them; the French had little time for the Spanish or Germans and vice versa; the Czechs were cliquey, preferring their own company; and the Germans and Austrians were unsociable with the East Europeans. The Russians favoured anyone and everything British; like the French, Italian and Yugoslav nationals, they were not nominated for prominent positions.

Not everyone admired the British. The French, former politicians and resistance leaders, were often critical; they felt bitter because France had been left in the lurch, 'dans la merde', at the time of Dunkirk with the evacuation of British troops. Their other gripe was that Paris could have been liberated by air long before the day of deliverance in August 1944, four long years after the start of the Occupation. Intellectual 'Red' Germans and Austrians, well versed in international politics, prominent Communists, anti-fascists, fallen fascists and the 'Green' criminal element were often damning of the British, in particular Churchill. I was lectured on British royalty, British aristocracy and British Jewry. Wasn't it true that the British were first to set up a concentration camp? Didn't they persecute and exploit the blacks in the colonies? The British had little to be proud of in the way of morals and principles towards black people and the low-born. This was a sample of the prattle I was obliged to listen to. I knew practically nothing about politics, nor was I in a mood to be instructed on a subject which tended to inflame passions. Having learned in Buchenwald that diplomacy was the wisest course to follow, I was attentive, nodding and shaking my head as the discussions proceeded.

Incredibly, there were fanatical Germans and Austrians who were still faithful to Hitler, and considered the invasion by the Allies of German territory to be an affront. They were convinced that their freedom from the camp would come with a general pardon, when Hitler's sensational secret weapon, currently being talked about, would turn the war in Germany's favour and effect a military occupation of England. Whether it was fact or simply another rumour one couldn't be sure, but disturbing news was circulating of a formidable weapon in the shape of a flying torpedo aimed at destroying London and other English cities. It was a topic that generated great optimism for a German victory among the guards and their prisoner-allies.

My status in the camp was an enigma, causing me much concern. I had become a figure of curiosity, a prisoner without a number or insignia, drawing attention and speculation, something I desperately wanted to avoid. At roll-calls I stood detached from the main body of prisoners from my Block, at the head of the ranks and two paces to the right, to be counted 'und ein'. Invariably, the SS teller would stare at me and ask of my Block-chief 'Warum?' The Spaniard would shrug his shoulders and reply, 'Ich weiss nicht, Herr Unteroffizier.' He didn't know why, nor did I. Ill-omened or not, I learned that I was not the first British national to be publicly paraded without the characteristic markings. A short while before, 47 Allied airmen together with several British agents, were in the same spot. They were forced to work in the notorious 'Arbeitskommando Wienergraben', the quarry with 186 break-neck steps of descent into a massive basin of blasted granite, overshadowed by a rockface with a 200 foot drop into a stagnant pond.

The quarry, where up to 2,000 men worked at one time and where life-expectancy was reckoned at just one shift or less, was overseen by some of Mauthausen's worst brutes, among them the German-born Unterscharführer (Corporal) Andreas 'blue lips' Trumm and his close friend of the same rank, Josef Niedermayer. Both in their mid-twenties, they were well-known for 'moonlighting', escorting parties of children to the gas chamber to die a lingering death by a preparation of blue crystals that let off a high concentration of cyanide acid on contact with air. This was a formula known as Zyklon B.

Supervising the work in the quarry, it appeared, was of secondary importance to the kicks derived from violence and murder. Bored guards and Kapos selected Jews, priests and what they called the 'Religiös verrückten' (mad Jehovah's Witnesses) for baiting. Obersturmführer Grau, the veteran Hauptscharführer Spatzenegger and Kapo Hans played major roles in the orgy of violence and murder.

The 186 steps leading down into the basin, broken, uneven and precipitous, giving a sensation of giddiness to those affected by heights, were first approached by a rough sloping track; midway, at the highest point, there was an open gap overlooking the rockface screened by a scrub of bracken and small thin trees. It was from this point that hundreds of men broke ranks. In desperation they chose to leap to their deaths; countless others were propelled over the chasm by force, singly, in pairs, and in a chain of linked hands. The guards had a fancy for nicknaming sites where some of the worst cruelties were recorded. Hence this was the Parachutists' Leap. Below men were crushed on the jutting rocks beneath or drowned in the 'Swimming Pool'. Here, too, live Jews from the tent camp were reported to have been fed into a mechanical stone-crusher.

It was risky enough for a fit man to descend the 186 steps, a hard fate for those in poor shape and encumbered by footwear that rapidly disintegrated over rough surfaces. But it was the uphill climb that was more frightening and which took the greatest toll. Blocks of granite, weighing up to 50 kilograms, were carried on hods strapped to backs and on bare shoulders when the hods were in short supply. And it took hours to marshal a column of ten men widthwise and one hundred metres from head to tail, those up front taking the strain of waiting for the order to move off. The non-starters were heaped up and removed from the quarry by stretcher-bearers.

Shoulder to shoulder, top-heavy, the climb to the top proved treacherous. It was futile labour. At the widest point the ascent measured just twelve feet. Since each of the 186 crumbling steps was aligned to the average size 'clip-clop', men with large feet were forced to climb splay-footed. Sometimes men, overcome by exhaustion, fits, strokes and madness, let go their granite blocks; as a result, many of those bringing up the rear suffered crushed bones. The flashpoint having been reached at the summit, the front ranks waited for the battered column to be rebuilt. This was the most dangerous, unpredictable stage, hinging on the breed and moods of the guards standing by up front. Foul play, a regular practice, was to gun-butt the front rank; in the debacle that followed, an avalanche of men and blocks were skittled to the bottom of the steps.

Unnerving reports from the quarry were commonplace. I had already seen great evil, therefore I had no reason to question the accuracy of these chilling stories told by sane men. The extremists among the guards – Trumm and Niedermayer and a score of Kapos and SS-conscripted Ukrainian nationals were among the leading psychopaths overseeing the quarry detail – comprised a mere minority against the moderately violent element commonly found among the older brigade of guards, and there were a cringing few who turned their backs and put their hands over their ears at the absolute cruelty.

Marcus Bloom, an English Jew and a wireless-operator with the Special Forces, was described to me as a big man with red hair. Healthy and strong at the time of his capture, he was detailed to the quarry to work. Goaded by whips, he must have guessed that the end of his young life had been determined. In a burst of rage, he was seen to bring his granite block down on a guard's head, crushing the man's skull. A bullet ploughed into Bloom's leg. Many witnesses, rejoicing at the incident confirmed what followed next. The 'Engländer' roared like a mad bull. He picked up a granite block. Clutching it to his chest 'comme un rugbyman', he dragged his injured leg and charged into every Kapo and guard barring his path, knocking them to the ground like skittles. It was Andreas Trumm who killed Bloom, with a play of bullets to the head and chest fired from a machine-pistol. Marcus Bloom was just one of the much-talked-about heroes in camp Mauthausen.

Surprisingly, I was not put to work. I joined the swollen ranks of the written-off, loitering outside my Block in the freezing cold, shifting aimlessly along the crowded streets from dawn to dusk, and stepping over and shying away from sprawled out bodies dead or dying in the churned-up slush. It was prudent to keep a watchful eye open for the Camp chief and Kapos making sneak incursions into the streets to pick men at random for clearing snow from around the SS barracks and shrink back to a safe distance.

Christmas was near. It would be my sixth in captivity. I was limping badly, my right thigh festering in two places. At roll-calls I stood with my drained weight leaning on my left leg to conceal my disability. I had declined the offer of a crutch for the reason that any visible aid to mobility gave priority of place in the queue for the gas chamber. But my wounds were rapidly deepening, gangrenous germs were eating into the flesh and the smell was proof enough that I was dangerously close to becoming a candidate for the flesh pit. I had taken a glimpse into this open chamber near the crematory building where stricken men and women lay stewing in their own toxic gases, without whole arms, without whole legs, with feet missing. From the raw, bleeding joints turned black and green hung strips like cords of limp spaghetti trailing in a thick yellowish fluid on a cement floor.

When permission was granted by my Block-chief to remain in my bunk after I could no longer hobble about, I was counted among the sick at roll-calls by the SS teller who came to the Block soon after dawn and in the early evening. Nicolas and Barnado – both had survived quarantine and were housed in Block 11 – collected my food rations and helped me to the lavatory. But time was running out for me; if anyone spent more than three days confined to their bunk it was noted in the teller's book of reports. There was a real risk that I would be labelled a 'Drückeberger', a lazy loafer taking up space and receiving food rations.

Nicolas, in poor health himself, suffering from the seeds of consumption, hit upon a former fellow-student, a sympathetic English-speaking Czech named Alex who did duty in the SS infirmary. Alex had some pull with the Czech prominenten; his uncle, a Professor of medicine, worked in the prisoner hospital where only selected patients were given treatment. Alex paid me a visit. His diagnosis was straightforward; I was in great danger of losing my leg, and that was the least of my troubles.

I was left wallowing in self-pity, imagining how I might cope with a peg-leg back on civvy street. Losing an arm, I told Nicolas, wasn't half as bad. I had no choice, nor did a thousand and one others in the same predicament and worse, he said. At least, he went on, I was being shown preferential treatment; the Professor had agreed to see me, for which I should count my blessings. And Nicolas tried to console me; plain wooden legs which caused small rascally boys to poke fun were things of the past, he assured me. Surgical appliances to correct and conceal deformities were constantly improving, an artificial leg would be engineered to fit comfortably and with almost as much manoeuvrability as the real thing; given time, I would learn to walk without a limp and undertake most things. I was not bowled over by that promise.

Soon I was carried by stretcher to the prisoner hospital, a building on the main street attached to the crematory Block. The 'operating theatre' was small, badly lighted, unclean, its stained walls flaking distemper. It reminded me of a squalid, back-street barber-abortionist from the dark ages; a high-backed chair fitted with a head-rest was sited in front of a cracked mirror, a table with a blanket overlay stood in the centre of the room; and on what might once have been a hotel tea-trolley, a crude-looking assortment of instruments was spread out – scissors, pincers, tooth-edged blades and cut-throat razors, stock-in-trade that would cause even the bravest of men to shudder. Stacked at random on a shelf were broad paper bandage rolls and glass jars filled with coloured ointments.

A tall, balding man in his late sixties, with his hands firmly stuck in the pockets of his off-white cotton coat, studied my naked thigh. Laid out on the table with my feet dangling over the end, I looked up into a craggy, dour face filled with despair, perhaps affected by many years surrounded by death and disease and defeatism. I saw a wide brow wrinkle. And then the Professor shook his head from side to side in a way which, to me, was a signal bereft of hope. He spoke in Czech to Alex, and I braced myself for the worst.

Interpreting the Professor's decision, Alex said that the wounds were too high on the thigh for extensive surgery; an amputation would be too great a gamble under prevailing conditions. There was just one alternative, he said; if I could put up with the pain, the Professor would gouge out the infected parts; they were dangerously deep, there was no guarantee of the wounds healing, 'positively none'.

I was too demoralized to think about pain. Dangerous though the treatment might be I was grateful for an opportunity denied the majority. Reports were circulating that some camps in Germany had been overrun by the Allies; even the merchants of doom were predicting the end of the war with the start of the new year and I desperately wanted to hang on to my life.

I swallowed a good measure of colourless liquid which tasted like methylated spirits. It was a stimulant Alex said, a generous one. A web belt was passed under the table and strapped around my ankles, and another was wound around my chest and pulled taut. A pair of strong hands gripped my shoulders. Through narrowing eyelids I watched Alex heat a pair of long-nosed scissors over the flame of a burner, reminding me of my mother's kitchen surgery and the times when she operated on boils on the back of my neck as a young boy, first sterilizing her sharpest hat pin in hot coals before jabbing the point into the head of the swelling which caused me to howl and jump up to the ceiling.

Dazed, I was conscious of Nicolas at my side telling me that the bread ration was going to be increased for Christmas Day, a kilo loaf divided into six portions instead of the usual eight, sometimes ten. In addition, the soup would be upgraded with meat and potatoes and every prisoner could look forward to three cigarettes apiece – an extravagant and incredible pledge.

I thought about my last Christmas Day at home with my father and mother and my sisters. At Christmas time my mother's meagre housekeeping money was always spent unstintingly on her children. Two whole days of fun and laughter, card games and dancing; a late breakfast of oven-baked pork and haricot beans; a roast duck dinner with crisp potatoes, brussels sprouts and thick brown gravy, and a supper of ham sandwiches and pickles and mince pies and we children suffered the consequences of gluttony. Oh for one Christmas Day far removed from cruelty and barbarism!

Granted a short period of recuperation, I had a bed to myself in a sick bay occupied by three others similarly favoured with peace and seclusion almost beyond recollection. Propped up in bed I was brought food; my lavatory was a tin chamber-pot brought whenever I called for its use, and my leg was dressed each day. Such tender care when within earshot so many were suffering inexcusable injustices and torments. And from my warm cot in the stark but dirt-free room, I had a scenic view of a snow-white rural landscape with a stretch of the river Danube flowing gently past. Such tranquillity, if only a brief encounter!

The strains of energetic singing came to my ears. It was Christmas evening. In their barracks, the off-duty guards had downed their punishing tools, their rubber truncheons and their whips. With well-lubricated voices accompanied by some strident music, they were singing their theme song about triumph, good fortune and sweeping all before them. They were in a festive, blustering mood not shared by their prisoners, except perhaps the Kapos and the bosses among the Prominenten, who were junketing on their own intoxicating brew ... and therefore at their most dangerous.

Escape from Block 20

Unlike British prisoner-of-war camps where escapes were painstakingly and elaborately planned and executed, with forged papers, documents, clothing, money and food (and without the certainty of damnable reprisals in the event of recapture), prisoners in concentration camps were faced with impossible odds. To the community at large, a scrawny, shabby and anaemic-looking individual with a cut of hair like that of a Pawnee Indian or a growth of two inches with a broad shaven path running through the middle was instantly recognized as a criminal on the loose, a 'fiend' to be put down like a rabid dog. Yet despite the repeated warnings transmitted over the loud-speaker systems, despite the inevitable back-lash, and the mutilated 'sinners' – often maltreated by their civilian captors – who were put on display, there were many prepared to take the gamble.

The escape from Block 20 on the night of 2 February 1945 will stay unique in the annals of those who, persecuted and treated with tyrannical injustices, make a bid for freedom. Block 20, a prison within a prison, housed mainly Russian officers and men, some French, and a small number of Yugoslav partisans, 700 in total confined to one hut. Surrounded by tall granite walls topped with electrified barbed-wire and a sentry in a watch-tower armed with a heavy machine-gun, the building stood without glass in many of its windows, just yawning gaps in the side walls that let in the driving wind and the freezing cold.

Huge pits were being dug outside the perimeter of the camp for communal burials, each hole in the ground designed to accommodate many thousands of bodies. Although strictly isolated, Block 20 learned that they were going to be exterminated en masse. The tip-off was backed up by the fact that they had not received food rations for three days. A quick decision was reached among the senior ranks – there were no dissenters. Towards the latter part of the evening, the Block-chief, a 'Green', and his retinue of assistants, already in a state of unease, were quietly set upon and strangled. This done, the men started to dismantle the furniture and fittings in the two dormitory rooms and the wash-room; they ripped up floorboards and joists, broke up the plumbing, and collected hard footwear, all to be used as missiles.

I was in my bunk, scratching as one inevitably did for relief from blood-sucking marauders before slipping into a troublesome sleep. Apart from crawling pests, there were other irritants that prevented a night of sound sleep – we were always cold, always damp, always hungry, and then there were those poor wretches with respiratory seizures who cried out for help; others in pain, in tears, and in conflict. And, of late, we had a new rumour to contend with; because of typhus in the quarantine camp, we believed the whole camp was marked for liquidation at a stroke.

The wind, too, grated on one's nerves. It sighed and moaned like a thousand suffering souls and whipped up snowflakes against the windows. I was thinking how miserable and unfriendly the place would be even without the camp and all the ugliness associated with it, when a sudden fracas started an alarm. Whoops and screams like those of Red Indians on the warpath came to our ears and reverberated through the streets. I heard warning shouts ... 'flammen, flammen' ... 'verbrennen' ... 'lance-flames'. The flame-throwers we had been dreading were probably about to sear through the thin wooden walls of the hut. We thought we were going to be incinerated alive.

I hooked a leg over the edge of the bunk and tumbled to the floor. My patched up thigh was trampled on in the scrimmage to get out of the hut through the door and the windows. Outside, on the hardened snow, I slithered on all fours, taking an erratic course through the crowds in the direction of the barbed-wire perimeter. Put in great fear from an imaginary inferno, the mobs crawled and ran in all directions in the grey light trying to hide their heads in holes in the ground. The uproar and clamour attracted the fury of the guards.

Approaching Block 15, the hut which was parallel to Block 20 but divided by the tall granite wall sandwiched between, I could see the cause of the turmoil clearly. With the searchlights and arc-lamps switched on, silhouettes of frenzied men, screaming loudly and imitating animal cries, were in full view on the roof of Block 20. A heavy machine-gun was firing; missiles were being thrown; dressed and half-dressed guards were running pell-mell along the track bordering the perimeter, and bullets fired haphazardly from machine-pistols were splintering the walls of Blocks 14 and 15. Amidst howls from men who had been hit, I retreated rapidly, scampering like a frightened rabbit back to the comparative safety of Block 12.

More than half the complement of men had been cut down before the heavy machine-gun had been silenced and the guard in the tower overpowered and thrown to the ground. Hunt down the 'hares', ordered Kommandant Franz Ziereis. So outraged was he by the audacity of the men in Block 20, that he demanded that those who had run, crawled and limped blindly into the bleak, hostile Austrian countryside be brought back alive. The search for the escapees was widespread. At first light, Block-chiefs, Kapos and trustees joined the guards searching the woods and the surrounding countryside. Frozen bodies were sledged back to the camp and dumped outside the crematorium. Reports were reaching a deeply worried Franz Ziereis of prisoners breaking into houses in search of food and clothing. Farmers found shotguns missing and lost horses. In the village of Mauthausen, the inhabitants claimed they had been terrorized by gangs looting their homes. There had been skirmishes; villagers alleged that they had been punched and hit with sticks but many of the prisoners, too weak to resist the fury of the natives, were beaten to death.

Franz Ziereis was more concerned about his own responsibility for the mass break out than he was about the safety of Austrian civilians coming face to face with desperate men, many of whom had been reported to be fleeing along the railway line in the direction of Perg and the city of Linz. But the sub-zero temperature and the violence from the inhabitants in the hamlets into which flagging and disorientated men stumbled were more than enough to abort the efforts of the great majority.

They were brought back to the camp in ones, twos and small straggling groups, bloody, beaten, blue, half-clothed and near naked. Heads bent, heads held high, with a nod to the onlookers, a limp wave of a hand, a greeting, even a smile, they hobbled, they shuffled, they were carried, and they were whipped through the wide open gate into the main street. Watched by a huge assembly of prisoners, dry-tongued and wet-eyed, the luckless men were cudgelled, booted, decapitated and disembowelled by guards and Kapos wielding axes and sharp-edged spades.

In the following days, three men were brought back from Vienna and two from the Czechoslovakian border. At the height of the escape, a small number were known to have disappeared into the camp's entrails where they were given shelter and new identities by their fellow countrymen. Only six, all Russians, reached Moscow safely.

The 'Ice' General

In the dreary, dragging existence of a prisoner, boredom could be a killer. There was much to cry about, little to be engrossed in, nothing to joke or laugh about, except for an occasional incident which raised a chuckle and a quiet round of applause – tales told by eyewitnesses on the crematory detail and by guards and Kapos who, in their daily humdrum, were greatly amused by the misfortunes and mishaps befalling their own kind.

Andreas Trumm, he who gave little children sweets and led them by the hand to their awful deaths, was attacked by a gypsy woman before she was bundled into the gas-chamber. The brave woman lunged at Trumm with a metal spoon sharpened to a point at the handle which caused lacerations to the Corporal's face. A child in the arms of its mother managed to poke a finger into Josef Niedermayer's eye, and to add to the pain, a consumptive woman spat blood into his face. These were minor incidents compared to what befell an unnamed guard escorting women from neighbouring camps; he was pulled into the gas chamber before the door banged to, and his screams were smothered by the sixty victims wailing and chanting.

Polish Colonel Morawski, an intelligence officer and a prisoner-of-war at a place called Grossborn, arrived in camp Mauthausen with several colleagues. They were prepared for execution, having been 'graciously' granted the last rites by a prisoner-priest before they were led to the grim execution Block to be killed by 'Kugel Aktion', the well-tried 'height-measuring' device which fired an unexpected bullet into the back of the victim's neck. However, on this occasion the officers were accompanied by Kommandant Ziereis, his deputy Georg Bachmayer and a retinue of other top-notchers, all wanting to witness the officers' humiliation and to be in at the kill.

First, in order to prolong the anguish, the condemned were conducted on a tour of the building and were shown the 36 tiny interrogation cells on the upper floor, then they descended into the basement where they were invited to look through the Judas spy-hole in the door of the gas chamber. High-ranking military officers and civilian personages sometimes looked through this when the chamber was in operation, to witness for themselves the struggling contortions of the victims as they choked on the lethal fumes.

Next, the men looked into the dissecting room, a cold dank stone chamber with an elongated dish-shaped stone table where operations were carried out to salvage gold in teeth and to skin off exotic tattoos from bodies to incorporate into pieces of craft work. A short walk along a narrow, darkish corridor brought the men to the crematory ovens; and to conclude the tragic farce, which preceded their murder, they were guided to the execution cellar where the method of garrotting was explained. Here, a practical demonstration was arranged in which a prisoner from the tent camp was stood on a short stool under the noose. When the wire apparatus was placed around the live model's neck, a scuffle broke out. Franz Ziereis was seen to shoot Colonel Morawski in the back with his pistol. The wounded Pole turned and grappled with the Kommandant and punched him hard in the face before falling. A Polish major, already incapacitated by sickness, hit out at Georg Bachmayer with the stool and knocked him to the floor; and a young naval officer kicked an Obersturmführer in the testicles.

In a separate incident, a Russian general, Boris Dworkin, left his mark on an Oberscharführer, he punched the man in the mouth and broke his teeth.

General D. M. Karbyshev was a man in his sixties when he arrived in camp Mauthausen. He had a distinguished career, serving in the Imperial Russian army as an officer in the Corps of Engineers. By 1917, he had reached the rank of lieutenant colonel. Shortly after the revolution, he joined the Red Army and in 1919 he was Inspector of Fortifications with the Bolshevik Southern Army Group. Between the wars, he was a senior lecturer at the Staff Academy and in 1939 he sat on a committee which revised the Russian army's training manuals.

But, as I had seen many times before, our captors had total disregard for men, even women, of honour and fame, especially if they were Russian, Polish or Jewish. The brutal murder of General Karbyshev, together with a group of some two hundred men of various nationalities who arrived in the camp, cold, hungry and weary after a long cross-country footslog, was an act of extreme violence and unequalled cruelty, if only because of the numbers involved.

It was February, a typical cold day with ice underfoot, when Karbyshev and his ragged companions were marched into the main street to be corralled between the disinfectant hut and Block 1, the 'A' section of which served as a brothel with small intimate rooms where selected women prisoners, volunteers, pledged their well-fed bodies to the hierarchy of prisoner prominenten. What to do with the new arrivals? The killing machines were working overtime; the four crematory ovens were burning continuously day and night, incinerating some fifty-four bodies each hour; the communal graves were overspilling. Space to house the thousands of evacuees arriving from overrun camps was running out; we were two to a bunk, with others queuing for leg and head room, perhaps hoping for someone to surrender his place by dropping down dead.

The main street and side streets were littered with the dead and dying; great mounds of stiffened bodies formed walls which were broad and high. Passing them, we could see arms and legs shifting, muscles twitching, eyes blinking and mouths opening and closing as if wanting to communicate. Brutality was commonplace and knew no bounds. A hardened prisoner, and I considered myself to be such, could easily turn away from scenes of revolting horror. Seeing a man booted to death no longer shocked, but there were some ruthless examples of great wickedness that compelled me to record in my memory – so as to inform the civilized world, if such a place existed and if I survived – what members of the human species were capable of inflicting on their fellow-men.

One example was a stack of women's bodies dumped haphazardly outside the crematory chute. By all evidence, they were very young women, perhaps just girls, who must have been arrested recently, because they had full heads of hair and showed no signs of malnutrition. Nicolas guessed that they were aged from twelve to sixteen, with a few in their twenties. The clothing on the partially clothed bodies was identical, and we were sure that they were in the uniforms of schoolgirls, perhaps the entire complement coming from an upper-class boarding-school together with their teachers. But what was so stomach-churning was that the bodies, with the exception of the faces, had been violated with instruments for sadistic pleasure. Nicolas described whip marks across thighs and buttocks, flesh from bellies stripped like peel from an orange and hanging in curls, breasts missing and gaping holes between the legs. The work of madmen.

I stood with Nicolas and Barnado outside Block 6. The wind was punishing, but I was somewhat protected from the extreme cold by a cardboard 'vest' next to my skin – an invaluable asset – and a threadbare assortment of glad rags, a thick woollen nightshirt tucked well down into a pair of breeches, army puttees, a greatcoat and a hood with eye-slits pulled down over my head. Coverings like these were as priceless as bread.

General Karbyshev and his companions, thinly protected, in ranks four deep, were ordered to undress. Those who howled protests or were slow to comply were flayed with fists and whips. Serviceable clothing, discarded on the frozen ground, was removed by trustees to be fumigated and cleaned before marketing. Once stripped, the weakest quickly foundered, their raw and livid limbs thrown into spasms as they struck the ground. The General, who had cried out his name and rank to the crowd of lookers-on blocking the cobbled pavement and windows fronting the functional brothel, was seen to rally those crying on their knees, calling upon them to rub their limbs, shift about, and to perform feats of agility to ward off the cold and to stay upright.

With the approach of darkness, those still standing and able to take a few steps were herded into the shower block. The men might have hoped for deliverance when a short fall of warm water energized their frozen limbs. But no, regret or pity was not part of the system which reigned over us; to kill a man at one stroke was often too convenient, a soft option which was boringly unoriginal.

'Die Wasserbehandlung?'* What our guards called 'Unterhaltung', a little amusement. Such unfathomable cruelty! Karbyshev and his few remaining companions, still naked and dripping with warm water, were forced back into the open where hoses were played on their bodies, a performance that was repeated – warm water followed by cold – until every man collapsed. At first light, one could see the result. Blackened, grotesque corpses, some cemented together by ice, lay face down, face up, crouched and stooped in a new fall of snow. Axes and sharp-edged spades cleaved them apart. Only one man had refused to yield and remained on his two feet. General Karbyshev was upright, leaning against the 'Wailing Wall' with his arms folded across his chest and his naked body encased in a mantle of ice.

Descent from Heaven to Hell

February, like all the previous winter months, had produced a great natural toll of human lives. At the turning point in the calendar, we were fed on rumours and precious little else. Unconfirmed reports, hearsay, whispers, no matter how far-fetched, tempered even the minds of those who were hopelessly despondent and on the verge of ending their own lives. No one, not even our jailers, could dispute that the war was petering out. Buchenwald had been liberated by the Russian army and Mauthausen had become the dumping ground for men, women and children from the evacuated camps of Bergen-Belsen, Natzweiler, Sachsenhausen, the women's camp at Ravensbrück and other places previously unheard of. It was impossible to understand what was in the minds of the Germans. Their armies were at a critical disadvantage in the war and nearing the point of total defeat. Transporting hundreds of

---

* The water treatment. General Karbyshev was spared the form of torture when water hoses were forced down a prisoner's throat and up the backside.

thousands of prisoners over hundreds of miles must have placed a heavy burden on their dwindling resources.

The current talk in the camp was of a superhuman American army general, by the name of Patton, a knight in shining armour coming to our rescue. His army, we heard with great rejoicing, was bowling along, skittling down the enemy and anyone attempting to put obstacles in his way. This was credible news, attributed to a hidden wireless and from the mouths of dispirited guards, which brought many close to tears and took some of the sting out of the hostility among the community.

A nine days wonder! General Patton was at Munich, at Salzburg, even closer – at Linz. A 'few' days, 'une semaine', 'zwei Wochen', no more than three before our salvation. I could be home in the middle of March, well in time to greet a glorious spring. What a beautiful thought! What a wonderful promise! 'Vive le Général!' 'Dreifaches auf der Generaloberst!' Alas, no one predicted another seventy-five days before the coming of the Americans and an acceleration in thuggery and murder.

It was a freakish day, sunny and warmish with blue skies, and there was not a cloud to be seen. I was just one among a multitude squatting and sprawled out on dry ground in the side streets, bare to the waist and enjoying the physical pleasure of the sun's rays. There were those like me with their open wounds uncovered in the belief that the sun contained natural healing qualities; others were studiously searching the depths of their clothing for that elusive louse, the many-tentacled pest which stubbornly resisted annihilation.

It was unusually peaceful, just the occasional crack-crack of small-arms fire disturbing our therapy; the administration, too, was taking advantage of the favourable atmospheric conditions. I was catnapping, in the company of the consumptive Nicolas and the reserved Barnado; with us were two newcomers to the camp, John Starr, a lame Englishman who claimed he was an agent with the Special Operations Executive captured in Paris and shot in the leg whilst on the run,* and an American army captain, Jack Taylor, taken prisoner after parachuting into Yugoslavia. Taylor, a tall scrag-faced man – like John Starr, not yet physically on the downward path – told of a planned visit to the camp by a delegation from the Swiss Red Cross, bringing with them a consignment of food and clothing together with a medical team. Incredible news, if true. But late in the day, I thought.

---

* I had learned to be wary of those who claimed to be members of the 'cloak-and-dagger' brigade, no matter what nationality, in the belief that principled agents should remain tight-lipped and not boast about their undercover activities to all and sundry; airy-fairy tales of escapism and playing at spies were two-a-penny, inherited, in all probability, from novels and the cinema screen.

The advancing American army knew about Mauthausen and the many smaller camps within the area of Upper Austria, according to Jack Taylor. We could expect some form of direct action, he said; a few hundred parachute troops descending on to the village and the camp with supplies of arms and ammunition were all that were needed to put our guards to flight. Such a venture, no one doubted, would save many thousands of lives and the war would be over sooner. Such a 'tour de force' would receive a thunderous applause.

There was a formidable army of prisoners in and around Mauthausen; a total of 24,000 at the nearby Gusen camps; 18,000 in Ebensee; 10,000 in Melk; 6,000 in Linz; and smaller numbers at many other subsidiaries … men and women still reasonably strong in mind and body, professional soldiers and veteran resistance fighters, and tens of thousands suffering from moderate to serious physical disadvantages but equally determined to join in an uprising given the chance and the weapons. Angry, revenge-seeking hordes on the loose, especially the Russian hoi-polloi, would cause chaos for the military and civilian population alike. Berlin, we imagined, might be forced to divert some of their reserves to the region and away from the vital lines of battle. It was a satisfying thought!

But the cynics and those who claimed to be experts in the field of international politics – there were, among us, many who once held high office in the service of their respective governments – were resigned to the fact that deliverance would not come from the sky over Mauthausen. It would only happen at the bitter end of hostilities. I became confused, even concerned, by the conjectures and the theories put forward by clear-headed and clear-sighted men of twice and three times my age. I listened attentively and anxiously. The British and American governments had known about German concentration camps and the huge destruction of lives for a long time, and so had the Vatican State. They had done nothing to condemn the widely reported atrocities. Any priest in camp Mauthausen would admit to being haunted with shame for the tolerance shown by the Vatican towards the Nazi regime. Did I really think that someone in London was concerned about me? Look around, I was told. What did I see? Nothing but human waste! Were the powers that be, guzzling and drinking in the safety of their private clubs in Westminster and Washington, going to be wet-eyed and worked up because of us, the scapegoats of war? 'Non' … 'Nein.' Well, someone might shrug their shoulders and be heard to tut-tut, but no one would lose any sleep over us. It would even be said that war was a necessary evil, to pick out and get rid of the insignificant millions like us. If one had to single out an example of ruthless capitalistic policy, said those who supported Communism, it was the 1914–1918 war which took out more than a million 'suckers'. And French infantrymen of that era told of the huge, needless sacrifice of young lives in the trenches, because of the madness, the negligence and the incompetence at international government level.

Insensitive fools, I was told, were still around, manipulating the war from their arm-chairs whilst drinking 'le Scotch', they were not going to move heaven and earth to save people already known to be at death's door. It was a matter of economics, not charity. One million sick and crippled survivors might be acceptable; two million and possibly more falling to the responsibility of the British and American governments would be too much. It stood to reason, no matter how unreasonable and callous it might seem, that a rescue would not be mounted on grounds of compassion.

'Bien sûr!' Of course, there would be an outcry after the war when the full account of the atrocities was broadcast to the world. Questions would be raised. Lies and deceit would be fed. Trials would be held. Those found guilty of crimes would be punished by death, imprisonment, shown leniency and set free. Monuments would be built. People would come to camp Mauthausen to stare, to pray and to cry. People would read books about Hitler's concentration camps written by historians and imaginative novelists, see the violence depicted, even glamorized on cinema screens and, after a while, laugh at sick jokes about gas chambers. And fathers would be persuaded to buy military-style playthings as Christmas presents for their sons, virile-looking figures in combat uniforms armed with gimmicky weapons and flying things with RAF roundels, American stars and Nazi swastikas.

Mistrust. Envy. Opposing views. My ears were sensitive to the verbal strife among the varied nationals; there was no place to hide from the continuous political wrangles which often ended in fisticuffs or worse. But on this day in late February when the mobs were allowed to laze about the side streets unmolested, the warming sun had a magical effect on even the worst of temperaments; and in a friendly, if temporary togetherness, we were listening to weird and wonderful music. A young Jew with bulging eyes was blowing into the mouthpiece of a battered saxophone; another, an older man, was performing an accompaniment with a tinny violin. Nevertheless, it was a sweet diversion and catchy, ironically played in the spirit of jazz – American-style.

Quite suddenly, a diversion of a more urgent kind; ten thousand heads turned upward. A few kilometres to the west and at no great altitude, a formation of aircraft was on an unwavering course, dominating the sky, returning from a mission somewhere, perhaps in Yugoslavia. Then a small group peeled away simultaneously, to break the journey 'home'. Bombs dropped on the marshalling yards at Linz, just twenty kilometres away. Was this the promised day of rescue, when help was so vital to save thousands of lives? Despite the arguments against, I had faith in the Allies, and though I was counted among the disadvantaged – a shortness of breath, a painful throat, dizziness and a drag in my steps – I was goaded by the anger stored within my body to make ready for a rough and tumble should it come. Given a gun, I had the will to pull the trigger.

As always when watching friendly aeroplanes passing over Mauthausen I looked on with envious eyes, thinking of the crews, young men of about my own age, blush-coloured, rakish, sound in wind and limb, returning to base, to a round of applause, to a welcoming and well-deserved tea of eggs and bacon, bread and butter and fruit cake; an evening unbending, a song and dance, a few beers and to bed with a girl.

For a few moments, I was completely abstracted from the wraiths around me. Then came calamity; from the rearguard of a second, smaller formation, came a laggard, its nose dipping and lifting away from the pack. A wisp of smoke, then a broad black ribbon streaked from an engine; the bomber was seen to ripple its wings; and we heard the engines screaming at a high pitch. White puffs were ejected from the body; these unfolded into parachutes that floated gently earthwards before the stricken machine exploded into a ball of fire. John Starr gasped: 'God, do they know on what ground they are falling?'

There were six, five walking, one being carried into the camp, apparently unconscious. Those in good condition were just as I had imagined, sturdy young men in warm flying jackets, ruddy of complexion, bright but watchful eyes, dark- and fair-haired. Arranged with their backs to the 'Wailing Wall', a metre apart they looked neither to the left nor to the right. Eyes straight ahead, they must have been shocked to see the mounds of rigid corpses thawing out in the sun all along the length of the main street, and they may have suspected that the stench wafting up their nostrils came from burning human flesh. Nevertheless the five were in complete control of their feelings.

They stood bolt upright, chins up and hands at their sides. First to inspect the catch were the sadistic friends, Andreas Trumm and Josef Niedermayer, taking time off from the quarry. The toe of Trumm's boot probed the body of the slumped airman, turning the head from one side to the other. Others made sport of the occasion; they teased smoke into the airmen's faces from cigarettes seized as contraband of war – 'Camels', Jack Taylor said, recognizing the packets being offered round.

Heels clicked smartly when the Kommandant, Franz Ziereis, blustered on to the scene, closely followed by his deputy, the vicious Georg

Bachmayer. The silence was uncanny, cat watching mouse, as Ziereis and Bachmayer studied the men's faces and fingered their garments with their large pockets and flaps, quality clothing that would go to relatives or friends, no doubt.

Then, through an Obersturmführer who spoke some English, questions were put to the airmen, first in a civil manner, with a touch of the cap. Having spoken to them blandly, one at a time with unfaltering patience and having achieved nothing, not one answer. The Obersturmführer dropped his gentlemanlike artifice, bunched his gloved fist and punched each man in the face.

Jack Taylor, standing at my side, said in a dry voice: 'They'll get nothing out of those boys, not one damned word.'

The gloved fist assault was a signal for rankers and higher grades to join in a free-for-all. From where we stood, we could clearly hear the gasps of pain; fists and boots rocked the men and felled them to the ground. On their knees, they struggled back to their feet, stood rigidly erect, only to be floored again. Blood trickled from their heads and their eyes puffed up so that they looked like slits – those large, clear eyes that only a few minutes before shone with defiance. Not once did they speak or cry out as they were beaten mercilessly. Almost blinded, and in a state of near collapse, they marched off to the interrogation building as though they had been instilled with a new vitality, their backs were straight, their shoulders square and their heads held high. One could see the tremendous effort they were making to go right through to the bitter end, unconquered and unconquerable.

Distraught, we turned away, thinking only of the day when the account would be settled. Lanky Jack Taylor choked back his tears, tried miserably to whistle a few bars of the American national anthem and, in a cracked voice, recited some of the lyrics: 'And this be our motto: In God is our trust. And the star-spangled banner in triumph shall wave o'er the land of the free and the home of the brave ... '

Note: There were conflicting reports on the killing of the American airmen. Two, the more senior crew members, were said to have been garrotted by Andreas Trumm with the help of Josef Niedermayer. Georg Bachmayer was suspected of having shot all five with a machine-pistol. By whom, and by what method, was a matter of conjecture; one can be certain that the manner of killing was prolonged and painful.

The six airmen were never positively identified. However, it was thought they were from Bombardment Group 99, flying aircraft model B-17G, serial number 44-3187.

Another atrocity involving captured American aircrew was reported to have occurred two months later, on Wednesday, 25 April, less than two weeks before the end of the war, when, again, I heard of cruel acts and Georg Bachmayer implicated in the crimes.

Jack Taylor, agent of the Office of Strategic Services (OSS), was the main prosecutor at the trial of former SS personnel (Mauthausen) held at Dachau, Germany, in 1946.

The Murder of Catholic Priests

Mauthausen, the 'Mother' camp, was not set up to get rid of only Jews. True, Jewish people were top of the list for extermination, but hatred, brutality and wholesale murder were directed towards all religious, political and non-political creeds, towards dark-skinned people like gypsies and negroes, Jehovah's Witnesses, homosexuals and, sadly, what was termed 'nutzlos Dreck', old people and many thousands of incurables previously locked away in institutions.

Priests were looked upon unfavourably. More than 350 were tortured and murdered in the Mauthausen complex. They were labelled 'Soul-Sellers', 'Robe-Slutters', 'Robe-Bugs', 'Heaven-Comics' and 'Pulpit Jews' and were frequently the objects of humiliation.

At the nearby sub-camp of Gusen, they had it doubly hard because of their priesthood and their Polish nationality. As early as 1939, over 1500 prisoners were sent to Mauthausen from the temporary camp of Dachau's penal labour force; and with the transports arriving from Buchenwald, there came more than 200 Polish priests of the Roman Catholic Church, some pastors of Poland's Protestant Church and several German and Austrian priests.

Priests were forbidden to work in the secretarial departments or to hold any position of conciliation. All Polish priests had to work in the open, this meant the terror of the quarry detail using picks and shovels and hauling granite blocks manually up the steps of death in all weathers. They were treated abominably, badly clothed and starved. Hence, the life-span, generally, of these prisoners, especially of the 'low-worth' Poles, and this included Polish priests, was short ... very short. Father Franciszek Mogarski, for example, born on 4 October 1880, arrived in the sub-camp of Gusen on 25 May 1940. The very next day he was killed in the quarry in the early hours of the evening. The cause of death was listed as 'General weakness', and his story is repeated in the records again and again.

There can be no doubt that the great majority of priests and rabbis arrested, transported and incarcerated in the dungeons of prisons and concentration camps throughout occupied Europe showed exemplary courage. Whilst they had their own miseries to contend with, they could be seen tending the sick and injured and comforting the dying. And I would never forget one, a French Catholic priest on the transport from Compiègne to Buchenwald, who kept the torch of his courage shining bright throughout that terrible journey, singing music-hall songs and telling smutty jokes. When it came to the test, after the door of the truck was discovered damaged and forced apart and seventy men were

missing, that silver-haired man in his long black soutane, who had
stayed behind with those too old or too sick to jump from the truck on
to the rails and run for their lives, never flinched. Calmly, he stepped
forward to the edge of the gaping splintered exit; half-blinded from the
light of a powerful torch pointing up at him, he stood firm when the
transport master, a young SS officer in a black leather trench coat, held a
pistol at arm's length and, hysterically, yelled 'Sabotage!' The priest
hunched his shoulders and fingered a medallion hanging from a chain
around his neck. Questioned on who was answerable for the damage, I
saw a faint smile break out on the priest's chubby face. Slowly he raised
a finger, pointing it upwards. 'Lui ... le bon Dieu, en haut, Capitaine,'
he said.

The first priest to arrive in camp Mauthausen on 5 September 1939,
was the Austrian, Herman Kagerer, who came with a transport of skilled
workers as a cabinet-maker from camp Dachau. Herman Kagerer's
prisoner-number was 495. A few months later, on 8 March 1940, came
the Polish priest, Joseph Galuszka from Buchenwald. He immediately
met Father Kagerer, who gave him a piece of bread, informed him about
the camp conditions and advised him not to publicize his priesthood
but, if asked about his trade, to say he was a teacher.

Joseph Galuszka soon came to know of the many dangers facing
priests. Any religious conversation with the other prisoners, as well as
any form of religious activity, care for the souls of the sick and distressed, the saying of Mass or cultural activities, were strictly forbidden
in camp Mauthausen between the years 1938–45, almost up to the very
day of liberation. Even to be caught praying or saying 'God bless you'
was a punishable offence that often led to the death penalty, a thrashing
at least. The possession of rosaries, crosses, necklaces, holy pictures and
prayer books resulted in punishment by the most brutal methods. The
harsh camp life, long working hours, little food and dreadful living conditions made any associations almost impossible. Priests also had to be
wary of the Kapos and Block-chiefs, and there were countless ordinary
prisoners ready to denounce them for a crust of bread and small favours.
Priests were surrounded by bad neighbours and blackmailers.

The antagonistic attitude towards the Church, which was also evident
during the training of members of the SS and the indoctrination of SS
recruits in the Nazi theory of the 'Master-race', as well as the deep-
seated intolerance of all SS personnel, created an atmosphere under
which all religious prisoners suffered. Every day we saw the barbaric
intimidations and chicanery, severe beatings and murder inflicted on
priests by SS officers and men of low grades and by certain prisoners
easily recognized as 'Prominenten' by their beefy build, by their swanky

mode of dress and swinish complexions. The ordinary prisoner had much to fear from these self-important big-mouths.

For example, on the afternoon of 13 August 1940, during a spell of very hot weather, all prisoners working outside were ordered to run at their jobs because two inmates had attempted to escape. This involved running up and down hills carrying heavy granite blocks. Whether it was a sixty-year-old priest or a twenty-year-old student of Theology made no difference, they suffered equal punishment. At short distances stood watchful SS guards. Kapos, armed with whips and sticks beat without mercy anyone not running fast enough. The following night, Poles on outside work were selected for continued maltreatment; having 'forfeited' their meal of the day, they were ordered to spend the night standing to attention in front of their barracks. Those still standing at daylight were moved out to their places of work. Those left on the ground were shot if they still showed a sign of life. As a result of the attempted escape, the neighbouring camp, Gusen, reported many deaths among priests, recorded as due to 'Heart attack' or 'General weakness'. Father Franciszek Woschke was known to have died two days later.

Two priests, the Austrian, Lenz, and the German, Mayer, were transferred from camp Mauthausen to join the Gusen penal company. Together with rabbis, Lenz and Mayer were forced to work under the normal inhuman conditions; every day they had to empty the latrines and carry the body substances in boxes and barrels tied to long poles and strictly at the double ... 'schnell, schnell!' Regularly, and with bare hands, they had to lift the dead out of the stinking pits where they had fallen when trying to empty their bowels. To see a priest covered from head to foot in bloody excreta, carrying away the bodies for burning, provoked shrieks of laughter from guards and Kapos alike.

'Wunderbar!' Marvellous! The cry went up. Suddenly, in late 1940 something happened which was bewildering for all concerned: the living conditions of Polish priests (not the ordinary Polish inmates) was unexpectedly made a little more bearable. The reason which was not disclosed to the priests, was the direct intervention of the Vatican to the German government. On Saturday, 16 November, twenty-seven younger Polish priests were detailed to archaeological diggings – Kommando Spielberg. The priests were personally informed about the nature of their work by Gusen's camp Kommandant, the cutthroat SS Karl Chmielewski, formerly the head chemist. He asked them to work 'langsam', slowly and easily, and, unbelievably, addressed them as 'Sie', a respectful form that made an unprecedented change from the normal 'Schweine' and 'Dummköpfe'. Furthermore, Chmielewski announced an increase in their daily bread ration, one kilogram loaf between four instead of the usual six, even eight. All this was such an absolute sensation that it spread through the camp 'telegraph' system at lightning speed. At the same time, Polish priests were withdrawn from the quarry and stone-carrier commandos and transferred to other work-groups. This was heartening news for all prisoners. Were the SS about to depart from their normal callous indifference to their prisoners and show mercy?

Old hands were sceptical, even suspicious. The well-intentioned SS, the 'gutgemeint', they said, were the dead ones rotting in the ground; there was no such thing as fair-minded or charitable SS. The idea that the SS were going to release the priests, the 'scum' they hated to extinction, and put them back on the streets, was laughable, they declared. Nevertheless, on 7 December, all religious prisoners suitable for transport were called together in Gusen, Karl Chmielewski's camp. On the same day, some 180 prisoners, the majority priests, said 'auf wiedersehen' to Mauthausen and were transferred out of Austria to camp Dachau, Germany. Except for a few, all were in bad physical condition and most had to be transported by trucks. They looked on the transfer as an escape from the traumatic experience of Mauthausen and Gusen; but those who expected Dachau to be soft, some kind of sanatorium, were sadly to be disillusioned. For Dachau was, in many ways, just as terrible a place. Priests were selected for live medical experiments and many were sent to Castle Hartheim, Austria, the centre for extermination by gassing.

At least one of the priests, Karol Zwaka, did not arrive at Dachau alive; he died on the rail-transport. Not all the priests were transferred as expected. Among those who stayed behind was the twenty-seven-year-old army priest, Father Stefan Ringwelski, born in Nowo Poleszki, and the able-bodied Dr Johannes Gruber, who was tortured and strangled to death by the one-time Gusen camp Kommandant, SS Fritz Seidler, a corpulent brute. Dr Gruber earned recognition in the sick-barracks as a male nurse to the sick priests and for his efforts to obtain medication for them. Whilst he was responsible for the stocking and transport of archaeological finds in Gusen, he gained an almost legendary name for the constant and systematic care he gave to Polish children and youth prisoners.

The Polish accountant, Zdislaw Rakowski, prisoner number 46511, gave the following report about Dr Gruber ' ... one felt his concern, he had friends of all nationalities, he was unafraid, constantly searching for new sources from which he might help. He had much to bear. When he was caught distributing little gifts of love, he was often beaten. In the spring of 1943, he managed to establish a secret means of communication with the world outside ... ' In fact information about the atrocities at Mauthausen and its sub-camps was leaked out regularly, not only from Austria but also from camps in Germany. On 11 January 1942, the London *Sunday Times* reported that hundreds of Jews had been murdered in camp Mauthausen. At least one other reputable English national newspaper carried the story. Did no one care?

In 1943 Dr Gruber had secured an illegal contact by letter with people in the city of Linz, some twenty kilometres from Mauthausen (probably with others who were working in the quarry and the civilians working in the factories); he was said to have informed the world about the conditions, the facts about the wholesale slaughter of men, women, and children, about the mass shootings, the hangings and the gassings. In the beginning of 1944, the Vienna Gestapo received information on Dr Gruber's activities and he was transferred from Mauthausen to camp Gusen and strict camp-arrest. Here, the SS authority expected him to commit suicide. The impatient brute, Fritz Seidler, strangled the brave Dr Gruber on Good Friday 1944.

Priests of all nationalities were sent to Castle Hartheim, the euthanasia centre on the road to Passau, Alkoven, Austria described by Simon Wiesenthal as a 'school for mass murder'. As Wiesenthal wrote in *The Murderers Among Us*:

> No one will ever know exactly how many people were put to death in Castle Hartheim, the renaissance building with its magificent colonnade. No memorial for the victims of Hartheim – most of them Austrian and German Christians – has been erected. The records of the registry office have not been found ...
>
> Hartheim graduates later became teachers of future cadres of scientifically-trained killers. After some practice, the 'students' became insensible to the cries of the victims. The 'teachers' would watch the reaction of their 'students.' It was a brilliant psychological touch to use Austrians and Germans as victims in the basic training for mass murder. If a 'student' did not break when he had to kill his own people, he would have no moral scruple about exterminating thousands of 'Untermenschen'. A 'student' who couldn't take it was sent to the battle fronts, where his commander would assign him to a Himmelfahrtkommando, 'a suicide squad'.

When at last liberation came to camp Mauthausen, all priests who were physically able dedicated themselves to the care of sick prisoners. Within a short time temporary chapels were set up in Block 18 and Block 19. American military-priests donated various objects, such as prayer-books, vestments, chalices and hosts – consecrated wafers of unleavened bread.

Murder had been run down but no amount of praying, medication or nursing could halt the death-rate which continued to be distressingly high among those too far gone. The chance of life had come too late for many hundreds. A few days, even a few hours, would have made a difference.

To Sleep, not to Awake

Sick in body and soul, I longed to find a quiet place to lie down and sleep. Near to despondency, I wished only for eternal rest to come in sleep, without the humiliation, the agony and the violence that encompassed us. The rescue by air had not come about, and the general supposition was that it never would. Nicolas was dead, his pitiful end caused by consumption among other damnable things; so, too, was Barnado, who had chosen to die by simply walking to the electrified barbed-wire, a way of death currently popular among the hopelessly deranged.

I knew I was dangerously ill, at the point of my own death. I retched on an empty stomach; I tried dunking my bread in my soup, but nothing would pass down my burning throat. I trembled constantly, could not bring my eyes into proper focus and stumbled about almost legless. For a place in a lower bunk, I traded my rations; here, by the grace of my Block-chief, now more tolerant because of the threat of deliverance and the day of reckoning, I was granted a respite from the dreaded outdoor roll-calls.

Through the heavy curtains of my semi-consciousness, the noise in the hut was amplified a hundred times, until it became like a hammer thudding away in my head. The cacophony of tempers, of hysterics, grieving and weeping was unremitting. I wept too. Tears of foolish, boyish homesickness sprang to my eyes and began to trickle down my cheeks. I hid my head under my blanket, not wishing others to see my weakness, for if I did not take hold of myself, I would soon be across the narrow dividing line between sanity and madness.

When I was awake again, thousands of strange little objects darted in front of my eyes and my bunk seemed to be tossing about like a punt in a storm. It was strangely quiet, almost peaceful, and when I slewed my pillowed head to one side and adjusted my vision I saw I was in a confined space with figures stirring stealthily around me. I heard John Starr's very British voice in my ear. 'How d'you feel, old boy?' he asked. 'We thought you were going to kick the bucket, you know!'

I took a deep swallow and found my tongue. 'How long have I been in here?' I asked Starr.

'Going on four days,' he replied. 'Thanks to Alex, he pulled a few strings and had you brought here. You've had a nasty dose of diphtheria, you know. Thank Christ for being British … '

I had been blessed with more than the nine lives of a cat. I was feeble, just skin and bone, unable to sit up, but I could breathe with little trouble, peck like a bird at my bread and take liquids. Alex warned me of possible complications. There was no medicine available, not even an aspirin, the only antidote was to grin and bear the malaise and to see it through unbeaten.

That I was obliged to do. My death had been averted only because of the privilege granted to my nationality, that much I knew; which left me with a twinge of uneasy conscience when there were many hundreds capable of life and deserving of attention. But there appeared to be good news for everybody holding on to life. Amazingly, the Swiss Red Cross had made contact with the camp and a few dozen food parcels had been unloaded at the gate for distribution. Unfortunately the consignment proved to be a nice bonus for the Kommandant and his cronies, although at least the Red Cross had come into contact with us, though entry into the entrails of the camp had not been permitted.

So far, the best news was for John Starr, and this time it was not a rumour, but a confirmed report. The Englishman was due to be released, and was officially informed that he was on a list of some 180 to be removed from the camp by the Swiss authorities. Why Starr was among those chosen was a mystery to him. Whatever the reason, it was a psychological lift for Jack Taylor, myself and all of us left behind. We might profit by the setting free of the 180; it would no longer be necessary for the Swiss to enter the camp to see the horror for themselves, the drama would be unfolded by those released and broadcast to the world.

Given renewed hope, and mindful of the short respite allowed in my hospital bed before being returned to the fold, I was resolved to get back on to my feet unaided and as quickly as my spindly legs would allow. I took short, shuffling steps around the room hanging on to the sides of the other three bunks occupied by my neighbours, making my way unassisted to the washroom and lavatory in a deep recess in the corridor outside the door. It was here, on a bench seat in the corridor where I paused to take breath, that I came across a rare sight – a young, leggy girl, dark-haired and attractive, who was dressed neatly in a grey-coloured cotton coat over a skirt. Thinking her to be a member of the SS medical personnel, I went by the rules, hauled myself to my feet and observed a servile respect until she passed me by, without so much as a glance.

Who was this unfaded creature with the sad brown eyes? Alex

enlightened me: twenty-three years of age, Lena worked as a prisoner-nurse in the SS infirmary, making occasional visits to the SS medical laboratory attached to the prisoner-hospital building, a sinister corner which no one cared to discuss. A Czech national, she was just one of a small group most women prisoners looked upon with suspicion as shameful opportunists who had given the kiss of Judas; it was an imputation which was sometimes perhaps misplaced, sometimes perhaps justified, particularly so with regard to the whores in the brothel block who were known to be ready volunteers.

Lena was a 'protégée' under the wing of an SS doctor, it was revealed. But, said Alex, not from choice; like many pretty young girls of intelligence and with nursing experience, Lena had bowed to a threat. She had seen her father executed in Prague, and her mother and older sister had been incarcerated in nearby Gusen camp to toil in the penal columns. Because Lena had agreed to conditions forced upon her, her mother and sister had been transferred to the military textile factory at Lenzing, thus sparing them from the rigours of heavy, killing work. To spit at Lena, to damn her, and to put her in the same category as the brothel women was, perhaps, warped judgement.

I chanced to see Lena again the following day. I risked a smile and a 'bonjour ... wie geht's, Mademoiselle?' I didn't click; she quickened her step and darted brusquely by with her head held high. Undaunted, I watched for her return and tried a different approach. I said, cheerfully, in English and French: 'Hello, Lena, I'm Alex's friend ... l'ami anglais de Alex!' She stopped in her tracks, hesitated, turned her head, looked me blankly straight in the face then went on her way.

I felt disappointment. What did I have in mind? I had hoped to hear a soft answer, see a twinkle in her sad brown eyes, feel a touch of her hand. It was a long time since a pretty girl had looked at me with wistful eyes; a long time since I had thrilled to the sizzling passion of full red lips on mine and frenzied fingers quickening my pulses in a fever of excitement. Oh, for just one fabled day of Romainville; fond looks from a woman; blown kisses; the love letters that had me tossing and turning in my sleep; the adulation; the amorous intentions. Lucy ... dear Lucy, often said, often spiritedly, that I was 'un jeune homme, peu mondain, le plus beau'. Eighteen months had passed. Now, when I dared to look at myself in the mirror hanging on the wall in the washroom, I saw a face which was unshapely and haggard, with deep lines and hollowed eyes. I looked an old person – 'gaga'. Would my face ever be pressed to a woman's naked bosom again?

On what should have been the last day of my convalescence before I was returned to my Block, I was given a reprieve. It was Lena who approached me in the corridor; her voice was low and urgent and her eyes darted about. In passable English, she said: 'I'm sorry if you thought me rude. Alex spoke to me. Watch for me tomorrow.' She pressed something into my hand. 'No one must see,' she said as she hurried away.

She was gone in a flash, before I could return a reply. Cautiously I crept into the washroom and found a vacant cubicle; behind the closed door, I opened my loosely clenched fist and saw an egg. It was brown and boiled hard by the feel. I cracked it gently, putting aside the fragments of shell. I remembered how my mother fed sick birds, crumbling an egg into the smallest of pieces so as not to choke their gullets. I followed her lesson, placing each crumb in my mouth, chewing thoroughly and, between breaths, swallowing the mash with saliva. I was convinced there was nutriment in the shell. I pulverized the fragments in the palms of my hands until they were just grains and lapped them up. I felt I had eaten a meal.

Because of Lena's magical intervention, which I wasn't going to question, my release from the hospital bunk was postponed for a few precious days. This remission gave me the time to upgrade my five senses and improve my motive power. I continued to receive my food rations, brought to me in my room by orderlies so that I did not have to stand in quarrelsome and riotous lines. And Lena, at great risk, was meeting me in the corridor to pass me food appropriated from speculative sources.

Yet another consignment of food parcels had been delivered to the camp but into the wrong hands. How careless of the Red Cross! Lena had seen a distribution to SS officers. It went to their families quartered in the Mauthausen area; nothing reached the prisoners.* The rank-and-file guards were tightening their own belts, short on food rations, drink and tobacco. One heard of unrest, some desertions, and many soldiers were seeking leave to join the troops in action on the battle fronts with a fair chance of ending the war as prisoners and escaping the expected wrath of mobs liberated from years of torment who were bent on revenge. For the same reason, Kapos and many other top-ranking criminal prisoners were volunteering for the scenes of battle, hell-bent

---

* The President of the International Red Cross, Professor Karl Burckhardt, received permission from Gestapo Chief Ernst Kaltenbrunner to instruct the Swiss delegates to enter camp Mauthausen to undertake the distribution of food parcels themselves. But Kommandant Ziereis pretended to be grieved by the mistrust this implied; he said that he was perfectly competent to make the distribution himself without anyone looking over his shoulder. Ziereis, understandably, did not want the delegates nosing around the interior of the camp. However, delegates did not have to go beyond the gates to grasp the situation, corpses were littered everywhere; had they looked down on the SS football field at the end of the approach road, they might have counted ten thousand bodies filling a communal grave.

on avoiding threatened retribution in the safe-keeping of the advancing Americans.

Right now, Kommandant Ziereis was in deep trouble with Mauthausen's civilian population. Demoralized, they were petitioning Ziereis to turn away the incoming transports cluttering the station and its surroundings and to clear away the trail of human mess. On a brief visit to the village, Lena had noticed groups of nervous people wandering around the market square, bemoaning the disastrous turn of events. Undoubtedly, the villagers had heard about the liberation of Buchenwald by the Russian army, when countless numbers of starving prisoners had gone on the rampage, breaking into homes, attacking the inhabitants and searching for food and clothing. Hadn't they suffered an example of what might come to them when they were confronted by a few stragglers after the escape from Block 20? To the villagers, who perhaps deserved a stint of nervousness and misery, the blot on their landscape had become a real hornet's nest.

The plea fell on deaf ears. To get rid of the human 'mess' was a Herculean task. It was impossible for Ziereis to turn back the transports, because there was no place for them to go. He was reported to have told the villagers that they had to share the responsibility for the 'Unordnung'. If they wanted a clean village they would have to set about the work themselves; he had better things to do.

At last, the Swiss delegates arrived to collect an anxious John Starr, who had started to think that some kind of hoax was being played on him and that he wasn't due to go home after all. Once more Kommandant Ziereis refused the delegates entry; their lorries were driven into the main street by the SS whilst they hung about outside. After the loading of those selected to leave, the lorries were driven out, handed over and escorted to a road away from the village centre.

John Starr had been well briefed by Jack Taylor, who had told him: 'For Christ's sake don't disown us, John. You're our only hope of getting us out of here in one piece; if you have to draw a picture, make it stick out, but we *must* have help ... that's an order, John! Our faith is in you; in the next few days our necks will be stretched up at the sky. Think about that, John!'

We had watched his departure with envious looks. After he had passed through the gate seated in the back of a lorry, and had vanished from view, Jack Taylor turned to me with a baffled expression and said: 'I don't know what to make of that guy.'

If Kommandant Franz Ziereis was worried about the approaching Americans, he didn't show it; he made no attempt to halt the murder. On the contrary, the executioners went to work in fits of madness, machine-gunning new arrivals in batches. Incredibly, special cases were often treated with time-consuming ceremony: public hangings with lurid pageantry, including the camp's earnest prisoner-musicians with violin, accordion and brass instruments.

Reveille was still at 5.15 am; roll-call half an hour later. Working hours were maintained at thirteen hours daily and longer for penal commandos. Food rations had become irregular and pitifully small, just a smell and a lick. Child-prisoners, mainly Jews and gypsies from Hungary, were shown no mercy. Paralysed by fear, the children were introduced to a new menace recruited to the ranks of the guards – 'half-pint' soldiers of the Hitler Youth, equalling their elders in callousness. And they were scheming; when they joined in the kind of recreation normally seen in a school playground – football, rounders, and hop-scotch – there was a sinister purpose behind the show of friendliness towards the captive children. The Hitler Youth experimented in games of impropriety; boy and girl prisoners were encouraged to perform acts of bestiality with each other for rewards and, pretending they were going to give out sweets, the Hitlerite bullies offered to take the children for a stroll. Hand in hand, singing, they went along the main street and into the gas-chamber.

Lena warned me to look for a hiding place in the event of Kommandant Ziereis carrying out his threat to blow up the camp and bring in the flame-throwers. Along with others desperate to see the conclusion of the war and the punishment of the vile criminals controlling us, I spent many hours wandering from one end of the camp to the other searching for a hole where I might hide. There was no place bomb- or fireproof. But now that the crematorium had been run down for lack of fuel, some enterprising prisoners were hiding among the mounds of corpses during the hours of darkness, waiting to be carted to the communal graves for burial by porters employed on the night shift. They ran a great risk of being bayoneted, but once outside, and if undiscovered, slipped away from the wagons into the countryside.

Face to Face with a Monster

I was in possession of a pistol, a Walther P38 with a full clip of ammunition. To possess it was as indiscreet as walking about with a whole loaf of bread under my arm. As a schoolboy, I had fun with a water-pistol bought from Woolworth's; never had I handled anything more lethal. Lena had passed the P38 to me. It was not hard to guess where it had been swiped from and from whom. There were others in possession of guns, Lena assured me. A Russian major and an Austrian colonel were plotting an uprising – an order to resist would be given at the first sign of danger. How, I asked myself, could a few guns take on an estimated 2,000 heavily-armed guards? It would be no more than slinging ink pellets at them.

We were well into the season of spring, the closing days of April. The milder weather was welcome, but the conditions had become infinitely worse. Sealed trucks stood immobilized at Mauthausen's station, the poor souls within suffocating and maddened by thirst. Despite the late hour and regardless of the heavy demand on military manpower and the futility of it all, the transfer of prisoners from one camp to another in the region went on in the normal way. Women arriving from the evacuated Ravensbrück camp were immediately selected for fitness and sent, unfed, to places on the road to Vienna to clear debris from bomb damage. An untold number fell victims to air-raids.

News was filtering into the camp from several sources. Lena – I was still snatching a few seconds with her each day and receiving life-saving bread – said she had seen guards and some of their officers trying on civilian clothing and packing bags. We heard about Dresden; the city had been levelled to the ground with one hundred thousand being killed. Pleasing news! We heard deplorable reports of captured Allied airmen being bludgeoned to death and lynched by townspeople. And the German High Command was ruthless with their own; deserters had been seen hanging from roadside trees as an example to others with unsoldierly intentions.

John Starr's release had proved non-productive. There was general bitterness within the camp; prisoners were griping that the Allies had written everybody off. There was some justification for the accusations going the rounds, because an air-drop of arms and ammunition when the SS garrison was at breaking point would have been very effective.

It was unfortunate that we were denied the opportunity of a proper battle for our survival. A confrontation would have neutralized the conflict within the camp: a great deal of blood was being shed among prisoners at loggerheads with one another. Murder had become rife, the motive being bread, and it was the sick and the weak who took the brunt of the violence. Bread was irregular, and when an allocation of soup was announced, room-assistants armed with cudgels escorted the containers from the cookhouse to the Blocks to prevent starving youths from dipping tin mugs into the liquid and making off as fast as their stick-like legs could scuttle. Scuffles were the rule, resulting in containers spilling into the dirt; the hit-and-miss raiders, down on their knees and lapping up the soup, seemed immune to the blows that split open their heads. Many accepted punishment by hanging and without showing fear; a chair, a short rope and a hook in the ceiling of a hut was the scaffold. The craving for food had driven some men to cannibalism; it was not an epidemic, but examples were open to view, and there were those who, unashamedly, acknowledged that the flesh of corpses alone was giving them lifeblood. Who could argue?

Fresh supplies of poison had arrived for the gas-chamber; the crematory ovens were revived and the killing industry was running on oiled wheels around the clock again. I watched Maria Baranbanov pass by, on her way from the quarantine camp to join the queue for asphyxiation, an agonizing and long drawn out death for those in full grasp of their senses. I had no way of knowing if she was in her proper state of mind. A year and a half had gone by since that red-letter day in both our lives when I had become acquainted with the lovely Maria on Romainville's enchanted ground. Now the beauty had wilted more than enough to make my heart bleed, she looked like a rag doll that had been dragged through a quagmire; unshapely, she reeled as she walked and her frail arms thrashed at the air; her once long glossy fair hair, viewed with envy by Romainville's young women, now hung down in thick matted cords; and her dress, in shreds and unfastened, bared her breasts which drooped over a sunken chest like blackened tongues. I had a mind to call out: 'Maria, I love you … we'll meet again, soon!' But I restrained myself and turned my head away. There was nothing I could do for Maria.

The camp was awakened by a huge explosion. Fear swept through the Blocks yet again. We poured out into the streets, through the doors and the windows in another rough and tumble. It was still the small hours. Panic, for the moment, marked time in the main camp. Pandemonium came from beyond the perimeter: one of the Jewish tent camps had been dynamited. Daylight revealed the carnage; whole bodies and limbs had been tossed on to the roofs of Block 5 and Block 10. It was a crime without explanation which presaged more evil. Later in the day, 2,000 sick men from the 'Russenlager' were machine-gunned beside the SS football field.

The month of May blossomed and the camp was treated to an extraordinary sight. A tremendous roar which deafened ears and skittled rickety prisoners to the ground streaked over the rooftops like a gust of hot wind. It was an aeroplane! The machine waggled its wings, lifted its nose up and disappeared, breathing out an overpowering smell of fumes in its wake. 'A two-engined American reconnaissance plane,' Jack Taylor whooped. There was great excitement; caps were thrown into the air, men whistled and hurrahed as never before, and the queue for the gas-chamber thinned with the wild abandonment of discipline, the resilient breaking away to take refuge among the many thousands milling about in the side streets.

Was this winged phenomenon at last the curtain-raiser to an air-drop? With the guards put in a flap, it was a moment for rejoicing, when hunger and antipathy between certain factions mattered little. To the north of the camp, fighter planes could be seen over the Danube, streaking out from the clouds and strafing an enemy stampeding in terror. Prisoners, pushing their luck, clambered on to roofs for a grand-stand view. But the machine-guns in the watch towers remained silent, their handlers lurking half-visible in the background.

Masses were spoiling for a fight. There was boastful talk, calling for a rush at the gate. But it was suspended when the fighter planes were seen to fly away without so much as a nod or a wink, and when guards and Kapos were hotfooted in from work-parties to strengthen a weakening garrison and restore order to the streets.

Lena said there was wrangling within the administration: some wanted to made a quick exodus whilst there was time; others, fanatical Hitler devotees believing in miracles, were relying on the elite SS divisions and their new all-powerful tanks to outmatch the Americans and repel the advance. And Lena was very concerned: her 'guardian' had voted with the officers preparing to quit the scene and, in no-nonsense talk, had told her she was to accompany him.

Lena was in a tight corner. She had no desire to leave Mauthausen under pressure with someone unacceptable. Her first priority was her mother and sister, both now returned to camp Gusen and holding on to life. With Alex's help, her intention was to wait until the very last minute, then adopt a disguise and gain admittance to the women's quarantine camp.

'Hey, Engländer!' It was the term of address to which I was accustomed, that or 'Brite'. The caller, a Czech prominent I recognized from the Political Section, sounded hard-pressed. Sweating, he said he had been searching for me all over the place. He had a message: Hauptsturm-führer Georg Bachmayer wanted to see me immediately.

It was the afternoon of the third day of May. Trees could be seen in full bloom. Shrubs were thickening. There was a definite bluishness about the River Danube, sunbeams were shimmering on the gently flowing water. Fragile mayflies were flitting about on a warm breeze. No birds were to be seen but a myriad of flying and crawling insects with bloated abdomens picnicked on human remains and on those in a dying state. There was no queue for the gas-chamber, no roll-call, no rations; nervous Block-chiefs and prominenten chewed on their dwindling store of bread guarded against discovery.

In the cluttered streets, sullen, cursing men, half-naked, naked, drifted about aimlessly and wallowed in self-pity. They squatted on the ground, stretched out, face down, twitching, brooding, rambling, weeping, suffering, dying. Bony fists brandished, they damned the god-forsaken sky and tongue-lashed the Allies for promising hope then failing to rescue them. My feelings were similar: disappointment, bafflement, anger.

I had come a long way. The big guns were within earshot – thunderous booms and muffled thumps – and I did not want to die without seeing the final result ... the pay-off. Now, as I followed in the messenger's footsteps, gulping for breath, I was at an unexpected psychological crisis. One of the most feared degenerates, Georg Bachmayer, was waiting to see *me*. What little blood I possessed in my body jellied.

There was no need for alarm, the Czech said, speaking in French, I would be returning to my Block 'dans très peu de temps', a promise which did nothing to relieve my anxiety and suspicion. Why should the monstrous Hauptsturmführer send for me? A thousand things went through my mind. My involvement with Lena? The stolen food? My witness to murder? Keeping my head, I contrived to flick the safety-catch of my pistol to the 'feuer' mark; the weapon lay snug in the deep hollow of my stomach, tightly secured by a thin belt of plaited rags. If the worthless Bachmayer intended to do me harm, then I would do my damnedest to shoot him before turning the pistol on myself.

Committed, I passed through the gate. Outside, there was a great deal of activity, guards running around in circles and loading boxes and bundles on to trucks. I was ushered through the door of a one-storeyed building, along a narrow corridor to a door affixed with the name: Hauptsturmführer G. Bachmayer. The Czech messenger knocked gingerly, with the knuckle of a finger. My heart pounded. A voice, jaunty-sounding, called out: 'Bitte, eintreten.' I took three awkward paces into the monster's den.

At that very instant, the fearless Lutchez's words of wisdom came back to me. 'SS officers? I shit in their faces. It's the fancy uniform that make some knees knock, undress the bastards and what do you see, eh?' Lutchez's contemptuous tone was easily recalled when my eyes fell on Bachmayer. It was the first time I had seen him at close quarters and bareheaded. He looked harmless enough, not the kind of man whose name would go down in history's black book. A cigarette burned between his lips; he lounged behind a desk, one slippered foot across it; his jacket hung at the back of his chair; his braces hung loose and his shirtsleeves were rolled above his elbows; his darkish hair was thinning and sloped back from his forehead. Bachmayer looked normal, like a sociable person relaxing after toiling in his garden; his eyes were soft and not, as one might have expected of a killer, steely and callous.

He half smiled. 'Bitte, sitzen,' he said, politely pointing to a cushioned chair, the only other piece of furniture in the room. I sat down, crossed my legs and folded my arms. Bachmayer offered me a cigarette which I declined with a respectful 'Nein danke, Herr Hauptsturmführer.' Did I speak German? Again I replied in a servile manner. 'Nein, nichts, Herr Hauptsturmführer.'

Bachmayer turned to the Czech. He spoke to the man in soft, remorseful-sounding tones and I was easily able to understand what was being communicated before the interpretation into French. First came 'an apology'. The Hauptsturmführer, said the Czech, had not been made aware of my presence in the camp; had he been informed earlier he would have made it his business to include me among those removed by the Swiss authorities.

That feigned regret disposed of, Bachmayer continued with a torrent of words; 'sagen' him this, 'sagen' him that, inhaling on a cigarette, gesticulating with his unimpaired hand – the other was crippled – and occasionally glancing in my direction. I kept a straight face, trying not to bat an eyelid, shifting uncomfortably on my seat in an effort to ease the pressure on the leaking ulcers trapped under my backside. I was attentive. The war, it was explained to me in pious tones, had been a dreadful event for the British and German peoples alike. It was the all-powerful Jewish influence in the world which was responsible for the war. Did I understand?

'Mais oui, bien sûr,' I answered readily. Had my head not been on the block I might have yawned and added, 'de nature fatigante'. But I wasn't going to strike a dramatic pose and challenge Bachmayer's twisted ideology with the Americans knocking at the door; and not for one moment did I think the man had called me into his presence to offer me an apology or rant about Jews. He wasn't responsible for the conditions in the camp, he wanted me to know. Nor had he ever raised a hand to a prisoner, a thousand people would testify to that. He had striven for better terms, but he was in the minority, one small voice which didn't carry much power. I had to understand that there were bad men in every army; he blamed the Russians for the hunger and sickness, it was the Russkies who had deliberately bombed food depots and who had destroyed medical supplies meant for the camp. And Bachmayer expressed his relief for the coming of the Americans before the Russians. For that we should thank God he said. Claptrap, I thought to myself.

Bachmayer got up from his chair. He adjusted his trouser braces and left the room to fetch me some bread to eat. When the door closed, the Czech came to the crucial point. I was astounded. Bachmayer, the Czech said, was in need of a safe passage out of the camp, 'un renseignement' written in English to be presented to the Americans if challenged. All that was wished of me was to write down on paper my full name, nationality, place of birth and a few words to exonerate Bachmayer from blame. Several other nationalities had made a contribution. 'C'est tout simple,' the Czech said.

It was preposterous! Bachmayer was clutching at a straw to save himself. Not only was he evil, he was moronic. Who in their right mind was going to accept the words of an insignificant nobody like me? Why seek my help when Jack Taylor was a creditworthy person? He had the qualifications, was older by more than ten years and was a captain in the American army, a rank which matched Bachmayer's. I was about to recommend Taylor when, suddenly, it occurred to me that his presence in the camp might not be known to Bachmayer. Taylor wouldn't thank me for putting him at risk.

'Vous êtes avec indécision?' the Czech asked sternly, thinking I was hesitant.

'Mais non, Monsieur!' I replied. I had no thought of playing the hero. A brave man might have said: 'To hell with the Hauptsturmführer!' Jack Taylor, made of sterner stuff, might have told Bachmayer to 'go jump in the Danube'. Not me! Tact was the best policy. To put my tongue out at Bachmayer would be to lose my head; I wouldn't be around to receive an ovation or a medal.

I took the pen and paper, steadied my right hand and wrote down my home address in block capitals: '1 LES MARAIS COTTAGE, BEAUMONT, SAINT PETER'S, JERSEY, CHANNEL ISLANDS. BRITISH SUBJECT. CHURCH OF ENGLAND. AGE 24.' I wrote with extra care, as I had done at school when I was awarded the prize for clarity and neatness, and opened with a form I had often seen as the heading on official communications: 'To whom it may concern: The American Army, Airforce, Navy, Marines.' The last-named was meant to ridicule, but I wanted to be neither too clever nor infantile, not knowing whether the note would be put to the test by some astute brain gifted in the English language. I kept the composition short and simple, in terms which I hoped would carry conviction and insure me from harm over the next twenty-four hours. I added my signature in the realization that the note did not indemnify me against Bachmayer's treachery.

The wooden-faced Czech took a long look at what I had written. His eyes passed over it and his lips moved silently, nodding what seemed to be an approval without asking questions. When Bachmayer returned, carrying a half-loaf of black bread and a fat piece of sausage, the Czech perked up and said 'Alles in Ordnung, Herr Hauptsturmführer.' Bachmayer took the note, gave some attention to it and asked the Czech a couple of questions. Satisfied with the answers, Bachmayer folded the paper carefully, as if it was a rare piece of parchment. He placed it into his wallet; that done, he turned to me, put out his good hand and said 'vielen Dank' and 'auf wiedersehen'.

Greatly relieved, I made my exit. With the sausage in a pocket and the bread hidden inside my jacket, tucked under an armpit, I was escorted back into the camp's entrails. Scarcely pricked by conscience, I went in search of Jack Taylor. 'Hardly treason,' I said to him after I explained where I had been and the result. 'I even shook hands with the man. Tell me, what would you have done?'

Jack Taylor made short work of a share of the bread and sausage. Mouth full, he said: 'I'd have kissed the son of a bitch's ass for a whole loaf.'

Lena had been on edge, having learned of my summons to Bachmayer's office. When we came together for a few minutes in the storage room at the hospital she warned me to be on guard. Bachmayer, she said, was tricky. I wasn't safe. I took Lena's advice, abandoning my Block and adopting another identity, that of a Russian, having stripped the clothing from a body. Now, for the remaining hours of daylight, I looked over my shoulder wherever I drifted. At nightfall, I lay down in the open. I slept fitfully.

The fourth day of May dawned. Sharp-eyed, I resumed my wanderings, mingling with the lethargic hordes. No roll-call. No work-parties assembled. No guards to be seen other than those mounting the towers and now strolling the perimeter in pairs, and the crematory chimney was producing no smoke.

On tenterhooks, I watched for Lena. The time dragged. It was mid-afternoon before she appeared, after having been put to some difficulty at the gate, she explained. Bachmayer was still about, she said; but Franz Ziereis had left immediately after hearing of the Americans fighting on the approaches to Mauthausen, news which failed to quicken my pulses into a fever of excitement.

For the first time, Lena and I sat down and held hands. Calmly, we discussed the future, now staring us in the face. First, Lena wanted to be reunited with her mother and sister, to see to their well-being was her priority. She asked me if I would go with her to her home in Prague; there, she said, I would have the opportunity to recover my strength throughout the months of summer. Later, if my plans were to go to England, she had her heart set on accompanying me.

The offer of convalescing in Prague appealed to me for a very good reason; and providing there were no strings attached I would help Lena get to England if that was her wish. I owed it to her; there was no doubt in my mind that she had made a vital contribution to my survival. At the point of breaking down, she spoke plainly of her relationship with her SS protector, a man more that twice her age, an involvement which she admitted she had accepted willingly, but in the particular circumstances.

One could but praise, not condemn, Lena. She was just one innocent casualty of war and terrorism and blackmail. I, for one, was full of admiration for her and, perhaps, in time, might see myself falling in love with her, because if I was to form a lasting attachment with a woman I thought I would prefer a partner who had endured the many traumas of concentration camp life. She would understand the frame of mind which I had developed since that unforgettable day when I entered the slums of Compiègne, the gateway to all the wickedness.

I was sick, chronically sick if the truth could be ascertained. Even if I were fit and well there would be difficulties. I was without means, without prospects and job qualifications. I had no desire to live in England; nor did I want to return to my native Jersey, an island, for me, of fond memories overshadowed by bitter disillusionment. For the moment I accepted Lena's generous offer gratefully.

Towards the latter part of the day, twilight falling, a party of heavily-armed guards entered the camp to shoot the prisoners held in the interrogation building. Jews from the tent camps were gunned down in batches by machine-guns until they became mere silhouettes in the bad light.

The Lust for Revenge

Only the dead slept that night. Throughout the long hours of darkness, the camp was alerted to the raucous commands and conflicting sounds coming from behind the walls; rubber-wheeled and tracked vehicles with heavy revving engines were heard to leave the SS garages, their noise sinking to an uncanny whine then silence as they rolled out of earshot down the twisting hill heading towards the village, leaving us with little doubt that a great evacuation was under way.

There was tension and friction on the crowded streets; quarrelsome groups were clustered outside the Blocks bandying words about in several languages. Blacked out, discipline was difficult to referee. Young Russians and Poles were calling for a breakout in the belief that the entire garrison had decamped. Maddened by hunger, they clamoured for blood, brandishing knives taken from the cookhouse and heavy piping ripped out from washrooms. With bad grace, the ringleaders were dissuaded from going on the rampage; senior Russians and Austrians came out into the open, a scant few with pistols in their fists. Blinkered almost, they addressed the mob and called for restraint; to rush at the gate was to stick one's neck out, it was said. Wise counselling; the glow of cigarettes from the machine-gun posts along the cat-walk indicated that these and other strategic points were still manned and, by lurking within spitting distance of the wall, one could hear the odd cough and a shifting of feet on boards. There was another warning for those bent on going it alone: the barbed-wire still held enough electric power to kill.

Alex was disturbed. Lena had failed to put in an appearance at the agreed time. Though she was many hours overdue, I watched the gate from the shadows of the brothel block, now out of service. The gate remained firmly closed, and as the hours dwindled away I could only think that her delaying tactics had misfired and some obstacle had been put in her way. I was not unduly worried, convinced that she had gone into hiding in the locality, even in the village, and would surface at daylight or when the Americans arrived.

At long last, the first streak of daylight revealed the true situation; silhouettes in uniform, almost invisible to poor and tired eyes, stood paralysed behind the machine-guns and gradually became clear as the sky brightened. A sea of faces gaped up at the towers and cat-walk. Baffled, those in the foreground could see a marked difference in the uniforms of the guards. In ignorance, many thought they were soldiers of the American army and cheered loudly. But the uniforms seemed to be dark, black almost, and the men looked middle-aged and over, gaunt and apprehensive. They were a mixed bag of policemen and firemen drafted in from Vienna to replace the SS and they had little stomach for the assignment forced upon them.

With a white flag flying over the Fortress of Mauthausen, and the promised Americans on their way, Jack Taylor and I were admitted to the hospital's washroom where we shaved off a rough growth of beard and cleansed the dirt from our bodies with carbolic soap and warm water. Revived, we put on outfits of clean clothing taken from the best in the store. Well turned out, sweet-smelling, we went to meet our liberators.

It was mid-morning when they arrived. Not the great armada expected with food, doctors and medicines, only a small unit of arm-oured cars 'stumbling on the hideous place'. Jack Taylor greeted a corpulent, cigar-smoking sergeant and disclosed his name and rank. 'Where the hell have you been? What kept you?' he asked sharply.

How often had I dreamed of this day! Now it had dawned, I found myself, like so many, curiously unmoved – apathetic almost. Here was the ally, about whom I had heard so much, come to shake my hand and remove me far beyond the bloody amphitheatre of barbarism and murder. All at once, my body began to tremble in an excess of rage, it was not a moment of sudden and uncontrollable passion, but the accumulation of months, no, years, of hatred.

It was meant to be a day for rejoicing. Prisoners with enough strength were hopping about whooping and clapping hands. A great number, consigned to oblivion, floundering, weeping, were unresponsive – beyond caring. I could not demonstrate my gratitude, not even a token, only echo Jack Taylor's sentiment, ungracious as it seemed.

It would be too easy to allow myself to be whisked away without turning my head and saying goodbye to Alex and the few friends I had made during my eight months in the camp. Besides, there was Lena. I had to determine whether or not she was safe and unharmed. Another few days in the camp didn't matter. I wasn't pressed for time.

I shook hands with Jack Taylor – he had no reason to wait – and watched him being helped into one of the grey, squat cars with white stars emblazoned on their turrets; it headed a column in the direction of the village, a straggling line of dejected, captive Viennese police and firemen walking in between the two armoured cars. And when the column disappeared from sight, a wit was heard to say: 'Voilà la danse qui va commencer!'

The 'fun' was about to begin. The American soldiers, who had been sickened by what they had seen during their brief stay, had left promising to return with reinforcements within a day or so.* Meanwhile, food had to be sought, some order had to be maintained to prevent restless hordes from breaking out to plunder the countryside and, foreseeably, go on the warpath against the inhabitants. Moreover, it had been confirmed that roaming bands of armed SS men, with no place to go, were hiding in the vicinity.

Reliable men, nominated from all nationalities, were handed weapons and ammunition which had been seized from the armoury and retrieved from where they had been abandoned. Groups were directed to mount guard in the watch-towers and around the perimeter. Understandably, the reaction to this was mixed, seen by many as an affront – a new threat from their own side – they hissed and jeered when they saw guns pointing at them. When food was promised, the majority responded with two cheers.

To find enough food and feed so many hungry thousands was a

---

* United States official records state that Mauthausen Concentration Camp, containing some 16,000 inmates, was uncovered on 5 May 1945, by Troop D, 41st Cavalry Reconnaissance Squadron (Mechanized) of the 11th Armored Division. The camp was subsequently taken over by the 21st Armored Infantry Battalion, Combat Command B. Officers in command: Major General H.E. Dager, Colonel Wesley W. Yale, Lt Col M. W. Keach and Lt Col Herbert M. Hoy, Jr.

formidable task. Whilst fires were lit under the cauldrons and water put
to the boil, teams were sent to forage the village and surrounding farms;
in many instances force was used on anyone showing resistance to the
'hijackers' and 'rustlers'. But there was a premium to pay for the booty
brought back on requisitioned vehicles; bands of SS men and armed
civilians fired the first shots. First to be picked off was Badia, a swaggering, unpalatable, anti-British, Spanish deputy Block-chief who had spent
many years in Spanish, French and German prisons only to die after
revelling in just two hours of freedom.

And there were violent skirmishes in the immediate area, in the dense
woods surrounding the quarry with wounded and killed on both sides.
SS men were rounded up; a pitiable number had made a desperate
attempt to infiltrate the prisoner community, shaving their heads,
putting on shabby clothing and dirtying themselves, a ruse which failed
to get past scrutineers warned to be vigilant, those who were too heavy,
too sound, too pink, too intense were eliminated.

I was designated to sit in judgement on those captured and returned to
the camp. Some showed fright, pleading innocence; some maintained
their arrogance, coming to attention, a click of the heels, a hand raised
and a 'Heil Hitler!' They were a mixed bag; 'Junglinge', pimply, barely
shaving, those in their late twenties and hardened veterans. They were
weedy, squat, lanky, rugged. They broke down, cried, offered excuses,
opened their pocketbooks and held up photographs of mothers, wives
and children, and they stood firm and sullen.

It was true, as many claimed, that batches had been drafted into the
camp only days before; spent, ill, they had arrived straight from the
battle lines to replace guards who were fit enough for combat. But others
had come from camps overrun by the Allies and were very much at home
with the policy of violence and extermination. Culpable or not, all had
vowed their allegiance to an evil regime and donned the 'hallowed'
uniform of the 'Totenkopf' divisions.

The 'tribunal' of ex-prisoners was not concerned with the charge that
it was an improperly constituted assembly thirsting only for revenge.
Wrongs were best dealt with on the spot, before one's eyes, not by
long-drawn-out court trials some time in the distant future with blank-
minded legal pundits arguing for and against, resulting in unsatisfactory
conclusions, punishment by half measures, even acquittal. The 'chair-
man', artless, clownish, a Spaniard with his two feet across a table and
chewing on a peppermint gum, communicated the sentences with two
fingers to the side of his head and in a few words: 'Schiessen, amigo!
Kaputt, compris?' And there were more than enough volunteers to carry
out the executions.

Luckless guards and Kapos who fell directly into the hands of those wanting to settle old scores were not awarded the merciful bullet in the neck, but a lethal dose of their own medicine – a climb, bare-footed, up the 186 death steps humping a granite block and a push over the 'parachutists' cliff'. Perhaps more ruthless, a method of retribution to which I could not subscribe, was the spread-eagling and staking down of guards to the road before driving a truck loaded with chanting ex-prisoners over the screaming wretches.

When, by late evening, an hour before darkness, Lena had not turned up, Alex and I took a break in the duties to which we had been assigned, ate a portion of tangy and solid soup, and went about looking for a clue to Lena's disappearance. We found the small dormitory-room where she had been quartered with other women who had been employed in the same capacity. We were alarmed by what we saw. The six bunks which took up half the floor space were disarranged, some of the bedclothing was bloodstained and the doors of the steel lockers were wide open, one locker resting at an angle spewing out garments. We left the building convinced there had been a scrimmage of sorts.

Inquiries took us to a refuse tip near to the SS hospital. A number of women had been victims of sadism, apparently killed immediately before the decampment. Some of the bodies had been burned beyond identification: they were blackened effigies. Others, still smouldering, were charred to some degree or untouched by the fire. The women had been abused, shot and strangled. These were not commonplace creatures from the general community, it was believed, but included women from the brothel block. Sickened and unable to establish whether Lena was among the victims, but suspecting she might be, we returned to the camp.

Night fell and, flagging after a long day of activity but with hunger appeased, I went with Alex to the SS hospital where we bedded down between sheets on soft mattresses. There were many beds conspicuously empty, not everyone fancied sleeping outside the walls of the camp because of a morbid fear of the enemy still roaming the area in scattered numbers. I was too tired to care whose head had rested on the pillow before mine; I slept soundly, a machine-pistol loaded with a full magazine at hand, until, in the early hours, the building was awakened by a volley of shots and an explosion which rattled the windows. Some zealot burst into the room; frantically waving a torch, he shouted: 'Aus … aus … schnell … zwei deutsche Panzer kommen!'

Two German tanks heading up the approach road! In the darkness, I joined in the scramble for the door, my machine-pistol in one hand and my clothing clutched under an arm. In a blue funk, I tore up to the gate, falling to the ground and cutting my bare feet on the sharp stone and grit, the smell of cordite wafting up my nose and both my ears tuned to the clatter of rolling steel.

The cause of the alarm held in check and outmanoeuvred, but at some cost, we all thanked God for the daylight. Brilliant sunshine beamed down on the camp to soothe the great epidemic which reached out for as far as the eye could see. Official wireless sources told us that the war had ended, news which left no one intoxicated with excitement. People were still in great pain, crying out for help and dying needlessly.

Vantage points, the cookhouse roof, watch-towers and cat-walks, were dense with people scanning the countryside for the promised aid. The foraging for food was maintained; bread was scarce, barely enough to share out among those risking the wrath of householders and farmers. Potatoes, green vegetables, oatmeal, flour, milk, animal food and hidden stores of dried foodstuffs were carted into the cookhouse in quantities sufficient to feed the camp one meal. And a few farm animals were brought in on the hoof. The sight of these helpless creatures standing forlorn, neighing, bellowing, bleating, squealing, estranged from their natural environment and waiting to be dispassionately bludgeoned, would, thereafter, remain deeply embedded in my mind and would greatly affect my outlook and my attitude to life.

I was forced to abandon the reckless pursuit of SS stragglers, my legs could no longer support my body; I was weak-eyed and a tremor of the hands left me with no choice but to surrender my machine-pistol. Frustrated, I was confined to a chair. Then, more bad news which left me even more wretched; Alex, perhaps over-confident and playing a danger-ous cat-and-mouse game with the enemy as many were still doing before the Americans returned in force, was brought back to the camp, shot by a sniper in the village. Conscious but without the power of speech, he held on to my hand and died as the first ambulance drove through the gates.

Camp Mauthausen entered the black book of history ... to serve as a warning and 'remind future generations of what Hitler's Germany meant', from which little would be learned.

Stretcher-bearers carried me gently to an ambulance; then on a lengthy journey over cratered roads to a bed in a military field-hospital. A portable wireless played soothing background music to sick and wounded patients. America's rising star, Bing Crosby, pulling at the heart-strings, crooned: 'Hello Mum'.

Postscript

SS Standartenführer Franz Ziereis, born in the city of Munich, was only in his fortieth year when he fled camp Mauthausen in an attempt to evade his enormous responsibility for the crimes. More than two weeks later he was recognized hiding near Spittal. Shots were exchanged and he was wounded by a patrol of American soldiers. Dying, with a soft cushion to comfort his head and an ex-prisoner doctor in attendance, he made a confession and passed peacefully away on the evening of 24 May 1945.

Hauptsturmführer Georg 'of the crippled hand' Bachmayer, with whom I spent a nasty half-hour, perhaps the worst of the villains if one had to put them in order of merit, avoided arrest and trial. Some nine miles from the camp, at a place called Perg, his body was dug up and identified. Georg committed suicide after killing his eleven-year-old daughter.

Camp Mauthausen and its many sub-camps in Austria were polluted with perverts, sadists and killers on both sides of the walls. Not all faced a tribunal for their crimes. Hundreds of guards, Kapos and 'prominenten' who aided and abetted in the tortures and murders evaded capture; they adopted aliases and were easily lost among the multitudes of displaced persons.

Among the more notorious hanged were: Obersturmbannführer Johann Altfuldisch, aged 34; Hauptsturmführer Adolf Zutter, 57; August Eigruber, Gauleiter of Linz, 57; Unterscharführer Andreas Trumm, 25; Josef Niedermayer, 26; Anton Kaufmann, born in the village of Mauthausen, 38.

Among the evil doctors, psychiatrists and medical professors on the staff were: Eduard 'Needle' Krebsbach, hanged in 1947; Dr Helmut Vetter, previously with the firm I G Farben; Dr Werner 'mercy-killer' Heyde, a professor of psychiatry at the University of Wurzburg, captured in 1962 and committed suicide before his trial; Dr Rudolf Lohnauer, chief physician from Linz who committed suicide with his family after the war.

A long list of SS personnel, including guilty Austrian, Czech, Yugoslav, Hungarian and Spanish civilians employed by the military authorities, had their death sentences commuted to life imprisonment which, in effect, meant release after only a few comfortable years in detention. Others, accomplices in multiple murder, received ten, five, three and as little as one year in detention, farcical sentences which hardly matched their dreadful crimes. Shamefully, many directly involved in war crimes were not brought to trial because they were found to be useful in the developing fields of science, technology and medicine. A number were to find sanctuary in America and England, received with open arms by those governments and safeguarded well.

In the years after the war I often felt that I had never left the camp, had never been granted the right to leave when others, more deserving, more worthy, had been denied their liberty. As with ex-concentration camp prisoners I met on my travels, not a day went by without my conscience reminding me of my good fortune. My eventual return was an obligation, a debt to those ill-fated friends who helped me when I was at death's door whilst they struggled with their own miseries.

When Mary and I arrived at the great double entrance doors leading to the former reception quadrangle and SS garages, where a huge Nazi eagle once scowled down on new arrivals, only the rusted twisted ties remained. On the day of the liberation, a cheering mob with a rope had pulled down the symbol of evil.

Parked in the vast silent enclave beyond the entrance were a taxi, a mini-bus and a coach, all with snow-chains attached to the wheels. At the far end, where once the immaculately-uniformed Franz Ziereis stood on his diminutive granite balcony to cast an eye over what he called 'Futter' (fodder) to feed the crematory ovens, a large black cat with a stern expression sat hunched on the snow-capped wall, engrossed in our approach.

'Franz Ziereis reincarnated,' I quipped.

'That's unkind to the cat,' Mary answered.

We climbed the wide granite steps to a higher level, leading to the former administration quarters and the camp itself. Half-way up, screwed to a wall, a notice depicting a domestic animal modelled on contemporary lines – matchstick legs and body and a sizable dot for the head with a broad vertical stripe interjected – caught Mary's eye.

'Does that mean what I think?' she asked.

'Hunde verboten,' I replied. 'No dogs allowed.'

Dominating the entrance into the camp is the most poignant memorial of all. The Russian, General D. M. Karbyshev, aptly named the 'Ice General,' stands tall and erect on his flower-bedecked pedestal, a strong chin tilting upwards, arms folded defiantly and his beautifully sculptured body encased in a mantle of 'ice'. For several minutes I stood and brooded over this historical hero; it was difficult to tear myself away from a symbol whose death brought tears to the eyes of ten thousand witnesses.

The door into the main street was ajar. We walked through. There were a few people braving the frigid weather. Two stout women swathed in fur coats were peering through a grime-stained window of the brothel block. Constructionally, as far as I could see, little had changed; the remains of the camp have been well-preserved. It was cold, the wind was mournfully complaining as it always did; green grass thrived along the bank outside Block 11; birds, once conspicuous by their absence, had returned; and, swimming in the gutters, a mile of discarded cigarette-ends reminded me that tobacco was a commodity men fought for and killed for.

My immediate thoughts were interrupted by a command-like shout. I turned to see a swarthy-looking individual beckoning, brandishing what looked like a ticket in his hand. 'Zurückkommen, mein Herr! Zahlen, nix frei!' he called out loud enough for the dead to hear.

The man's German had a Spanish accent. Mary and I retraced our steps. Stabbing a thumb in my chest, I retorted, somewhat bluntly but so that he would understand: 'Ich nix figging Deutsch! Wir von England, Britisch, compris?'

'Ja, ja, pardon,' the man said defensively. 'Sprechen spanisch?' he asked.

I shook my head. 'Vous parlez français, sans doute?'

'Oui,' he said, his face immobile. He touted the ticket at me. 'Payez la monnaie pour une visite, Monsieur! Compris?'

Mary laughed. 'You have to dig into your pocket to go in,' she said.

'A joke! Une blague, mon vieux,' I said turning to the Spaniard. 'J'ai payé ... cher! One thousand times!'

The man shrugged impatiently. One had to pay for the upkeep! For the wages! Did I understand?

Mary squeezed my hand. 'It's only a few Austrian schillings,' she said.

'Nothing to do with cost,' I replied. 'It's the principle!'

'Voyez-vous, Monsieur,' the Spaniard explained, 'seulement les ex-prisonniers et leurs familles entrent gratis. Compris, un billet de faveur?'

'Fair enough! That lets me out,' I said to Mary. 'Moi, prisonnier ici, au Block douze,' I informed the man.

Did I have a paper, a certificate or anything else as proof? I looked at him blankly and shook my head. Under my breath, I said: 'Just a few fucking scars.'

Mary took the ticket and pressed a banknote into his hand, much more than the sum demanded. 'Merci beaucoup, Monsieur,' she said, taking my arm and leading me away.

'I didn't expect to have to buy shares in the place,' I said.

The 'Wailing Wall', eight feet high and topped with five strands of – now defunct – electric barbed-wire, with its iron rings embedded in the granite on which men were tethered by the hands and feet and crucified, is, in itself, a startling memorial to those who suffered the torments of hell. Opposite, the 'Disinfektionkammer' and the 'Wäscherei' have been incorporated into a chapel of remembrance. Here, before the flags of many nations, visitors stop to pray.

A well-trodden trail along the snow-covered main street led us to the most feared building of all. We turned the corner by the cookhouse, once comfortably insulated from the freezing winters for those chosen to work therein, and climbed the twelve steps to reconnoitre the 36 tiny cells where men, British and American among them, were interrogated and cruelly tortured, their pitiful cries and screams often reaching my ears across the street in Block 12. Between the long rows of cells, the broad, stone corridor has the eerie silence of a mausoleum. The 36 heavy doors, each with a 'Judas' spy-hole in the centre panel, were open for inspection. Visitors step from cell to cell in silence, almost on tip-toe. With long faces, they exchange glances, they peep, contemplate and imagine; but it is not easy to grasp the insufferable realities, when strong men were reduced to broken, whimpering and demented animals.

The cobblestone courtyard at the rear of the building led us down a short flight of steps to a sequence of small, grotesque, almost medieval chambers, each breathing horror. First, the gas-chamber, no bigger than a high-street butcher's storage refrigerator, into which more than sixty prisoners were squeezed at one time. The low ceiling is plumbed as for a shower-bath with a series of perforated nozzles meant to deceive but from which water never flowed. White tiles, extending over the four walls, are broken and chipped from a million finger-nails clawing in the last agonizing struggles of the victims as they choked on the fumes of Cyclone B gas.

Along a narrow, darkened passage-way, in an ante-room, stands one piece of furniture – the gruesome-looking dissecting table hewed out of stone, concave and slanting at one end with a channel and a drain to receive the blood of the victims whose gold teeth were extracted without anaesthetic, whose rectums were probed with rods and inspected for hidden pieces of jewellery, and where colourful tattoos were skinned off bodies to make lampshades, book-covers and fancy work.

The execution chamber is small. The short length of wire noose for garrotting hangs from a steel girder below ceiling height; directly underneath is the round drain where blood, urine and excrement were washed away. Here, too, is the 'height measuring device' (Kugel Aktion) where unsuspecting victims stood with their backs to a wall to receive a shot in the neck from the hidden gunman.

To complete the tour of the chambers of horror is the crematorium, its brick-built ovens and steel stretchers blackened by fierce, salt-fed flames which consumed more than fifty bodies every hour, every day, seven days a week. It mattered not if those engulfed still had a breath of life.

Fresh and plastic posies adorned the gaping mouths of the ovens. Mary and I stopped to watch an old peasant-looking woman go down on her knees to pray. I saw the soles of her shoes, thin and down at the heels; the long black coat she wore hung from scrag-like shoulders, it was frayed at the hem and sodden with mud. I saw her as a copy of the thousands who were herded like cattle into camp Mauthausen, women from the outbacks, prematurely aged by hard work outdoors in all weathers, raw-boned, crook-backed, bow-legged and with arthritic joints; mothers, grandmothers and great-grandmothers, 'old witches' they were dubbed by the guards who made them objects for scorn and 'sportive' abuse.

Mary took the old woman by an arm and helped her to her feet. She wiped her tears with a soiled khaki handkerchief and said 'danke'. She pointed to a miniature photograph set in a round frame, one among a great number embedded in the walls of the crematorium. 'Mein Sohn, Miklos, neunzehn Jahr alt Mauthausen kommen,' she said in a faltering voice.

Her story was not exceptional. Coming from a small farming community in the hinterland of Yugoslavia, a daughter violated and killed, a husband fighting with the partisan leader, Josip Tito, captured and hung, and a nineteen-year-old son killed in camp Mauthausen. The old woman is alone in the world with her sad memories, travelling over a great distance to the memorial camp is an annual pilgrimage for which she puts a little money away each month to pay the train fare. 'Wenn Gott erlaube' (if God permits), she will come back next year and for as long as she has breath in her body.

Small chubby children, well-behaved, somewhat bewildered, with rosy cheeks and wet noses, stand on their toes to peer into the ovens. 'Brot Backöfen, liebling' (bread ovens, darling), I heard one mother explain. From the crematorium synthetically smooth stairs lead to the museum, once the hospital where, in my last weeks, I was befriended by Lena who disappeared on the eve of the liberation. The many rooms have since been integrated into a comprehensive repository for the exhibition of artistic handiwork designed and made by prisoners. Not so easy on the eye, but a magnetic attraction to the visitors who shift about and talk in whispers, are the many instruments of torture safeguarded under glass. Most commonly used on heads and shoulders was the 'Gummi Schlauch', a sand-filled rubber truncheon sixteen inches long with a leather lace at one end, often introduced to the unacquainted as the 'Dolmetscher' (interpreter). Meant to cause excruciating and lasting pain were the wooden pins which spread fingers wide apart. Ugly-looking needles and syringes, handy sizes and large models for injecting poisons into veins. And the 'Trog', one of a specimen employed in the quarry, a purpose-made hod which was strapped to a man's back by webbing so that he could haul a heavy granite block up the 186 death steps.

Perhaps the most poignant pictorial evidence of an atrocity recorded by SS photographers is that of the Dutch grammar-school teacher, number 13922, a thirty-year-old crippled dwarf who was injected with a lethal poison and dissected into sections for analysis. After the flesh was removed from his bones, his head, torso and limbs were wired together for a further experiment. Woeful, too, is the SS photograph of Hans Bonare-witz, a twenty-two-year-old Austrian escapee aboard a flat cart with his sack of personal belongings slung over a shoulder, being pulled to the scaffold by a group of prisoners in striped uniforms and preceded by the camp's musicians and a strutting baton-wielding bandmaster in a cocked hat.

I asked myself, who was the Britisher by the name of John Alater with a Polish friend – Tanek? Where was Alater born? How did he come to Mauthausen? And why? Had he a poetical imagination? Perhaps an artist? Did he sketch a game of football on what looked like a chain of blank bus tickets? Did he put together the scrappy English/German dictionary open at a page composed of words suggested by confinement?

> fought/
> caught/
> to pay/
> to think/
> to hear/
> to feel/
> to weep/
> to sleep/
> to dream/

What became of John Alater? And his 'good friend', Tanek? Were they killed? Are they buried in one of the communal graves? Unsung heroes. No posies. No laurels. The mystery, one of a million, remains.

To have preserved camp Mauthausen in its entirety would have been impossible with limited financial resources, requiring, too, a caretaking labour force not easy to recruit in the bleak isolation of the huge necropolis. Only those Blocks fronting the main street have been kept from decay; they stand as they were relinquished but cleaned of the viruses, the venom, the mistrust, the self-pity, the tears and those who treated their fellow-prisoners with persistent taunts and devilry. And, as I stood on the foundation of Block 12, I became almost paralysed with emotion, because I was one who often flinched from the bullies, the soulless, self-important auxiliaries who beat men indiscriminately before sending them the forty paces across the street to the place of execution.

Visitors stand on a raised tract of ground surrounded by four high granite walls. They consult their guide books, listen to their hired tape-recordings, narrated in several languages, which tell the events of the escape from Block 20. Unless one was a witness, it is impossible to imagine the fracas, the fighting and the catastrophe that occurred when, on that freezing night in February 1945, nigh on 700 despairing men entered into a compact, unprotected from violent and cruel death.

There are areas which need no attention, nature preserves. The quarry, 'Wienergraben', where, before the war, slaves were used to hew and shape granite blocks and facings for sale to private building contractors and the Vienna city authorities, is a daunting enclosure. The approach from the main gate of the camp is along a rough sloping track; half-way down, one's attention is drawn to the notorious gap in the cliff top – the 'Parachutists' Leap' over which the vanguard of Dutch Jews were forced to jump of their own free will or be pushed to their deaths. Here, the Democratic Republic of Germany has created a fitting memorial. The gap has been corralled with four thick strands of sculpted 'barbed wire'.

The steps leading down into the basin of the quarry have been repaired to carry those visitors keen to attempt the precarious descent; others, understandably, haven't the stomach; they pause to sit down or shrink back up the trail. One feels nervous just looking down. There is an atmosphere of evil about the place, an uncanny silence, the silence of an ancient battlefield. The trees and the tall shrubbery on the edge of the boulder-strewn arena bend to the whimpering winds and, with an ear close to the ground, one can receive the impression of a chorus of voices weeping and wailing.

Tears came to Mary's eyes when we watched a deer, scared of the hunters' shotguns, burst through the dense shrubbery. Breathing hard, the worried animal pulled up at the edge of the pool, bent its head as if to drink, then, recoiling made a hasty retreat. Indignant, Mary quoted

Leonardo da Vinci's prophecy: 'Some day men will look upon the killing of an animal as today we look upon the killing of a human being.' And she recited a poem by Walter de la Mare.

In the basin of the quarry, at the bottom of the steps and fixed to a facing rock, a corroding plaque bears the British-sounding names of the Allied agents who were put to work in the quarry and who were murdered on 6 September 1944:

G. Norman	M. Bloom
J.C. Young	S.C. Jones
E. Wilkinson	R. Newman
J. Dane	L. Punt

These men, who were killed so brutally and who were regarded with such high respect by their fellow-workers in the quarry detail, deserve a more worthy commemoration. How was it, I asked myself, that I wasn't among those selected to sweat blood in this monstrous boneyard? Taking account of the 186 almost vertical steps, I might have been able to climb them once, but not twice.

Alone with my thoughts, I wandered about the area, stepping over boulders abandoned where they had been dropped on the last day of labour. Nervous people are reluctant to move around unaccompanied. Tales are told of hammerings, pingings, thuds, and rustlings and human voices coming from the dense undergrowth. I was not perturbed, even though I had the feeling I was being watched. I paid a small homage to the misty shadows, nodded and passed the time of day in three languages.

Whilst bumbledom permits the harassment and shooting of four-legged creatures in and around the woody neighbourhood there are warning notices posted to trees commanding visitors to respect the ground they walk on. Forbidden are 'Ballspielen' (ball-playing), 'Baden' and 'Tauchen'. Who would wish to bathe or swim in a pool of infamy? Also taboo is 'Autowaschen'. Even without the signs prohibiting it, who would dare to picnic on dedicated ground?

From the top of the death steps, we walked along a track bordering the perimeter where the escapees from Block 20 crawled and limped in blind confusion into the frozen countryside. We came across the 'Asche-häufen', simply marked by a plain wooden cross. Here, many tons of ash from men, women and children incinerated in the crematory ovens were dumped unceremoniously over a slope to form a huge mound. Close by, a handyman was busy repairing a fracture in the wire fencing, to prevent visitors from sneaking into the camp without paying.

One could spend a whole day going the rounds of the magnificent memorials erected by various nations whose peoples perished in the huge slaughter. Many are grand, artistically contrived and skilfully sculptured in granite. The Italian monument is highlighted with an abundance of synthetic flowers in tins and jam jars, with family mementos and the familiar miniature photographs in weatherproof frames of husbands, brothers and sons among the 6,000 Italians reported dead in the camp. Many are portrayed in an intimate style: in formal suits, slick dinner jackets and bow ties, plastered-down hair and wide-brimmed trilby-hats. Full-faced, some bear the fierce expressions which reminded me of the secret groups of Sicily who, in the 1920s, emigrated to Chicago to join the lawless syndicates. In Mauthausen, all the Italians, whether they were good, proud partisans, army deserters or fascists loyal to Mussolini, were lumped together and cold-shouldered.

Darkness approaching, we made our way back to the gate and paused for a short while with the caretaker, Garcia Manuel, until a mini-bus arrived to take us back to the village. Garcia fetched hot coffee from the canteen and I laced his cup and mine with a measure of whisky from my flask. A long-term prisoner in Block 11, he lives with his wife and young son in part of the former SS officers' quarters, earning a modest wage but doing a worthwhile job. His wife lends a hand, tending the graves and the monuments, arranging flowers and cutting grass. In the better seasons they are kept busy with additional help; from dawn to dusk, many hundreds of visitors arrive daily from all over the world. Each May, on the first Sunday, there is a reunion; ex-prisoners, families and friends, and government representatives, honour the occasion in their thousands.

Strange noises, unseen things and unidentified voices reported to Garcia are not thought twice about, and he laughs when he hears stories about ghosts roaming the village at night, or rising out of the mists of the Danube. 'Les fantômes,' he said, are his friends, he talks to them as he makes his last round of the camp, taking a short cut through the execution chamber and the crematorium to lock up the museum.

'Et pourquoi?' he asked. What was it all about? The great sacrifice was for nothing. What has changed? 'Nothing at all!' The hostility, the persecution, the terror, the cruelty and the hunger did not end with the liberation of the concentration camps and the defeat of Nazism. And Garcia pointed a finger at the ground. Our friends underground, he said, had no peace of mind, knowing as they did that they had been betrayed by man's continued hatred, violence, greed and the threat of a new holocaust.

I took note of Garcia's condemnation of the world's dictatorial politicians and warring governments, vented in the same harsh words I had heard many times before in prisons and camps. I understood and wholly agreed with his point of view. Strangely, however, I was not embittered by my years in captivity, harsh as it was; in many ways, the camaraderie and the passion at Romainville and, by contrast, the isolation, the prejudice, the intimidation and the defiance at camps Buchenwald and Mauthausen proved to be an important education for me. And although I value my freedom, constantly under threat, I will never be persuaded that bad and immoral laws must be left unchallenged even to this day.

PICTURE CREDITS

Anthony Faramus's birthplace *author's collection*

The Forum Cinema *Jersey Museums Service*

German gun emplacement *Jersey Museums Service*

Entrance to the Fort de Romainville *author's collection*

The courtyard in front of the prison building *author's collection*

Stairs from the ground floor to Room 26 *author's collection*

The *Appel Platz* during roll call at Buchenwald *Wiener Library*

An illegal photograph of malnourished prisoners in Buchenwald *author's collection*

The first glimpse of Mauthausen concentration camp *author's collection*

New arrivals in the reception area at Mauthausen *Wiener Library*

The death steps at Mauthausen *Wiener Library*

The quarry at Mauthausen *Rijksinstituut voor Oorlogsdocumentatie*

Prominent Nazis visiting Mauthausen

Hans Bonarewitz is led to the gallows by the camp orchestra *Wiener Library*

Tony and Mary courting on Hampstead Heath *author's collection*

Anthony Faramus as a POW in *The Colditz Story author's collection*

INDEX